Hard Choices

Hard

Choices

An
Iowa Review
Reader

Edited by
David Hamilton

University of Iowa Press
Iowa City

University of Iowa Press
Iowa City 52242
Copyright © 1996 by
the University of Iowa Press
All rights reserved
Printed in the United States of America

No part of this book may be reproduced or used
in any form or by any means, electronic or mechanical,
including photocopying and recording, without
permission in writing from the publisher.

Printed on acid-free paper

Library of Congress Cataloging-in-Publication Data

Hard choices: an Iowa review reader / edited by David Hamilton.
    p.   cm.
  ISBN 0-87745-536-8
  1. American literature—20th century. I. Hamilton,
David B. II. Iowa review.
PS536.2.H36   1996
810.8'0054—dc20   95-43433
                                                   CIP

Cover and part title art reproduces earlier covers of the *Iowa Review* and is used with permission of the artists or their families: Alexander S. Gourlay (cover and "The Seventies"), Rikki Ducornet ("The Eighties"), and Ulfert Wilke ("The Nineties").

01   00   99   98   97   96   P   5   4   3   2   1

The publication of this book was supported by the generous assistance of the Offices of the Provost and the Vice President for Research.

Contents

Notes for the Next Century / ix

The Seventies
Under the Maud-Moon *Galway Kinnell* 1970 / 3
In the Brontë Country *William Stafford* 1970 / 6
Requa *Tillie Olsen* 1970 / 7
The Tale *Charles Simic* 1970 / 39
Poem *Donald Justice* 1971 / 42
Farm Wife *Ellen Bryant Voigt* 1972 / 43
Zaydee *Philip Levine* 1973 / 44
The Secret of Poetry *Jon Anderson* 1973 / 46
Gemini *Louise Glück* 1973 / 47
Oleum Misericordiae *John Ashbery* 1975 / 48
Nightmare Begins Responsibility
 Michael S. Harper 1975 / 50
Power *Audre Lorde* 1975 / 51
Problems of Art *James Alan McPherson* 1975 / 52
The Return of Julian the Apostate to Rome
 Ishmael Reed 1975 / 71
A Goldfinch *Marvin Bell* 1976 / 73
Reply to Lapo Gianni *Charles Wright* 1977 / 73
Continuing *A. R. Ammons* 1977 / 74
Centerfold Reflected in a Jet Window
 Sandra McPherson 1977 / 75
Weed *Robert Hass* 1977 / 75
Phantom Silver *William Kittredge* 1977 / 76
View Finder *Raymond Carver* 1978 / 89
Swift *Mary Swander* 1978 / 93
At the Store *Jane Kenyon* 1978 / 94
For Mark Rothko *Jorie Graham* 1979 / 95

A Working Day *Robert Coover* 1979 / 97
Diamond Breakfast *Marianne Boruch* 1979 / 135

The Eighties
They Shall Not Pass *Ai* 1980 / 139
Three Secrets for Alexis *Jane Miller* 1980 / 141
Remembering Brother Bob *William Stafford* 1980 / 145
Instructions for the Next Century
   Stephen Dunn 1980 / 145
Johnnieruth *Becky Birtha* 1981 / 147
√Travel Notes *Michelle Cliff* 1981 / 153
Each Bird Walking *Tess Gallagher* 1981 / 157
Problems of Translation: Problems of Language
   June Jordan 1981 / 159
Philosophy in Warm Weather *Jane Kenyon* 1981 / 162
The Meal *Sharon Olds* 1981 / 163
For Ethel Rosenberg *Adrienne Rich* 1981 / 164
Confiteor *Henri Coulette* 1981 / 169
The Houses *W. S. Merwin* 1982 / 169
The Power of Toads *Pattiann Rogers* 1982 / 174
Epistemology, Sex, and the Shedding of Light
   Lynne Sharon Schwartz 1983 / 175
The End of an Era *James Tate* 1983 / 183
Cooley and Kedney *Peter N. Nelson* 1984 / 184
Ghosts *Jack Gilbert* 1985 / 220
In Umbria *Jack Gilbert* 1985 / 221
Alma in the Dark *Linda Gregg* 1985 / 222
Everything Else You Can Get You Take
   Robert Dana 1986 / 222
From Commerce to the Capitol: Montgomery, Alabama
   Andrew Hudgins 1986 / 223
Elegy for Cello and Piano *Donald Justice* 1986 / 226
In the Basilica of San Francesco *Laurie Sheck* 1986 / 228
The Trail *Tim McGinnis* 1986 / 229
Wonderland *C. S. Godshalk* 1987 / 232
We Are Americans Now, We Live in the Tundra
   Marilyn Chin 1987 / 249

Reading Aquinas *Michael Heffernan* 1987 / 250
Amazing *Laura Jensen* 1987 / 251
East Grandville School *Sandra Nelson* 1989 / 253
In the Workshop after I Read My Poem Aloud
    Don Colburn 1989 / 255
The Battle of Manila *Laura Kalpakian* 1989 / 256
R for Rosemary *Gerald Stern* 1989 / 285

The Nineties
Saul and Patsy Are Pregnant *Charles Baxter* 1990 / 289
Peelings *Mary Swander* 1990 / 320
Long, Disconsolate Lines *Jane Cooper* 1990 / 322
Midwestern Villanelle *Robin Behn* 1990 / 323
One Continuous Substance *Albert Goldbarth* 1990 / 324
Across These Landscapes of Early Darkness
    Dionisio D. Martínez 1990 / 325
Dove *Stanley Plumly* 1990 / 327
Both Definitions of Save *Albert Goldbarth* 1991 / 328
Waiting for Lesser Duckweed: On a Proposal of Issa's
    Sandra McPherson 1991 / 375
Dominion *Debra Hines* 1992 / 378
Numberless *Heather McHugh* 1992 / 380
Journey One *Radcliffe Squires* 1992 / 382
The Envoy *Radcliffe Squires* 1992 / 383
Another Elegy *Donald Hall* 1992 / 384
Work *Yusef Komunyakaa* 1992 / 390
The Adulterers *Kenneth Mason* 1992 / 391
Fortunate Traveller *Lynda Hull* 1993 / 412
The Spring House *Katherine Soniat* 1993 / 416
At School *Marianne Boruch* 1993 / 417
Girl Writing a Letter *William Carpenter* 1993 / 418
Memorywork *Susan Malka Choi* 1993 / 420
Party *Norman Sage* 1993 / 434
The Book of the Dead Man (#6)
    Marvin Bell 1993 / 438
The Departure *James Laughlin* 1993 / 440
At the End *James Laughlin* 1993 / 441

Untitled, 1968 *James Galvin* 1994 / 441
Translations from Colonial Swahili
    Sue Standing 1994 / 442
Emma Enters a Sentence of Elizabeth Bishop's
    William H. Gass 1994 / 444
Circe *Laura Gerrity* 1994 / 450
We Go to a Fire *James Tate* 1994 / 463
Abundance and Satisfaction *Pattiann Rogers* 1995 / 464
Empties *Rochelle Nameroff* 1995 / 466

Permissions / 469

The *Iowa Review*, 1970–1995 / 473

Notes for the Next Century
DAVID HAMILTON

What you hold in your hands is a retrospective anthology drawn from the first twenty-five years of the *Iowa Review*, and little need be said by way of introduction. Readers who would know more of our history can surmise much from the appendix. Beyond that, what we hope you will find is that though these were hard, they are worthy choices.

Our contents represent less than four percent of what we have published since 1970. A few blanket decisions guided us. Though the *Review* began with strong critical intentions, that is not how it has mostly continued, and so we have left out critical essays. We left out translations as well, though we have carried many, because so far it seems that our essential work has been publishing stories and poems in English written by contemporary North American writers.

Two years ago, twenty-three graduate students helped me through a systematic reading of all we had published to that point, reminding me of stories and poems I had forgotten and arguing forcefully at times for others I had valued less highly than they. When they taught me well, their favorites added to my own and entered this collection.

At our best moments as readers, I believe we read as fans, critical fans to be sure, but fans nevertheless, and share with the writer some feel for that to which she or he aspires. So we sense and admire an apt turn of phrase, the shape of a line, the way words here prepare for and are fulfilled by words there, the curve of a story as it arcs in its flight, all the way out of the park sometimes, leaps and passes that amaze us.

Now and then we think we glimpse the perfect beyond what anyone is likely to bring to the page, and it is a range of such moments that we sought to gather. My own working title has been "Notes for the Next Century," which is to say work that we, and we hope others, will want to keep around. More than that, work that will give us an angle on what we are getting into.

Hints of our history show in our including two pieces each by a small set of poets. I do not mean those few cases where two poems by the same poet fall together, both being short and both from the same issue of the *Review* anyway. I mean instead a few times when you find a poet and then find her or him again, usually after years, and so after some interval of pages. The careers of half of these writers have grown more or less in step with our magazine. The others were ahead of us and served as guides. Usually we have published them all several more times than the two represented here. Together they seem a core that represents well what we have found we are after, and we wanted to reflect that in this anthology.

Raymond Carver is a special case since we couldn't do so easily for prose what we did for poetry. As nominations of stories moved to a short list, four or five of his stood out. "What's in Alaska," "Put Yourself in My Shoes," and "The Calm" were all contenders. We could have made these selections a "Raymond Carver Carnival" with no detriment to the quality of the volume. At length, however, we chose to go with a much less well known story, "View Finder," precisely because it is almost hidden, and also because it prefigures "Cathedral."

Once the decisions were made and we sought permission of the writers, and of their later publishers when necessary, everyone was remarkably cooperative. A few writers did not respond to our invitation for reasons of their own. Their being out of town, or whatever, amounted to our final decisions. The response of others was so overwhelmingly positive and quick that we did not need to make a second round of invitations as I had thought likely.

This magazine has been a community effort. The names are too numerous for exhaustive mention, but I want to list several. John Gerber, Richard Lloyd-Jones, John Raeburn, Ed

Folsom, and Adalaide Morris, chairs of English over these years, have always been supportive and have sometimes participated closely. While directing the Writers' Workshop, John Leggett, Frank Conroy, and Connie Brothers have been equally supportive, especially in helping us locate valuable assistants. The rest of the Workshop faculty during my time—Marvin Bell, Vance Bourjaily, James Galvin, Jorie Graham, Donald Justice, James Alan McPherson, Marilynne Robinson, and Gerald Stern—have been marvelous in both keeping their hands off and, now and then, being ready to assist. Though many colleagues have helped with an emphasis or a feature here or there, the late Sherman Paul stands out as one who was always ready with ideas and advice and uncomplaining when I did not follow them. Mary Hussmann has been invaluable, my closest companion as a reader.

This magazine came into being under the sponsorship of Duane C. Spriestersbach, then dean of the Graduate College and vice president for research. He and Associate Dean Charles Mason kept us going for many years, with the support of Willard Boyd, James O. Freedman, and Hunter Rawlings, our presidents. Though the NEA has helped significantly, the University of Iowa has steadily provided bedrock support even if it has, now and then, thought twice about it. Without Spriestersbach and Mason, we would have folded early. Leslie Sims, David Skorton, and Peter Nathan, more recently of the administration, have been steadfast and inventive. A few years ago, in a year of doubt and of no salary increases, our faculty rallied astonishingly to an emergency campaign that saved us. Consequently, if we should dedicate this volume, let that dedication be to the University of Iowa, where we have mostly prospered, and to the writers from all over who have looked to this *Review* as one in which they wish to appear.

The Seventies

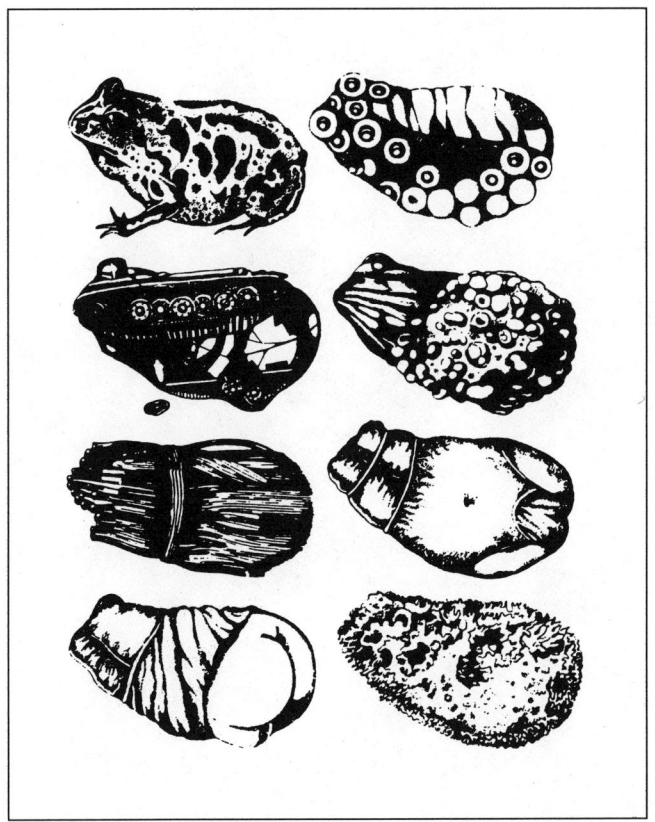

Under the Maud-Moon
GALWAY KINNELL

1
A fat-
cheeked girl-child comes awake
in her crib, chortling
and yodelling
to the day, the green
swaddlings tear open, a filament
or vestment tears,

and she who is born,
she who sings and cries,
she who begins the passage, her hair
sprouting out,
her gums budding for her first spring on earth,
the mist still clinging
about her face, puts
her hand into
her father's mouth to clutch
his song.

2
It is all over, little one,
the flipping
and overleaping, the watery
somersaulting alone in the oneness
under the hill,
under the old lonely bellybutton
pushing forth again
in remembrance,
the drifting there furled in the dark, pressing
a knee or elbow down the slippery
wall, sculpting existence

with a foot, streams
of omphalos blood singing all about you.

3
Her head
enters the headhold
through which she starts rising:
being itself
clamps down all over her, gives her
into the shuddering grip
of departure, the huge, agonized clenches
making the last perfect molds of her
as she goes.

4
The eye
of darkness opens, the pupil
droozed with black hairs
stops, the chakra
on top of the brain
throbs a long moment in world light.

And she skids out on her face into light,
this peck
of stunned flesh clotted
with celestial cheesiness, glowing
with the astral violet
of the underlife. And as they cut
her tie to the darkness, she dies
a moment, turns
blue as a coal, the limbs shaking
as the memories rush out of them. And when
they hang her up by the feet
she sucks
air, she screams
her first song—and turns rose,

the slow,
beating, featherless arms
already clutching at the emptiness.

5
When it was cold
on our hillside, and you cried
in the crib rocking
through the darkness on wood
knifed down to the curve
of the smile, a sadness
stranger than ours, all of it
flowing from the other world,

I used to come to you
and sit by you
and sing to you. You did not know,
and yet you will remember,
in the silent
zones of the brain, a spectre,
descendant of the ghostly forefathers, singing
to you in the night-time—not the songs
of light streaming
through the golden hair of the angels—
a blacker
rasping flowering on that tongue.

6
For when the Maud-moon
glimmered in those first nights, and the Archer
lay sucking
up the icy beestings
of the cosmos, in his crib
of stars,

I had crept down
to riverbanks, their long

rustle of being and perishing, down to marshes
where the earth oozes up
in cold streaks, touching the world
with the underglimmer
of the beginning,

and there learned my only song.

7
And in the days
when you find yourself orphaned,
emptied of wing-singing, of light, pieces
of cursed bread
on your tongue,

there shall come back to you
a voice, spectral,
calling you
sister! from everything which dies.

And then
you shall open
this book, even
if it is the book of nightmares.

In the Brontë Country
WILLIAM STAFFORD

Emily's room looks out on the graves.
A sampler by each daughter fades
in the cupboard. The moss
would not leave her thoughts alone.

She tried to do what the moss
began. Moss will finish it.

On the moor a track wears deep
on the hillside; gorse leans in.
Water stands in the grass, in brown
pools on the soaked upland. Miles
from the sea, gulls drift over
that brown tide. Buffeted, they
leave in the air their international cry.

At Top Withens black stones
of the wall cling, stubborn, deaf.
To look far you have to ignore them.
The wind at your shoulder says over
and over, "I knew them all." In a stunned
second you are one of the rocks
and the heath has taken all your friends.

You understand what the bird that
followed you was saying. The wind
falls away and goes still. This earth
tells time by the stars, and is telling
you something:
this is the way the world will be, after.

Requa

TILLIE OLSEN

It seemed he had had to hold up his head forever. All he wanted was to lie down. Maybe his uncle would let him, there in that strip of pale sun by the redwoods, where he might get warm.

I got those sittin kinks, too, his uncle said, but you don't see *me* staggerin round like an old drunk . . . Here, shake a leg and let's get wood for a fire. Dry pieces if there is any such. I'll catch the fish.

But he had to heave. Again.

You can't have 'ary a shred left to bring up. Remind me not to take you noplace but by streetcar after this . . . Alright, stretch out; you'll see you're feeling better.

Everything slid, moved, as if he were still in the truck. He had been holding up his head forever. The spongy ground squished under him, and the wet of winter and spring rains felt through the tarp. He was lying on the ground, *the ground*. There might be snakes. The trees stretched up and up so you couldn't see if they had tops, and up there they leaned as if they were going to fall. There hadn't even been time to say goodbye to the lamppost that he could hug and swing himself round and round. Round and round like his head, having to hold it up forever. Being places he had never been. Waiting   moving   sliding   trying. Staying up to take care of his mother, afraid to lie down even if she was quiet, 'cause he might fall asleep and not hear her if she needed him.

Even the sun was cold. Wes took off his mackinaw and threw it over to him. He squinched himself together to try and fit under it. Moving   sliding   The road was never straight, the pickup bumped and bumped and he had to hold up his head. Even when he threw up, his uncle wouldn't stop. Maybe it was the whiskey they'd had when they got back from   that place   made him sick. Or the up all night up and down sorting and packing, throwing away and loading. Then too dark on the auto ferry so he didn't even get to see the new bridge they were building, and anyway, that wet, hoohoo wind.

The trees *were* red, like blood that oozed out of old meat and nobody washed the plate. Under them waved—ferns? Baddream giant ones to the baby kind they put around flowers for   too sick people.

He had been holding up his head forever. The creek was slipping and sliding too. His uncle came from nowhere and put three fishes too close to him on a rock. They flopped and moved their sides, trying hard to breathe like too sick people.

He pulled the tarp farther down to the next stripe of sun. A wind made the skinny fire cough gallons of smoke and him shiver even more. Curling and curling till he got all in a ball under the mackinaw and didn't have to see or smell.

When he woke up, he was warm. Fog curled high between the trees, the light shone rosy soft like a bedroom lamp lit somewhere. By the fire, a harmonica in his hand, his uncle was sleeping. Across the creek, just like in the movieshow or in a dream, a deer and two baby deers were drinking. When he lifted his head, they lifted theirs. He and the doe looked into each others eyes for a long time. Then swift, beautiful, all were gone—but her eyes kept looking into his.

Wes was mad to have conked out like that. Six more hours to go—that's if this heap holds up and we don't get stuck 'hind a load going up a grade. I'll have to put out at work like always tomorrow, and it's sure not any restin we been doin these gone days.

Just like before, but colder. Moving sliding. Having to hold up his head. Bumproad twisty in a dark moving tunnel of trees. The lumber trucks screamed coming round the bends, and after it was dark their lights made the moving fog look scary. Sometimes he could sleep, sagged against his uncle who didn't move away. Cold or jolts would wake him. He didn't understand how it was that he was sitting up or why he didn't have a bed to lie down in or why or where he was going. All he wanted was to lie down
    forever

•

A long bridge with standing stone bears. His uncle said: Klamath, almost there. *(Underneath in the night, yearling salmon slipped through their last fresh waters, making it easy to the salt ocean years.)* When the car stopped, there wasn't even a street lamp to see by. A lady came out to help; the light from the open door made the dark stand taller than even the redwoods and *that* leaned like it might fall on him too. The wind or something blew away her words and his uncle's words. His feet were pins and needles   too many boxes and bundles   too many trips down and back a long hall like a cave. A feather cape or something hanging got knocked down. His head gasped back and forth like the sides of the fish on the rock   Something about: we didn't throw away nothin   well I'm sure not goin to miss where I've been   hot milk or coffee?   but he didn't answer, just lay down on a cot with the bundles stacked around him and went into a dream.

So he came to Requa   March, 1932   14 years old.

•

He stands with his back clamped hard against the door Wes has left open, and he has jumped up from the cot to close.

Hey. Leave it open. My can's still draggin. A block behind.

(No smile. Skinny little shrimp. Clutching at the door knob, knuckles white, nostrils flaring. Funny animal noises in his throat.)

Sleeping—all day? Cmon, you had to at least take a leak and put something into that belly . . .   Mrs. Ed or Yee didn't stick their nose in? You didn't see nobody? . . .   Well (looking around), one thing, you sure weren't neating up the place.

(Pale. Ol ghostboy   Silent Cal.   Natural—its plenty raw yet.) I been sleepin too—on my feet AND gettin paid for it. That's talent. *(No smile)* I wasn't bawlin you out, we can get squared away tonight or tomorrow . . . Sure you have to come to eat. It'll only be them that stays here. We all get along. You don't bother them, they don't bother you.

•

They are taking away the boxes and bundles, his low little walls.

That one on top: left over groceries. Into the kitchen, Yee.
Forget takin it off the weeks board, Mrs. Ed, they didn't cost
me nothin. Bedding stuff, Bo: up to the attic. Pots and kitchen
things, Hi. Attic. . . . Well who'd I leave them for and I
thought they might be worth a dime or two. Listen, you'd be
surprised how many's been in tryin to sell Evans their pots and
blankets and everywhich things. Even guns and fishin gear,
and thats get-by when nobodys workin. (Lowered voice) Just
her clothes, Mrs. Ed, you know anybody? Mrs. Ed's room.
Lamps and little rugs, Stevie *said* they was theirs. Sure lay it
down, save me a splinter. Looks good. . . . Anyone for a
lamp? (Funny noises in the kid's throat.) Gear. *He'll* put 'em
away, Mrs. Ed. The bottom drawer, kid, yours and room to
spare. Just a mitt? no ball, no bat? . . . Oddsies, endsies. Yah,
a radio. Even works: Kingfish and Madam Queen, here we is.
Stevie, Mrs. Edler is talking at you: you got clean stuff for
school or does Yee have to wash? No, we never talked is he goin
to school or what. . . . I'll tell you this, though, he's not goin
through what me and Sis did: kicked round one place after an-
other, not havin nobody. Nobody. Right, Stevie? Can you use a
clock, High? Attic. . . . Was you startin to say something,
Stevie? (*Ghostboy!* Swallowing, snuffling.) Naw, that last box
stays: our ketchall; it'll take time, goin through it.

Wait, Bo, maybe I'll chase along after all IF you got the
doremi. Sattiday night, isn't it? and I feel the week. (*What am
I doing, what am I goin to do with this miserable kid?*) Stevie's
for the shuteye anyway, aren't you, kid.

Are you for the shuteye, Stevie?

Scratch of a twig on the window. All he has to lull to, who
has rocked his nights high on a tree of noise, his traffic city.

Blind thick dark, whose sleep came gentled in streetlamp
glow.

And the head on his pillow bulging, though still he is
having to hold it up somewhere   And the round and round
slipping   sliding   jolting   moved to inside him, so he has

to begin to rock his body; rock the cot gently, down and back.

Down and back. It makes a throb for the dark. A clock sound.

That man Highpockets who stuck his hand out at supper and said "Shake, meet the wife" and everybody laughed, he had their clock that stood by the bamboo lamp. A tiny lady in a long dress leaned on it and laughed and held up a tinier flower branch. It had been one of his jobs to wind it and it wheezed while he was winding.

Jobs.

He couldnt remember, was it Bo had taken the lamp? Telling everybody at the table like it was a joke or important   Would you believe it? He's never been fishin never been huntin never held a gun never been in a boat.

Never   Forever

Down and back.   The army blanket itched. When he was a kid he'd really believed that story about they were that color and scratchy because of blood and mud and poo and powdered licy things from the war that never could get washed out

Down and back   A clock sound   It keeps away

What had happened with the bloody quilt? Soft quilt   She hadn't even asked how he was when they let him in after all that waiting and waiting to see her   Just: did you   soak my quilt   Burning eyes

Gentle eyes that looked long at him   blood dripping from where should be eyes   out in the hall swathed bodies floating like in bad movies   never touching the ground   At the window

Down and back   down and back

If he had the lamp   the boxes

You promised   and see I'm someplace else again   dark and things that can get me and I don't know where anything is. Don't expect *me* to be 'sponsible

down and back

they should have put the clock and lamp in with her   the boxes and bundles and wall and put them round her   everything would be together   he wouldn't have to try and remember   or hold up his head that wouldn't lay down inside the one on the pillow and let him sleep

   down and back   down and back

•

All that week he would be lying on the cot in the half dark when Wes got home from work; jump up to re-close the door; lie down again until Wes made him wash up, go in to supper.
At the table he looked at no one, answered in monosyllables, or seemed not to hear at all, stared at the wall or at his wrist, messed the food on his plate into the form of one letter or another, hardly ate
Supper over, he would walk somnambule back to the gaunt room, take off his shoes, get under the covers and lie there, one hand over his eyes.
Bo, Hi, crowded in chattering alongside the radio or playing a quick round of cards; Wes oiling his boots for work, tinkering with fishing-hunting gear, playing the harmonica;   or the room empty: lying there, his arm over his eyes snuffling   scratching   swallowing

One Monday (let him be a while, Mrs. Ed had said), Wes, on his way to work, left the boy at the Klamath crossroads to wait the school bus.
He stands motionless in the moist fog that is almost rain, in Bo's too big fishing slicker. Blurs of shapes loom up and pass. Once a bindle stiff plods by. The across-the-road is blotted out.

When the bus stopped and the door snorted open, he still does not move. The driver tried three honks,   poked his head out and yelled: c'mon New, whatever your name, I'm late. You can do your snoozing inside.
Laughter from in the bus. In hoots.
Slowly, as if returning from an infinite distance, the boy focuses his eyes on the driver, shaking his head and moving his lips as if speaking. He was still mutely shaking "No," as the

[13]

faces at the grimy windows began to slip by fast and faster, contorted or vacant or staring.

On *his* face, lifted to the fog, is duplicated one by one, the expressions on the faces of his fellow young. Still he stood, his lips moving. When he had counted thirteen cars passing (a long while), he crossed and went back down the road, the way his uncle had brought him.

•

Days.

This time when Wes got home, his neatly made bed is torn up, its blanket bunched round the boy stretched out in dimness near the window.

At the expected convulsive jumpup, Wes stepped back and grabbed the doorknob himself. Alright, alright, I'm closin it. The law aint chasin *me*. Are they chasin you?

(*but the boy had not moved at all*)

He felt like yelling: why do you do that or: look at me, for once say hello.

Instead he sat down heavily in the big chair, unlaced his boots. No, I won't ask what he's been doin. Nothin. He'll say it in nothin, too.

Night scratched at the window and seeped from the room corners. No other sound but rising river wind.

The work of the day (of the week, of years) slumped onto Wes. For a minute he let go, slept: snored, great sobbing snores. In a spasm of effort, jerked awake, regarded the shadows, the rumple on the floor by the window.

Something about the light, the radio, not being snapped on, the absence of the usual attempted pleasantries, some rhythm not right, roused the boy from the trancing secret tremble of leaves against the low glowing sky. Was that his mother or his uncle sagged there in the weight of weariness, and why were her feet on the floor?

Get back   he said implacably   Your footstools gone too In a box or throwed away or somebody else resting their tootsies on it   Serve you right   How you going to put up your feet and rub on the varicose like you like to, now?

(Blue swollen veining)   (Are you tired, Ma? Tired to death, love.)

What are you twitchin your muscles like a flybit horse for? asked Wes. And stop swallowin snot.

He slept again   This man he hardly knew who came and took everything and him and put him in another place he did not know where he was.   Slumped, sagged, like . . .

Wes, if you set your feet up on something. *WES*

If I what?

If   you set your feet up on a box

A box. For Crizake

Or a chair   and rub where your feet hurt

A box. Say, did you do up that box today like I told you?

It rests them, Wes. You rub up, not down

Answer me. Did you? No. You leave the only thing I ask you to do, for me to do, on my day off   My one day   Just look at this place   You didn't help High neither when I asked you   You think the candlefish run is goin to last forever? Maybe you might of brung in a basket or two   Mrs. Ed would've took it into consideration   You cost boy   ghostboy don't you know that? My Saturday night for one thing   my one night to howl   you're costin

(Shrimp!) (I'd better watch it; I'm really spoiling tonight.) A rancorous: What's goin to be with you, you dummy kid? raps out anyway.

Sounding a long plaintive mockcowboy howl, switching on the light, yanking him up (God, he's skinny) and with a shove that is half embrace, steers the kid in to dinner.

Where he'd pushed the boiled salt salmon and potatoes away, the crack on his plate made: *Y. You cost, boy, you cost.*   In his wrist a little living ball pushed, as if trying to get out   Where the visiting nurse put her pinky and counted . . . too sick people

Sagged with weariness   like Wes, her stockings rolled down   rubbing rubbing where the blue veins swoll

On the wall the bottom of the Indian bow made: *U*.   No, a funny *V*.   *Y*.   *V*.   Vaud-e-ville. He'd stay for it twice and the feature twice and maybe the serial too   while the light the silvery light   Face bigger and bigger on the screen   Closer   Vast glutinous face   Sour breath   *IS YOU DERE, CHARLIE?*

Bo. Only Bo. Everybody at the table laughing

And now the faces start up   bigger than the room   on the fast track   Having to hold up   Hurry

At the door, Wes heard it again, that faint rhythmic creak. The first time, nights ago, he had thought: is the little bastard jacking off? but it wasnt that kind of a sound. Switching the light on, he saw the boy—as usual—lying on the cot, arm over his face—yes, and rolled into *his* blanket. The sound had stopped.

Sit up. Don't you know enough to excuse yourself when you leave a table sudden? Mrs. Edler was askin me, could you go upriver with her tomorrow to the deer or jumpdance or some such Indian thing they're having up at Terwer. She must want company bad.

Is you dere, Charlie? You jumped a mile when Bo yelled that into your mug. Serves you right, sitting there night after night like you're no place at all, hardly answerin if people talk to you. Why are you such a snot? *Why* (savagely:) IS YOU DERE?

> *(Somewhere.*
> *But the stupor, the lostness, the torpor   the safety*
> *Keep away you rememorings   slippings   slidings*
> *having to hold up my head   Keep away you trying*
> *to get me's*
> *Become the line on a plate, on a wall   The rocking*
> *and the making warm   the movement of leaves against*
> *sky*

    I work so hard for this safety   Let me a while   Let me)

    C'mon. Set up like you belong. We're going to get shed of that box. Right now. But first you make up my bed. Just *keep* that blanket you dragged round the floor, and give me yours.

    C'mon, tuck those corners in. We keep things neat around here. Monday you're starting school. For sure this time. No more of this laying round.

    Neat, I said. Now, where's that goddamn box. And quit making those damn noises.

Scooping onto the bed: boy-sitting-on-a-chamber-pot ash tray
    Happy Joss   Hollywood California painted fringed
    pillow cover   kewpie doll   green glass vase, cracked
Jesus, what junk
    tiny India brass slipper ash tray   enamel cigarette case,
    Fujiyama scene (thrown too close to the edge of the
        bed, it
    slithers off, slips down behind)   pencils, rubber banded
Junk is right. We sure throwed it in in a hurry
    coiled brass snake   Plush candy box: sewing stuff:
        patches
    buttons in jars,   stork scissors,   pincushion doll,
        taffeta
    bell skirt glistening with glass pinheads
Now you got a dolly to play with   Ketch   Can't you even ketch?
    Red plush valentine box: nestled in the compartments:
    brown baby hair, ribbon tied   perfume bottle   empty
    china deer miniature, the fawn headless   heart locket,
        stone
    missing   sand dollar, gull feather
            close quick
Now why did we . . .
    tarnished mesh purse: in it a bright penny   lipstick
    rouge-powder compact, slivered mirror   powder sifts

      close quick
  Pictures: palm size, heart shaped frame
onto the bureau
  celluloid frame, tin laddered back stand
onto the bureau
    stained oblong cardboard, smaller snapshots clipped
     round
    the large center one (His hand falters, steadies)
onto the bureau
    More boxes, slender, rubber banded: in the first,
    letters tied in a man's handkerchief, tin collar
    button, red garter band, ribboned medal pinned to
    a yellow envelope
    In the second (vicious the rubber band snaps)
     DON'T

  The boy rigid on the floor, eyes glazed, mouth open, fixed, face contorted. A fit?

  Steve? Stevie?

  Crawling now, a snake. Rising. With the pillow batting the box out of Wes's hands, flailing at him. *Put it back.* With the pillow shoving everything off the bed into the box. *Put it back. If you was dead you'd put it back* With the pillow pushing the box into the hall slamming the door *all of it dead bury buried* Runs to the chamberpot vomits jabs at Wes when he tries to help him runs to the door to run out sees the box runs back takes the coverlet to him and rocks

  Alright alright Easy Some other day Where was my marbles? Phew Just a bad day, Stevie mine was a Lulu Alright, it's over It was too soon, I know All her things and she's not . . . Alright Easy

  Heaving again.

  You through? I'll get it out of here. (Almost falling over the box on his way to empty the slop.) (No, nobody home I can bum a drink off of. Sattiday night . . .) *(What am I doing what am I going to do with this miserable kid?)*

  Bawling now like a girl.

Alright! It's over, Stevie   It got me too   Easy   You got to grab hold ... It's no good for you, all this layin round   never goin out like normal   Monday you'll start   School   Keep you busy   You'll be with other kids, play ball, have somebody to fish with   Not lay around all the time   thinkin about her, feelin bad.

Stopping his rocking. I don't. I don't.

Easy. It's all right; it's natural. But now you got to take hold.

Shut up bastard. Jabbing at his uncle. Shut up. I told you I don't think about her, I don't feel bad. She's dead. Don't you know she's dead, don't you know?

Fending him off   nodding wordlessly   *(don't I know?)* Edging him back to the cot   Easy   Do I have to paste you one? Forget it, try to sleep, fella   There's just so much I can stand   Easy   I'm so tired I could drop   I'll help you to catch hold, Steve, I promise I'll help   Stop now   Try to sleep Holding him down to the cot   I'm tryin. Doing the best I can, even if it turns out worse like usual   But tryin. You try too. You hear that, Stevie? You try too.

Having to hold up

The pictures stayed, untouched, face down on the dresser. Wherever the box went, Wes assumed it was to the attic. Days later, making his bed, he found the cigarette case, slipped it into a drawer against that far time he might no longer have to roll his own, could afford tailor-mades.

The boy would not rouse. Shaken awake, would not come to breakfast, refused to go out with him and Bo. "We was goin to start you practice shootin today, try for some fish, maybe even let you take the wheel a while. *You're* the loser." But he did not do much urging, wanting to get away from the incomprehensible moil of with-that-boy.

Before he went, he left instructions: Don't lay down *once*, not once. Neat up this room. If there's going to be any hot water, get yourself scrubbed up for school tomorrow   Squeak clean. Find out has Yee got some work you can do; God, what in hell CAN you do. Get outside   even if its raining   down to the river   throw rocks or something. Keep yourself moving   Hear? And don't try to con me.

Asleep in the big chair when Wes got back; no, not asleep (hair still wet and an almost phosphorescent shine on his face) *(ghostboy)*   so   *gone*, Wes's breath stopped for a moment. Maybe I ought to get a doc, or ask Mrs. Ed to look in the doctor book. But what would she look for?   laying around? throwin up?   actin nuts?

Then the dazed, shocked eyes looked at him   but the voice said, perfectly normal: I did everything like you told. Yee cooked him and me rice chow yuk so I don't have to go in for supper tonight, do I. How was your fishing, Wes?

He did not go to school.

Clean to his one white shirt with its streaks of bluing, clutching his and Wes's lunch pails, he sat silent in the pickup till Wes slowed for the crossroads stop where, three weeks before, he had been left for the school bus. Quickly he is over the side.

Hey, *I'm* takin you. You forget? WAIT! Where do you think you're heading?

Plodding back toward Requa.

Get back here. Listen, don't pull no girl tantrum. Get in.

Having to pull over to the shoulder, park, run after him. His violent grab missing, so that he tears the sleazy jacket, half yanking down the boy.

I'm not going, Wes.

Get up, you're going all right. If I have to drag you.

I'd leave soon as you were gone, Wes.

Starting down the road again.

Spinning him around, socking him a good one, steering him back into the car.   *(What am I doing, what am I going to do   )*

What you got against school anyway?

You're headed straight for the nuthouse, layin round like you've been doing. Just nuttier every day. I'm not goin to let you.

I'll have the truant officer, see? Wait, is 14 or 16 the limit?

You're goin, see. What the hell else you got to do? C'mon, dust yourself off. I can't be late.

Starting to climb out again.

Really hurting him; pinning him back, banging and banging his head against the wheel, against the seat. You *have* to go, see?

Wes   (in a strangled voice)   Wes   you're hurting   If I find me a job?

A job!   Releasing him in disgust. You ARE in a nutworld. Half the grown men in the county's not working, High's down to two days, and this dummy kid talks about a job.

In Frisco then, Wes? Maybe set up pins again. Or ship?

In Frisco, my God. It's worse there, you know that. And how you goin to make that 500 miles? And who you got in your corner there? Nobody. You NEED learnin.

Starting up the motor.

Wes, I'll jump.

Socking him again. Hard.

Wes, if I go with you? Ask Mr. Evans, can I help? A learn job, Wes. By you.

Something in the boys voice . . . This time Wes's hands on his shoulders are gentle. Steve, don't fight it no more. It's five, maybe six weeks to vacation . . . fishin   You'll have school buddies. Maybe you're even goin to like school. And even if you don't, sometimes in this life you got to do what you *don't* like. *(Sometimes!)*   Evans ain't about to put anybody on—if he did, Ez would be first choose; every week Ez is in askin: can he have his job back. . . .   Evans don't have it, Stevie. Sometimes its slow even for me. And everythings credit or trade-in; when we get a nickel, he bites it, makes sure its real. I'm surprised he pays *me*.

Ask him, Wes. You said: I'll help you, Steve. You said it. He

don't have to pay me. You hurt me bad Wes. A learn job. By you. You promised.
>   Not school
>   Never
>   Forever

•

Gas   Butane   Sportsmens Goods
Auto Parts   Fittings   Tools
Lumber   Rags   Scrap Iron
Electric/plumbers/builder   supply
>   Housefurnish things
>   Auto Repair   Towing   Wrecking
>   Machining   Soddering   Welding
>   Tool & Saw Sharping   Glasswork
>   Boat caulking/repair

(Leaky, appraising eyes) Sure, why not? Favor to you, Wes. Anything he gets done, we're that much ahead. But if he's in the way, or it don't work out, that's it. And he's *your* headache. Anybody sticks their nose in, he's helping you, not working for me. Don't get him expecting anything for the piggy bank, either. Used stock sometime maybe, whatever I think it's worth   and he's worth. Catch?
>   NEW   USED
>   U NAME IT——WE GOT IT
>   U ASK IT——WE FIX IT

Tumble of buildings and sheds, stockpiles and junk—a block from the bridge—sprawled in the crotch between 101 going north/south and the short crooked upriver road to game and Indian country.

Landscape of thinghillocks and mounds innumerable. Which shed is which? The wind blows so. Too close: scaly, rapid river; too close: dwarfing, encircling: dark massive forest rise.

Stumbling the mounds in his too thin jacket or Bo's too big

slicker after Wes. *(got to figure out what's simple enough he can do. Keep him up. Moving. Paying attention.)* Helping haul   drag   break apart;   find the right sized used tire, generator, lumbersash; hand the measure   the part   the tool

> I said the red devil   Red devil glass cutter   Your ears need reaming?
> Does that even *look* like a 16 × 120? Even the thing they throw peanuts at could figger it
> What you breathin like that for? I showed you: if you lift it this way, she goes easy. Easy. A right way and a wrong way—easy is the right way.
> Is that a shimmy or a shiver? I ought to take me a razor cut, see is it blood or icewater runs in your carcass

The mess heap. Your baby to red up when I'm not needin you. Stack everything, that's what's here, everything—with its own kind. If theys a pile or shed already for it, get it over there   Whats too far gone or cant be burnt, leave. Get them rotten carpets   mattresses out first. Then them batteries   Pile 'em so.   Where I expect to spot you when you're not workin with me, see?

Into the toolshed when it rains. Sort outa the bins into these here washboilers: like, pipe fittins: brass here   copper there: elbows   flanges   unions   couplings   bends   tees. Check out the drawers, see just what belongs is in 'em; get acquainted: like this row: wing nuts   castellated   slotted   quarter inch   *Pay attention!*

> Heaps   piles   glut   accumulation
>   Sores   cuts   blisters on his hands
>   Don't look: scaly rapid river   dark forest encircling
>
> Cold   hardly comprehending   wearing out so quick
>
>   Didn't you hear me callin? Answer me. What you staring at?   You paralyzed?   *(ghostboy)*   Drop that

[23]

carpet and get out of sight till you can come to   Do
I have to paste you one?
(The stiff mouldy rug breaks like cardboard in his
hands. Underneath maggot patterns writhe)
Can't you tell the difference between taper and spiral
   fluted?   (lock or finish washer?)   (adapter, exten-
sion?) can't you? can't you?
Who said you could come in here and lay down? You
   sure tire instant   Get yourself back to the burn pile
and throw that filthy ragquilt out of here. No wonder
you're always scratching.

Is that all you got done and I let you alone all mornin
for it? What's there goin to be to show Evans you're of
use   Yah, useful as a tit on a bull   O for Crizake,
you're not here at all

   More and more wrapped in the peacock quilt, rocking, scratching, snuffling. Rain on the toolshed roof; the little kerosene stove hissing warmth through its pierced crown. Wes looming in the doorway, the grey face of evening behind him. C'mon, useless. 6:30. You killed another day. I *knowed* this was never going to work.
   And once, in the most mournful of voices: Can't you do no better? I can't stand it, Stevie. You're ending up in the dummy or loony house, for sure.

   But the known is reaching to him, stealthily, secretly, reclaiming.
   Sharp wind breath, fresh from the sea. Skies that are all seasons in one day. Fog   rain. *Known weather of his former life.*
   Disorder twining with order. The discarded, the broken, the torn from the whole: weathereaten   weatherbeaten: moldering, or waiting for use-need. *Broken existences that yet continue.*

   Hasps   switches   screws   plugs   faucets   drills
   Valves   pistons   shears   planes   punchers   sheaves
   Clamps   sprockets   coils   bits   braces   dies

How many shapes and sizes; how various, how cunning in application. Human mastery, human skill. Hard, defined, enduring, they pass through his hands—link to his city life of man made marvel.

Wes: junking a towed-in car, one hundred pieces out of what had been one. Singing—unconscious, forceful—to match the motor hum as he machines a new edge, rethreads a pipe. Capable, fumbling; exasperated, patient; demanding, easy; uncomprehending, quick; harsh, gentle: *concerned* with him. *The recognizable human bond.*

The habitable known, stealthily, secretly, reclaiming.
The dead things, pulling him into attention,
   consciousness.
The tasks: coaxing him with trustworthiness, pliancy,
   doing as he bids
                              having to hold up

Rifts:
Wes sets the pitch, the feed, the slide rest to chase a thread. "Wes, *let me.* We're learning it in shop. It's my turn again Monday."

(Monday! What Monday? A Monday cobweb weeks miles gone life ago) Hard, reassuring, the lathe burrs; spins under his hands. (Somewhere in cobweb mist, a school—speck size Somewhere smaller specks that move speak have faces)

Watch it! O my God, you dummy. How'm I goin to explain *this* one to Evans.

Painted wheat wreathes on a tin breadbox he is tipping to empty of rain Remembered pattern. Forgotten hunger peanut butter, sour french bread Remembered scene, face, hand wavering beneath his face reflected in the rusty agitated water

He lifts the wrecking mallet, pounds. Long after the spurting water has dried from his face and the tin is shreds in great muddy earth gouges, he still mindlessly pounds.

Later, dragging a mattress to the burn pile, his face contorts, fixes rigid, mouth open. The rest of the day in the toolshed, to lie immobile, and will not get up even to Wes's kick of rage.

Rags stiff and damp   Green slime braids with the rope coils, white grubs track his palm
Bottle fly colors luster the rotting harness   rusty tongueless bells fall

He is warmer now. An old melton coat with anchor buttons that Evans let Wes take from the clothes shed. Faint salt of a seaman's many voyagings seem to nest in it, and deep in the pockets, mysterious graininesses crumble. Afternoons, if the strong northwest winds of May clear the sky an hour or two, the coat distills, stores the sun about him as he moves through mound-sheltered warmth in and out of the blowing cold; or sits with Wes, poncho over the muddy ground, eating their baloney and bread lunch in the sun-hive the back of the scrap-iron pile makes.

Weeds, the yellow wild mustard and rank cow parsnip, are already waist high, blow between him and the river. Blue jays shrill, swoop for crumbs; chipmunks hover. Wes gabs, plays his harmonica. The boy lies face down in his pool of warmth. In him something keeps trembling out in the wind with the torn whirled papers, the bending weeds, the high tossed gulls.

Only the rain saves him—otherwise, before lunch, he practices shooting. Buckets, cans, are spotted in a semicircle for targets, the rococo scroll of a carpet beater nailed to a post. Sight. Squeeze. Anticipatory wince. Shuddering rock of the recoil.

Who barks more, Wes or the gun? If you'd been concetrating   if you'd just been concetrating. I want you good as me, Stevie. See? 200 yards   right on target everytime.

The bruise on his shoulder—from when? Wes's beating the day he would not go to school?—purples, spreads.

Maybe this is better'n school for you now, Stevie   Keep you outdoors, build you up   I got so much to learn you   All your life you can use it.

Helping at the gas pump, he keeps his head lowered so that he knows the grease spots on the ground and how they change from day to day, but not who is in the cars. Even when the speech comes glottal, incomprehensible, Indian, he will not look up on the faces, nor on those of the riggers and swampers, checking the chains tight around the two-three giant logs that make up their load.

Grease spots, and how they change from day to day; loggers muddied boots, flowerets and pine needles embedded; pliant redwood hair strands loosened from the logs and blowing across the road; the cars of the regulars; Evans dry ghost cough from the store, and that a certain worn-to-bareness tire tread brings him watchfully into hearing distance: these he comes to know—but never faces.

Once, checking tires (young swaggering voices in the car), a girl steps out on the running board, so close he can smell her, round his hand to her bared thigh, the curve of her butt.

Relentless, vehement: clamor congests   engorges. Gas bite, the soaked rag held to his nostrils, will not help.

Wes, don't call me to the pumps any more.

You'll do as you're told, you snotty kid   Snotty's right Everytime I look at you. Wipe that nose. You need a washer in there?

relentless
engorged
clamorous
stealthily secretly reclaiming

Terrible pumps:
Evans out more and more.

Davis does what *I* say, see? Pay on the line or no tow. Yep, no dough, no go. I don't care *how* many kids you got stuck in your jalopy, or how far you had to hitch to get here. Sure we got a used transmission. We got a used everything. But for do-re-mi. Don't ask *me* how you're going to manage without a heap. . . . You can junk it.

No, not even for five gallons trade, I won't take that mattress. I got a shed full now. There's maybe four hundred families the fifty miles around; they're sleeping on something already; who's going to buy 'em off me? No. That spare hasn't got a thousand miles left. Well maybe the gun.

Ten gallons gets you up—say—Grants Pass. How do *I* know how you'll make it to your brothers in Chehalis. One thing we *don't* sell here is a crystal ball.

Whisper: Over here, Wes. I don't want ol Skinflint to spot me. You think you might have some link chain like this? An/8th or maybe a/4th. I got this idea, see? Sports season coming, and you know how they like to bring back a souvenir. Well, Christmas we didn't know what to do, so I whittled the boys up little lumber trucks—load of logs, chain and all—they're still playing with 'em. I thought till the woods open up again, I might pick up some loose change makin 'em to sell. Esty's doing up dolls out of redwood hair. Real cute. Evans won't help me out, but you will, won't you Wes. I'm about out of my mind.

When I call you I don't mean tomorrow sometime next week. If I catch you cuddlin up to that stove again, I'll turn you every which way but loose

•

The smell or the whiskey is making him sick   is making him happy   is making him sleepy   The brights and the ragtime making him happy   Lights lights little lights over the fireplace going on and off and on and off and on and off and on if you wink your eyes in time in time   I love you lights   Are you howling Wes   is that how you howl your night to howl? O Wes   in the blue of smoke and breaths tapdancing with Bo and that lady Esty in the middle and that fatso man   Stop you don't know how to tap, Wes   The keys on the player piano nickel in the slot piano know how   jigging and tapping and nobodys playing them because I'M playing them   long distance   knowing how   tapping and dancing luxurious round the table   round the dollars   his fingers tapping round and round

What you going to do with those two big beautiful cartwheels honey? Tapdance my fingers round and round them what he didn't answer her and should have   because   because   and here the breathblue smokeblue clouds into his head   And on and off   and round   tiniest sparkle on the wall   calendar snow scene, moose locking horns   sparkly I love you   O I like that ragtime   kitten on the keys   I *am* the keys   What did you say that's so ha ha Wes?   wave wave dance my hand (no nobody's looking) highstep my fingers   o highstep and off and on and round   I wanta go to a movie show   and round   Red light that squiggles to you in the fog and when you get closer says   E A T   but nobody's eating   they're dancing   they think its dancing   chewing the rag and swiggling and off and on and sparkle and round and fire jumping and Wes howling

> *Stop that, Bo*

sticky and cold, the whiskey doused over him. *Best hair tonic there is, I'm tellin you, kid, use it myself every celebratin night   and it stinks so purty*

It doesn't   it doesn't   and it doesn't wipe off and the smell is on his sleeve now so when he has to wipe his nose or wave his arm   is making him sick and off and on   and round   o put another nickel in   reeling waltz   I wanta go to a picture show   a man crying (Fatso)   *sobby sentimental stew*   O ma, that's funny, a sobby sentimental stew

Liar   You promised   and see I'm another place again   no movies and no stores and no Chinatown and cold water in the faucet you have to pump   not even lights   just tonight   little prickle kind and one squiggle sign   just tonight

   and round and round and off and on   push on the keys   dance   tap   float on the sadness   sleep pushing down clouding with the air and   Sure I'm listening Wes   No thanks you just gave me another nip   Yah *how you keep Evans from catching on that I'm not all there*   Yah   and round sparks like blows from a fist   the fire?   over the fireplace, branching antlers, sad deer eyes   in the fire, branching antlers   glowing eyes   am going to be sick

aaagh
aaagh

•

A dream?   The yard   lithe Bo tapdancing the mounds   Wes in the furnish shed handing out bottles   gurgling from one himself   bootleg   he don't know I know he's peddlin hooch but I do, gettin in on it just when it's goin to get legal   end hard times   Turning round and round a musical saw wheel dry whispery papery sad sound   *they have taken her to Georgia*   Wes's harmonica prowl   papery sad   *there to wear her life away*   making his saddest trainwhistle sounds
round   and   round

•

The damp rushing air slaps slaps the boys face: *wake up* the lurching in his belly, the pitching truck: *wake up*. Wes slapping too, jabbing him away with his elbow every lurch he is thrown against him; waves of drunk smell from Wes's breath or is it his own sleeve: *wake up*. Wes driving jolty, not like Wes at all: shouting   singing   mumbling   beating on the dash. Crooning: poor ol shrimp cant sit up poor ol shrimp passin out   Take him out to celebrate   Evans shakin loose two smackers and he cant take it   cant celebrate FOOderackysacky want some seafood momma shrimpers and rice are very nice   poor ol shrimp   (pounding on the dash) YOU'RE A SHIT EVANS   YOU HEAR ME (whispering) he don't know though does he (elbow jab) he don't know   you're not all there   (loud) cause I cover up good don't I Stevie? We'll have a heaver on that, hey? Me, not you, shrimp. Am taking care of you like I promised. Right?

Vamp me honey kitchaleecoo   anything you'll want we'll do   Jab. Forever long to get to Mrs. Eds. Not the same way they came. Jolt, jolt. Is it even a road? Headless shadows in the carlights. Stumps. *Not all there*   Sparks like blows   Hurtled, falling   falling   Wet on his face   fir needles   leaves. Blood?

C'mon, up, up, see if you're hurt. Well I did stop sudden. You're fine, kid, sound as a dollar. Go ahead, puke. I got to go to this place down here, see?

Thick   oblivious   laughing   mumbling   pawing the floor of the truck for something, throwing the poncho at him, hard. *Cover up*   Dont want you ketching cold. You're running out of snot as is. Counting, recounting his silver by the light of a flash. Expansively: Keep 'em, Stevie, keep 'em; don't need 'em.

Need what? Thick black   His trembling body redoing the hurtling fall over and over   all scraped places burning. His shoulder . . . Far down in trees a weak light   whorled, spectral, veined   Eyes

Wes, wait, wait for me. Tripping over the poncho. On the ground again, his nose bubbling blood.

Easier to just lie there   roll into the poncho   shrink into the coat   cry   (In one soft pocket his fingers tap round and round the silver dollars; in the other, hold the tongueless bell.) Put another nickel   Some celebrating!   *Not all there*

Faint salt smell   from drying blood?   the coat?   Warm. Round and round   not even minding the dark

Sudden the knowledge where Wes has gone. *Annie Marines*, she sells it. Nausea. Swelling, swollen aching. Relentless. Helpless, his hand starts to undo the coat layer (*meet the wife, meet the wife*).

Slap. On his face. Another slap. Great drops. *Rain.* Move, you dummy. Pushing himself up against a tree, giant um-

[31]

brella in the mottled dark. Throb sound in and around him (his own excited blood beat?) Rain, hushing, lapping.

City boy, he had only known rain striking hard on unyielding surface, walls, pavement; not this soft murmurous receiving: leaves, trees, earth. In wonder he lay and listened, the fir fragrance sharp through his caked nostrils. Warm. Dry.

Gently he began to rock. The hardness had gone down by itself.

Far down where Wes was, a branch shook silver into the light. Rain. *His mothers quick shiver as the rain traced her cheek. C'mon baby, we've got to run for it.*

Laughing. One of her laughing times. Running fast as her, the bundles bumping his legs. Running up the stairs too. Tickling him, keeping him laughing while she dried his face with the rough towel.

Twisting away from the pain: trying to become the cocoa steam, the cup ring marking the table, the red checked tablecloth. *Her shiver.* How the earth received the rain, how keen its needles. Don't ask *me* where your umbrella got put, don't expect *me* to be 'sponsible, you in your leaky house.

Her shiver. Rain underneath, swelling to a river, floating her helpless away   *Her shiver*

Twisting from the pain: face contorted, mouth fallen open fixed to the look on her dying, dead face.

When Wes lurched down the path, he still did not move. The helpless pain came again. For Wes this time, drunk, stumbling, whispering: O my God, I've had better imagines

Stevie! Where the hell are you? You scared the hell out of me . . . Get in. I feel lower than whale shit, and that's at the bottom of the ocean.

The light was still on. Wes must have carried or walked him in, been too drunk to make him wake up, undress. Wes hadn't undressed either, lay, shoes muddy on his bed, he, who was always the neat one.

The boy stared at the bulb staring at him; then, painfully, got up, pulled off his clothes, went over and knelt by Wes's bed to tug off the offending shoes and cover him.

One of Wes's fists trembled; a glisten of spit trickled out of the corner of his mouth. His fly was open. How rosy and bud-like and quiet it sheathed there.

The blanket ends wouldn't lap to cover. He had to pile on his coat, Wes's mackinaw, and two towels, patting them carefully around the sleeping form. *There now you'll be warm*, he said aloud, *sleep sweet, sweet dreams* (though he did not know he had said it, nor in whose inflections).

He was shivering with cold now. *Dummy or crazy house not all there* Though he put his hands out imploringly to protect himself the blows struck at him again. His uncle moaned, whispered something; he leaned down to hear it, looked full on the sleeping face. Face of his mother. His face. Family face

For once he was glad to turn off the light and have the shutting darkness: hugged the pillow over his face for more. At the window spectral shapes tapped; out in the hall, swathed forms floated, wrung their hands. Later he hurtled the fall over and over in a maggoty sieve where eyes glowed in rushing underground waters and fire branched antlers, fir needle after shining needle.

•

accurately threaded, reamed and chamfered
    Shim   Imperial flared
        cutters   benders   grinders   beaders
            shapers   notchers   splicers   reamers
                  how many shapes and sizes,
                  how various, how cunning in
                      application

What did Toots and Casper want? Did I hear them asking for two gallons of gas? *Two* gallons? Where they coming from anyway? I thought that kind were all riding 99.

Tentacle weeds pierce the dishpan he is trying to pry up. Orange rust flowerings flake, cling to the quivering stalks, embroider the gaping pan holes.

Beauty of rot   rust   mold

Wingding anchors   bearing sheaves   plated, crackle, mottled blue, satin, finish

Are you dreamin or workin? That carbon should of been clean chipped off by now. I *promised* that motor. O for Crizake, you ain't here at all.

Something is different at Mrs. Eds. Is it the longer light? How clear everyone is around the table, though still he does not look into their faces. The lamps, once so bright and hung with shadows, are phantom pale now; the windows, once black mirrors where apparitions swam, show green and clear to heads of trees, river glint, dark waver of hill against sunset sky.

Highpockets is gone. When had he gone, and why? The blurredness will not lift. A new man, thready, pale, sits in his place and has his room.

The talk eddys around him: aint going to be no season, not in Alaska Vancouver or Pedro . . . like crabs feedin on a dead man, like a lot of gulls waitin for scraps . . . the Cascades the Olympics the Blues . . . nickel snatchin bastards

He sees that it is not shadows that hang on the wall around the bow, but Indian things: a feathered headdress, basket hats, shell necklace. Two faces dream in shell frames. One, for all the beard, Mrs. Ed's.

                her family face

•

    sharping   hauling   sorting   splicing
    burring   chipping   grinding   cutting
    grooving   drilling   caulking   sawing
                             the tasks, coaxing
    rust gardens

Nippers. You bring nippers. Did you think I was going to *bite* the wire? Try it with *your* choppers.

Pilings on pilings. Rockers, victrolas, flyspecked mirrors, scroll trundle sew machines, bureaus, bedsteads, baby buggies.
  Wes, I can't hardly open the door, it won't go in, there's no room.
  No room, you make room, dummy. That's the job. You good for *any*thing?
  The wind blows the encircling forest to a roar. Papers fly up and blind; a tire is blown from his hand. He scrambles the scrapiron pile to the shelter side, stands, coat flapping, blown riverspray wet on his face, hallooing and hallooing to the stone bears on the bridge.
  Loony, loony, get down. You see that canvas needs tackin? Tack.

Miming Wes's face   Sounding Evans dry ghost cough   Gentling his bruised shoulder. Sometimes stopping whatever he is doing, his mouth opening: fixed to the look on her dying face

We'll be able to start burnin today or tomorrow if the wind stays down, says Wes. Don't this sun feel good? Just smell.
  Meld of rose bay, forest, river, earth dryings. The sun stirring the brew to a great fragrant steaming. In it, every metal scrap, every piece of glass, glances, flashes, glitters, spangles, ripples light.
  Wes stands in fountains of light: white sparkles as he moves the wheel for knife sharpening; blue jettings as he welds a radiator.
  I didn't know you could sing, Stevie. You practicing for the Majors Amateur Hour?
  It's for my head, Wes.
  Outa your head, you mean.
  The baking warmth, the dazzle, the windlessness.

Toward noon the next day, they set the burn pile. Wes lets him douse on the gasoline, but the boys look is so unnatural—spasms of laughing and spastic body dance as the flames spurt—Wes cuffs him away.

You a firebug nut or something? Get away, loony.

The wordless ecstasy will not contain. Quiver and dazzle are magnified in the strange smoking air. Baking mud sucks at his shoes as he runs from flash to flash. Stench of burning rubber and smoldering wet rags layer in with the heady sweet spring vapors. A stately rain of ash begins. It drives him down by the river, but the stench and dazzle are there too, and flashing rainbow crescents he does not know are salmon leaping. There, on a sandy spit, where the blue water greens the edging forest, the climbing fir trees blue the sky, sun drenched, he lays himself down.

Only when they turn at Panther Creek for the Requa cutoff do they leave the smoke. They ride west into setting sun blare. The road is gold, black leaves shake out sungold, and from the low gilded deer brush there reels a drunken wild-lilac smell.

Ten more days to huntin, Stevie. You don't know how much I want them few days . . . I shouldn't have got so mad at you; you're doin almost o.k. lately sometimes as much help as trouble. Even your shootin

Four days in a half stupor, pumping for breath.

Why do you have to go and pull something like this for? Now I'll have to work Decoration Day, be far enough ahead so he'll give me them three days off . . .

Mrs. Ed, come here, isn't there anything you can do to help this poor kid catch his breath?

He stands beside her negligently, as if he is not there at all, stooping his newly tall, awkward body into itself while she introduces him to the preacher, families, other young.

Better go in, Stephen, you shouldn't be standing here in this strong wind. Betty'll show you where to sit, won't you, Betty?

    his Dad . . . afore he was born . . . AEF . . .
    never knew him . . . his mother . . . just a few months
       ago
    . . . Wes Davis   uncle . . . all he has
  His sleeves don't pull down to cover   ugly scabs   peely walls   *That these dead shall not have*   Mrs. Edler's arm light on his hurt shoulder   *He breaketh the bow and snappeth the spear asunder*   cobwebs under the backless benches   Spiders?   his skin crawls   scratching the itch places he can reach   scratching blood   somebody giggling whispering dead fly in the hymn book
    There is a fountain filled with blood
sweet voice   a girl or lady in back
    and there may I, as vile as he
    wash all my sins away
somebody giggling whispering   The sleeves don't pull down

•

  At the first cemetery, he waits for her under the Requiescat in Pace gate. People came by, carrying wreaths and flowers and planting flags. If you were a dead soldier, you got a flag. The flags made crackle noises in the wind—like shooting practice—and kept getting blown down and having to be planted again.
  A girl—that Betty maybe?—called his name, so he had to walk to a tangled part where nobody else was. His foot kicked over something—a glass canning jar—rust and dried things that might once have been flowers in it. Did it belong to the marble hand pointing to the sky, Leo Jordan, 1859–1911, He is Not Dead but Sleeping, or to the kneeling stone lamb, almost hidden by the tall blowing weeds?
  Carefully he bent down and stood it by the lamb. Milena Willett was carved on it, 1 yr. old
          Budded on earth
          Blooming in Heaven
      He had to pull away the weeds
and scratch out sandy dirt to read the rest:

>   Thy mother strives in patient trust
>   Her bleeding heart to bow
>   For safe in God   the Good   the Just
>   Her babys sleeping now

That part was sunk in the ground.

How warm it felt down there in the weeds where nobody could see him and the wind didn't reach. The lamb was sun warm too. He put his arm around its stone neck and rested. Red ants threaded in and out; the smell was sweet like before they set the burn pile; even the crackling flags sounded far away.

The sleep stayed in him all the way to the second cemetery. Other people were in the car, they had stopped at back dirt roads to get them. You always get out and open the car door for ladies, Stephen, Mrs. Edler had said. But they weren't ladies, they were Indians.

The sun baked in through the car window and their trouble talk floated in haze   He says the law on his side   legal   *but it's ours*   the Sheriff   bones don't prove it he says the law

This cemetery he didn't get out of the car, pushed and rattled by the wind. Trees, bent all their lives that one way, clawed toward the windows. There were firing sounds here too, but maybe they were ocean booms. He thought he could see ocean, lashing beyond the trees.

•

What did you do to him, Wes asked Mrs. Edler. When I heard where you went, I expected sure he'd get back near dead, bad as in the beginning. But he's been frisky as a puppy all day. Chased me round the junk heaps. Rassled   went down to the river on his own   threw skimmers   sharped a saw perfect   Paid attention. Curled up and fell asleep on the way home.

That's where he is—still sleeping. Lay down second we got home and I can't get him up. Blowing out the biggest bubble of snot you ever saw. Just try and figger that loony kid.

                    (stealthily   secretly reclaiming

The Tale
CHARLES SIMIC

INVENTION OF THE INVISIBLE

And always someone's missing
and the light left for him in the window
is now the oldest one on earth
and still each day his shirt, bowl, and spoon
are washed by his mother and sister
and the front door is unlocked just before nightfall
because that's the time
when the ones who have been gone so long
like to return

but nothing happens
although we heard his messengers
behind the wall
and yet when we go looking for them
there's only his empty chair
around which, the old ant,
now barely able to move
has almost made a circle.

INVENTION OF THE KNIFE

Its blade imagined by the hanged man
in that split of a second as he glimpses
with raised eyes the rope for the last time

yields itself to his executioners
who then go home at daybreak
over the snow that makes no sound
to cut the bread fresh from the oven.

INVENTION OF A COLOR

Already it's thousands of years old.
Who can say its name?
Neither black nor white.
No one sees it twice.

How strangely everything is soaked in it:
that finger straining to lift itself and that face.
Even the trees and the animals are still,
that is to say, if there were any here.

This color announces a visitor.
Somewhere no doubt a door has been opened.
It is a color of waiting, color of patience.
No one comes. It is a color of an idea
               which will not complete itself in our lifetime.
The more I speak about it, the more
I realize that it doesn't exist,
like the steady dripping of a faucet
which, all of a sudden, has ceased.

INVENTION OF NOTHING

I didn't notice
while I wrote here
that now nothing remains of the world
except my table and chair.

And so I said:
(for the hell of it, to abuse patience)
Is this the tavern
without a glass, wine, or waiter
where I'm the long awaited drunk?

The color of nothing is blue.
I strike it with my left hand and the hand disappears.

Why am I so quiet then
and so happy?

I climb on the table
(the chair is gone already)
I sing through the throat
of an empty beer-bottle.

errata

Where it says snow
read teeth-marks of a virgin
Where it says knife read
you passed through my bones
like a police-whistle
Where it says table read horse
Where it says horse read my migrant's bundle
Apples are to remain apples
Each time a hat appears
think of Isaac Newton
reading the Old Testament
Remove all periods
they are scars made by words
I couldn't bring myself to say
Put a finger over each sunrise
it will blind you otherwise
That damn ant is still stirring
Will there be time left to list
all errors to replace
all hands guns owls plates
all cigars ponds woods and reach
that beer-bottle my greatest mistake
the word I allowed to be written
when I should have shouted
her name

Poem

DONALD JUSTICE

This poem is not addressed to you.
You may come into it briefly,
But no one will find you here, no one.
You will have changed before the poem will.

Even while you sit there, unmovable,
You have begun to vanish. And it does not matter.
The poem will go on without you.
It has the spurious glamor of certain voids.

It is not sad, really, only empty.
Once perhaps it was sad, no one knows why.
It prefers to remember nothing.
Nostalgias were peeled from it long ago.

Your type of beauty has no place here.
Night is the sky over this poem.
It is too black for stars.
And do not look for any illumination.

You neither can nor should understand what it means.
Listen, it comes without guitar,
Neither in rags nor any purple fashion.
And there is nothing in it to comfort you.

Close your eyes, yawn. It will be over soon.
You will forget the poem, but not before
It has forgotten you. And it does not matter.
It has been most beautiful in its erasures.

O bleached mirrors! Oceans of the drowned!
And it does not matter what you think.

These are not my words now.
This poem is not addressed to you.

Farm Wife

ELLEN BRYANT VOIGT

Dark as the spring river, the earth
opens each damp row as the farmer
swings the far side of the field.
The blackbirds flash their red
wing patches and wheel in his wake,
down to the black dirt; the windmill
grinds in its chain rig and tower.

In the kitchen, his wife is baking.
She stands in the door in her long white
gloves of flour. She cocks her head and
tries to remember, turns like the moon
toward the sea-black field. Her belly
is rising, her apron fills like a sail.
She is gliding now, the windmill churns
beneath her, she passes the farmer,
the fine map of the furrows.
The neighbors point to the bone-white
spot in the sky.
                  Let her float
like a fat gull that swoops and circles,
before her husband comes in for supper,
before her children grow up and leave her,
before the pulley cranks her down
the dark shaft, and the church blesses

her stone bed, and the earth seals
its black mouth like a scar.

Zaydee
PHILIP LEVINE

Why does the sea burn? Why do the hills cry?
My grandfather opens a fresh box
of English Ovals, lights up, and lets the smoke
drift like clouds from his lips.

Where did my father go in my 5th autumn?
In the blind night of Detroit
on the front porch, grandfather points up
at a constellation shaped like a cock and balls.

A tiny man, at 13 I outgrew his shirts.
I then beheld a closet of stolen suits,
a hive of elevator shoes, crisp hankies,
new bills in the cupboard, old in the wash.

I held the spotted hands that passed over
the breasts of airline stewardesses,
that moved in the fields like a wind
stirring the long hairs of grain.

Where is the ocean? the flying fish?
the God who speaks from a cloud?
He carries a card table out under the moon
and plays gin rummy and cheats.

He took me up in his arms
when I couldn't walk and carried me
into the grove where the bees sang
and the stream paused forever.

He laughs in the movies, cries in the streets,
the judges in their gowns are monkeys,
the lawyers mice, a cop is a fat hand.
He holds up a strawberry and bites it.

He sings a song of freestone peaches
all in a box,
in the street he sings out Idaho potatoes
California, California oranges.

He sings the months in prison,
sings salt pouring down the sunlight,
shoveling all night in the stove factory
he sings the oven breathing fire.

Where did he go when his autumn came?
He sat before the steering wheel
of the black Packard, he turned the key,
pressed the starter, and he went.

The maples blazed golden and red
a moment and then were still,
the long streets were still and the snow
swirled where I lay down to rest.

The Secret of Poetry
JON ANDERSON

When I was lonely, I thought of death.
When I thought of death I was lonely.

I suppose this error will continue.
I shall enter each grey morning

delighted by frost, which is death,
& the trees that stand alone in mist.

When I met my wife I was lonely.
Our child in her body is lonely.

I suppose this error will go on & on.
Mornings I kiss my wife's cold lips,

nights her body, dripping with mist.
This is the error that fascinates.

I suppose you are secretly lonely
thinking of death, thinking of love.

I'd like, please, to leave on your sill
just one cold flower, whose beauty

would leave you inconsolable all day
The secret of poetry is cruelty.

Gemini
LOUISE GLÜCK

There is a soul in me
It is asking
To be given its body

It is asking
To be given blue eyes,
A skull matted

With black hair
That shape
Already formed & detaching:

So the past put forth
A house filled
With asters & white lilac

A child
In her cotton dress,
The lawn, the copper beech—

Such of my own lives
I have cast off—the sunlight
Chipping at the curtains

And the wicker chairs
Uncovered, winter after winter,
As the stars finally

Thicken & descend as snow

Oleum Misericordiae
JOHN ASHBERY

To rub it out, make it less virulent
And a stab too at rearranging
The whole thing from the ground up.
Yes we were waiting just now
Yes we are no longer waiting.

Afterwards when I tell you
It's as though it all only happened
As siding of my story
I beg you to listen
You are already listening

It has shut itself out
And in doing so shut us accidentally in

And meanwhile my story goes well
The first chapter
                endeth

But the real story, the one
They tell us we shall probably never know
Drifts back in bits and pieces
All of them, it turns out

So lucky
Now we really know
It all happened by chance:
A chance encounter
The dwarf led you to the end of a street
And pointed flapping his arms in two directions
You forgot to misprize him
But after a series of interludes

In furnished rooms (describe wallpaper)
Transient hotels (mention sink and cockroaches)
And spending the night with a beautiful married woman
Whose husband was away in Centerville on business
(Mention this wallpaper: the purest roses
Though the creamiest and how
Her smile lightens the ordeal
Of the last 500 pages
Though you never knew her last name
Only her first: Dorothy)
You got hold of the water of life
Rescued your two wicked brothers Cash and Jethro
Who promptly stole the water of life
After which you got it back, got safely home,
Saved the old man's life
And inherited the kingdom.

But this was a moment
Under the most cheerful sun.
In poorer lands
No one touches the water of life

It has no taste
And though it refreshes absolutely
It is a cup that must also pass

Until everybody
Gets some advantage, big or little
Some reason for having come

So far
Without dog or woman
So far alone, unasked.

Nightmare Begins Responsibility
MICHAEL S. HARPER

I place these numbed wrists to the pane
watching white uniforms whisk over
him in the tube-kept
prison
fear what they will do in experiment
watch my gloved stickshifting gasolined hands
breathe *boxcar-information-please* infirmary tubes
distrusting white-pink mending paperthin
silkened end hairs, distrusting tubes
shrunk in his *trunk-skincapped*
shaven head, in thighs
distrusting-white-hands-picking-baboon-light
on this son who will not make his second night
of this wardstrewn intensive airpocket
where his father's asthmatic
hymns of *night-train*, train done gone
his mother can only know that he has flown
up into essential calm unseen corridor
going box carred home, *mamaborn,sweetsonchild
gonedowntown* into *researchtestingwarehousebatteryacid
mama-son-done-gone*/me telling her 'nother
train tonight, no music, nobreathstroked
heartbeat in my infinite distrust of them:

and of my distrusting self
white-doctor-who-breathed-for-him-all-night
say it for two sons gone,
say nightmare, say it loud
panebreaking heartmadness:
nightmare begins responsibility.

Power

AUDRE LORDE

The difference between poetry and rhetoric
is being ready to kill
yourself
instead of your children.

I am trapped on a desert of raw gunshot wounds
and a dead child dragging his shattered
black face off the edge of my sleep
blood from his punctured cheeks and shoulders
is the only liquid for miles and my stomach
churns at the imagined taste while
my mouth splits into dry lips
without loyalty or reason
thirsting for the wetness of his blood
as it sinks into the whiteness
of the desert where I am lost
without imagery or magic
trying to make power
out of hatred and destruction
trying to heal my dying son with kisses
only the sun will bleach his bones quicker.

The policeman who shot down a ten year old in Jamaica
stood over the boy with his cop shoes in childish blood
and a voice said "Die you little motherfucker" and
there are tapes to prove that.
At his trial this policeman said in his own defense
"I didn't notice the size or anything else
only the color," and
there are tapes to prove that too.

Today that 37 year old white man with 13 years of police
    forcing

was set free
by 11 white men who said they were satisfied
justice had been done
and one black woman who said "They convinced me"
meaning
they had dragged her 4'10" black woman's frame
over the hot coals of four centuries of white male approval
until she let go of the first real power she ever had
and lined her own womb with cement
to make a graveyard for our children.

I have not been able to touch the destruction within me
but unless I learn to use
the difference between poetry and rhetoric
my power too will run corrupt as poisonous mold
or lie limp and useless as an unconnected wire
and one day I will take my teenaged plug
and connect it to the nearest socket
raping some 85 year old white woman
and as I beat her senseless and set a torch to her bed
a greek chorus will be singing in 3/4 time
"Poor thing. She never hurt a soul. What beasts they are."

Problems of Art

JAMES ALAN MCPHERSON

Seated rigidly on the red, plastic-covered sofa, waiting for Mrs. Farragot to return from her errand, Corliss Milford decided he did not feel comfortable inside the woman's apartment. Why this was he could not tell. The living room itself, as far as he could see around, reflected the imprint of a mind as meticulous as his own. Every item seemed in place; every detail meshed into an overriding suggestion of order. This neatness did no damage to the image of Mrs. Farragot he had assembled, even before visiting her at home. Her first name was Mary, and she was thin and severe of manner. He recalled that her walnut-brown face betrayed few wrinkles; her large brown eyes were quick and direct without being forceful; her thin lips, during conversation, moved with precision and resolve. Even her blue summer dress, with pearl-white buttons up its front, advertised efficiency of character. The bare facts of her personal life, too, argued neatness and restraint; he had them down on paper, and the paper rested on his knee. Milford juggled his knee; the paper shifted, but did not fall. That too, he thought. It was part of why he felt uneasy. For a few seconds, he entertained the notion that the living room was no more than a sound stage on a movie lot. Somehow, it seemed too calculated.

Milford's suspicion of an undisclosed reality was heightened by the figure in the painting on the wall across the room. It was the portrait of a sad-eyed Jesus. Immaculate in white and blue robes, the figure held a pink hand just above the red, valentine-shaped heart painted at the center of its chest. Bright drops of red blood dripped from the valentine. Such pictures as this Milford had seen before in dimestores. Though it had a certain poignancy, he thought, it was . . . cheap. It conveyed a poverty of the artist's imagination and tended to undermine the sophistication of those who purchased such dimensionless renditions. Did not the Latin poor build great cathedrals? Even country Baptists wheeled their preachers about in Cadillacs. Why then, Milford asked himself, would a poor black woman compound an already bleak existence by worshiping before a dimestore rendition of a mystery? He recalled having heard someplace something about the function of such images, but could not recall exactly what he had heard. The plastic crinkled as he shifted on the sofa to review Mrs. Farragot's papers. She had been born in Virginia, but had lived for many years in Los Angeles. She was a widow, but received no compensation from her husband's social security.

She had been arrested for driving under the influence of alcohol, although she insisted that she was a teetotaler. About the only consistent factual evidence about her that Milford knew was her insistence, over a period of two weeks, that no one but a white lawyer could represent her at the license revocation hearing. For her firm stand on this, she was now notorious in all the cubbyhole offices of Project Gratis. Milford looked again at the portrait. Perhaps that explains it, he thought. Then he thought, perhaps it does not.

He leaned back on the sofa, impatient now for Mrs. Farragot to return. According to his watch it was 11:45 A.M. The hearing was scheduled for 1:30 P.M. The day was already humid and muggy, and would probably grow warmer as events developed in the afternoon. But Milford was used to it. For want of a better rationalization, he liked to call such occasions invigorating. Now he sighed and glanced again about the room, wondering just who would return with her to act as witness and corroborator. Since his mind was trained to focus on those areas where random facts formed a confluence of palpable reality, he became restless for easy details. His eyes swept over the brown coffee table; above the red, plastic-covered armchair across the room; past the tall glass china closet packed with jade-green and brandy-red and sunset-orange cut-glass ashtrays and knickknacks whose scalelike patterns sparkled in the late morning sunlight streaming lazily through the open window on bright particles of dust; beyond the china closet to the yellow-white door leading into the quiet, smell-less kitchen from which sounded the hum of a refrigerator; past the doorframe, quickly, and to the sofa's edge on his right to where a group of pictures in cheap aluminum frames stood grouped on a brown plywood end table. These he examined more closely. The larger one was of Mrs. Mary Farragot. It was a close-up of her face as it must have looked ten years ago. There were fewer wrinkles and no strains of gray in her ebony black hair. She was smiling contentedly. This, Milford thought, was not the face of an alcoholic. It reflected strength and motherly concern. Next to this picture was a small color print of two white children. Both were smiling. One, a blond boy seated in a blue high chair, grinned with his spoon raised above a yellow dish of cereal, as if about to strike. The little girl, with dark brown hair, posed extravagantly beside the chair, her skinny right arm raised in anticipation of the falling spoon. The picture was inscribed: "To Aunt Mary, Love, Tracy and Ken." Corliss Milford did not pause to examine their faces. Instead, his eyes were drawn to the third picture. This was a faded black and white enlargement of a very weak print. Behind the glass stood a robust black man in army uniform, saluting majestically. His grin was mischievous and arrogant; his nostrils flared. The thumb of his raised hand stood out prominently from his temple; a few inches above the hand the edge of an army private's cap hung casually over his forehead like an enlarged widow's peak.

This is a good picture, Milford decided. He picked it up and examined its details more closely. The man stood in what was obviously an exaggeration of attention. He saw that the man's left brogan was hooked nonchalantly around his right ankle. In the background a flagpole whistled up some six or eight feet above the man's head. The flag was snapping briskly in what might have been the morning breeze, although the faded condition of the print obscured the true direction of the sun. Milford counted the number of stars in the flag. Then he peered deeper into the background, beyond the pole, and saw what might have been palm trees, and beyond these mountains. His eyes moved from the mountains back to the flagpole and down the pole past the saluting soldier to the bottom of the picture, where the grass was smooth as a billiard table. His eyes fastened on a detail he had missed before: a bugle stood upright on its mouth just at the soldier's feet; in fact, the man's left brogan was pointing slyly at the bugle. This was why the man was grinning. Near the bugle, at an angle, someone, probably the soldier, had written: "To Mary Dear, Lots of Love, 'Sweet Willie.'" There was a flowing line just below this inscription, as if the signer had taken sudden inspiration.

Corliss Milford shifted his eyes to the papers on the sofa

beside him. Mrs. Farragot had reported that she was a widow. He had written that down. But now he recalled she had actually said "grass widow," which meant that Sweet Willie was still around. It also explained why she was not drawing social security. Perhaps, he thought, it also justified her frustration if indeed she had been drunk when arrested. There was no doubt that it accounted completely for the bitterness which had compelled her to request specifically the services of a white lawyer. From his picture, Milford concluded, Willie Farragot seemed to reek of irresponsibility. Perhaps all the men she knew were like him. This would account for the difficulty she seemed to be having in getting a witness to corroborate her story that she had not been drunk or driving when arrested.

Now he shifted his eyes to the print on the wall, but this time with more understanding. He had re-entered the living room on another level, and now he could sympathize. Still, he did not like the painting. A disturbing absence of nuance undermined the face: the small brown eyes were dimensionless, as if even they did not believe the message they had been calculated to convey. The pigeon nose had no special prominence, no irregularity suggestive of regality; even the lips, wafer-thin and pink, suggested only a glisten of determination. In the entire face, from forehead to chin, there was not the slightest hint of tragedy or transcendence. To appreciate it, Milford concluded, required of one an act of faith. The robes, though enamel white and royal blue, drooped without majesty from shoulders that were round and ordinary. And the larger-than-life valentine heart seemed to have been merely positioned at the center of the figure's chest. The entire image suffered badly from a lack of calculation. It did not draw one into it. Its total effect did no more than suggest that the image, at the complete mercy of a commercial artist, had resigned itself to being painted. The face reflected a nonchalant resignation to this fate. If the mouth was a little sad it was not from the weight of this world's sins but rather from an inability to comprehend the nature of sin itself.

Milford was beginning to draw contrasts between the figure and the picture of Sweet Willie when Mrs. Mary Farragot opened the door and stepped quickly into the room. A heavy-set brown-skinned man followed behind her. "May Francis Cripps wouldn't come," she announced in a quiet, matter of fact voice, "but Clarence was there too. He seen it all. Clarence Winfield, this here's Mr. Milford from that free law office round there."

Milford stepped to the center of the room and extended his hand.

"How do?" the man, named Winfield, boomed. He grasped Milford's hand and squeezed it firmly. "Everything Miss Mary told you, she told you the truth. I was there and I seen it all. Them cops had no call to arrest her. She warn't drunk, she warn't driving, and I know damn well she warn't going nowheres in that car." While saying this Winfield ran the thumb of his left hand around the inside of his belt, tucking his shirt more neatly into his trousers. "Like I say," he continued, dropping Milford's hand, "I was there and I seen the whole thing."

Corliss Milford stepped back and considered the man. He wore a light brown seersucker suit and a red shirt. A red silk handkerchief flowered from the pocket of his jacket. A red silk tie dangled in his left hand. He had obviously just finished shaving because the pungent scent of a cheap cologne wafted from his body each time he moved. There was something familiar about the cologne, Milford thought; he imagined he had smelled it before, but could not remember when or where. He turned and sat on the plastic-covered sofa, crossing his leg. "I'm from Project Gratis," Milford announced. "Did Mrs. Farragot tell you about my interest in her case?"

Clarence Winfield nodded. "When Miss Mary told me what happen I put on my business clothes and rush right on over here. I told her"—and here he threw a comforting glance at Mrs. Farragot, who stood several feet behind him—"I told her, I say, 'Miss Mary, you don't have to beg May Francis and Big Boy and them to testify for you.' Anyway, that

[57]

nigger Big Boy couldn't hit a crooked lick with a straight stick."

"Speak good English now, Clarence, for the Lord's sakes," Mrs. Farragot called. "We got to go downtown. And there's one thing I learnt about white people: if they don't understand what you saying they just ain't gonna hear it." She looked conspiratorially at Milford.

The lawyer did not say anything.

Clarence Winfield glanced again at Mrs. Farragot. "I knows good English," he said. "Don't you forget, I worked round white folks too. They hears what they wants to hear." Then he looked at Milford and said, "No offense intended."

The lawyer studied the two of them. Over Winfield's broad shoulder he saw Mrs. Farragot leaning against the chair, directly under the painting. With both hands placed firmly on her hips, she stood surveying the two men with something close to despair playing over her face. Milford noticed her high brown cheeks twitch slightly. Her lips were drawn and thin. She seemed about to say something to Winfield, but no words came from her mouth. The big, middle-aged black man remained standing in the middle of the room as if waiting for something to happen. The longer Milford studied him, the more he became convinced that it was not the smell of the cologne but something else, possibly something about his carriage, which made him seem so familiar. The man seemed eager to be in motion. He seemed self-conscious and awkward standing at attention. Corliss Milford took up the papers from the sofa. He flipped a page to the statement of facts he had typed before leaving the office. "Now Mr. Winfield," he said, "please tell me what you saw the night of August 7 of this year."

Clarence Winfield cleared his throat several times, then glanced once more at Mrs. Farragot. "That there's a night I remember well," he began slowly. "It was hot as a sonofabitch. I was setting on my porch with May Francis Cripps and Buster Williams. It warn't no more than eight-thirty 'cause the sun had just gone down and the sky up the street was settling in from pink to purple to black. I remember it well. We had us some beer and was shooting the shit and the only sound was the crickets scraping and a few kids up the block raising hell when all at once there come this loud honking. I look 'cross the street and seen Miss Mary here come running out her door and down the stairs. I knowed it was her 'cause she left the door open and the light from in here come out through the screen and spotlight her porch like a stage. Yeah, come to think of it, just like a stage. See, there was this car right behind hers that was park so close the headlights was burning right into Miss Mary's tail end, and right up close behind *him* was another car. Well, the guy was trap and couldn't get out. I don't know who was in that car, but that guy kept honking his horn 'cause he couldn't move without scratching against Miss Mary's car. I never found out who that guy was, but man he played Dixie on that horn. See, he couldn't back back either 'cause that car behind had him squeezed in like a Maine sardine. That's the way it is round here in summertime. There's so many big cars park end to end it look like some bigtime I-talian gangsters was having a convention. For folks poor as these round here, I don't know where in the *hell* all these here cars come from. Me, I drive . . ."

"You see what I mean, Clarence?" Mrs. Farragot interrupted. She walked toward Winfield, her hands still on her hips. "The man didn't ask about no *gangsters*! All he want is the *facts*!" Then she threw up her hands, cast a look of exasperation at Milford, and dropped into the plastic-covered armchair beneath the painting.

"It's all right," Milford told the two of them. He set down his notes and watched Mrs. Farragot. She was sprawled in the armchair; her arms were folded, her legs were crossed, and there was great impatience in her face. Milford attempted to communicate to her, with a slight movement of his pencil, that he had no objection to the mode of Winfield's presentation.

For his own part, Clarence Winfield grinned bashfully. Then he said, " 'Scuse me, Miss Mary; you right." Then he swallowed again and proceeded, this time pausing tentatively before each sentence. "Well, me and May Francis and Buster listen to all this racket and we seen Miss Mary here, plain as day, open up her car and start it up and cut on the headlights. Now *her* car was lighting up the taillights of the car in front of her, and it reflect back on her behind the wheel. I seen that. And I heard this guy steady honking on his horn. Well, just about then who should drive up the street in his new Buick but Big Boy Ralston. He lives up the block there, 'bout five houses down from me. Big Boy a security guard down to the bank and I guess he just naturally take his work serious. I mean he bring it home when he come. Anyway, he drives up just about even with this guy that's honking and he stops and calls out, 'Who that making all that motherfucking racket?' Well, this makes the other guy mad and then he *really* tore into that horn. By this time the street is all lit up like a department store. All three of 'em got they headlights and brakelights on so the street's all white and yellow and red and Big Boy car is fire engine red and the sky is black and purple now, with just a little bit of pink way over West yonder where the sun done gone down. But this guy is still playing Chopsticks on that horn. Big Boy holler, 'If you don't quit that racket I'ma put my foot up your ass as far as your nose!' Well, that there just shell old Buster's peanuts. He scream out, 'Stomp on his ass, Big Boy!' Big Boy lean out the window and look over at us setting on the porch. He holler, 'That go for you too, Buster. I'm tired of this shit every night. Ain't y'all got nothing else to do but set on them motherfucking steps selling wolf tickets?' But this guy is honking hard and strong now, and he don't pay Big Boy no mind. So Big Boy scream, 'You blowing your own funeral music, chump!' And he jerk open the door of his Buick. But right about then I seen Miss Mary pull out of her spot and go *fa*ward about three feet. I seen that, 'cause my eyes got pulled in that direction when her brakelight went off and the red in the back of her car went all yellow and white. Well, Big Boy leaves his motor running and he jumps out his car and slam the door. Old Buster laugh and say to me and May Francis, 'Watch old Big Boy *bogart* this motherfucker. I ain't seen a Friday go by yet he don't floor somebody.' I think old Buster was right. When Big Boy round his car his shoulders was hunched like he was fixing to clean house. The light was shining on his brown uniform and that red Buick and I tell you the truth, you couldn't hardly tell the steel in that Buick from the steel in him. He moved round that car like six feet and three hundred pounds of mad nigger in a *po*-lice uniform fixing to clean him somebody's *plow*!"

Here Winfield paused to chuckle. "Lawd," he said, not looking at anyone in particular, "that there was a *night*! We just set and watch and drunk our beer. People run out they houses. Some look out they windows. Some of them bad kids round here commence to sic Big Boy on. Well, this guy in the car warn't no fool. He must of knowed he didn't have a snowball's chance in hell against Big Boy. He cut his wheels fast and scrunch out of that space like a flash. Fact is, he just miss swatting Big Boy as he wheeled round that Buick. Well, old Big Boy rush back round his front end to get in his car and go after the guy. But just then, who should I see but Miss Mary here come back backing up real slow-like into her old parking space. Well, just then *four* things happen, all at the same time. Them wild kids yell; Miss Mary's brakelights come on fast and red; there was a real loud *scrruunch*!; and Big Boy scream, 'Mother-*fuck*!' See, Miss Mary here done back-back right into the side of his red Buick."

Milford sat transfixed. He leaned forward on the sofa, oblivious to anything but the big man in the brown seersucker suit standing quietly in the center of the room. He did not notice Mrs. Mary Farragot, seated in the armchair beneath the picture of Jesus, draw her crossed arms tighter about her breasts.

"*Now*," Clarence Winfield continued, wetting his lips slowly, "now we come to the part *you* interested in. See, when Big Boy mad he don't have no respect for *nobody*! He run over to Miss Mary's car, pull open the door, and commence to give her hell. Buster Williams spit on the sidewalk and said to us, 'Oh shit! Now they go'n be some *real* trouble. The one thing *nobody* can do is mess with Big Boy Buick. Me, I seen the time he near kilt a guy for putting a dent in his *bumper*, so you know they's hell to pay now with the side all smash in. Somebody better run and call up the *po*-lice!' He nudge May Francis and she taken and run up to her place to call up the law. And just in time too. I heard Big Boy tell Miss Mary here, 'Woman, what the fuck you mean backing into my car that way? If you was a man I'd kick your ass to kingdom come!' Lawd, he cuss this poor woman here something awful . . ."

"Please, Clarence," Mrs. Farragot called from behind him. "Just get the thing told." She looked at Milford while saying this. "This man ain't got all day."

Corliss Milford said nothing. Nor did he allow his eyes to respond to Mrs. Farragot's searching expression. Instead, he kept his face turned toward the big man standing before him and touched his pencil to the paper on his lap.

Clarence Winfield smiled, as if the gesture had reassured him. "Okay," he said, to no one in particular. "Me and Buster run on over before Big Boy could swing on Miss Mary here. Like I say, Big Boy don't much care *who* he swing on when he gets mad. Poor Miss Mary here just standing there in her peejays crying and carrying on, she so excited, and there was dogs barking and them wild kids was running round whooping and hollering in the floodlights of them two cars, and by this time the sky was all black and purple with no pink. I tell you, man, it was a sight. Buster, he run down the corner for more beer and Miss Bessie Mayfair, up the block, lean out her window and scream, '*Fish sandwiches! Hot fresh fish sandwiches,* just out the *pan!* Don't *rush,* they's *plenty. Fifty cents!*' Miss Bessie don't miss a chance to make a dollar. Anyway, long about then a squad car come screaming up with red and white lights flashing and it screech to a stop right longside Big Boy's red Buick and this white cop lean out the passenger window and holler, 'Stand back! Don't nobody touch the body. The law is here to take *charge!*' Big Boy push me away from him and look at that cop. He stare him dead in the face and say, 'Drop dead yourself, creampuff!' Hot damn! That's what I heard him say.

That street was all lit up like a department store with red and white lights flashing on all them people in blue and brown and pink clothes. Lawd, it was a sight! But even in all them lights I saw this white cop turn red in the face; his own strobe lights made his face look like it was bleeding. I seen that. I seen the driver get out of the car. It was a colored fellow and he walk like he was ready to do somebody in. He walk up real close to Big Boy and look him dead in the eye. He say, real cool-like, 'What it is, feller?' and Big Boy say, 'Plenty! This here woman done *ruin* my new Buick Electra with *push-*button drive and *black leather* bucket seats! There ain't a worser thing that could of happen to me.' So the colored cop begin to question Miss Mary. She was so mad and angry and crying so much I guess he thought she was drunk, 'cause he ask her to walk the line. He just walk over to the sidewalk and point the toe of his shoe to a crack. Well, Miss Mary here look at him and say, 'No. No, *sah. N.O. Naw*!' That's what I recollect she said. Then I heard him tell her the law was writ so that if she refuse she was bound to lose her license. Well, by this time there was so much commotion going on till I suspect Miss Mary here was too embarrassed to even *think* about walking no line. Folks was laughing, drinking beer, grabbing for fish sandwiches, and raising so much hell till I reckon a private person like Miss Mary here would rather lose her license than walk the line in her *pee*jays. So she refuse. Well, them two cops put her in the car and taken her off to jail. Like I said, I seen it all, and I done told you the truth of all I seen. And I'm ready anytime to go down and tell the same thing to the judge."

Corliss Milford completed his notes. He had scribbled sporadically during the recitation. Now he looked up at Clarence Winfield, who shifted impatiently as though confirming his eagerness to be on his way downtown. Then he looked at Mrs. Mary Farragot, still seated in the armchair behind Winfield, her arms locked tightly across her breasts. "His story corroborates yours in all essential details," Milford called to her.

"Of course it do," Mrs. Farragot answered. "That ain't the problem." She shrugged. "The problem is how in the *hell* can

I tell a white judge something like all that Clarence just said without being thrown out of court?" She paused and sighed, raising her head so that her hair almost touched the edge of the picture frame. "What I wanted me in the first place," Mrs. Farragot added slowly, "was a white boy that could make some *logic* out of all that."

Now both she and Winfield looked imploringly at Corliss Milford.

At 1:45 P.M. the three of them sat waiting outside the hearing room of the Department of Motor Vehicles. During the drive downtown, Milford had attempted to think through the dimensions of the situation; now he decided that Mrs. Farragot had been right all along. Since this was not a jury case, there was no way a judge would allow Clarence Winfield to tell his version of the story. As Mrs. Farragot had anticipated, any defense she offered would have to be confined to the facts. Milford cast a sidewise glance at the woman, seated on the bench beside him, with new appreciation of her relative sophistication. In the car she had disclosed that she did domestic work for a suburban stockbroker; from listening in on conversations between the broker and his wife, she must have discerned how a bureaucracy, and the people who made it function, must of necessity be restricted to the facts. And as colorful as were the circumstances of her case, there was not the slightest possibility that any responsible lawyer could include them in her defense.

A pity, too, Milford thought, turning his gaze to Clarence Winfield. Despite the imprecision of his language, the man possessed a certain rough style. He watched Winfield pacing the waxed tile floor of the corridor. The black man had put on his tie now, but because of the excessive heat allowed it to hang loosely about his collar. At one point, with Milford looking on, Winfield lifted his right foot and polished the pointed toe of his shoe against the cloth of his left trouser leg. When he saw Milford watching, Winfield grinned. A pity, the lawyer concluded. Now he would have to restrict the man's statement to yes or no answers to specific questions. He motioned for Winfield to come over to the bench. "Now listen," Milford said, "when you talk to the hearing officer, restrict your statement to the *last* part of your story, the part about her *not* being drunk when she was arrested. You understand?"

Clarence Winfield nodded slyly.

"And don't volunteer anything, please. I'll ask all the questions."

Winfield nodded again.

"Do like he tell you now Clarence, hear?" Mrs. Farragot said, leaning sideways on the bench. "Don't mess up things for me in front of that man in there." Then she said to Milford, "Clarence one of them from downhome. He tend to talk around a point."

"Ah hell!" Winfield said, and was about to say more when the door to the hearing room opened and a voice called, "Mary Farragot?"

It was a woman's voice.

Corliss Milford stood. "I'm representing Mrs. Farragot," he said. "I'm with Brown and Barlow's Project Gratis."

"Well, we're ready," the woman called, and she stepped out into the corridor. She was short and plump, but not unattractive in a dark green pantsuit. Her silver blond hair was cut short. Dark eyelashes, painted, Milford suspected, accentuated her pink face. "I'm Hearing Officer Harriet Wilson," she announced.

As she stood holding open the door, Milford noticed Mrs. Farragot staring intently at Hearing Officer Harriet Wilson. The expression on her face was one he had not seen before. Suddenly he remembered the photograph of Mrs. Farragot on her plywood end table, and the expression became more familiar. He touched her shoulder and whispered, "Let's go on in." They filed into the hearing room, Mrs. Farragot leading and Clarence Winfield bringing up the rear. Over his shoulder, Milford saw the hearing officer sniffing the air as she shut the door. The room was humid. Over on the window sill a single electric fan rotated wearily, blowing more humid air

[65]

into the small room. They seated themselves in metal chairs around a dark brown hardwood table. Only Hearing Officer Harriet Wilson remained standing.

"Now," Hearing Officer Wilson said, "we're ready to begin." She smiled round the table pleasantly, her eyes coming to rest on the red silk handkerchief flowering out of Clarence Winfield's coat pocket. It seemed to fascinate her. "Now," she said again, moving her eyes slowly away from the handkerchief, "I'll get the complaining officer and we'll begin." She moved toward a glass door at the back of the room.

"Lawyer Milford," Mrs. Farragot whispered as the glass door opened and shut. She tugged his coat. "Lawyer Milford, I thought it was men that handled these hearings."

Milford shrugged. "Times change," he answered.

Mrs. Farragot considered this. She glanced at the glass door, then at Winfield seated on her right. "Tell you what, Lawyer Milford," she said suddenly. "Actually, Clarence don't do too bad when he talk. Maybe you ought to let him tell his story after all."

"I thought we had already agreed on procedure," the lawyer muttered. He found himself irritated by the mysterious look which had again appeared in Mrs. Farragot's eyes. She looked vaguely amused. "We can't change now," he told her.

"Miss Mary," Winfield volunteered, "I can't tell it exactly like I did before."

"Clarence, that don't matter, long as you hit on the facts. Ain't that right?" she asked Milford.

He had no choice but to nod agreement.

"Good," Mrs. Farragot said. She straightened in her chair and brushed her hand lightly across her sweating forehead.

It seemed to Milford she was smiling openly now.

Hearing Officer Harriet Wilson re-entered the room. Behind her, carrying a bulky tape recorder, stepped the arresting officer. He was a tall, olive-brown-skinned man who moved intently in a light gray summer suit. Cool dignity flashed in his dark brown eyes; his broad nose twitched, seeming to sniff the air. He placed the recorder on the table near Hearing

Officer Wilson's chair, then seated himself at the head of the table. He crossed his leg casually. Then he gazed at the three seated on his right and said, "Officer Otis S. Smothers."

"How do?" Winfield called across the table.

Milford nodded curtly.

Mrs. Farragot said nothing. Her eyes were fixed on the tape recorder.

Hearing Officer Harriet Wilson noticed her staring and said, "This is not a jury matter, dear. At this hearing all we do is tape all relevant testimony and forward it on to the central officer at the state capital. The boys up there make the final decision."

Milford felt a knee press against his under the table. "I should of knowed," Mrs. Farragot whispered beside him. "Won't be long they gonna just give you a lie detector and railroad you that way."

Milford shushed her into silence.

From the head of the table Officer Smothers seemed to be studying them, quiet amusement tugging at the corners of his plump lips.

Officer Wilson placed a finger on the record button and looked round the table. Milford felt Mrs. Farragot tense beside him. A desperate warmth seemed to exude from her body. Officer Wilson smiled cheerily at Clarence Winfield, but sobered considerably as her eyes came to rest on Officer Smothers. She pressed the record button. After reciting the date and case record into the microphone, she swore in the parties. Then she motioned for Officer Smothers to make his statement. It seemed to Milford that Smothers, while taking his oath, had raised his right hand a bit higher than Mrs. Farragot and Winfield. Now he told his version of the story, presenting a minor masterpiece of exactness and economy. His vocabulary was precise, his delivery flawless. When he reached the part of his testimony concerning the sobriety test, he pulled a sheet of paper from his coat pocket and recited, ". . . suspect was informed of her legal obligation to submit to the test. Suspect's reply was . . ." and he touched a lean brown finger to the

[67]

page "... 'I ain't go'n do *nothin*'!'" These words, delivered in comic imitation of a whine, stung Milford's ears. Even Mrs. Farragot, he noticed, winced at the sound. And Clarence Winfield, slouching in his chair, looked sheepish and threatened. To Milford the action seemed especially cruel when Smothers looked over at Hearing Officer Wilson and said in crisp, perfect English, "That's all I have to say," as though he intended to end the recital of facts without some account of his own response to the refusal. Milford watched Smothers as he leaned back in his chair, looking just a bit self-righteous.

"If you have no questions," Hearing Officer Harriet Wilson said to Milford. Her finger was already on the off button of the recorder.

"You *did* offer her a test, then?" Milford asked, stalling for time to reconsider his position.

"Of course," Smothers replied, his fingers meshed, his hands resting professionally on his knee.

"And you had already concluded there was probable cause to believe she was drunk?"

"Certainly."

"How?"

"Her breath, her heavy breathing, and her slurred speech."

"Could you have mistaken a Southern accent for slurred speech?"

"No, I couldn't have," Smothers answered nonchalantly. "I'm from the South myself."

Across the table Hearing Officer Harriet Wilson smiled to herself, her finger tapping the metal casing just above the off button on the recorder.

"Let me say something here," Clarence interrupted. "I was there. I seen the whole thing. It warn't like that at all."

Hearing Officer Wilson looked at Winfield out of the corner of her eye. "Do you want this witness to testify now?" she asked Milford.

But before the lawyer could answer he felt the pressure of Mrs. Farragot's hand on his shoulder. Looking up, he saw her standing over him. "Nome, thank you," he heard her say in a voice very much unlike her own. She was facing Hearing Officer Wilson but looking directly at the recorder. Her face was expressionless. Only her voice betrayed emotion. "I'm innocent," Mrs. Farragot began. "But who go'n believe me, who go'n take my word against the word of that officer? Both of us black, but he ain't bothering his self with that and I ain't concerning myself with it either. But I do say I'm innocent of the charges he done level against me. The night this thing happen I was inside my house in my pajamas minding my own business. I wasn't even *fixing* to drive no car . . ."

She told her side of the story.

While she talked, in a slow, precise tone, Milford watched the two officers. It was obvious that Hearing Officer Harriet Wilson was deeply moved; she kept her eyes lowered to the machine. But Officer Smothers seemed impervious to the woman's pleadings. His meshed fingers remained propped on his knee; his eyes wandered coolly about the room. At one point he lifted his left hand to rub the side of his nose.

When Mrs. Farragot had finished speaking she eased down into her chair. No one spoke for almost a minute; the only sounds in the room were the soft buzz of the recorder and the hum of the window fan. Then Clarence Winfield cleared his throat noisily. Officer Harriet Wilson jumped.

"Tell me something, Officer Smothers?" Milford said. "If you did offer a test, which one was it?"

"I asked her to walk the line, as both of us have already testified," Smothers answered.

"That was the only test you offered?"

"That's right," Smothers said in a tired voice.

"But doesn't the statute provide that a suspect has the right to choose one of *three* tests: *either* the breathalyzer, the blood, or the urine? As I read the statute, there's nothing about walking the line."

"I suppose that's right," Officer Smothers said.

"Are you authorized to choose, arbitrarily, a test of your own devising?"

"My choice was *not* arbitrary!" Smothers protested. "The

policy is to use that one on the scene. Usually, the others are used down at the station."

Now Milford relaxed. He smiled teasingly at the olive-skinned officer. "*Was* this lady offered one of the other tests down at the station before being booked?"

"I don't really know," the officer answered. "I didn't stay around after filing the report."

Milford turned to Mrs. Farragot, new confidence cooling his words. "*Were* you offered any other tests?"

"No, suh," she said quietly, her voice almost breaking. "They didn't offer me nothing in front of my house and they didn't offer me nothing down to the jail. They just taken me in a cell in my pajamas."

"We've had enough," Hearing Officer Harriet Wilson said. Her pink face seemed both sad and amused. She pressed the off button. "You'll hear from the board within thirty days," she called across the table to Mrs. Farragot. "In the meantime you can retain your license."

They all stood abruptly. Milford smiled openly at Officer Smothers, noting with considerable pleasure the man's hostile glare. Milford offered his hand. They barely touched palms. Then the lawyer took Mrs. Farragot's arm and steered her toward the door. Clarence Winfield came behind, tearing off his tie. Just before Winfield closed the door, Hearing Officer Harriet Wilson's voice came floating after them on the moist heat of the room: "Otis, tell the boys that in the future . . ."

Milford and Clarence Winfield waited by the bench while Mrs. Farragot rushed down the corridor toward the ladies' room. Winfield walked around, adjusting his trousers. Milford felt pleased with himself. He had taken command of a chaotic situation and forced it to a logical outcome. Absently, he followed Clarence Winfield over to the water fountain and waited while Winfield refreshed himself. "This meant a lot to her," Milford observed.

Winfield kept a stiff thumb on the metal button. The cold water splashed the side of his face as he turned his face upward and nodded agreement.

"All this sweat over one freak accident," Milford observed.

"Yeah," Winfield said. He straightened and wiped his face with the red silk handkerchief. "Many's the time I've told Miss Mary about that drinking."

"What's a beer on a hot night," Milford said, bending to drink.

Clarence Winfield chuckled. "Man, Miss Mary don't drink no *beer*!" He leaned close to Milford's ear. "She don't drink nothing but Maker's Mark." He laughed again. "I thought you *knowed* that."

Turning his head, Milford saw Mrs. Farragot coming up the hall. Her blue dress swished gaily. It seemed to him that she was strutting. He observed for certain that she was smiling broadly, not unlike the picture of her next to Sweet Willie on the coffee table in her home.

Clarence Winfield nudged him, causing the cold water to splash into his eyes. "Don't you pay it no mind," Winfield was saying. "Between the two of us, why we ought to be able to straighten her out."

The Return of Julian the Apostate to Rome
ISHMAEL REED

Julian
Come back
It can't be long
For the emperor

He sees plots everywhere
Has executed three postmen
Rants in print against his
Former allies

Imagines himself a
Yoruba god
Has asked the Bishops to
Deify him

Not only is he short
He's nuts

Julian come back
The people are shitting
In the temples
Barbarian professors

Are teaching one god
They are ripping the limbs
Off our fetishes
They are carving the sea
Monsters from our totems
They made a pile of our
Wood sculpture and set fire
To it

Julian
Come back
Rude hags
Have crashed the senate
And are spitting on the
Elders

Meanwhile, Julian
The perennial art major
Ponders in the right wing
Of the monastery museum

The Egyptian collection

A Goldfinch
MARVIN BELL

The Baltimore oriole, seldom an Iowan,
was last thought seen to be bathing
where we took coffee on a sweltering morning
yet in Iowa, a fan failing at our feet.
It was a sign, not of betrayal either.
That yellow breast of hers looked cool
and the white bars on her black wings
returned to us the formal in weather
without shape, shimmery. So a goldfinch.
The mind is a wonder, is my summary.

Reply to Lapo Gianni
CHARLES WRIGHT

Lapo, we're all slow orphans under the cruel sleep of heaven.
We're all either creased and sealed or somebody's cough.

Outside the window, twilight slips on its suede glove.
The river is fine balsam, fragrant and nicked by cold feathers.
Under the grass, the lights go on in their marled rooms.

Lapo, the dreams of the dog rose are nothing to you and me.

Continuing
A. R. AMMONS

Considering the show, some prize-winning
leaves broad and firm, a good year,
I checked the ground
for the accumulation of
fifty seasons: last year was
prominent to notice, whole leaves
curled, some still with color:
and, underneath, the year
before, though paler, had structure,
partial, airier than linen:
but under that,
sand or rocksoil already mixed
with the meal or grist:
is this, I said to the mountain,
what becomes of things:
well, the mountain said, one
mourns the dead but who
can mourn those the dead mourned;
back a way
they sift in a tearless
place: but, I said,
it's so quick, don't you think,
quick: most time, the mountain said, lies
in the thinnest layer: who
could bear to hear of it:
I scooped up the sand which flowed
away, all but a cone in the palm:
the mountain said, it
will do for another year.

Centerfold Reflected in a Jet Window
SANDRA MCPHERSON

There is someone naked flying alongside the airplane.
The man in the seat in front of me is trying to hold her.
But she reflects, she is below zero, would freeze the skin
off his tongue.

Beside me also someone is flying.
And I don't say, "Put on your sweater."
And I don't say, "Come back in this minute,"
though she is my daughter:

And there is an old woman riding inside the earth.
Metal shoulders wear her dresses.
She believed she would be an old woman flying alongside
    heaven
because she loved, because she had always loved.

Weed
ROBERT HASS

    Horse is Lorca's word, fierce as wind
or melancholy, gorgeous, Andalusian:
    white horse grazing near the river dust;
and parsnip is hopeless,
    second cousin to the rhubarb
which is already second cousin
    to an apple pie. Marrying the words
to the coarse white umbels sprouting
    on the first of May is history

but conveys nothing; it is not the veined
    body of Queen Anne's lace
I found, bored, in a spring classroom
    from which I walked hands tingling
for the breasts that are meadows in New Jersey
    in 1933; it is thick, shaggier, and the name
is absurd. It speaks of durable
    unimaginative pleasures: reading Balzac,
fixing the window sash, rising
    to a clean kitchen, the fact
that the car starts & driving to work
through hills where the roadside thickens
    with the green ungainly stalks,
        the bracts and bright white flowerets
of horse-parsnips.

Phantom Silver
WILLIAM KITTREDGE

The great white horse rears above the rolling horizon, which is golden and simple in the sunset, and those sparkling hooves strike out into the green light under the dark midsummer thunderclouds. Far away there is rain, and barn swallows drop like thrown rocks through clouds of mosquito near the creek. A single planet and then stars grow luminous against the night, and the great horse is gone. Moths bat against the screen around the veranda porch, and we are left in that dreamed yesteryear where the masked man rides away, leaving his silver bullet behind. The light is cold in the early morning, and the silver bullet rests on the mantle like a trophy. Only in the morning is it possible to think of that masked man as old and fat and slow and happy.

They were all brave and unmasked in that beginning, before the Cavendish gang burned down the crew of clean-shaven Texas Rangers, and left him for dead and alone, all his comrades sprawled around him and killed. They had ridden into an entrapping box canyon, and the rifle fire crackled from the surrounding rims. They were ambushed; horses reared and screamed; the good men fell, and in only a few beats of the heart it was over. The Cavendish boys walked the stony ground amid the bodies, and smiled as if they would live forever.

But he was not dead, only scarred.

Tonto found him, saved him, and revenge became his great obsession, revenge and justice. They were notions that served him like two sides of a coin.

Right then, like a stone into gold, he changed. He rode that white stallion named Silver, he disguised himself behind that mask, he traveled with his dark companion, the Indian named Tonto, and they began their endless conquest of wrongdoing. There was ranch after ranch saved from eastern bankers and monied second sons from Baltimore. Always another gold shipment to be rescued. Another sodbuster and his family to be protected. Another evil lawman to be confounded. Another wagon train to be jerked away from the clutches of circling savages—anyone would have grown weary, or even bored. How many rustlers died, how many homesteaders' wives stood in the doorway of plain unpainted cabins with that silver bullet still warm in their hands while they wondered aloud who that masked man could have been, while the great stallion reared, before the Lone Ranger and Tonto galloped away?

And now, why is the great stallion running alone? Do we believe the real beginning of this end could have been only boredom? Could there have been a mortal family, a strong-handed father and a mother who could split wood and still stay a woman, two children, a brother and a sister, all of them having come west to Texas after the Civil War? Could they have been living happily in a juniper-log cabin alongside the Brazos River before that summer morning when Comanche came down like slaughtering, screaming rain? Of course.

They thought they were safe. The Comanche had been corraled for seven years on the Oklahoma Territory, eating mainly on dole meat, and the father was a slow-spoken German other white men did not deal with easily, and so left mostly alone. But there on that bright morning was the truth, Comanche out of season, and killers. But look away from that cabin and the killing for a moment.

Down there in the bullrushes near the water of the Brazos there was another morning sort of time, there was the dumb blankness of eyes rolled back to their extreme station, the hardness of lean hipbones under the flesh, handholds as this brother mounts his sister from behind, the younger brother, the older sister, her skirt tossed up where they were down there on the matted grass, hidden from the house by tules and nodding downy cattails, the sister on her knees and elbows and the brother plugged in from behind, going weak and dizzy that morning with her and afraid the screaming he heard so distantly might be her or even himself, but that was foolish, they were practiced and wouldn't. He stopped, crouched over her, listening, and she thrust herself back against him.

"Don't you quit now," she said.

But he did. He had. The screaming he heard was not really screaming, not fearfulness, that came later, but high-pitched joyous whooping and kiyiing, and now he could hear the horses, the hooves beating down the hardpacked wagon road. Sure as hell there were lots of them, and riding hard.

"Don't you stop," she said, but it was too late for that, already he had fallen back away from her, turning, knowing there was no way to see anything from where they were, that was why they were safe there on those hidden mornings down near the river. Already he was frightened, and later he would sense she had always been stronger, had always cared more than he did about what was going on right at the time; later he would understand it was an undivided mind that gave her what proved in time to be the strength of her indifference.

"Dammit," she said. "Then get yourself together."

What she meant was for him to pull up his pants and tuck in his shirttail, and to do it quietly. It was she who kept him quiet and crouching there those next hours as the smoke from the burning cabin and the barns rose thin and white into the clear sky, after the first bellowing from their father and their mother's frantic shrieking, after the horses had gone away, as the smoke dwindled and twilight came and the frogs called to one another in the quiet. It was she who kept him crouching and hidden there, until the next day they were saved, at least saved in the sense that they could walk away, they were not killed and not captured, not bloody and hairless like the bodies of their father and their mother.

She was sixteen that summer of 1867, and he was two years younger, and for a few months, after they had walked those miles upstream to the nearest homestead on the Brazos, toward the Palo Pinto, they were pitied and fed. Then October began to settle into fall, and in November the green-headed mallards and the Canada geese and the sandhill crane began coming south, circling and calling as they settled toward the river. The clump of pink-blooming roses on the south wall of the cabin froze, the tamarack hung darker red against the gray hillslopes, and the big cottonwood flared yellow one morning in the sun, but the real cold came all in one day the week before Thanksgiving, weather a line of shadow on the morning horizon, the air greasy and hushed all that day, then at twilight a hard norther and driven sleety rain. But they didn't leave until after the Thanksgiving meal, goose and all the fixings. It was she who decided.

"We are going," she said.

By Christmas they had hooked wagon rides south to San Antonio, and she would no longer let him touch her. "If we had been going to stay there we would have stayed forever," she said, and after the beginning of the new year she took to leaving him alone for days while she went around to the taverns on the banks of the San Antonio River, and she came home with money. She had her blankets in the room they shared, and she would not let him come under them with her. "You have done me what damage you could," she said. It was not that she did not love him, she explained, it was simply that the damage was done. He took to breaking horses for a livery stable. He had always been good with horses. He could not remember his parents, they had gone away into those scalped bodies the Comanche left behind, he could not think about them at all, and the thing he hated most was the notion of horses he had loved being driven north toward the territories by those savages.

Three summers later, when he was seventeen, she left him behind altogether. "You are man enough," she said. "You take care of yourself like I am going to take care of myself." She was loading just a few things into saddlebags, rich-looking carved-leather bags provided by the tubercular-looking white-haired man she was with, a man who wore one quick gun and claimed to be a medical doctor, although no one had ever known him to cure anything. "We are going to settle in the north," she said, talking about her reasons for traveling, as though the white-haired man meant nothing. "He is going to do some work," she said, talking about the eastern Wyoming Territory around Laramie. "Things are cleaner in the north," she said, before she rode off alongside her man. "But you stay around here. You can be what you want to be around here."

By the next summer he was riding with the Texas Rangers, all of them young and clean-handed and shaven, except for the older ones with brushy mustaches, and he was thinking about the man she had ridden away with, going north to some trouble centering around the long-horned cattle being driven that way out of Texas in the great herds, thinking about how he was going to learn this law business clean, getting set for another one-day meeting with that white-haired medical doctor. He could not stop thinking about her with that man, in his bed, on her knees and her elbows as she had been when the

Comanche struck. He knew she was that way with the white-haired man, and he watched them in the darkness and kept his hands off himself, getting ready.

Then, in the spring of 1876, it happened, the Cavendish gang did them in, left him there shot in the face, thinking him dead on the rocky dry riverbed, and he changed, like a stone into gold.

There came along a single Indian, a man without a tribe, the rider on the paint horse, the good dark man named Tonto, who found him and nursed him, and he recalled that long-ago morning the Comanche struck and knew this was a different life. As he recovered, he knew childishness was behind, that somewhere in the dark kindness of this new companion there was a force he would hold always steady against that, until now, he had thought he loved: her white flesh in the sunlight that morning while she crouched with her skirt thrown forward.

For a long while things were so easily clear, there was this dark new friend and there was the great white horse, and both were sides of what was right, like the Indian and buffalo on the United States nickel. And the mask, the silver bullets, were emblems of the need to be austere and distant if you were to be great and right. He understood emblems were only emblems, ways of getting the work done, even though the mask covered that dark purple scar, the twisted hole that had been his nostrils before the Cavendish gang shot him down and rode away, thinking he was dead, seeing as he looked drowned in blood.

And what luck that he could shoot so perfectly without any sense of aiming, the silver bullets being after all part of him, the way he thought, the shooting more a business of balance and intent than anything he understood, the bullets just going where he thought they would, as though he could see a pistol in the hand of some craven man and shoot it away with only a thought.

Those were the legendary wandering years, when he did not think about his sister. There was plenty of time; time was a trapeze that only swung you back and forth. Those were the years our union advanced in its skip-step way toward the Pacific and the meeting of fresh water with salt tides in the Golden Gate, the years our passenger pigeons were clubbed out of trees and Indian children were clubbed out of bushes as the nation made ready for the clubbing of Cuba and the Philippines and China. The Pony Express riders mounted their quickly saddled horses at a run while savages burned the way stations behind them; all but the impounded remnants of our sixty odd million buffalo were slaughtered for their tongues and humps and hides and bones; the long-horned cows wore their way north to the grassy plains of Montana and Wyoming, surviving stampede while the lightning flashed, surviving quicksand on the Platte, only to perish in the snowy blizzard of 1885. The horse-drawn stages scattered dust between towns like Helena and Butte, Goldfield and Tonopah, carrying treasure in their strongboxes and enticing weak black-hatted men into banditry; the railroads came, building their graded roadbeds inexorably up through the passes, over Donner Summit and through the Marias in the northern Rockies; the nesters fought the cattle barons; the cattle men fought the sheep men; the rich fought the poor; the barbed wire went up and fought the wind; the sodgrass was plowed under; the streets of Carson City were paved with brick that had served as ballast on sailing ships from China; Joseph and Looking Glass fought off tourists in Yellowstone, which was already a National Park, before losing everything they had suffered for in the Bear Paw Mountains. Somewhere far away the last visionary chiefs were dying. Crazy Horse was dead, and what there was to defend was somehow over as the first popping of the internal combustion engine began to be heard. There was nothing right left to do most of the time, nothing at all to do, and our man who began down on the Brazos was not yet fifty years of age, still quick-handed as he had ever been, and bored.

In 1912 Tonto found a woman and stayed in Grants Pass, Oregon, amid blossoming spring apple and cherry trees and what the masked man called wine-berries. The woman had come west as a child from the plains after her toes were frozen off in the aftermath of the great Ghost Dance massacre on the Pine Ridge Reservation of South Dakota in December of 1891. "We were like animals," the woman said, "so they let us run."

The earth shook San Francisco, where he knew she was, where she had to be, that most sin-filled and elegant city, with water all around. The trench warfare began in Europe, and he was too old. Over there they fought each other from craft in the air, he would have liked that, it seemed right, and he was too old. Then the war was over and he started toward the coast, rode the white horse through the mountains of northern New Mexico, along the old trails that had been graded into roadways, wintered alongside a lake in the Sierras, and in spring drifted down to the valley towns of California, wondering what next, trying to stay furtive now, hiding out, taking his time on his way to San Francisco, perfecting disguises.

He was growing old, alone with the white horse, almost seventy and getting ready for San Francisco, thinking of her hair, the dark marks of age on her hands, which would be like his. The man she left San Antonio with was no doubt dead, but she would have another. There would be something. In some elegant house on one of those hills she would be pouring tea from a silver service, pouring steadily, her hands not shaking at all. He would lift the delicate cup made of fragile English porcelain, and perhaps she would smile.

In those days they still had room for horses.

The summer day was cool that close to the ocean as he came up the old mission road, the El Camino, into the Mission District of San Francisco. Off west the Twin Peaks were green with forest and above them the gray fog stood like an arrested wave. The Pacific was over there, and he had never seen the ocean, never seen real waves coming from Asia. The solid ground felt precarious, like it might tip, as though it could slip away without the strength of the continent spread around. He wished he were back on the solid ground of the interior, and smiled at himself, wishing he had come here years earlier when he was not old, when he would have liked this walking on eggs, this vast uneasiness, so much more important to confront than some fool with a model 1873 Colt revolver. So he stabled the white horse, in those days when there was still room for horses, in a barn on the swampy ground of the upper Mission, and he rode an electrified trolley car out toward the ocean, to see what it was.

It was like he was invisible, disguised as an old man with a shot-off nose that was impossibly ugly to look at. The black man in the livery stable had treated him like a customer, and the people crowding around him on the trolley car talked and laughed like nothing at all was the matter, like this was what they did all the time.

As though his wound were only a matter of accident. Four seats down there was an old woman with an enormous goiter on the side of her neck, and no one looked at her either. Except for him, he watched her, and once she looked up and caught him and smiled.

They passed beyond the Twin Peaks, beneath the fog and out onto the grassy dune-land that descended toward the sea, and it was necessary to walk. The trolley-line ended, and a board walk went on. He strolled, feeling he was coming toward the edge of what he had always been. But it wasn't. It was heavy with dampness, the fog thick around him, the waves gray and white the little way out he could see, but it wasn't like the edge of anything. He took off his boots and left them in the sand, and walked down to the water, which was cold as hell lapping on his blue-white feet. He backed out and rolled himself a cigarette, pulled a few drags of smoke, and flicked the cigarette into the water. It was like being at the center of something, standing barefoot on warm damp ground beside the house where you have always lived in the center of Kansas. He fired one shot out into the very center of that gray circle of oncoming water and fog and smiled at himself because there was nothing there to disarm.

Of course she wasn't up there in those hills, in some rich man's house. He knew that. She would not have gone that way. Down on Market Street, the next day after he slept in the stable beside the white horse, that was where she would be. She would understand that much, and be in the right place, down there with the injured, where arrogance was equal to foolishness. Over the years she would have figured it out. She would have left the white-haired man before he died, she would have gone right and poor.

But she was not there. This day he went without his guns, without his mask and the gun-belt stocked with silver bullets. The white horse stayed where it was stabled, munching oats calmly as if this were not a new world, and he walked the bar-rooms, expecting to see her laughing and quarreling, maybe selling flowers on a street-corner. That night he stayed in a room which smelled of urine and ammonia, slept on sheets that smelled of old nervous sweat, not really sleeping, just resting there and dreaming, feeling she was nearby somewhere, knowing she was there, close by, waiting. But she was not. He walked the muddy streets toward the outskirts of the city as a common man, and she was not there.

At least he had not recognized her.

So it was her turn.

He went back to the only things there were: his mask, his silence, those guns, the great white horse. No matter what the comforts of nearby water, he would not be a common man. Trussed out in his black leather gun-belt, so she would see, he would be what he had always been, so totally prepared for whatever happened he had always been able to see the moment of his own death: the lurking coward, the high-powered rifle and the shot from behind, the loud after-crack echoing where the Staked Plains fall off the Cap Rock in west Texas, swallows flushing and turning through the afternoon, deer in thickets by the river lifting their heads after the impact, as the darkness closed and the faraway silence began. These last gun-less days of searching in this city, where even the sound of the last rifle shot would be lost amid the cobbled streets, as he went aimlessly where she might be, that moment of dying had seemed closer.

But he would not die dumb and amiable. So he made inquiries. Who was the most evil and wretched man in this town? She would see, he thought, as the great horse cantered on the bricks. He would not be a common man.

There was no worst man, but there was the man who owned the worst men. There from far away we see the city on the hills in the sunlight of that morning, the water gleaming around the ferry boats, the sidewalk crowds along Market Street and the trolley cars clanging, the square black automobiles and the masked man on his white horse riding proudly between the stone buildings, up from the Mission and then down Market toward the building where the ferry boats were docking. The white horse prances and his mane blows in the sea breeze. The masked man stops before an Irish tavern, and calms his horse. In through the gleaming clean windows of the tavern he can see faces peering out, old men and old women, and great depths. In his deep, steady voice he calls out the worst man in San Francisco, an old Chinese gentleman with a white thin beard and hundreds of killer functionaries, both white and oriental, some brutal, some cunning. The masked man sits on his horse with his hands poised at his guns. At least he will not die amiable, that old magic will bring down one or two before he goes, even though the deer along the Brazos will never hear of it. But the old Chinese gentleman comes out alone, wearing a long brocade gown decorated with silver and gold thread, and he holds his hands together before him, as though praying.

"You come in," he says in his quavering voice, gesturing at the masked man.

"You come in with us," he says.

"You shake your hands at your sides," he says, "and you feel the sun on your back, and the great knot will untie itself."

"Feel the warmth," he says, "move your fingers."

"Twist your head on your neck, and feel the cracking as things come loose. Feel the movement of each finger, the warmth of the sun, and the coolness of the sea." The Chinese gentleman begins moving his hands up and down at his sides in motions like those of newborn birds, the deep sleeves on his embroidered gown flapping as if he might at any moment fly.

As if his body were at last doing what it wanted with him, the masked man found his fingers flexing and unlocking and his head slowly turning from one side to the other, lifting and falling as he twisted and the small old bones of his upper spine began to crack apart from one another. "Feel the movement of each finger," the Chinese gentleman says, "and the aching in your joints as it all comes loose."

Like a child out on that street astride his great white horse, as his arms begin to lift and his fingers feel like feathers, the masked man knows it is important now, in this old age, to risk foolishness. Something new has begun, and the heavy revolvers at his sides will never again be part of what he is; he feels light and only encumbered by these trappings of greatness, the guns and heavy silver bullets in the stiff leather belt. "Step down," the Chinese gentleman says, "and accept this present from an old man." From the folds in his gown the Chinese gentleman produces an orange, which he holds as a gift toward the masked man.

"They are the sweetest and oldest in all the world," the Chinese gentleman says, "the golden apples of the Orient. In the south of China they are like fire amid the emerald leaves."

Thus the masked man comes to stand in the cool and cavernous darkness of the tavern with his fingers feeling like feathers, and a China orange before him on the hardwood surface of the bar. "The outside is golden," the Chinese gentleman says, "and the inside is sweet."

The people crowding around the masked man are old, and they are talking as old people will, standing in clusters and sometimes gesturing, sometimes talking angrily, but talking. A fat old woman with bright red lipstick and a pink flowered dress, who could never have been his sister, rubs at his neck, digging her thumbs into the knot he feels now between the blades of his shoulders, and there, as the masked man stands twisting his head on his neck, listening to the cracking of small bones loosening themselves from one another, he knows the knot is coming undone, untying him from what he has always been, and the guns at his side are more and more a heavy and foolish weight.

"You stay here with us," the Chinese gentleman says. "We know there is nothing to be done about any of that out there."

"Tell us," the Chinese gentleman says, "what all that was like, out there."

The masked man carefully lifts his guns from their holsters and places them carefully on the worn mahogany surface of the bar, and alongside them he places a silver bullet. "Everybody knows," the masked man says, "what it was like out there."

The masked man orders a drink, a round for the house, for what he calls his friends, and an Irish bartender in a stiff collar sets him up a bottle of whiskey and accepts the silver bullet as payment. The masked man peels off his mask and stands barefaced beside the aged Chinese gentleman and does not feel mutilated as he sips his drink and listens to this society he has joined, the old Finns and the French and Britishers around him talking, the cackling of old men, old women telling of childbirth after raising the drinks he has bought to toast him silently. "There was a morning," the masked man says, "down by the river, when the Comanche came . . ." No one is listening. The masked man begins to peel the soft glowing China orange, stripping the peel away in long spooling motion and then separating the sections and aligning them before him on the bar before eating the first one. The juice is cool and rich and sweet. For him it is over. In the time left he will spend a lifetime of silver. He will be ancient when the great fires blossom over Dresden and Japan, after the millions died, and he will not know he should care. Now the salmon die in turbines and he does not know at all.

But there was a moment when great silence descended, and beyond the Staked Plains and the Cap Rock of west Texas, where the swallows flushed and turned through the afternoon, deer in the thickets by the Brazos lifted their heads. In that silence down there amid the bullrushes by the river, a girl crouched on her knees with her skirt thrown forward, and her flesh was so perfectly white under the fresh morning sun. "Don't you stop," she said. And for us there is still that great white horse rearing above the rolling horizon, which is golden and simple in the sunset, those sparkling hooves striking out into the green light under dark midsummer thunderclouds. Far away there is rain, the stars growing luminous, and the white horse always running.

View Finder

RAYMOND CARVER

A man without hands came to the door to sell me a photograph of my house. Except for the chrome hooks, he was an ordinary-looking man of fifty or so.

"How did you lose your hands?" I asked, after he'd said what he wanted.

"That's another story," he said. "You want this picture of the house or not?"

"Come on in," I said. "I just made coffee."

I'd just made some jello too, but I didn't tell him that.

"I might use your toilet," the man with no hands said.

I wanted to see how he would hold a cup of coffee using those hooks. I knew how he used the camera. It was an old Polaroid camera, big and black. It fastened to leather straps that looped over his shoulders and around his back, securing the camera to his chest. He would stand on the sidewalk in front of a house, locate the house in the view finder, depress the lever with one of his hooks, and out popped the picture in a minute or so. I'd been watching from the window.

"Where'd you say the toilet was?"

"Down there, turn right."

By this time, bending and hunching, he'd let himself out of the straps. He put the camera on the sofa and straightened his jacket. "You can look at this while I'm gone."

I took the photograph from him. There was the little rectangle of lawn, the driveway, carport, front steps, bay window, kitchen window. Why would I want a photograph of this tragedy? I looked closer and saw the outline of my head, *my head*, behind the kitchen window and a few steps back from the sink. I looked at the photograph for a time, and then I heard the toilet flush. He came down the hall, zipped and smiling, one hook holding his belt, the other tucking his shirt in.

"What do you think?" he said. "All right? Personally, I think it turned out fine, but then I know what I'm doing and, let's face it, it's not that hard shooting a house. Unless the weather's inclement, but when the weather's inclement I don't work except inside. Special-assignment type work, you know." He plucked at his crotch.

"Here's coffee," I said.

"You're alone, right?" He looked at the living room. He shook his head. "Hard, hard." He sat next to the camera, leaned back with a sigh, and closed his eyes.

"Drink your coffee," I said. I sat in the chair across from him. A week before, three kids in baseball caps had come to the house. One of them had said, "Can we paint your address on the curb, sir? Everybody on the street's doing it. Just a dollar." Two boys waited on the sidewalk, one of them with a can of white paint at his feet, the other holding a brush. All three boys had their sleeves rolled.

"Three kids were by here a while back wanting to paint my address on the curb. They wanted a dollar, too. You wouldn't know anything about that, would you?" It was a long shot. But I watched him just the same.

He leaned forward importantly, the cup balanced between his hooks. He carefully placed the cup on the little table. He looked at me. "That's crazy, you know. I work alone. Always have, always will. What are you saying?"

"I was trying to make a connection," I said. I had a headache. Coffee's no good for it, but sometimes jello helps. I picked up the photograph. "I was in the kitchen," I said.

"I know. I saw you from the street."

"How often does that happen? Getting somebody in the picture along with the house? Usually I'm in the back."

"Happens all the time," he said. "It's a sure sell. Sometimes they see me shooting the house and they come out and ask me to make sure I get them in the picture. Maybe the lady of the house, she wants me to snap hubby washing his car. Or else there's junior working the lawnmower and she says, *get him, get him*, and I get him. Or the little family is gathered on the patio for a nice little lunch, and would I please." His right leg began to jiggle. "So they just up and left you, right? Packed up and left. It hurts. Kids I don't know about. Not any more. I don't like kids. I don't even like my own kids. I work alone, as I said. The picture?"

"I'll take it," I said. I stood up for the cups. "You don't live around here. Where do you live?"

"Right now I have a room downtown. It's okay. I take a bus out, you know, and after I've worked all the neighborhoods, I go somewhere else. There's better ways to go, but I get by."

"What about your kids?" I waited with the cups and watched him struggle up from the sofa.

"Screw them. Their mother too! They're what gave me this." He brought the hooks up in front of my face. He turned and started pulling into his straps. "I'd like to forgive and forget, you know, but I can't. I still hurt. And that's the trouble. I can't forgive or forget."

I looked again at the hooks as they maneuvered the straps. It was wonderful to see what he could do with those hooks.

"Thanks for the coffee and the use of the toilet. You're

going through the mill now. I sympathize." He raised and lowered his hooks. "What can I do?"

"Take more pictures," I said. "I want you to take pictures of me and the house both."

"It won't work," he said. "She won't come back."

"I don't want her back," I said.

He snorted. He looked at me. "I can give you a rate," he said. "Three for a dollar? If I went any lower I'd hardly come out."

We went outside. He adjusted the shutter. He told me where to stand, and we got down to it. We moved around the house. Very systematic, we were. Sometimes I'd look sideways. Other times I'd look straight into the camera. Just getting outside helped.

"Good," he'd say. "That's good. That one turned out real nice. Let's see," he said after we'd circled the house and were back in the driveway again. "That's twenty. You want any more?"

"Two or three more," I said. "On the roof. I'll go up and you can shoot me from down here."

"Jesus," he said. He looked up and down the street. "Well, sure, go ahead—but be careful."

"You were right," I said. "They did just up and move out. The whole kit and kaboodle. You were right on target."

The man with no hands said: "You didn't need to say word one. I knew the instant you opened the door." He shook his hooks at me. "You feel like she cut the ground right out from under you! Took your legs in the process. Look at this! This is what they leave you with. Screw it," he said. "You want to get up on that roof, or not? I've got to go," the man said.

I brought a chair out and put it under the edge of the carport. I still couldn't reach. He stood in the driveway and watched me. I found a crate and put that on the chair. I climbed onto the chair and then the crate. I raised up onto the carport, walked to the roof, and made my way on hands and knees across the shingles to a little flat place near the chimney. I stood up and looked around. There was a breeze. I waved, and he waved back with both hooks. Then I saw the rocks. It was like a little rock nest there on the screen over the chimney hole. Kids must have lobbed them up trying to land them in the chimney.

I picked up one of the rocks. "Ready?" I called.

He had me located in his view finder.

"Okay," he answered.

I turned and threw back my arm. "Now!" I called. I hooked that rock as far as I could, south.

"I don't know," I heard him say. "You moved," he said. "We'll see in a minute," and in a minute he said: "By God, it's okay." He looked at it. He held it up. "You know," he said, "it's good."

"Once more," I called. I picked up another rock. I grinned. I felt I could lift off. Fly.

"Now!" I called.

Swift

MARY SWANDER

Now it is loose in the room, ashes falling
from its wings, falling from the ceiling,
the large black flakes, the large black
wings pressed against the cold window glass,
my grandmother waving a long yellow broom.

Now it comes down again and again,
moves inside the pipes of the house, flutters,
knocks, pounds, the water rising around it,
its head down, body bent down, mouth open,
now closed, trailing a long streamer of paper.

Now there are twenty, thirty piled by the chimney.
I lie down and they come out of my skin,
cover me completely. I pick them up and they
dissolve in my hands—feather and bone, a splinter,
one thin wafer the size of the moon filling the room.

Then they are gone. December, my grandmother
and I sit before the fire and drink tea.
She smoothes the napkin over her thigh,
rattles her saucer, brings the cup to her lips.
This is lovely, I say, *lovely*, a huge white bird in my arms.

At the Store
JANE KENYON

Clumps of daffodils along the storefront
bend low this morning, late snow
pushing their bright heads down.
The flag snaps and tugs at the pole
beside the door.

The old freezer full of Maine blueberries
and breaded scallops mumbles along.
A box of fresh bananas on the floor,
luminous and exotic . . .
I take what I need from the narrow aisles.

Cousins arrive like themes and variations.
Ansel leans on the counter,
remembering other late spring snows,
the blue snow of '32:

Yes, it *was*, it was *blue*.
Forrest comes and goes quickly
with a length of stovepipe, telling
about the neighbors' chimney fire.

The store is a bandstand. All our voices
sound from it, making the same motley
American music Ives heard;
this piece starting quietly,
with the repeated clink of a flagpole
pulley in the doorway of a country store.

For Mark Rothko
JORIE GRAHAM

Shall I say it is the constancy of persian red
that permits me to see
this persian red bird
come to sit now
on the brick barbecue
within my windowframe. Red,

on a field made crooked
as with disillusion or faulty
vision, a backyard in winter
that secretly seeks a bird. He has
a curiosity
that makes him slightly awkward,

as if just learning
something innate, and yet
there is no impatience,

just that pose of his
once between each move
as if to say, and is *this* pleasing?

When I look again he is gone.
He is easy to imagine
in flight: *red extended flame*
I would say, or, *ribbon
torn from a hat rising once
before it catches*

on a twig, or
flying painted mouth . . .
but then how far
have we come?
He could fly now
into a moment of sunlight

that fell from the sun's edge
ten thousand years ago,
mixed in with sunlight
absolutely new.
There is no way to understand
the difference. Some red

has always just slipped from
our field of vision, a cardinal
dropping from persian to magenta to white so slowly
in order that the loss
be tempted
not endured.

A Working Day
ROBERT COOVER

She enters, deliberately, gravely, without affectation, circumspect in her motions (as she's been taught), not stamping too loud, nor dragging her legs after her, but advancing sedately, discreetly, glancing briefly at the empty rumpled bed, the cast-off nightclothes. She hesitates. No. Again. She enters. Deliberately and gravely, without affectation, not stamping too loud, nor dragging her legs after her, not marching as if leading a dance, nor keeping time with her head and hands, nor staring or turning her head either one way or the other, but advancing sedately and discreetly through the door, across the polished floor, past the empty rumpled bed and cast-off nightclothes (not glancing, that's better), to the tall curtains along the far wall. As she's been taught. Now, with a humble yet authoritative gesture, she draws the curtains open: Ah! the morning sunlight comes flooding in over the gleaming tiles as though (she thinks) flung from a bucket. She opens wide the glass doors behind the curtains (there is such a song of birds all about!) and gazes for a moment into the garden, quite prepared to let the sweet breath of morning blow in and excite her to the most generous and efficient accomplishments, but her mind is still locked on that image, at first pleasing, now troubling, of the light as it spilled into the room: as from a bucket ... She sighs. She enters. With a bucket. She sets the bucket down, deliberately, gravely, and walks (circumspectly) across the room, over the polished tiles, past the empty rumpled bed (she doesn't glance at it), to draw open the tall curtains at the far wall. Buckets of light come flooding in (she is not thinking about this now) and the room, as she opens wide the glass doors, is sweetened by the fresh morning air blowing in from the garden. The sun is fully risen and the pink clouds of dawn are all gone out of the sky (the time lost: this is what she is thinking about), but the dew is still on every plant in the garden, and everything looks clean and bright. As will his room when she is done with it.

*

He awakes from a dream (something about utility, or futility, and a teacher he once had who, when he whipped his students, called it his "civil service"), still wrapped in darkness and hugged close to the sweet breast of the night, but with the new day already hard upon him, just beyond the curtains (he knows, even without looking), waiting for him out there like a brother: to love him or to kill him. He pushes the bedcovers back and sits up groggily to meet its challenge (or promise), pushes his feet into slippers, rubs his face, stretches, wonders what new blunders the maid (where is she?) will commit today. Well. I should at least give her a chance, he admonishes himself with a gaping yawn.

*

Oh, she knows her business well: to scrub and wax the floors, polish the furniture, make the master's bed soft and easy, lay up his nightclothes, wash, starch, and mend the bedlinens as necessary, air the blankets and clean the bathroom, making certain of ample supplies of fresh towels and washcloths, soap, toilet paper, razor blades, and toothpaste—in short, to see that nothing be wanting which he desires or requires to be done, being always diligent in endeavoring to please him, silent when he is angry except to beg his pardon, and ever faithful, honest, submissive, and of good disposition. The trivial round, the common task, she knows as she sets about her morning's duties, will furnish all she needs to ask, room to deny herself, a road (speaking loosely) to bring her daily nearer God. But on that road, on the floor of the bathroom, she finds a damp towel and some pajama bottoms, all puddled together like a cast-off mop-head. Mop-head? She turns and gazes in dismay at the empty bucket by the outer door. Why, she wants to know, tears springing to the corners of her eyes, can't it be easier than this? And so she enters, sets her bucket down with firm deliberation, leans her mop gravely against the wall. Also a broom, brushes, some old rags, counting things off on her fingers as she deposits them. The curtains have been drawn open and the room is already (as though impatiently) awash with morning sunlight. She crosses the room, past the (no glances) empty rumpled bed, and opens wide the glass doors leading out into the garden, letting in the sweet breath of morning, which she hardly notices. She has resolved this morning—as every morning—to be cheerful and good-natured, such that if any accident should happen to test that resolution, she should not suffer it to put her out of temper with everything besides, but such resolutions are more easily sworn than obeyed. Things are already in such a state! Yet: virtue is made for difficulties, she reminds herself, and grows stronger and brighter for such trials. *"Oh, teach me, my God and King, in all things thee to see, and what I do in any thing, to do it as for thee!"* she sings out to the garden and to the room, feeling her heart lift like a sponge in a bucket. *"A servant with this clause makes drudgery divine: who sweeps a room, as for thy laws, makes that and th'action fine!"* And yes, she can still recover the lost time. She has everything now, the mop and bucket, broom, rags, and brushes, her apron pockets are full of polishes, dustcloths, and cleaning powders, the cupboards are well stocked with fresh linens, all she really needs now is to keep—but ah! is there, she wonders anxiously, spinning abruptly on her heels as she hears the master relieving himself noisily in the bathroom, any *water* in the bucket—?!

*

He awakes, squints at his watch in the darkness, grunts (she's late, but just as well, time for a shower), and with only a moment's hesitation, tosses the blankets back, tearing himself free: I'm so old, he thinks, and still every morning is a bloody new birth. Somehow it should be easier than this. He sits up painfully (that divine government!), rubs his face, pushes his feet into slippers, stands, stretches, then strides to the windows at the far wall and throws open the tall curtains, letting the sun in. The room seems almost to explode with the blast of light: he resists, then surrenders to, finally welcomes its amicable violence. He opens wide the glass doors that lead out into the garden and stands there in the sunshine, sucking in deeply the fresh morning air and trying to recall the dream he's just had. Something about a teacher who had once lectured him on humility. Severely. Only now, in the dream, he was himself the teacher and the student was a woman he knew, or thought he knew, and in his lecture "humility" kept getting mixed up somehow with "humor," such that, in effect, he was trying, in all severity, to teach her how to laugh. He's standing there in the sunlight in his slippers and pajama bottoms, remembering the curious strained expression on the woman's face as she tried—desperately, it seemed—to laugh, and wondering why this provoked (in the dream) such a fury in him, when the maid comes in. She gazes impassively a moment (yet humbly, circumspectly) at the gaping fly of his pajamas, then turns away, sets her bucket down against the wall. Her apron strings are loose, there's a hole in one of her black stockings, and she's forgotten her mop again. I'd be a happier man, he acknowledges to himself with a wry sigh, if I could somehow fail to notice these things. "I'll start in the bathroom," she says discreetly. "Sir," he reminds her. "Sir," she says.

*

And she enters. Deliberately and gravely, as though once and for all, without affectation, somewhat encumbered by the vital paraphernalia of her office, yet radiant with that clear-browed self-assurance achieved only by long and generous devotion to duty. She plants her bucket and brushes beside the door, leans the mop and broom against the wall, then crosses the room to fling open (humbly, authoritatively) the curtains and the garden doors: the fragrant air and sunlight come flooding in, a flood she now feels able to appreciate. The sun is already high in the sky, but the garden is still bejeweled with morning dew and (she remembers to notice) there is such a song of birds all about! What inspiration! She enjoys this part of her work: flushing out the stale darkness of the dead night with such grand (yet circumspect) gestures—it's almost an act of magic! Of course, she takes pleasure in *all* her appointed tasks (she reminds herself), whether it be scrubbing floors or polishing furniture or even scouring out the tub or toilet, for she knows that only in giving herself (as he has told her) can she find herself: true service (he doesn't have to tell her!) is perfect freedom. And so, excited by the song of the birds, the sweet breath of morning, and her own natural eagerness to please, she turns with a glad heart to her favorite task of all: the making of the bed. Indeed, all the rest of her work is embraced by it, for the opening up and airing of the bed is the first of her tasks, the making of it her last. Today, however, when she tosses the covers back, she finds, coiled like a dark snake near the foot, a bloodstained leather belt. She starts back. The sheets, too, are flecked with blood. Shadows seem to creep across the room and the birds fall silent. Perhaps, she thinks, her heart sinking, I'd better go out and come in again . . .

*

At least, he cautions himself while taking a shower, give her a chance. Her forgetfulness, her clumsiness, her endless comings and goings and stupid mistakes are a trial of course, and he feels sometimes like he's been living with them forever, but she means well and, with patience, instruction, discipline, she can still learn. Indeed, to the extent that she fails, it could be said, *he* has failed. He knows he must be firm, yet understanding, severe if need be, but caring and protective. He vows to treat her today with the civility and kindness due to an inferior, and not to lose his temper, even should she resist. Our passions (he reminds himself) are our infirmities. A sort of fever of the mind, which ever leaves us weaker than it found us. But when he turns off the taps and reaches for the towel, he finds it damp. Again! He can feel the rage rising in him, turning to ash with its uncontrollable heat his gentler intentions. Has she forgotten to change them yet again, he wonders furiously, standing there in a puddle with the cold wet towels clutched in his fists—or has she not even come yet?

*

She enters once and for all encumbered with her paraphernalia which she deposits by the wall near the door, thinking: it should be easier than this. Indeed, why bother at all when it always seems to turn out the same? Yet she cannot do otherwise. She is driven by a sense of duty and a profound appetite for hope never quite stifled by even the harshest punishments: this time, today, perhaps it will be perfect . . . So, deliberately and gravely, not staring or turning her head either one way or the other, she crosses the room to the far wall and with a determined flourish draws open the tall curtains, flooding the room with buckets of sunlight, but her mind is clouded with an old obscurity: When, she wants to know as she opens wide the glad doors to let the sweet breath of morning in (there are birds, too, such a song, she doesn't hear it), did all this really begin? When she entered? Before that? Long ago? Not yet? Or just now as, bracing herself as though for some awful trial, she turns upon the bed and flings the covers back, her morning's tasks begun. "Oh!" she cries. "I beg your pardon, sir!" He stares groggily down at the erection poking up out of the fly of his pajama pants, like (she thinks) some kind of luxuriant but dangerous dew-bejeweled blossom: a monster in the garden. "I was having a dream," he announces sleepily, yet gravely. "Something about tumidity. But it kept getting mixed up somehow with—" But she is no longer listening. Watching his knobby plant waggle puckishly in the morning breeze, then dip slowly, wilting toward the shadows like a closing morning glory, a solution of sorts has occurred to her to that riddle of genesis that has been troubling her mind: to wit, that a condition *has* no beginning. Only *change* can begin or end.

*

She enters, dressed crisply in her black uniform with its starched white apron and lace cap, leans her mop against the wall like a standard, and strides across the gleaming tile floor to fling open the garden doors as though (he thinks) calling forth the morning. What's left of it. Watching her from behind the bathroom door, he is moved by her transparent earnestness, her uncomplicated enthusiasm, her easy self-assurance. What more, really, does he want of her? Never mind that she's forgotten her broom again, or that her shoe's unbuckled and her cap on crooked, or that in her exuberance she nearly broke the glass doors (and sooner or later will), what is wonderful is the quickening of her spirits as she enters, the light that seems to dawn on her face as she opens the room, the way she makes a maid's oppressive routine seem like a sudden invention of love. See now how she tosses back the blankets and strips off the sheets as though, in childish excitement, unwrapping a gift! How in fluffing up the pillows she seems almost to bring them to life! She calls it: "doing the will of God from the heart!" *"Teach me, my God and King, in all things thee to see,"* she sings, *"and what I do in any thing, to do it as for thee!"* Ah well, he envies her: would that he had it so easy! All life is a service, he knows that. To live in the full sense of the word is not to exist or subsist merely, but to make oneself over, to *give* oneself: to some high purpose, to others, to some social end, to life itself beyond the shell of ego. But he, lacking superiors, must devote himself to abstractions, never knowing when he has succeeded, when he has failed, or even if he has the abstractions right, whereas she, needing no others, has him. He would like to explain this to her, to ease the pain of her routine, of her chastisement—what he calls his disciplinary interventions—but he knows that it is he, not she, who is forever in need of such explanations. Her mop fairly flies over the tiles (today she has remembered the mop), making them gleam like mirrors, her face radiant with their reflected light. He checks himself in the bathroom mirror, flicks lint off one shoulder, smoothes the ends of his moustache. If only she could somehow understand how difficult it is for me, he thinks as he steps out to receive her greeting: "Good morning, sir." "Good morning," he replies crisply, glancing around the room.

He means to give her some encouragement, to reward her zeal with praise or gratitude or at least a smile to match her own, but instead he finds himself flinging his dirty towels at her feet and snapping: "These towels are damp! See to it that they are replaced!" "Yes, sir!" "Moreover, your apron strings are dangling untidily and there are flyspecks on the mirror!" "Sir." "And another thing!" He strides over to the bed and tears it apart. "Isn't it about time these sheets were changed? Or am I supposed to wear them through before they are taken to be washed?" "But, sir, I just put new—!" "What? *WHAT*—?!" he storms. "Answering back to a reproof? Have you forgotten all I've taught you?" "I—I'm sorry, sir!" "Never answer back if your master takes occasion to reprove you, except—?" "Except it be to acknowledge my fault, sir, and that I am sorry for having committed it, promising to amend for the time to come, and to . . . to . . ." "Am I being unfair?" he insists, unbuckling his belt. "No, sir," she says, her eyes downcast, shoulders trembling, her arms pressed tight to her sides.

*

He is strict but not unkindly. He pays her well, is grateful for her services, treats her respectfully, she doesn't dislike him or even fear him. Nor does she have to work very hard: he is essentially a tidy man, picks up after himself, comes and goes without disturbing things much. A bit of dusting and polishing now and then, fold his pajamas, change the towels, clean the bathroom, scrub the floor, make his bed: really there's nothing to complain about. Yet, vaguely, even as she opens up the garden doors, letting the late morning sunshine and freshness in, she feels unhappy. Not because of what she must do— no, she truly serves with gladness. When she straightens a room, polishes a floor, bleaches a sheet, or scrubs a tub, always doing the very best she can, she becomes, she knows, a part of what is good in the world, creating a kind of beauty, revealing a kind of truth. About herself, about life, the things she touches. It's just that, somehow, something is missing. Some response, some enrichment, some direction . . . it's, well, it's too repetitive. Something like that. That's part of the problem anyway. The other part is what she keeps finding in his bed. Things that oughtn't to be there, like old razor blades, broken bottles, banana skins, bloody pessaries, crumbs and ants, leather thongs, mirrors, empty books, old toys, dark stains. Once, even, a frog jumped out at her. No matter how much sunlight and fresh air she lets in, there's always this dark little pocket of lingering night which she has to uncover. It can ruin everything, all her careful preparations. This morning, however, all she finds is a pair of flannelette drawers. Ah: she recognizes them. She glances about guiltily, pulls them on hastily. Lucky the master's in the bathroom, she thinks, patting down her skirt and apron, or there'd be the devil to pay.

*

Something about scouring, or scourging, he can't remember, and a teacher he once had who called his lectures "lechers." The maid is standing over him, staring down in some astonishment at his erection. "Oh! I beg your pardon, sir!" "I was having a dream . . . ," he explains, trying to bring it back. "Something about a woman . . ." But by then he is alone again. He hears her in the bathroom, running water, singing, whipping the wet towels off the racks and tossing them out the door. Ah well, it's easy for her, she can come and go. He sits up, squinting in the bright light, watching his erection dip back inside his pajamas like a sleeper pulling the blankets over his head (oh yes! to return there!), then dutifully shoves his feet into slippers, stretches, staggers to the open garden doors. The air is fragrant and there's a morning racket of birds and insects, vaguely threatening. Sometimes, as now, scratching himself idly and dragging himself still from the stupor of sleep, he wonders about his calling, how it came to be his, and when it all began: on his coming here? on *her* coming here? before that, in some ancient time beyond recall? And has he chosen it? or has he, like that woman in his dream, showing him something that for some reason enraged him, been "born with it, sir, for your very utility"?

*

She strives, understanding the futility of it, for perfection. To arrive properly equipped, to cross the room deliberately, circumspectly, without affectation (as he has taught her), to fling open the garden doors and let the sweet breath of morning flow in and chase the night away, to strip and air the bed and, after all her common tasks, her trivial round, to remake it smooth and tight, all the sheets and blankets tucked in neatly at the sides and bottom, the upper sheet and blankets turned down at the head just so far that their fold covers only half the pillows, all topped with the spread, laid to hang evenly at all sides. And today—perhaps at last! She straightens up, wipes her brow, looks around: yes! he'll be so surprised! Everything perfect! Her heart is pounding as the master, dressed for the day, steps out of the bathroom, marches directly over to the bed, hauls back the covers, picks up a pillow, and hits her in the face with it. Now what did he do that for? "And another thing!" he says.

*

He awakes, feeling sorry for himself (he's not sure why, something he's been dreaming perhaps, or merely the need to wake just by itself: come, day, do your damage!), tears himself painfully from the bed's embrace, sits up, pushes his feet into slippers. He grunts, squinting in the dimness at his watch: she's late. Just as well. He can shower before she gets here. He staggers into the bathroom and drops his pajamas, struggling to recall his dream. Something about a woman in the civil service, which in her ignorance or cupidity, she insisted on calling the "sybil service." He is relieving himself noisily when the maid comes in. "Oh! I beg your pardon, sir!" "Good morning," he replies crisply, and pulls his pajamas up, but she is gone. He can hear her outside the door, walking quickly back and forth, flinging open the curtains and garden doors, singing to herself as though lifted by the tasks before her. Sometimes he envies her, having him. Her footsteps carry her to the bed and he hears the rush and flutter of sheets and blankets being thrown back. Hears her scream.

*

He's not unkind, demands no more than is his right, pays her well, and teaches her things like, "All life is a service, a consecration to some high end," and, "If domestic service is to be tolerable, there must be an attitude of habitual deference on the one side and one of sympathetic protection on the other." "Every state and condition of life has its particular duties," he has taught her. "The duty of a servant is to be obedient, diligent, sober, just, honest, frugal, orderly in her behavior, submissive, and respectful toward her master. She must be contented in her station, because it is necessary that some should be above others in this world, and it was the will of the Almighty to place you in a state of servitude." Her soul, in short, is his invention, and she is grateful to him for it. *"Whatever thy hand findeth to do,"* he has admonished her, *"do it with all thy might!"* Nevertheless, looking over her shoulder at her striped sit-me-down in the wardrobe mirror, she wishes he might be a little less literal in applying his own maxims: *he's drawn blood!*

*

He awakes, mumbling something about a dream, a teacher he once had, some woman, infirmities. "A sort of fever of the mind," he explains, his throat phlegmy with sleep. "Yes, sir," she says, and flings open the curtains and the garden doors, letting light and air into the stale bedroom. She takes pleasure in all her appointed tasks, but enjoys this one most of all, more so when the master is already out of bed, for he seems to resent her waking him like this. Just as he resents her arriving late, after he's risen. Either way, sooner or later, she'll have to pay for it. "It's a beautiful day," she remarks hopefully. He sits up with an ambiguous grunt, rubs his eyes, yawns, shudders. "You may speak when spoken to," he grumbles, tucking his closing morning glory back inside his pajamas (behind her, bees are humming in the garden and there's a crackly pulsing of insects, but the birds have fallen silent: she had thought today might be perfect, but already it is slipping away from her), "unless it be to deliver a message or ask a necessary question." "Yes, sir." He shoves his feet into slippers and staggers off to the bathroom, leaving her to face (she expects the worst)—shadows have invaded the room—the rumpled bed alone.

*

It's not just the damp towels. It's also the streaked floor, the careless banging of the garden doors, her bedraggled uniform, the wrinkled sheets, the confusion of her mind. He lectures her patiently on the proper way to make a bed, the airing of the blankets, turning of the mattress, changing of the sheets, the importance of a smooth surface. "Like a blank sheet of crisp new paper," he tells her. He shows her how to make the correct diagonal creases at the corners, how to fold the top edge of the upper sheet back over the blankets, how to carry the spread under and then over the pillows. Oh, not for his benefit and advantage—he could sleep anywhere or for that matter (in extremity) could make his own bed—but for hers. How else would she ever be able to realize what is best in herself? "A little arrangement and thought will give you method and habit," he explains (it is his "two fairies" lecture), but though she seems willing enough, is polite and deferential, even eager to please, she can never seem to get it just right. Is it a weakness on her part, he wonders as he watches her place the pillows on the bed upside down, then tug so hard on the bottom blanket that it comes out at the foot, or some perversity? Is she testing him? She refits the bottom blanket, tucks it in again, but he knows the sheet beneath is now wrinkled. He sighs, removes his belt. Perfection is elusive, but what else is there worth striving for? "Am I being unfair?" he insists.

*

He's standing there in the sunlight in his slippers and pajama bottoms, cracking his palm with a leather strap, when she enters (once and for all) with all her paraphernalia. She plants the bucket and brushes beside the door, leans the mop and broom against the wall, stacks the fresh linens and towels on a chair. She is late—the curtains and doors are open, her circumspect crossing of the room no longer required—but she remains hopeful. Running his maxims over in her head, she checks off her rags and brushes, her polishes, cleaning powders, razor blades, toilet paper, dustpans—oh no . . . ! Her heart sinks like soap in a bucket. The soap she has forgotten to bring. She sighs, then deliberately and gravely, without affectation, not stamping too loud, nor dragging her legs after her, not marching as if leading a dance, nor keeping time with her head and hands, nor staring or turning her head either one way or the other, she advances sedately and discreetly across the gleaming tiles to the bed, and tucking up her dress and apron, pulling down her flannelette drawers, bends over the foot of it, exposing her soul's ingress to the sweet breath of morning, blowing in from the garden. "I wonder if you can appreciate," he says, picking a bit of lint off his target before applying his corrective measures to it, "how difficult this is for me?"

*

He awakes, vaguely frightened by something he's dreamt (it was about order or odor and a changed condition—but how did it begin . . . ?), wound up in damp sheets and unable at first even to move, defenseless against the day already hard upon him. Its glare blinds him, but he can hear the maid moving about the room, sweeping the floor, changing the towels, running water, pushing furniture around. "Good morning, sir," she says. "Come here a moment," he replies gruffly, then clears his throat. "Sir?" "Look under the bed. Tell me what you see." He expects the worst: blood, a decapitated head, a bottomless hole . . . "I'm—I'm sorry, sir," she says, tucking up her skirt and apron, lowering her drawers, "I thought I *had* swept it . . ."

*

No matter how much fresh air and sunlight she lets in, there is always this little pocket of lingering night which she has to uncover. Once she found a dried bull's pizzle in there, another time a dead mouse in a trap. Even the nice things she finds in the bed are somehow horrible: the toys broken, the food moldy, the clothing torn and bloody. She knows she must always be circumspect and self-effacing, never letting her countenance betray the least dislike toward any task, however trivial or distasteful, and she resolves every morning to be cheerful and good-natured, letting nothing she finds there put her out of temper with everything besides, but sometimes she just cannot help herself. "Oh, teach me, my God and King, in all things thee to see, and what I do in any thing, to do it as for thee," she tells herself, seeking courage, and flings back the sheets and blankets. She screams. But it's only money, a little pile of gold coins, agleam with promise. Or challenge: is he testing her?

*

Ah well, he envies her, even as that seat chosen by Mother Nature for such interventions quivers and reddens under the whistling strokes of the birch rod in his hand. "Again!" "Be . . . be diligent in endeavoring to please your master—be faithful and . . . and . . ." Swish—*SNAP!* "Oh, sir!" "Honest!" "Yes, sir!" She, after all, is free to come and go, her correction finitely inscribed by time and the manuals, but he . . . He sighs unhappily. How did it all begin, he wonders. Was it destiny, choice, generosity? If she would only get it right for once, he reasons, bringing his stout engine of duty down with a sharp report on her brightly striped but seemingly unimpressionable hinder parts, he might at least have time for a stroll in the garden. Does she—*CRACK!*—think he enjoys this? "Well?" "Be . . . be faithful, honest, and submissive to him, sir, and—" Whish-*SLASH!* "And—*gasp!*—do not incline to be slothful! Or—" *THWOCK!* "Ow! Please, sir!" Hiss-*WHAP!* She groans, quivers, starts. The two raised hemispheres upon which the blows from the birch rod have fallen begin (predictably) to make involuntary motions both vertically and horizontally, the constrictor muscle being hard at work, the thighs also participating in the general vibrations, all in all a dismal spectacle. And for nothing? So it would seem . . . "Or?" "Or lie long in bed, sir, but rise . . . rise early in a morning!" The weals crisscross each other on her flushed posteriors like branches against the pink clouds of dawn, which for some reason saddens him. "Am I being unfair?" "No—no, s———" Whisp—*CRACK!* She shows no tears, but her face pressed against the bedding is flushed, her lips trembling, and she breathes heavily as though she's been running, confirming the quality of the rod which is his own construction. "Sir," he reminds her, turning away. "Sir," she replies faintly. "Thank you, sir."

*

She enters once and for all, radiant and clear browed (a long devotion to duty), with all her paraphernalia, her mop and bucket, brooms, rags, soaps, polishes, sets them all down, counting them off on her fingers, then crosses the room deliberately and circumspectly, not glancing at the rumpled bed, and flings open the curtains and the garden doors to call forth the morning, what's left of it. There is such a song of insects all about (the preying birds are silent)—what inspiration! "Lord, keep me in my place!" The master is in the shower: she hears the water. "Let me be diligent in performing whatever my master commands me," she prays, "neat and clean in my habit, modest in my carriage, silent when he is angry, willing to please, quick and neat-handed about what I do, and always of an humble and good disposition!" Then, excited to the most generous and efficient accomplishments, she turns with a palpitating heart (she is thinking about perfect service and freedom and the unpleasant things she has found) to the opening up and airing of the bed. She braces herself, expecting the worst, but finds only a wilted flower from the garden: ah!

today then! she thinks hopefully—perhaps at last! But then she hears the master turn the taps off, step out of the shower. Oh no . . . ! She lowers her drawers to her knees, lifts her dress, and bends over the unmade bed. *"These towels are damp!"* he blusters, storming out of the bathroom, wielding the fearsome rod, that stout engine of duty, still wet from the shower.

*

Sometimes he uses a rod, sometimes his hand, his belt, sometimes a whip, a cane, a cat-o'-nine-tails, a bull's pizzle, a hickory switch, a martinet, ruler, slipper, a leather strap, a hairbrush. There are manuals for this. Different preparations and positions to be assumed, the number and severity of the strokes generally prescribed to fit the offense, he has explained it all to her, though it is not what is important to her. She knows he is just, could not be otherwise if he tried, even if the relative seriousness of the various infractions seems somewhat obscure to her at times. No, what matters to her is the idea behind the regulations that her daily tasks, however trivial, are perfectible. Not absolutely perhaps, but at least in terms of the manuals. This idea, which is almost tangible—made manifest, as it were, in the weals on her behind—is what the punishment is for, she assumes. She does not enjoy it certainly, nor (she believes—and it wouldn't matter if he did) does he. Rather, it is a road (speaking loosely), the rod, to bring her daily nearer God—and what's more, it seems that she's succeeding at last! Today everything has been perfect: her entry, all her vital paraphernalia, her circumspect crossing of the room and opening of the garden doors, her scrubbing and waxing and dusting and polishing, her opening up and airing and making of the master's bed—everything! True service, she knows (he has taught her!), is perfect freedom, and today she feels it: almost like a breeze—the sweet breath of success—lifting her! But then the master emerges from the bathroom, his hair wild, fumbles through the clothes hanging in the wardrobe, pokes through the dresser drawers, whips back the covers of her perfectly made bed. "What's this doing here—?!" he demands, holding up his comb. "I—I'm sorry, sir! It wasn't there when I—" "What? *What*—?!" He seizes her by the elbow, drags her to the foot of the bed, forces her to bend over it. "I have been very indulgent to you up to now, but now I am going to punish you severely, to cure you of your insolent clumsiness once and for all! So pull up your skirt—come! pull it up! you know well enough that the least show of resistance means ten extra cuts of the—*what's this*—?!" She peers round her shoulder at her elevated sit-me-down, so sad and pale above her stockings. "I—I don't understand, sir! I had them on when I came in—!"

*

Perhaps he's been pushing her too hard, he muses, soaping himself in the shower and trying to recall the dream he was having when she woke him up (something about ledgers and manual positions, a woman, and the merciless invention of souls which was a sort of fever of the mind), perhaps he's been expecting too much too soon, making her overanxious, for in some particulars now she is almost too efficient, clattering in with her paraphernalia like a soldier, blinding him with a sudden brutal flood of sunlight from the garden, hauling the sheets out from under him while he's still trying to stuff his feet into his slippers. Perhaps he should back off a bit, give her a chance to recover some of her ease and spontaneity, even at the expense of a few undisciplined errors. Perhaps . . . yet he knows he could never let up, even if he tried. Not that he enjoys all this punishment, any more (he assumes, but it doesn't matter) than she does. No, he would rather do just about anything else—crawl back into bed, read his manuals, even take a stroll in the garden—but he is committed to a higher end, his life a mission of sorts, a consecration, and so punish her he must, for to the extent that she fails, he fails. As he turns off the taps and steps out of the shower, reaching for the towel, the maid rushes in. "Oh, I beg your pardon, sir!" He grabs a towel and wraps it around him, but she snatches it away again: "That one's damp, sir!" She dashes out to fetch him a fresh one and he is moved by her transparent enthusiasm, her eagerness to please, her seemingly unquenchable appetite for hope: perhaps today . . . ! But he has already noticed that she has forgotten her lace cap, there's a dark stain on the bib of her apron, and her garters are dangling. He sighs, reaches for the leather strap. Somehow (is there to be no end to this? he wonders ruefully) it should be easier than this.

*

She does not enjoy the discipline of the rod, nor does he—or so she believes, though what would it matter if he did? Rather, they are both dedicated to the fundamental proposition (she winces at the painful but unintended pun, while peering over her shoulder at herself in the wardrobe mirror, tracing the weals with her fingertips) that her daily tasks, however trivial, are perfectible, her punishments serving her as a road, loosely speaking, to bring her daily nearer God, at least in terms of the manuals. Tenderly, she lifts her drawers up over her blistered sit-me-down, smoothes down her black alpaca dress and white lace apron, wipes the tears from her eyes, and turns once more to the unmade bed. Outside, the bees humming in the noonday sun remind her of all the time she's lost. At least, she consoles herself, the worst is past. But the master is pacing the room impatiently and she's fearful his restlessness will confuse her again. "Why don't you go for a stroll in the garden, sir?" she suggests deferentially. "You may speak when spoken to!" he reminds her, jabbing a finger at her sharply. "I—I'm sorry, sir!" "You must be careful not only to do your work quietly, but to keep out of sight as much as possible, and never begin to speak to your master unless—?" "Unless it be to deliver a message, sir, or ask a necessary question!" "And then to do it in as few words as possible," he adds, getting down his riding whip. "Am I being unfair?" "But, sir! you've already—!" "What? *What*—?! Answering back to a reproof—?" "But—!" "*Enough!*" he rages, seizing her by the arm and dragging her over to the bed. "*Please*—!" But he pulls her down over his left knee, pushes her head down on the stripped mattress, locking her legs in place with his right leg, clamps her right wrist in the small of her back, throws her skirts back, and jerks her drawers down. "*Oh, sir——!*" she pleads, what is now her highest part still radiant and throbbing from the previous lesson. "SILENCE!" he roars, lifting the whip high above his head, a curious strained expression on his face. She can hear the whip sing as he brings it down, her cheeks pinch together involuntarily, her heart leaps—*he'll draw blood!*

*

Where does she come from? Where does she go? He doesn't know. All he knows is that every day she comes here, dressed in her uniform and carrying all her paraphernalia with her, which she sets down by the door; then she crosses the room, opens up the curtains and garden doors, makes his bed soft and easy, first airing the bedding, turning the mattress, and changing the linens, scrubs and waxes the tiled floor, cleans the bathroom, polishes the furniture and all the mirrors, replenishes all supplies, and somewhere along the way commits some fundamental blunder, obliging him to administer the proper correction. Every day the same. Why does he persist? It's not so much that he shares her appetite for hope (though sometimes, late in the day, he does), but that he could not do otherwise should he wish. To live in the full sense of the word, he knows, is not merely to exist, but to give oneself to some mission, surrender to a higher purpose, but in truth he often wonders, watching that broad part destined by Mother Nature for such solemnities quiver and redden under his hand (he thinks of it as a blank ledger on which to write), whether it is he who has given himself to a higher end, or that end which has chosen and in effect captured him?

*

Perhaps, she thinks, I'd better go out and come in again . . . And so she enters. As though once and for all, though she's aware she can never be sure of this. She sets down beside the door all the vital paraphernalia of her office, checking off each item on her fingers, then crosses the room (circumspectly etc.) and flings open the curtains and garden doors to the midday sun. Such a silence all about! She tries to take heart from it, but it is not so inspiring as the song of birds, and even the bees seem to have ceased their humming. Though she has resolved, as always, to be cheerful and good-natured, truly serving with gladness as she does, she nevertheless finds her will flagging, her mind clouded with old obscurities: somehow, something is missing. "Teach me, my God and King, in all things thee to see," she recites dutifully, but the words seem meaningless to her and go nowhere. And now, once again, the hard part. She holds back, trembling—but what can she do about it? For she knows her place and is contented with her station, as he has taught her. She takes a deep breath of the clean warm air blowing in from the garden and, fearing the worst, turns on the bed, hurls the covers back, and screams. But it is only the master. "Oh! I beg your pardon, sir!" "A . . . a dream," he explains huskily, as his erection withdraws into his pajamas like a worm caught out in the sun, burrowing for shade. "Something about a lecture on civil severity, what's left of it, and an inventory of soaps . . . or hopes . . ." He's often like that as he struggles (never very willingly, it seems to her) out of sleep. She leaves him there, sitting on the edge of the bed, squinting in the bright light, yawning and scratching himself and muttering something depressing about being born again, and goes to the bathroom to change the towels, check the toothpaste and toilet paper, wipe the mirror and toilet seat, and put fresh soap in the shower tray, doing the will of God and the manuals, endeavoring to please. As he shuffles groggily in, already reaching inside his fly, she slips out, careful not to speak as she's not been spoken to, and returns to the rumpled bed. She tosses back the blankets afresh (nothing new, thank you, sir), strips away the soiled linens, turns and brushes the mattress (else it might imbibe an unhealthy kind of dampness and become unpleasant), shakes the feather pillows, and sets everything out to air. While the master showers, she dusts the furniture, polishes the mirrors, and mops the floor, then remakes the bed, smooth and tight, all the sheets and blankets tucked in neatly at the sides and bottom, the top sheet turned down at the head, over the blankets, the spread carried under, then over the pillows, and hanging equally low at both sides and the foot: ah! it's almost an act of magic! But are those flyspecks on the mirror? She rubs the mirror, and seeing herself reflected there, thinks to check that her apron strings are tied and her stocking seams are straight. Peering over her shoulder at herself, her eye falls on the mirrored bed: one of the sheets is dangling at the foot, peeking out from under the spread as though exposing itself rudely. She hurries over, tucks it in, being careful to make the proper diagonal fold, but now the spread seems to be hanging lower on one side than the other. She whips it back, dragging the top sheet and blankets partway with it. The taps have been turned off, the master is drying himself. Carefully, she remakes the bed, tucking in all the sheets and blankets properly, fluffing the pillows up once more, covering it all with the spread, hung evenly. All this bedmaking has raised a lot of dust: she can see her own tracks on the floor. Hurriedly she wipes the furniture again and sweeps the tiles. Has she bumped the bed somehow? The spread is askew once again like a gift coming unwrapped. She tugs it to one side, sees ripples appear on top. She tries to smooth them down, but apparently the blankets are wrinkled underneath. She hasn't pushed the dresser back against the wall. The wardrobe door is open, reflecting the master standing in the doorway to the bathroom, slapping his palm with a bull's pizzle. She stands there, downcast, shoulders trembling, her arms pressed to her sides, unable to move. It's like some kind of failure of communication, she thinks, her diligent endeavors to please him forever thwarted by her irremediable clumsiness. "Come, come! A little arrangement and thought will give you method and habit," he reminds her gravely, "two fairies that will make the work disappear before a ready pair of hands!" In her mind she doesn't quite believe it, but her heart is ever hopeful, her hands readier than he knows. She takes the bed apart once more and remakes it from the beginning, tucking everything in correctly, fluffing the pillows, laying the spread evenly: all tight and smooth it looks. Yes! She pushes the dresser (once he horsed her there: she shudders to recall it, a flush of dread racing through her) back against the wall, collects the wet towels he has thrown on the floor, closes the wardrobe door. In the mirror, she sees the bed. The spread and blankets have been thrown back, the sheets pulled out. In the bathroom doorway, the master taps his palm with the stretched-out bull's pizzle, testing its firmness and elasticity, which she knows to be terrifying in its perfection. She remakes the bed tight and smooth, not knowing what else to do, vaguely aware as she finishes of an unpleasant odor. Under the bed? Also her apron is missing and she seems to have a sheet left over. Shadows creep across the room, silent now but for the rhythmic tapping of the pizzle in the master's hand and the pounding of her own palpitating heart.

*

Sometimes he stretches her across his lap. Sometimes she must bend over a chair or the bed, or lie flat out on it, or be horsed over the pillows, the dresser, or a stool, there are manuals for this. Likewise her drawers: whether they are to be drawn tight over her buttocks like a second skin or lowered, and if lowered, by which of them, how far, and so on. Her responses are assumed in the texts (the writhing, sobbing, convulsive quivering, blushing, moaning, etc.), but not specified, except insofar as they determine his own further reactions—to resistance, for example, or premature acquiescence, fainting, improper language, an unclean bottom, and the like. Thus, once again, her relative freedom: her striped buttocks tremble and dance spontaneously under the whip which his hand must bring whistling down on them according to canon—ah well, it's not so much that he envies her (her small freedoms cost her something, he knows that), but that he is saddened by her inability to understand how difficult it is for him, and without that understanding it's as though something is always missing, no matter how faithfully he adheres to the regulations.

"And—?" "And be neat and clean in your—" whisp—*CRACK!* "—OW! habit! Oh! and wash yourself all over once a day to avoid bad smells and—" hiss—*SNAP!* "—and—*gasp!*—wear strong decent underclothing!" The whip sings a final time, smacks its broad target with a loud report, and little drops of blood appear like punctuation, gratitude, morning dew. "That will do, then. See that you don't forget to wear them again!" "Yes, sir." She lowers her black alpaca skirt gingerly over the glowing crimson flesh as though hooding a lamp, wincing at each touch. "Thank you, sir."

*

For a long time she struggled to perform her tasks in such a way as to avoid the thrashings. But now, with time, she has come to understand that the tasks, truly common, are only peripheral details in some larger scheme of things which includes her punishment—indeed, perhaps depends upon it. Of course she still performs her duties *as though* they were perfectible and her punishment could be avoided, ever diligent in endeavoring to please him who guides her, but though each day the pain surprises her afresh, the singing of the descending instrument does not. That God has ordained bodily punishment (and Mother Nature designed the proper place of martyrdom) is beyond doubt—every animal is governed by it, understands and fears it, and the fear of it keeps every creature in its own sphere, forever preventing (as he has taught her) that natural confusion and disorder that would instantly arise without it. Every state and condition of life has its particular duties, and each is subject to the divine government of pain, nothing could be more obvious, and looked on this way, his chastisements are not merely necessary, they might even be beautiful. Or so she consoles herself, trying to take heart, calm her rising panic, as she crosses the room under his stern implacable gaze, lowers her drawers as far as her knees, tucks her skirt up, and bends over the back of a chair, hands on the seat, thighs taut and pressed closely together, what is now her highest part tensing involuntarily as though to reduce the area of pain, if not the severity. "It's . . . it's a beautiful day, sir," she says hopefully. "What? *WHAT*—*?!*"

*

Relieving himself noisily in the bathroom, the maid's daily recitals in the next room (such a blast of light out there—even in here he keeps his eyes half closed) thus drowned out, he wonders if there's any point in going on. She is late, has left half her paraphernalia behind, is improperly dressed, and he knows, even without looking, that the towels are damp. Maybe it's some kind of failure of communication. A mutual failure. Is that possible? A loss of syntax between stroke and weal? No, no, even if possible, it is unthinkable. He turns on the shower taps and lets fall his pajama pants, just as the maid comes in with a dead fetus and drops it down the toilet, flushes it. "I found it in your bed, sir," she explains gratuitously (is she testing him?), snatching up the damp towels, but failing to replace them with fresh ones. At least she's remembered her drawers today: she's wearing them around her ankles. He sighs, as she shuffles out. Maybe he should simply forget it, go for a stroll in the garden or something, crawl back into bed (a dream, he recalls now: something about lectures or ledgers—an inventory perhaps—and a bottomless hole, glass breaking, a woman doing what she called "the hard part" . . . or did she say "heart part"?), but of course he cannot, even if he truly wished to. He is not a free man, his life is consecrated, for though he is *her* master, her failures are inescapably *his*. He turns off the shower taps, pulls up his pajama pants, takes down the six-thonged martinet. "I have been very indulgent to you up to now," he announces, stepping out of the bathroom, "but now I am going to punish you severely, so pull up your skirt, come! pull it up!" But, alas, it is already up. She is bent over the foot of the bed, her pale hinder parts already exposed for his ministrations, an act of insolence not precisely covered by his manuals. Well, he reasons wryly, making the martinet sing whole chords, if improvisation is denied him, interpretation is not. "Ow, sir! Please! *You'll draw blood, sir!*"

✱

"Neat and clean in habit, modest—" *WHACK!* "—in . . . in carriage, silent when—" Whisp—*SNAP!* "OW!!" "Be careful! If you move, the earlier blow won't count!" "I—I'm sorry, sir!" Her soul, she knows, is his invention, and she is grateful to him for it, but exposed like this to the whining slashes of the cane and the sweet breath of midafternoon which should cool his righteous ardor but doesn't (once a bee flew in and stung him on the hand: what did it mean? nothing: she got it on her sit-me-down once, too, and he took the swelling for a target), her thighs shackled by flannelette drawers and blood rushing to her head, she can never remember (for all the times he has explained it to her) why it is that Mother Nature has chosen that particular part of her for such solemnities: it seems more like a place for letting things out than putting things in. "Well? Silent when—?" "Silent when he is angry, willing to please, quick, and—" swish—*CRACK!* "and of good disposition!" "Sir," he reminds her: *THWOCK!* "SIR!" she cries. "Very well, but you must learn to take more pleasure in your appointed tasks, however trivial or unpleasant, and when you are ordered to do anything, do not grumble or let your countenance betray any dislike thereunto, but do it cheerfully and readily!" "Yes, sir! Thank you, sir!" She is all hot behind, and peering over her shoulder at herself in the wardrobe mirror after the master has gone to shower, she can see through her tears that it's like on fire, flaming crimson it is, with large blistery welts rising and throbbing like things alive: he's drawn blood! She dabs at it with her drawers, recalling a dream he once related to her about a teacher he'd had who called his chastisements "scripture lessons," and she understands now what he's always meant by demanding "a clean sheet of paper." Well, certainly it has always been clean, neat and clean as he's taught her, that's one thing she's never got wrong, always washing it well every day in three hot lathers, letting the last lather be made thin of the soap, then not rinsing it or toweling it, but drying it over brimstone, keeping it as much from the air as possible, for that, she knows, will spoil it if it comes to it. She finishes drying it by slapping it together in her hands, then holding it before a good fire until it be thoroughly hot, then clapping it and rubbing it between her hands from the fire, occasionally adding to its fairness by giving it a final wash in a liquor made of rosemary flowers boiled in white wine. Now, she reasons, lifting her drawers up gingerly over the hot tender flesh, which is still twitching convulsively, if she could just apply those same two fairies, method and habit, to the rest of her appointed tasks, she might yet find in them that pleasure he insists she take, according to the manuals. Well, anyway, the worst is past. Or so she consoles herself as, smoothing down her black skirt and white lace apron, she turns to the bed. *"Oh, teach me, my God and King, in all things thee to . . ."* What——? There's something under there! *And it's moving . . . !*

*

"Thank you sir." "I know that perfection is elusive," he explains, putting away his stout engine of duty, while she staggers over, her knees bound by her drawers, to examine her backside in the wardrobe mirror (it is well cut, he knows, and so aglow one might cook little birds over it or roast chestnuts, as the manuals suggest), "but what else is there worth striving for?" "Yes, sir." She shows no tears, but her face is flushed, her lips are trembling, and she breathes as though she has just been running. He goes to gaze out into the garden, vaguely dissatisfied. The room is clean, the bed stripped and made, the maid whipped, why isn't that enough? Is there something missing in the manuals? No, more likely, he has failed somehow to read them rightly. Yet again. Outside in the sleepy afternoon heat of the garden, the bees are humming, insects chattering, gentler sounds to be sure than the hiss of a birch rod, the sharp report as it smacks firm resonant flesh, yet strangely alien to him, sounds of natural confusion and disorder from a world without precept or invention. He sighs. Though he was thinking "invention," what he has heard in his inner ear was "intention," and now he's not sure which it was he truly meant. Perhaps he should back off a bit—or even let her off altogether for a few days. A kind of holiday from the divine government of pain. Certainly he does not enjoy it nor (presumably) does she. If he could ever believe in her as she believes in him, he might even change places with her for a while, just to ease his own burden and let her understand how difficult it is for him. A preposterous idea of course, pernicious in fact, an unthinkable betrayal ... yet sometimes, late in the day, something almost like a kind of fever of the mind (speaking loosely) steals over—enough! *enough!* No shrinking! "And another thing!" he shouts, turning on the bed (she is at the door, gathering up her paraphernalia) and throwing back the covers: at the foot on the clean crisp sheets there is a little pile of wriggling worms, still coated with dirt from the garden. "WHAT DOES THIS MEAN—?!" he screams. "I—I'm sorry, sir! I'll clean it up right away, sir!" Is she testing him? Taunting him? It's almost an act of madness! "Am I being unfair?" "But, sir, you've already—!" "What? *WHAT*—?! Is there to be no *end* to this—?!"

*

He holds her over his left knee, her legs locked between his, wrist clamped in the small of her back, her skirt up and her drawers down, and slaps her with his bare hand, first one buttock, reddening it smartly in contrast to the dazzling alabaster (remembering the manuals) of the other, then attacking its companion with equal alacrity. "Ow! Please, sir!" "Come, come, you know that the least show of resistance means ten extra cuts of the rod!" he admonishes her, doubling her over a chair. "When you are ordered to do anything, do not grumble or let your countenance betray any dislike thereunto, but do it cheerfully and generously!" "Yes, sir, but—" "What? *WHAT*—?!" Whish—*CRACK!* "OW!" *SLASH!* Her crimson bottom, hugged close to the pillows, bobs and dances under the whistling cane. "When anyone finds fault with you, do not answer rudely!" Whirr—*SMACK!* "NO, SIR!" Each stroke, surprising her afresh, makes her jerk with pain and wrings a little cry from her (as anticipated by the manuals when the bull's pizzle is employed), which she attempts to stifle by burying her face in the horsehair cushion. "Be respectful—?" "Be respectful and obedient, sir, to those—" *swish—THWOCK!* "placed—OW!—placed OVER you—AARGH!" Whizz—*SWACK!* "With fear and trembling—" *SMASH!* "—and in singleness of your heart!" he reminds her gravely as she groans, starts, quivers under his patient instruction. "Ouch! Yes, sir!" The leather strap whistles down to land with a loud crack across the center of her glowing buttocks, seeming almost to explode, and making what lilies there are left into roses. *SMACK!* Ker-*WHACK!* He's working well now. "Am I being unfair?" "N-no, sir!" *WHAP! SLAP!* Horsed over the dresser her limbs launch out helplessly with each blow. *"Kneel down!"* She falls humbly to her hands and knees, her head bowed between his slippered feet, that broad part destined by Mother Nature for such devotions elevated but pointed away from him toward the wardrobe mirror (as though trying, flushed and puffed up, to cry out to itself), giving him full and immediate access to that large division referred to in the texts as the Paphian grove. "And resolve every morning—?" "Resolve—*gasp!*—resolve every morning to be cheerful and—" He raises the whip, snaps it three times around his head, and brings it down with a crash on her hinder parts, driving her head forward between his legs. "And—*YOW!*—and good-natured that . . . that day, and if any . . . if any accident—*groan!*—should happen to—" swish—*WHACK!* "—to break that resolution, suffer it . . . suffer it not—" *SLASH!* "Oh, sir!" *SWOCK!* He's pushing himself, too hard perhaps, but he can't— "Please, sir! *PLEASE!*" She is clinging to his knee, sobbing into his pajama pants, the two raised hemispheres upon which the strokes have fallen making involuntary motions both vertically and horizontally as though sending a message of distress, all the skin wrinkling like the surface of a lake rippled by the wind. "What are you doing?! *WHAT DOES THIS MEAN—?!*" He spanks her with a hairbrush, lashes her with a cat-o'-nine-tails, flagellates her with nettles, not shrinking from the hard service to be done, this divine drudgery, clear-browed in his devotion to duty. Perhaps today . . . ! "SIR!" He pauses, breathing heavily. His arm hurts. There is a curious strained expression on her face, flushed like her behind and wet with tears. "Sir, if you . . . if you don't stop—" "What? *WHAT*—?!" "You—you won't know what to do *next*!" "Ah." He has just been smacking her with a wet towel, and the damp rush and pop, still echoing in his inner ear, reminds him dimly of a dream, perhaps the one she interrupted when she arrived. In it there was something about humidity, but it kept getting mixed up somehow with hymnody, such that every time she opened her mouth (there was a woman in the dream) damp chords flowed out and stained his ledgers, bleached white as clean sheets. "I'm so old," he says, letting his arm drop, "and still each day . . ." "Sir?" "Nothing. A dream . . ." Where was he? It doesn't matter. "Why don't you go for a stroll in the garden, sir? It's a beautiful day." Such impudence: he ignores it. "It's all right," he says, draping the blood-flecked towel over his shoulder, scratching himself idly. He yawns. "The worst is past."

*

Has he devoted himself to a higher end, he wonders, standing there in the afternoon sunlight in his slippers and pajama bottoms, flexing a cane, testing it, snapping it against his palm, or has he been taken captive by it? Is choice itself an illusion? Or an act of magic? And *is* the worst over, or has it not yet begun? He shudders, yawns, stretches. And the manuals . . . He is afraid even to ask, takes a few practice strokes with the cane against a horsehair cushion instead. When the riddles and paradoxes of his calling overtake him, wrapping him in momentary darkness, he takes refuge in the purity of technique. The proper stretching of a bull's pizzle, for example, this can occupy him for hours. Or the fabrication of whipping chairs, the index of duties and offenses, the synonymy associated with corporal discipline and with that broad part destined by

Mother Nature for such services. And a cane is not simply any cane, but preferably one made like this one of brown Malacca—the stem of an East Indian rattan palm—about two and a half feet long (give or take an inch and a half) and a quarter of an inch thick. Whing-*SNAP!* listen to it! Or take the birch rod, not a mere random handful of birchen twigs, as often supposed, but an instrument of precise and elaborate construction. First, the twigs must be meticulously selected for strength and elasticity, each about two feet long, full of snap and taken from a young tree, the tips sharp as needles. Then carefully combining the thick with the thin and slender, they must be bound together for half their length, tightly enough that they might enjoy long service, yet not too tightly or else the rod will be like a stick and the twigs have no play. The rod must fit conveniently to the hand, have reach and swing so as to sing in the air, the larger part of all punishment being the anticipation, not the pain of course, and immediately raise welts and blisters, surprising the chastised flesh afresh with each stroke. To be sure, it is easier to construct a birch rod than to employ it correctly—that's always the hard part, he doesn't enjoy it, nor does she surely, but the art of the rod is incomplete without its perfect application. And though elusive, what else is there worth striving for? Indeed, he knows he has been too indulgent to her up till now, treating her with the civility and kindness due to an inferior, but forgetting the forging of her soul by way of those "vivid lessons," as a teacher he once had used to put it, "in holy scripture, hotly writ." So when she arrives, staggering in late with all her paraphernalia, her bucket empty and her bib hanging down, he orders her straight to the foot of the bed. "But, sir, I haven't even—" "Come, come, no dallying! The least show of resistance will double the punishment! Up with your skirt, up, up! for I intend to—WHAT?! IS THERE TO BE NO END TO THIS—?!" "I—I'm sorry! I was wearing them when I came—I must have left them somewhere . . . !" Maybe it's some kind of communication problem, he thinks, staring gloomily at her soul's ingress which confronts him like blank paper, laundered tiffany, a perversely empty ledger. The warm afternoon sun blows in through the garden doors, sapping his brave resolve. He feels himself drifting, yawning, must literally shake himself to bring the manuals back to mind, his duties, his devotion . . . "Sir," she reminds him. "Sir," he sighs.

*

It never ends. Making the bed, she scatters dust and feathers afresh or tips over the mop bucket. Cleaning up the floor, she somehow disturbs the bed. Or something does. It's almost as if it were alive. Blankets wrinkle, sheets peek perversely out from under the spread, pillows seem to sag or puff up all by themselves if she turns her back, and if she doesn't, then flyspecks break out on the mirror behind her like pimples, towels start to drip, stains appear on her apron. If she hasn't forgotten it. She sighs, turns once more on the perfidious bed. Though always of an humble and good disposition (as she's been taught), diligent in endeavoring to please him, and grateful for the opportunity to do the will of God from the heart by serving him (true service, perfect freedom, she knows all about that), sometimes, late in the day like this (shadows are creeping across the room and in the garden the birds are beginning to sing again), she finds herself wishing she could make the bed once and for all: glue down the sheets, sew on the pillows, stiffen the blankets as hard as boards and nail them into place. But then what? She cannot imagine. Something frightening. No, no, better this trivial round, these common tasks, and a few welts on her humble sit-me-down, she reasons, tucking the top sheet and blankets in neatly at the sides and bottom, turning them down at the head just so far that their fold covers half the pillows, than be overtaken by confusion and disorder. *"Teach me, my God and King,"* she sings out hopefully, floating the spread out over the bed, allowing it to fall evenly on all sides, *"in all things thee to—"* But then, as the master steps out of the bathroom behind her, she sees the blatant handprints on the wardrobe mirror, the streamers of her lace cap peeking out from under the dresser, standing askew. "I'm sorry, sir," she says, bending over the foot of the bed, presenting to him that broad part destined by Mother Nature for the arduous invention of souls. But he ignores it. Instead he tears open the freshly made bed, crawls into it fully dressed, kicking her in the face through the blankets with his shoes, pulls the sheets over his head, and commences to snore. Perhaps, she thinks, her heart sinking, I'd better go out and come in again . . .

*

Perhaps I should go for a stroll in the garden, he muses, dutifully reddening one resonant cheek with a firm volley of slaps, then the other, according to the manuals. I'm so old, and still . . . He sighs ruefully, recalling a dream he was having when the maid arrived (when was that?), something about a woman, bloody morning glories (or perhaps in the dream they were "mourning" glories: there was also something about a Paphian grave), and a bee that flew in and stung him on his tumor, which kept getting mixed up somehow with his humor, such that, swollen, with pain, he was laughing like a dead man . . . "Sir?" "What? WHAT—?!" he cries, starting up, "Ah." His hand is resting idly on her flushed behind as though he meant to leave it there. "I . . . I was just testing the heat," he explains gruffly, taking up the birch rod, testing it for strength and elasticity to wake his fingers up. "When I'm finished, you'll be able to cook little birds over it or roast chestnuts!" He raises the rod, swings it three times round his head, and brings it down with a whirr and a slash, reciting to himself from the manuals to keep his mind, clouded with old obscurities, on the task before him: "Sometimes the operation is begun a little above the garter—" whish-*SNAP!* "—and ascending the pearly inverted cones—" hiss-*WHACK!* "—is carried by degrees to the dimpled promontories—" *THWOCK!* "—which are vulgarly called the buttocks!" *SMASH!* "Ow, sir! PLEASE!" She twists about on his knee, biting her lip, her highest part flexing and quivering with each blow, her knees scissoring frantically between his legs. "Oh, teach me," she cries out, trying to stifle the sobs, "my God and—" whizz—*CRACK!* "—King, thee—*gasp!*—to—" *WHAP!* "—SEE!" Sometimes, especially late in the day like this, watching the weals emerge from the blank page of her soul's ingress like secret writing, he finds himself searching it for something, he doesn't know what exactly, a message of sorts, the revelation of a mystery in the spreading flush, in the pout and quiver of her cheeks, the repressed stutter of the little explosions of wind, the—whush-*SMACK!*—dew-bejeweled hieroglyphs of crosshatched stripes. But no, the futility of his labors, that's all there is to read there. Birdsong, no longer threatening, floats in on the warm afternoon breeze while he works. There *was* a bee once, he remembers, that part of his dream was true. Only it stung him on his hand, as though to remind him of the painful burden of his office. For a long time after that he kept the garden doors closed altogether, until he realized one day, spanking the maid for failing to air the bedding properly, that he was in some wise interfering with the manuals. And what has she done wrong today? he wonders, tracing the bloody welts with his fingertips. He has forgotten. It doesn't matter. He can lecture her on those two fairies, confusion and disorder. Method and habit, rather . . . "Sir?" "Yes, yes, in a minute . . ." He leans against the bedpost. To live in the full sense of the word, he reminds himself, is not to exist or subsist merely, but to . . . to . . . He yawns. He doesn't remember.

*

While examining the dismal spectacle of her throbbing sit-me-down in the wardrobe mirror (at least the worst is past, she consoles herself, only half believing it), a solution of sorts to that problem of genesis that's been troubling her occurs to her: to wit, that change (she is thinking about change now, and conditions) is eternal, has no beginning—only conditions can begin or end. Who knows, perhaps he has even taught her that. He has taught her so many things, she can't be sure anymore. Everything from habitual deference and the washing of tiffany to pillow fluffing, true service and perfect freedom, the two fairies that make the work (speaking loosely) disappear, proper carriage, sheet folding, and the divine government of pain. Sometimes, late in the day, or on being awakened, he even tells her about his dreams, which seem to be mostly about lechers and ordure and tumors and bottomless holes (once he said "souls"). In a way it's the worst part of her job (that and the things she finds in the bed: today it was broken glass). Once he told her of a dream about a bird with blood in its beak. She asked him, in all deference, if he was afraid of the garden, whereupon he ripped her drawers down, horsed her over a stool, and flogged her so mercilessly she couldn't stand up after, much less sit down. Now she merely says, "Yes, sir," but that doesn't always temper the vigor of his disciplinary interventions, as he likes to call them. Such a one for words and all that! Tracing the radiant weals on that broad part of her so destined with her fingertips, she wishes that just once she might hear something more like, "Well done, thou good and faithful servant, depart in peace!" But then what? When she returned, could it ever be the same? Would he even want her back? No, no, she thinks with a faint shudder, lifting her flannelette drawers up gingerly over her soul's well-ruptured ingress (she hopes more has got in than is leaking out), the sweet breath of late afternoon blowing in to remind her of the time lost, the work yet to be done: no, far better her appointed tasks, her trivial round and daily act of contrition, no matter how pitiless the master's interpretation, than consequences so utterly unimaginable. So, inspirited by her unquenchable appetite for hope and clear-browed devotion to duty, and running his maxims over in her head, she sets about doing the will of God from the heart, scouring the toilet, scrubbing the tiled floor, polishing the furniture and mirrors, checking supplies, changing the towels. All that remains finally is the making of the bed. But how can she do that, she worries, standing there in the afternoon sunlight with stacks of crisp clean sheets in her arms like empty ledgers, her virtuous resolve sapped by a gathering sense of dread as penetrating and aseptic as ammonia, if the master won't get out of it?

*

She enters, encumbered with her paraphernalia, which she deposits by the wall near the door, crosses the room (circumspectly, precipitately, etc.), and flings open the garden doors, smashing the glass, as though once and for all. "Teach me, my God and King," she remarks ruefully (such a sweet breath of amicable violence all about!), "in all things thee to—oh! I beg your pardon, sir!" "A . . . a dream," he stammers, squinting in the glare. He is bound tightly in the damp sheets, can barely move. "Something about blood and a . . . a . . ." I'm so old, and still each day— "Sir . . . ?" He clears his throat. "Would you look under the bed, please, and tell me what you see?" "I—I'm sorry, sir," she replies, kneeling down to look, a curious strained expression on her face. With a scream, she disappears. He awakes, his heart pounding. The maid is staring down at his erection as though frightened of his righteous ardor: "Oh, I beg your pardon, sir!" "It's nothing . . . a dream," he explains, rising like the pink clouds of dawn. "Something about . . ." But he can no longer remember, his mind is a blank sheet. Anyway, she is no longer listening. He can hear her moving busily about the room, dusting furniture, sweeping the floor, changing the towels, taking a shower. He's standing there abandoned to the afternoon sunlight in his slippers and pajama bottoms, which seem to have imbibed an unhealthy kind of dampness, when a bird comes in and perches on his erection, what's left of it. "Ah—!" "Oh, I beg your pardon, sir!" "It's—it's nothing," he replies hoarsely, blinking up at her, gripped still by claws as fine as waxed threads. "A dream . . ." But she has left him, gone off singing to her God and King. He tries to pull the blanket back over his head (the bird, its beak opening and closing involuntarily like whipped thighs, was brown as a chestnut, he recalls, and still smoldering), but she returns and snatches it away, the sheets too.

Sometimes she can be too efficient. Maybe he has been pushing her too hard, expecting too much too soon. He sits up, feeling rudely exposed (his erection dips back into his pajamas like a frog diving for cover—indeed, it has a greenish cast to it in the halflight of the curtained room: what? isn't she here yet?), and lowers his feet over the side shuffling dutifully for his slippers. But he can't find them. He can't even find the floor! He jerks back, his skin wrinkling in involuntary panic, but feels the bottom sheet slide out from under him—"What? *WHAT*—?!" "Oh, I beg your pardon, sir!" "Ah . . . it's nothing," he gasps, struggling to awaken, his heart pounding still (it should be easier than this!), as, screaming, she tucks up her skirt. "A dream . . ."

*

She enters, as though once and for all, circumspectly deposits her vital paraphernalia beside the door, then crosses the room to fling open (humbly yet authoritatively) the curtains and the garden doors: there is such a song of birds all about! Excited by that, and by the sweet breath of late afternoon, her own eagerness to serve, and faith in the perfectibility of her tasks, she turns with a glad heart and tosses back the bedcovers: "Oh! I beg your pardon, sir!" "A . . . a dream," he mutters gruffly, his erection slipping back inside his pajamas like an abandoned moral. "Something about glory and a pizzle—or puzzle—and a fundamental position in the civil service . . ." But she is no longer listening, busy now at her common round, dusting furniture and sweeping the floor: so much to do! When (not very willingly, she observes) he leaves the bed at last, she strips the sheets and blankets off, shaking the dead bees into the garden, fluffs and airs the pillows, turns the mattress. She hears the master relieving himself noisily in the bathroom: yes, there's water in the bucket, soap too, a sponge, she's remembered everything! Today then, perhaps at last . . . ! Quickly she polishes the mirror, mops the floor, snaps open the fresh sheets and makes the bed. Before she has the spread down, however, he comes out of the bathroom, staggers across the room muttering something about a "bloody new birth," and crawls back into it. "But, sir—!" "What, what?" he yawns, and rolls over on his side, pulling the blanket over his head. She snatches it away. He sits up, blinking, a curious strained expression on his face. "I—I'm sorry, sir," she says, and pushing her drawers down to her knees, tucking her skirt up and bending over, she presents to him that broad part preferred by him and Mother Nature for the invention of souls. He retrieves the blanket and disappears under it, all but his feet, which stick out at the bottom, still slippered. She stuffs her drawers hastily behind her apron bib, knocks over the mop bucket, smears the mirror, throws the fresh towels in the toilet, and jerks the blanket away again. "I—I'm sorry, sir," she insists, bending over and lifting her skirt: "I'm sure I had them on when I came in..." What? Is he snoring? She peers at him past what is now her highest part, that part invaded suddenly by a dread as chilling as his chastisements are, when true to his manuals, enflaming, and realizes with a faint shudder (she cannot hold back the little explosions of wind) that change and condition are coeval and everlasting: a truth as hollow as the absence of birdsong (but they are singing!)...

*

So she stands there in the open doorway, the glass doors having long since been flung open (when was that? she cannot remember), her thighs taut and pressed closely together, her face buried in his cast-off pajamas. She can feel against her cheeks, her lips, the soft consoling warmth of them, so recently relinquished, can smell in them the terror—no, the painful sadness, the divine drudgery (sweet, like crushed flowers, dead birds)—of his dreams, Mother Nature having provided, she knows all too well, the proper place for what God has ordained. But there is another odor in them too, musty, faintly sour, like that of truth or freedom, the fear of which governs every animal, thereby preventing natural confusion and disorder. Or so he has taught her. Now, her face buried in this pungent warmth and her heart sinking, the comforting whirr and smack of his rod no more than a distant echo, disappearing now into the desolate throb of late-afternoon birdsong, she wonders about the manuals, his service to them and hers to him, or to that beyond him which he has not quite named. Whence such an appetite?—she shudders, groans, chewing helplessly on the pajamas—So little relief?

*

Distantly blows are falling, something about freedom and government, but he is strolling in the garden with a teacher he once had, discussing the condition of humanity, which keeps getting mixed up somehow with homonymity, such that each time his teacher issues a new lament it comes out like slapped laughter. He is about to remark on the generous swish and snap of a morning glory that has sprung up in their path as though inspired ("Paradox, too, has its techniques," his teacher is saying, "and so on . . ."), when it turns out to be a woman he once knew on the civil surface. "What? *WHAT*—?!" But she only wants him to change his position, or perhaps his condition ("You see!" remarks his teacher sagely, unbuckling his belt, "it's like a kind of callipygomancy, speaking loosely—am I being unfair?"), he's not sure, but anyway it doesn't matter, for what she really wants is to get him out of the sheets he's wrapped in, turn him over (he seems to have imbibed an unhealthy kind of dampness), and give him a lecture (she says "elixir") on method and fairies, two dew-bejeweled habits you can roast chestnuts over. What more, really, does he want of her? (Perhaps his teacher asks him this, buzzing in and out of his ear like the sweet breath of solemnity: whirr-*SMACK!*) His arm is rising and falling through great elastic spaces as though striving for something fundamental like a forgotten dream or lost drawers. "I—I'm sorry, sir!" Is she testing him, perched there on his stout engine of duty like a cooked bird with the lingering bucket of night in her beak (see how it opens, closes, opens), or is it only a dimpled fever of the mind? He doesn't know, is almost afraid to ask. "Something about a higher end," he explains hoarsely, taking rueful refuge, "or hired end perhaps, and boiled flowers, hard parts—and another thing, what's left of it . . ." She screams. The garden groans, quivers, starts, its groves radiant and throbbing. His teacher, no longer threatening, has withdrawn discreetly to a far corner with diagonal creases, where he is turning what lilacs remain into roses with his rumpled bull's pizzle: it's almost an act of magic! Still his arm rises and falls, rises and falls, that broad part of Mother Nature destined for such inventions dancing and bobbing soft and easy under the indulgent sun: "It's a beautiful day!" "What? *WHAT*—*?!* Answering back to a reproof?" he inquires gratefully, taunting her with that civility and kindness due to an inferior, as—hiss—*WHAP!*—flicking lint off one shoulder and smoothing the ends of his moustache with involuntary vertical and horizontal motions, he floats helplessly backwards ("Thank you, sir!"), twitching amicably yet authoritatively like a damp towel, down a bottomless hole, relieving himself noisily: *"Perhaps today then . . . at last!"*

Diamond Breakfast

MARIANNE BORUCH

Overnight, the windows have multiplied & eaten
the house. Boom! everything
is thinner, everything
manic with light. "Whirling dervish!" whispers
mother, screwing up her eyes
into little eyes. The children
lean like cactus in the doorway. Maybe
they are missing school. O rodeo, O Oklahoma shimmer.

Father clears his throat. "Things
are different now," he says, addressing the squints
from the breakfast nook. "That stove, for instance,
these eggs—all just a glimmer
of their former selves. Remember this.
This is like history." One boy agrees. He is
shielding his eyes as if an iceberg
had surfaced, he is planting
a blue flag.

Now they are eating, drinking: glossy oatmeal
shiny milk. Everything is a ghastly color. White & white
& white again. Outside, birds dive
into invisible walls
their small heads dashed against pure thought.

The Eighties

They Shall Not Pass
AI

Above me the sky is all Atlantic
and I taste vinegar, salt
and those hot yellow peppers
Natividad used to eat
with tamales and beer.
And the sweat above her lip—
I can taste that too.
And I have to remind myself
why I left Mexico,
why I'm lying here dying in Madrid
when I should be standing,
thumbs hooked in my belt loops,
a Lucky Strike caught in the corner of my mouth.

I was an IWW man like my father
and I always bought two drinks:
one for myself and one for the living ghost
of universal brotherhood,
with his tattered suitcase
and checkered tie
and a thirst for handshakes and hammers,
always leaning at the bar when I'd arrive,
with his *Joe, buy me a drink, just one more.*
He was in Vera Cruz the night I left,
he stood on deck with me before I sailed,
squinting at the dock, pointing out the ones
who were his.
And I stood there,
empty of everything
but what I believed:
that your brother was your brother
and you had to spare a dime,

that when you went down,
the next man would stand up
hand in his pocket,
that there were angels
who walked among the honored dead
carrying red sickles,
that Joe Stalin sat like Ole King Cole
top of the world
and I'd sit next to him someday
with the back pay of a thousand years
in my own hands.
I had a heart like a goddamn sponge.
You could fill me and fill me,
with slogans, with songs and marches,
with dead men—
like Sunshine.
He was next to me
when he split up the middle,
out of luck, out of dimes;
when there was terror no one told me existed,
betrayers, idealists; hysterical and uneven fighters.
Only this: they shall not pass.
I said it over and over to myself
as we defended the University of Madrid,
even when I took this slow glide down,
my blood like thick bolts of cloth,
hitting the ground as I fell
while the layers of ice and ash
floated down from Kingdom Come.

A chrome ship slides across the sky's smooth surface
and Franco himself lifts the Stars and Stripes sail.
My whole face is numb.
I wanted to hit the coast of Spain
like a fist ramming an old man's belly.
But instead found whatshisname

in the first bar I stepped into,
wearing a St. Patrick's day smile:
cold sober, Joe, he said, and he spat on the sawdust floor.
I'm my own man, first time in years.
You should try it.

And I did, with a carbine.
They told us a man can kill without hate,
that that's how it's done,
that Jesus Christ is the bullet
that makes everything right.
But it doesn't matter
now that the glorious perfumed air
is filled with butterflies
which have men's faces, men's feet,
now that the cocoon of flesh
that held me bursts
and I step left, right, left,
and whatshisname swaggers head of the line
and his voice floats over us
like the Holy Ghost:
victory, friends, brothers;
as we march
all in a row
into the motionless sea.

Three Secrets for Alexis
JANE MILLER

Eliot's lesson from Dante
that the poet be servant

not master of language
that he attend craft

and stretch
his emotional range

omits how to
begin the awesome

first draft.
Here technique

and emotional veracity
count but

like young wheat
we care less

for an act of mind
than a good

wind and countryside.
Birds pipe supper

and through the note
pleasure somehow

translates.
Good and good in itself,

I have two lovers,
one slower than summer

another like a sea comb,
empty and full.

I hear the old
habits of speech, for ex.,

in this country we say no
for yes

we bite into
a taco at the same time

slugging a beer.
Alexis,

eyes dreams lips and the night goes
was Pound's only line

I heard for years
because in heat its meter

undressed me. In empty space
magnetic fields exist

for no reason. How to use ideas
while living

a line, happy tension!
Turtles, quail,

a downpour
and two hailstorms

in one day are equal
access to knowledge.

Writers who work
in their separate mornings

join the woodchuck
and the missing cat

in the beauty of an act
you spoke about,

placing a candle in a tree.
Light

in a gravitational field
falling turns bluer,

the spruce's new needles
greener

for a poem in the form of an axe.
June, July, August

three secrets
whose time we use

as in sleep
differently to imagine

our sprint and the thrush's
fear when the tree falls,

your idea
about the candle catching fire.

Remembering Brother Bob

WILLIAM STAFFORD

Tell me, you years I had for my life,
tell me a day, that day it snowed
and I played hockey in the cold.
Bob was seven, then, and I was twelve,
and strong. The sun went down. I turned
and Bob was crying on the shore.

Do I remember kindness? Did I
shield my brother, comfort him?
Tell me, you years I had for my life.

Yes, I carried him. I took
him home. But I complained. I see
the darkness; it comes near: and Bob,
who is gone now, and the other kids.
I am the zero in the scene:
"You said you would be brave," I chided
him. "I'll not take you again."
Years, I look at the white across
this page, and think: I never did.

Instructions for the Next Century

STEPHEN DUNN

Instead of spouse say sailing ship,
   instead of dancing say
      ancient ruins.

When you want love
   don't say sailing ship, say
      seven-or-eleven.

When you want music say sacrifice,
   for if you dance
      to that music someone will say

secret police which means
   secret police and you'll be caught
      with all the wrong words.

Say cellar door
   when they take you in. Say it
      until it means something else.

Say whipped cream when you mean
   emptiness, say blue lagoon
      when you mean nightmare.

If all day you've planned to escape
   try to be silent. The most silent
      words are ocean floor.

Say ocean floor, blue lagoon, whipped
   cream over and over;
      you will not escape

but other prisoners might hear you
   and call it sacrifice, which will be
      music to the few who remember.

These are your friends. Say seven-or-eleven
   to them. Hold them in your arms
      and call it ancient ruins.

Johnnieruth

BECKY BIRTHA

Summertime. Nighttime. Talk about steam heat. This whole city get like the bathroom when somebody in there taking a shower with the door shut. Nights like that, can't nobody sleep. Everybody be outside, sitting on they steps or else dragging half they furniture out on the sidewalk—kitchen chairs, card tables—even bringing TV's outside.

Womenfolks, mostly. All the grown women around my way look just the same. They all big—stout. They got big bosoms and big hips and fat legs, and they always wearing runover house-shoes, and them shapeless, flowered numbers with the buttons down the front. Cept on Sunday. Sunday morning they all turn into glamour girls, in them big hats and long gloves, with they skinny high heels and they skinny selves in them tight girdles—wouldn't nobody ever know what they look like the rest of the time.

When I was a little kid I didn't wanna grow up, cause I never wanted to look like them ladies. I heard Miz Jenkins down the street one time say she don't mind being fat cause that way her husband don't get so jealous. She say it's more than one way to keep a man. Me, I don't have me no intentions of keeping no man. I never understood why they was in so much demand anyway, when it seem like all a woman can depend on em for is making sure she keep on having babies.

We got enough children in my neighborhood. In the summertime, even the little kids allowed to stay up till eleven or twelve o'clock at night—playing in the street and hollering and carrying on—don't never seem to get tired. Don't nobody care, long as they don't fight.

Me—I don't hang around no front steps no more. Hot nights like that, I get out my ten speed and I be gone.

That's what I like to do more than anything else in the whole world. Feel that wind in my face keeping me cool as a air conditioner, shooting along like a snowball. My bike light as a kite. I can really get up some speed.

All the guys around my way got ten speed bikes. Some of the girls got em too, but they don't ride em at night. They pedal around during the day, but at nighttime they just hang around out front, watching babies and running they mouth. I didn't get my Peugeot to be no conversation piece.

My mama don't like me to ride at night. I tried to point out to her that she ain't never said nothing to my brothers, and Vincent a year younger than me. (And Langston two years older, in case "old" is the problem.) She say, "That's different, Johnnieruth. You're a girl." Now I wanna know how is anybody gonna know that. I'm skinny as a knifeblade turned sideways, and all I ever wear is blue jeans and a Wrangler jacket. But if I bring that up, she liable to get started in on how come I can't be more of a young lady, and fourteen is old enough to start taking more pride in my appearance, and she gonna be ashamed to admit I'm her daughter.

I just tell her that my bike be moving so fast can't nobody hardly see me, and couldn't catch me if they did. Mama complain to her friends how I'm wild and she can't do nothing with me. She know I'm gonna do what I want no matter what she say. But she know I ain't getting in no trouble, neither.

Like some of the boys I know stole they bikes, but I didn't do nothing like that. I'd been saving my money ever since I can remember, every time I could get a nickel or a dime outta anybody.

When I was a little kid, it was hard to get money. Seem like the only time they ever give you any was on Sunday morning, and then you had to put it in the offering. I used to hate to do that. In fact, I used to hate everything about Sunday morning. I had to wear all them ruffly dresses—that shiny slippery stuff in the wintertime that got to make a noise every time you move your ass a inch on them hard old benches. And that scratchy starchy stuff in the summertime with all them scratchy crinolines. Had to carry a pocketbook and wear them shiny shoes. And the church we went to was all the way over on

Summit Avenue, so the whole damn neighborhood could get a good look. At least all the other kids'd be dressed the same way. The boys think they slick cause they get to wear pants, but they still got to wear a white shirt and a tie; and them dumb hats they wear can't hide them baldheaded haircuts, cause they got to take the hats off in church.

There was one Sunday when I musta been around eight. I remember it was before my sister Corletta was born, cause right around then was when I put my foot down about that whole sanctimonious routine. Anyway, I was dragging my feet along Twenty-Fifth Street in back of Mama and Vincent and them, when I spied this lady. I only seen her that one time, but I still remember just how she look. She don't look like nobody I ever seen before. I *know* she don't live around here. She real skinny. But she ain't no real young woman, neither. She could be old as my mama. She ain't nobody's mama—I'm sure. And she ain't wearing Sunday clothes. She got on blue jeans and a man's blue working shirt, with the tail hanging out. She got patches on her blue jeans, and she still got her chin stuck out like she some kinda African royalty. She ain't carrying no shiny pocketbook. It don't look like she care if she got any money or not, or who know it, if she don't. She ain't wearing no house-shoes, or stockings or high heels neither.

Mama always speak to everybody, but when she pass by this lady she make like she ain't even seen her. But I get me a real good look, and the lady stare right back at me. She got a funny look on her face, almost like she think she know me from some place. After she pass on by, I had to turn around to get another look, even though Mama say that ain't polite. And you know what? She was turning around, too, looking back at me. And she give me a great big smile.

I didn't know too much in them days, but that's when I first got to thinking about how it's got to be different ways to be, from the way people be around my way. It's got to be places where it don't matter to nobody if you all dressed up on Sunday morning or you ain't. That's how come I started saving money. So, when I got enough, I could go away to some place like that.

Afterwhile I begun to see there wasn't no point in waiting around for handouts, and I started thinking of ways to earn my own money. I used to be running errands all the time—mailing letters for old Grandma Whittaker and picking up cigarettes and newspapers up the corner for everybody. After I got bigger, I started washing cars in the summer, and shoveling people sidewalk in the wintertime. Now I got me a newspaper route. Ain't never been no girl around here with no paper route, but I guess everybody got it figured out by now that I ain't gonna be like nobody else.

The reason I got me my Peugeot was so I could start to explore. I figured I better start looking around right now, so when I'm grown, I'll know exactly where I wanna go. So I ride around every chance I get.

Last summer, I used to ride with the boys a lot. Sometime eight or ten of us'd just go cruising around the streets together. All of a sudden my mama decide she don't want me to do that no more. She say I'm too old to be spending so much time with boys. (That's what they tell you half the time, and the other half the time they worried cause you ain't interested in spending more time with boys.) Don't make much sense. She want me to have some girl friends, but I never seem to fit in with none of the things the girls doing. I used to think I fit in more with the boys.

But I seen how Mama might be right, for once. I didn't like the way the boys was starting to talk about girls sometimes. Talking about what some girl be like from the neck on down, and talking all up underneath somebody clothes and all. Even though I wasn't really friends with none of the girls, I still didn't like it. So now I mostly just ride around by myself. And Mama don't like that neither—you just can't please her.

This boy that live around the corner on North Street, Kenny Henderson, started asking me one time if I don't ever be lonely, cause he always see me by myself. He say don't I ever think I'd like to have me somebody special to go places with and stuff. Like I'd pick him if I did! Made me wanna laugh in his face.

I do be lonely, a lotta times, but I don't tell nobody. And I ain't met nobody yet that I'd really rather be with than be by myself. But I will someday. When I find that special place where everybody different, I'm gonna find somebody there I can be friends with. And it ain't gonna be no dumb boy.

I found me one place already, that I like to go to a whole lot. It ain't even really that far away—by bike—but it's on the other side of the Avenue. So I don't tell Mama and them I go there, cause they like to think I'm right around the neighborhood someplace. But this neighborhood too dull for me. All the houses look just the same—no porches, no yards, no trees—not even no parks around here. Every block look so much like every other block it hurt your eyes to look at, afterwhile. So I ride across Summit Avenue and go down that big steep hill there, and then make a sharp right at the bottom and cross the bridge over the train tracks. Then I head on out the boulevard—that's the nicest part, with all them big trees making a tunnel over the top, and lightning bugs shining in the bushes. At the end of the boulevard you get to this place call the Plaza.

It's something like a little park—the sidewalks is all bricks and they got flowers planted all over the place. The same kind my mama grow in that painted-up tire she got out front masquerading like a garden decoration—only seem like they smell sweeter here. It's a big high fountain right in the middle, and all the streetlights is the real old-fashion kind. That Plaza is about the prettiest place I ever been.

Sometimes something going on there. Like a orchestra playing music or some man or lady singing. One time they had a show with some girls doing some kinda foreign dances. They look like they were around my age. They all had on these fancy costumes, with different color ribbons all down they back. I wouldn't wear nothing like that, but it looked real pretty when they was dancing.

I got me a special bench in one corner where I like to sit,

cause I can see just about everything, but wouldn't nobody know I was there. I like to sit still and think, and I like to watch people. A lotta people be coming there at night—to look at the shows and stuff, or just to hang out and cool off. All different kinda people.

This one night when I was sitting over in that corner where I always be at, there was this lady standing right near my bench. She mostly had her back turned to me and she didn't know I was there, but I could see her real good. She had on this shiny purple shirt and about a million silver bracelets. I kinda liked the way she look. Sorta exotic, like she maybe come from California or one of the islands. I mean she had class—standing there posing with her arms folded. She walk away a little bit. Then turn around and walk back again. Like she waiting for somebody.

Then I spotted this dude coming over. I spied him all the way cross the Plaza. Looking real fine. Got on a three piece suit. One of them little caps sitting on a angle. Look like leather. He coming straight over to this lady I'm watching and then she seen him too and she start to smile, but she don't move till he get right up next to her. And then I'm gonna look away, cause I can't stand to watch nobody hugging and kissing on each other, but all of a sudden I see it ain't no dude at all. It's another lady.

Now I can't stop looking. They smiling at each other like they ain't seen one another in ten years. Then the one in the purple shirt look around real quick—but she don't look just behind her—and sorta pull the other one right back into the corner where I'm sitting at, and then they put they arms around each other and kiss—for a whole long time. Now I really know I oughtta turn away, but I can't. And I know they gonna see me when they finally open they eyes. And they do.

They both kinda gasp and back up, like I'm the monster that just rose up outta the deep. And then I guess they can see I'm only a girl, and they look at one another—and start to laugh! Then they just turn around and start to walk away like it wasn't nothing at all. But right before they gone, they both look around again, and see I still ain't got my eye muscles and my jaw muscles working right again yet. And the one lady wink at me. And the other one say, "Catch you later."

I can't stop staring at they backs, all the way across the Plaza. And then, all of a sudden, I feel like I got to be doing something, got to be moving.

I wheel on outta the Plaza and I'm just concentrating on getting up my speed. Cause I can't figure out what to think. Them two women kissing and then, when they get caught, just laughing about it. And here I'm laughing too, for no reason at all. I'm sailing down the boulevard laughing like a lunatic, and then I'm singing at the top of my lungs. And climbing that big old hill up to Summit Avenue is just as easy as being on a escalator.

Travel Notes

MICHELLE CLIFF

I wanted to be the lone figure on the landscape.
The cat burglar passing silent in the night.
The fast driver—unaffiliated—unnoticed.
This is not how it is.

Sometimes I see a small house—sometimes shacks attract me. I wonder how it would be to live hidden.

I am standing in the doorway of the dining room at Haworth Parsonage. *My sister Emily loved the moors. . . . Out of a sullen hollow in a livid hill-side, her mind could make an Eden.* —I stare at the horsehair sofa where Emily Brontë died.

Outside are the thousands of graves. Wind and rain obscuring the vision. Mosses cross the outer walls.

While inside glass cases display the tiny notebooks filled with stories. The needlework of the sisters.

Downstairs is the souvenir kiosk. The portraits of Keeper, Grasper, the hawk Hero. Views of the moors—heather—gorse. Top Withens. Kitchen. Churchyard. *She found in the bleak solitude many and dear delights; and not the least and best-loved was—liberty. Liberty was the breath of Emily's nostrils.*

Across from this kiosk is a bulletin board advising women of the existence of the Yorkshire Ripper and the necessity that we remain indoors.

The North Wind demolished their already weakened lungs—Anne and Emily. Charlotte died of pregnancy. Branwell of opium and drink. The old man of old age. Much earlier a mother and two other sisters: cancer, consumption, typhoid.

Back home—I find a suspect has been caught. He kept to himself. He was a shy man. He and his wife had no children. The police have his wife under guard. There are threats on her life.

"But we already know that women are oppressed," the student said to me. "I had hoped this course would deal with something else."

How do we keep their attention?
Our own.

*

As a child I saved maps. Haunted airports. Begged for travel brochures and posters of bazaars and castles. I wanted to go overseas. Always looked forward.

Traveling through my own time I often look back.

I am in Brighton where England's Neo-Nazis have headquarters. Where Fanny Imlay—Wollstonecraft's daughter—killed herself, wearing her mother's watch and undergarment. (Godwin did not claim her body, ashamed at her method of death.)

Brighton is an hour from Lewes—where Virginia Woolf walked into the River Ouse. I think about a memoir written by Woolf's cook—Louie Mayer—how she described the last afternoon: as Virginia wandered through the garden, bumping into branches. And Leonard suggested Virginia dust—but she lost interest.

These details crowd me.

What is left of Wollstonecraft's grave is a plaque by King's Cross Station.

In King's Cross once I saw a woman in the ladies' room—a large naked white woman accompanied by her belongings. She was standing in a corner against a wall, calmly washing herself. Wetting and soaping and drying herself with brown paper.

Other women came and went.

*

As a child I pressed my fingers against my closed eyes—watched the stars, planets, comets, and meteorites move against them. As if I could contain the universe behind my eyelids.

It is the anniversary of the first imprisonment of
   suffragists—
Annie Kenney and Cristabel Pankhurst.
Someone has left a bouquet of irises—purple
tied with ribbon—green:
the colors of the movement.

These lie in front of Emmeline Pankhurst's statue which stands to the side of the Houses of Parliament. The note attached to the bouquet is in a strong and older hand—perhaps of a woman who actually remembers 1905. The ink runs in the drizzle.

Now the meaning of green ribbon has shifted. They are killing black children in Atlanta—also elsewhere. Georgia Dean, a retired factory worker, suggests wearing an inverted V of green—the color of growing things.

Each newspaper report seems more clouded than before: today they claimed the children died at the hands of a "gentle" killer: does this translate as female? homosexual?

What are they getting at?

The Mark of the Beast—a special issue on the Klan. On the cover a member clasps a child; his eyes seem hollowed—the child's, I mean—the member is a woman.

*

I meet two women in Texas—they live on a farm in a small town north of Austin. Outside their kitchen is a pile of rocks where their cat stares down a diamondback.

They prepare a noose of cord—slide one rock back. The diamondback raises her head to strike. They slide the noose around her neck.

She stretches to her length. "Four feet of solid muscle"—one woman explains.

They place the snake in a garbage can—secure its lid by rope.

There is another snake in the rockpile—then another.

"We're lucky we had seven cans," says one woman—and a pickup to drive the diamondbacks twenty-five miles away and let them go: one by one.

A solid day's work.

Each Bird Walking
TESS GALLAGHER

Not while, but long after he had told me,
I thought of him, washing his mother, his
bending over the bed and taking back
the covers. There was a basin of water
and he dipped a washrag in and
out of the basin, the rag
dripping a little onto the sheet as he
turned from the bedside to the nightstand
and back, there being no place

on her body he shouldn't touch because
he had to and she helped him, moving
the little she could, lifting so he could
wipe under her arms, a dipping motion
in the hollow. Then working up from
the feet, around the ankles, over the

knees. And this last, opening
her thighs and running the rag firmly
and with the cleaning thought
up through her crotch, between the lips,
over the V of thin hairs—

as though he were a mother
who had the excuse of cleaning to touch
with love and indifference,
the secret parts of her child, to graze
the sleepy sexlessness in its waiting
to find out what to do for the sake
of the body, for the sake of what only
the body can do for itself.

So his hand, softly at the place
of his birth-light. And she, eyes deepened
and closed in the dim room.
And because he told me her death as
important to his being with her,
I could love him another way. Not
of the body alone, or of its making,
but carried in the white spires of trembling
until what spirit, what breath we were
was shaken from us. Small then,
the word *holy*.

He turned her on her stomach
and washed the blades of her shoulders, the
small of the back. "That's good," she said,
"that's enough."

On our lips that morning, the tart juice
of the mothers, so strong in remembrance, no
asking, no giving, and what you said, this
being the end of our loving, so as not to hurt
the closer one to you, made me look to see

what was left of us with our sex
taken away. "Tell me," I said,
"something I can't forget." Then the story
of your mother, and when you finished
I said, "That's good, that's enough."

Problems of Translation:
Problems of Language
JUNE JORDAN

dedicated to Myriam Diaz Diocaretz

1
I turn to my Rand McNally Atlas.
Europe appears right after the Map of the World.
All of Italy can be seen page 9.
Half of Chile page 29.
I take out my ruler.
In global perspective Italy
amounts to less than half an inch.
Chile measures more than an inch and a quarter
of an inch.
Approximately
Chile is as long as China
is wide:
Back to the Atlas:
Chunk of China page 17.
All of France page 5: as we say in New York:
Who do France and Italy know
at Rand McNally?

2
I see the four mountains in Chile higher
than any mountain of North America.
I see Ojos del Salado the highest.
I see Chile unequivocal as crystal thread.
I see the Atacama Desert dry in Chile more than the rest
of the world is dry.
I see Chile dissolving into water.
I do not see what keeps the blue land of Chile
out of blue water.
I do not see the hand of Pablo Neruda on the blue land.

3
As the plane flies flat to the trees
Below Brazil
Below Bolivia
Below five thousand miles below
my Brooklyn windows
and beside the shifted Pacific waters
welled away from the Atlantic at Cape Horn
La Isla Negra that is not an island La
Isla Negra
that is not black
is stone and stone of Chile
feeding clouds to color
scale and undertake terrestrial forms
of everything unspeakable

4
In your country how
do you say copper
for my country?

5
Blood rising under the Andes and above
the Andes blood
spilling down the rock

corrupted by the amorality
of so much space
that leaves such little trace of blood
rising to the irritated skin the face
of the confession far
from home:

I confess I did not resist interrogation.
I confess that by the next day I was no longer sure
of my identity.
I confess I knew the hunger.
I confess I saw the guns.
I confess I was afraid.
I confess I did not die.

6
What you Americans call a boycott
of the junta?
Who will that feed?

7
Not just the message but the sound.

8
Early morning now and I remember
corriente a la madrugada from a different
English poem
I remember from the difficulties of the talk
an argument
athwart the wine the dinner and the dancing
meant to welcome you you
did not understand the commonplace expression
of my heart:

the truth is in the life
la verdad es en la vida

Early morning:
Do you say *la mañanita*?
But then we lose
the idea of the sky uncurling to the light:

Early morning and I do not think we lose:
the rose we left behind
broken to a glass of water on the table
at the restaurant stands
even sweeter
por la mañanita

Philosophy in Warm Weather
JANE KENYON

Now all the doors and windows
are open, and we move so easily
through the rooms. Cats roll
on the sunny rugs, and a clumsy wasp
climbs the pane, pausing
to rub a leg over her head.

All around us physical life reconvenes.
The molecules of our bodies must love
to exist—they whirl in circles
and seem to begrudge us nothing.
Heat, Horatio, *heat* makes them
put this antic disposition on!

This year's brown spider
sways over the door as I come
and go. A single poppy shouts
from the far field, and the crow,

beyond alarm, goes right on
pulling up the corn.

The Meal
SHARON OLDS

Mama, I never stop seeing you there
at the breakfast table when I'd come home from school—
sitting with your excellent skeletal posture
facing that plate with the one scoop of cottage cheese on it,
forcing yourself to eat, though you did not want to live,
feeding yourself, small spoonful by
small spoonful, so you would not die and
leave us without a mother as you were
left without a mother. You'd sit
in front of that mound rounded as a breast and
giving off a cold moony light,
light of the life you did not want, you would
hold yourself there and stare down at it,
an orphan forty years old staring at the breast,
a freshly divorced woman down to 82 pounds
staring at the cock runny with milk gone sour,
a daughter who had always said
the best thing her mother ever did for her
was to die. I came home every day to
find you there, dry-eyed, unbent, that
hot control in the breakfast nook, your
delicate savage bones over the cheese
curdled like the breast of the mother twenty years in the
porous earth,
            and yet what I remember is your
spoon moving like the cock moving in the

body of the girl waking to the power of her pleasure,
your spoon rising in courage, bite after bite, you
tilted rigid over that plate until you
polished it for my life.

For Ethel Rosenberg
ADRIENNE RICH

convicted, with her husband, of "conspiracy to commit espionage"; killed in the electric chair June 19, 1953

1
Europe 1953:
throughout my random sleepwalk
the words

scratched on walls, on pavements
painted over railway arches
Liberez les Rosenberg!

Escaping from home I found
home everywhere:
the Jewish question, Communism

marriage itself
a question of loyalty
or punishment

my Jewish father writing me
letters of seventeen pages
finely inscribed harangues

questions of loyalty
and punishment
One week before my wedding

that couple gets the chair
the volts grapple her, don't
kill her fast enough

Liberez les Rosenberg!
I hadn't realized
our family arguments were so important

my narrow understanding
of crime   of punishment
no language for this torment

mystery of that marriage
always both faces
on every front page in the world

Something so shocking   so
unfathomable
it must be pushed aside

2
She sank however into my soul   A weight of   sadness
I hardly can register how deep
her memory has sunk   that wife and mother

like so many
who seemed to get nothing out of any of it
except her children

that daughter   of a family
like so many
needing its female monster

she, actually wishing to be   *an artist*
wanting out of poverty
possibly also really wanting
                              revolution

that woman   strapped in the chair
no fear and no regrets
charged by posterity

not with selling secrets to the Communists
but with wanting   *to distinguish*
herself   being a bad daughter   a bad mother

And I   walking   to my wedding
by the same token a bad daughter   a bad sister
my forces focused

on that hardly revolutionary effort
Her life and death   the possible
ranges of disloyalty

so painful   so unfathomable
they must be pushed aside
ignored for years

3
Her mother testifies against her
Her brother testifies against   her
After her death

she becomes a natural prey for pornographers
her death itself a scene
her body *sizzling   half-strapped   whipped like a sail*

She becomes the extremest victim
described nonetheless as *rigid of will*
what are her politics by then   no one knows

Her figure sinks into my soul
a drowned statue
sealed in lead

For years it has lain there   unabsorbed
first as part of that dead couple
on the front pages of the world   the week

I gave myself in marriage
then slowly severing   drifting apart
a separate death   a life unto itself

no longer *the Rosenbergs*
no longer the chosen scapegoat
the family monster

till I hear how she sang
a prostitute to sleep
in the Women's House of Detention

Ethel Greenglass Rosenberg   would you
have marched to take back the night
collected signatures

for battered women who kill
What would you have to tell us
would you have burst the net

4
Why do I even want to call her up
to console my pain   (she feels no pain at all)
why do I wish to put such questions

to ease myself   (she feels no pain at all
she   finally burned to death   like so many)
why all this exercise   of hindsight?

since   if I imagine her at all
I have to imagine first
the pain inflicted on her   by women

her mother testifies against her
her sister-in-law testifies against her
and how she sees it

not the impersonal forces
not the historical reasons
why they might have hated her strength

If I have held her at arm's length till now
if I have still believed it was
my loyalty, my punishment at stake

if I dare imagine her surviving
I must be fair to what she must have lived through
I must allow her to be at last

political in her ways   not in mine
her urgencies perhaps   impervious to   mine
defining revolution as she defines it

or, bored to the marrow of her bones
with "politics"
bored with the vast boredom of long pain

small; tiny in fact; in her late sixties
liking her room   her private life
living alone perhaps

no one you could interview
maybe filling a notebook herself
with secrets she has never sold

Confiteor
HENRI COULETTE

The blonde mane, the impossible blue of the eyes,
The black velvet jacket, the four gold frogs,
The white lace at the throat, at the white wrist,

And the blue vein, that small hammer at the wrist,
Like squaring the circle, or a grooming of griffins, or a black
    rose,
And the verdict in, kudos to the jury, the jury gone home,

And the judge shucking his black robe in his possible
    chamber,
And the verdict is guilty, and the sentence forever,
Forever the black rose, the blue eyes, the blonde mane . . .

What was your motive? I don't remember. I refuse to
    remember.
And the weapon? Guilty. And the weapon? Yes.
And the blue hammer, yes, impossible, mine, and forever.

The Houses
W. S. MERWIN

Up on the mountain where nobody is looking
a man forty years old in a gray felt hat
is trying to light a fire in the springtime

up on the mountain where nobody
except God and the man's son are looking

the father in a white shirt is trying
to get damp sticks to burn in the spring noon

he crumples newspaper from the luggage compartment
of the polished black Plymouth parked under the young leaves
a few feet away in the overgrown wagon track
that he remembers from another year
he is thinking of somewhere else as the match flame blows

he has somewhere else in mind that nobody knows
as the flame climbs into the lines of print and they curl
and set out unseen into the sunlight
he needs more and more paper and more matches
and the wrapping from hot dogs and from buns
gray smoke gets away among the slender trees

it does not occur to the son to wonder
what prompted his father to come up here
suddenly this one morning and bring his son
though the father looks like a stranger on the mountain
breaking sticks and wiping his hands on the paper
as he crumples it and blowing into the flames
but when his father takes him anywhere they are both
    strangers

and the father has long forgotten that the son
is standing there and he is surprised
when the smoke blows in his face and he turns
and sees parallel with the brim the boy looking at him
having been told that he could not help and to wait there
and since it is a day without precedents the son
hears himself asking the father whether he may
please see what is down the wagon track and he surprises
himself hearing the father say yes but don't go far

and be very careful and come right back
so the son turns to his right and steps over

the gray stones and leaves his father making
a smoky fire on the flat sloping rock
and after a few steps the branches close overhead
he walks in the green day in the smell of thawed ground
and a while further on he comes to a turn to the right
and the open light of cleared ground falling away
still covered with the dry grass of last year
by a dark empty barn he can see light through

and before the barn on the left a white house
newly painted with wide gray footsteps leading
up to the gray floor of the porch where the windows
are newly washed and without curtains so that he
can look into the empty rooms and see the doors
standing open and he can look out
through windows on the other side into the sky
while the grass new and old stands deep all around the house
that is bare in readiness for somebody
the wind is louder here than in the woods
the grass hissing and the clean panes rattling

he looks at rusted handles beside bushes
and with that thinks of his father and turns back
into the shadowy wagon track and walks
slowly tree by tree stone by stone under
the green tiers of leaves until he comes
to the smell of smoke and then the long pile of stones
before the clearing where his father is bending
over the fire and turns at the son's voice and calls him
a good boy for coming back and asks whether
he's hungry and holds out a paper plate
they stand in the smoke holding plates while the father
asks the blessing and afterwards the son tells him

of the white house the new paint the clean windows
into empty rooms and sky and nobody in sight
but his father says there is no such house along there

and he warns the son not to tell stories
but to eat and after a moment the son
surprises them both by insisting that he has
seen it all just as he said and again the father
scolds him this time more severely returning
from somewhere else to take up his sternness
until the son starts to cry and asks him
to come and see for himself after they have eaten

so when the plates have been burned and the fire
put out carefully and the car packed they walk
without a word down the wagon track where the light
seems to have dimmed as though rain might be on its way
and the trees are more remote than the boy
had thought but before long they reach the opening
where the track turns to the right and there is
the glare of the dry grass but no house no barn
and the son repeats I saw them but the father says
I don't want to hear any more about it

in a later year the father takes the boy
taller now and used to walking by himself
to an old farm in the middle of the state
where he busies himself in the small house he has bought
while the son having been told that he cannot help
walks down the lane past the vacant corn crib and barn
past the red shale banks where the lane descends
beside unkempt pastures with their springs and snakes
into the woods and onto a wooden bridge

still on his father's land he watches the dark water
flow out from under low branches and the small fish
flickering in glass over the black bed and as he
turns and climbs the lane on the far side he sees
to his right below him on the edge of the stream
a low house painted yellow with a wide porch

a gun leaning beside the front door and a dog's chain
fastened to the right of the steps but no dog visible

there appears to be no one in the house and the boy goes
on up the lane through the woods and across pastures
and coming back sees that nothing has changed
the gun still by the door the chain in the same place
he watches to see whether anything moves
he listens he stares through the trees wondering

where the dog is and when someone will come home
then he crosses the stream and returns to his father
indoors and in the evening he remembers
to ask who is living in the yellow house
in the woods on the far side of the stream
which he had understood was his father's land
but his father tells him there is no house there

by then they have left the farm and are driving home
and the son tells the father of the gun by the door
the dog's chain by the front steps and the father
says yes that is his land beyond the stream
but there is no building and nobody living there

the boy stops telling what he has seen
and it is a long time before he comes again
to walk down the lane to the woods and cross the bridge
and see on the far side only trees by the stream

then the farm is sold and the woods are cut and the subject
never brought up again but long after the father
is dead the son remembers the two houses

The Power of Toads
PATTIANN ROGERS

The oak toad and the red-spotted toad love their love
In a spring rain, calling and calling, breeding
Through a stormy evening clasped atop their mates.
Who wouldn't sing—anticipating the belly pressed hard
Against a female's spine in the steady rain
Below writhing skies, the safe moist jelly effluence
Of a final exaltation?

There might be some toads who actually believe
That the loin-shaking thunder of the banks, the evening
Filled with damp, the warm softening mud and rising
Riverlets are the facts of their own persistent
Performance. Maybe they think that when they sing
They sing more than songs, creating rain and mist
By their voices, initiating the union of water and dusk,
Females materializing on the banks shaped perfectly
By their calls.

And some toads may be convinced they have forced
The heavens to twist and moan by the continual expansion
Of their lung-sacs pushing against the dusk.
And some might believe the splitting light,
The soaring grey they see above them are nothing
But a vision of the longing in their groins,
A fertile spring heaven caught in its entirety
At the pit of the gut.

And they might be right.
Who knows whether these broken heavens
Could exist tonight separate from trills and toad ringings?
Maybe the particles of this rain descending on the pond
Are nothing but the visual manifestation of whistles
And cascading love clicks in the shore grasses.

Raindrops-finding-earth and coitus could very well
Be known here as one.

We could investigate the causal relationship
Between rainstorm and love-by-pondside if we wished.
We could lie down in the grasses by the water's edge
And watch to see exactly how the heavens were moved,
Thinking hard of thunder, imagining all the courses
That slow, clean waters might take across our bodies,
Believing completely in the rolling and pressing power
Of heavens and thighs. And in the end we might be glad,
Even if all we discovered for certain was the slick, sweet
Promise of good love beneath dark skies inside warm rains.

Epistemology, Sex, and the Shedding of Light

LYNNE SHARON SCHWARTZ

"Guess who I saw in a Chinese restaurant in Washington," Harry asked me. He had just returned from offering expert advice on disaster relief to government officials.

"Henry Kissinger."

Harry's eyes narrowed and his smile of anticipation vanished. "How did you know?"

"I don't know."

"Well, guess who he was eating lunch with?"

"Liv Ullmann."

Harry stopped combing his hair and regarded me with some bitterness. His eyes had that disappointed look Rachel's had when, a few years ago, she left the dinner table to go to the bathroom and returned to find Harry had finished her hamburger. He assumed she was done. She has never forgotten. "How did you know?"

"I don't know. I'm sorry. Tell me how they looked, anyway." That was not the whole truth. I read all the reviews of Liv Ullmann's recent autobiographical book and learned that she had once dated Henry Kissinger. Still, that doesn't account for my knowing.

I wasn't reading Harry's mind, either, as often happens. For example, five years ago he looked longingly at a box of saltine crackers on the supermarket shelf. "Do we need these?" he asked.

"We have saltines at home."

"Oh."

"Take them anyway. It's the box you want, isn't it?" It was a large square cardboard box with rounded corners, about five inches high. There were colorful flowers and curlicues painted on its sides. The metal lid in its center was round with raised edges, the kind that would have to be pried off with a spoon.

He looked distressed. "How did you know?"

"I know what you like. That's your kind of box. Take it. We'll empty the crackers into a canister."

He was tempted, but his upbringing was too powerful. "No." Harry is not self-indulgent, especially about spending money. Cash, that is. He prefers to write a check, or better still, whip out a credit card. As a result he buys big expensive things more willingly than small, cash-and-carry things. Penny wise and pound foolish, one might infer, except here the issue is not wisdom or folly, only the degree of abstraction of the money.

With the saltines my knowledge, though seemingly uncanny, might have been traced to certain fleeting perceptions stored in my brain cells. It was quite different with the case of Henry Kissinger and Liv Ullmann, a true epistemological mystery.

Similarly, I have unaccountable lapses. In the Central Children's Room at the Donnell Library two weeks ago my dear friend Emily from California, my daughter Rachel, and I admired a Gila monster on display in a jar of water. (Rachel was in the library to do research for a social studies report on Thomas Alva Edison.)

"Isn't it beautiful," I said. It was light orange and black, thick, powerful, coiled on itself. I felt an electrical charge of affinity with the Gila monster, though physically we have nothing in common, except that orange is my favorite color. After a while I added wistfully, "I think it's dead." Emily and Rachel burst out laughing.

"How could anything live in a jar of water?" Rachel said to me, with her twelve-year-old's stare of incredulity at my stupidity.

I was stupid indeed. I heard myself say in defense, "I guess I thought it was like a fish." I wonder how and why I could have assumed the Gila monster was alive. Apart from wishful thinking, I suspect it had something to do with the surprising appearance of Emily, whom I hadn't seen in over six months.

Emily was in New York on a flying visit; we spent an hour drinking in a bar near the Donnell while Rachel hunted for books about Edison. I was shocked when I first saw Emily, for she had cut off her hair and lost about fifteen pounds and was dressed in long black flowing garments.

"I'm thirty-eight years old," she explained. "I decided it was time to stop looking like a student at Music and Art."

"Well, you've succeeded," I said. "You look like a lady."

"Do I look like a lady poet?" She is in fact a poet.

"I think so. You look like a lady, anyway."

The transformation of Emily was so unexpected and disconcerting that perhaps it jolted something in my nervous system that subsequently made it possible for me to assume the Gila monster in the jar of water was alive. Perhaps.

At Hunter College the other day I asked my freshman students in Expository Writing to write an impromptu essay on a contention by Erich Fromm that education gives children a "fictitious picture of reality." I made quite sure to put "fictitious picture of reality" in quotes on the exam sheet so there would be no doubt those were Erich Fromm's words and not mine. One learns caution when teaching freshmen. I suggested they support their assertions with examples from their personal experience. After a half-hour of quiet writing, a boy with braces on his teeth came up to me and asked, "How is the word 'fictitious' used here?"

Surely the answer "as an adjective" was not what he sought. "What do you mean, how is it used?"

"I mean, well, what does it mean?"

One also learns, teaching freshmen, not to show surprise or any emotion that might discourage progress. "It means made up, not true, like a story."

"Oh. Thank you." He smiled happily and returned to his writing. I discussed this incident with a psychotherapist friend, who said that for her the real interest of the story was not that the boy did not know the meaning of the word "fictitious," but that he did not know how outrageous his not knowing would appear.

My own education, if more thorough, was equally unbalanced. As is the custom in schools, the teachers ignored connections and stressed facts, specifically facts regarding the Boxer Rebellion, Alexander Kerensky, the nature of scalene triangles, the names of the inns frequented or referred to by Chaucer, Shakespeare, and Dr. Johnson, the principal exports of Uruguay, and the names of Cabinet departments (St. Dapiacl, an acronym now an anachronism). Up until the age of twenty-five I remembered it all, then slowly, like a steep weather-buffeted slope, it began to erode, except for the Tabard and the Mermaid. The Tabard and the Mermaid, like seeds luckily blown to more fertile meadows, took root elsewhere in my brain, where I watered and nurtured them because I cared.

When Rachel first went off to be educated I used to pick her up every day on the Riverside Drive bus, taking along Miranda, two years younger. Once in a while our trips were graced by the glorious double-decker bus, whose erratic schedule we could never master, unfortunately. But most days, silent and absent, Miranda would gape morosely out the ordinary bus window with a finger in her mouth. I naturally inferred boredom and resentment. When Rachel learned to come home herself I said to Miranda, "I bet you'll be glad not to take that bus ride every day."

"But I won't get to see the statues."

"What statues?"

She confided that she had a private story explaining the free-standing statues dispersed along the Drive between 120th and 81st Streets, which she told herself every day, going and coming.

The first statue, a man on a pedestal, is a king, she told me. Beneath him, a soldier with a flag is holding a woman who is on her knees. The woman is really a princess but she's in rags. She is going to be put in jail and she's crying, "Let me go, let me go." (113th Street, erected in 1928 "by a Liberty Loving Race of Americans of Magyar Origin to Louis Kossuth the Great Champion of Liberty." Below Kossuth are a soldier and a long-haired old man in flowing robes; they are gripping hands.)

The next statue, Miranda related, is a man who looks like Abraham Lincoln, with a pedestal next to him. He is the father of the prince, and he is going to get a drink of water. (112th Street, Samuel J. Tilden, "1814–1886, Patriot Statesman Lawyer Philanthropist Governor of New York Democratic Nominee for the Presidency 1876 I Trust the People.")

The third is a man on a horse. He is the prince. He has heard the news about the princess and is going through the forest to rescue her. (106th Street, an equestrian labeled tersely, "Franz Sigel.")

Last is a lady on a horse. She is the same princess as in the beginning and she got rescued and that is the end. (Joan of Arc, 93rd Street, armed and bearing a torch, mounted on a rearing horse, "Burned at the Stake at Rouen France May 30, 1431, Erected by the Joan of Arc Statue Committee in the City of New York, 1915.")

I was disturbed by only one omission. "Why didn't you use the Buddha at 105th Street?" (The "Buddha" is Shinran

Shonin, 1173 to 1262, founder of the Jodo-Shinshu sect and presently adorning the doorway of the New York Buddhist Church.)

"Oh, him. He was too big." Seeing my dismay she added, "I did use him once. He was a magician. He was trying to stop the Prince, who was going through the forest. He's wearing a frown because the Prince got the Princess." She hesitated. "But he's really too big for the story."

"And I thought you were bored."

"I was, sometimes."

I asked Harry at dinner, the night he returned from Washington, if he had thought of going up to Liv Ullmann to tell her he enjoyed her performance in *A Doll's House*.

"Oh, no. They were looking for obscurity."

"What's 'obscurity'?" asked Miranda.

He told her. "Anyway, I eschew celebrities."

We laughed.

"What is 'eschew'?" asked Rachel.

"An obscure word meaning avoid," he said.

"I don't believe you."

"It is."

"That's ridiculous." At twelve, her only pejorative adjectives are "ridiculous," "gross," "disgusting," and "weird." "I don't believe there's such a word. It sounds weird."

"Go look it up in the dictionary." Harry spelled it for her.

"All right. But don't eat my dinner. I'm coming back."

"She'll never forgive me," he said. "She's like the elephant."

"Because you still do it," said Miranda. "You ate the M&M's I got from Willy's party."

"They were out on the table. I assumed they were common property."

"You should ask before you assume anything," said Miranda.

Rachel was chagrined to find "eschew" in the dictionary.

"While you're there," I called in to her, "please look up the Gila monster."

"God," she moaned, very put upon. She read me what it

said about the Gila monster. Of course I have forgotten most of it. I do remember that it has a "sluggish but ugly disposition," because I found the phrase, with its assonance, extremely suggestive, and I was intrigued by the choice of the connective "but." I also remember that there exists a "closely allied form" in Mexico named *H. horridum*. I will doubtless remember *H. horridum* forever. These facts made me love it more.

After Rachel returned to the table I reached for my purse, which I had set down in the center of the kitchen floor when I returned from giving my class the essay assignment on Erich Fromm's educational theories. Somehow its entire contents spilled out. Harry glanced over at the array of objects scattered on the floor. "Where is your eye of newt?" he asked.

Every now and then he says something that makes me recall with jubilation why I married him.

"Eye of newt," I laughed, crouching on the floor. "How do you know about eye of newt?" He reads mainly the *New York Times* and books on the structure of society and how it can be improved.

He shrugged.

"Come on, where do you know that from?" I challenged him. "Tell me where that comes from."

He paused, frowned, looked vaguely at the children for help not forthcoming. "Shakespeare?" he asked finally. *"Macbeth?"*

While I was putting my purse back together he said to Rachel, "By the way, how did you make out with the report on Thomas Edison?"

"OK. Did you know that Thomas Edison was deaf?"

"Yes," said Harry, and "No," said I, simultaneously.

"Was he born deaf," I asked, "or did he get deaf?"

"He got deaf, when he was around twelve or fourteen."

"How?"

"Thomas Edison," Rachel began in warm didactic tones, "had a job on a train, selling candy and stuff like that. When the train pulled out of the station he would grab hold of an open car above the wheels and pull himself up. One day he couldn't pull himself up so he was just hanging, and he knew that he could be killed, so a man standing in the car pulled him up by his ears. And Thomas Edison heard something pop in each ear and his ears really hurt for a while after that." She paused in reflective sympathy. "They really hurt a lot, and he began to get hard of hearing. And then his parents took him to a doctor, and the doctor examined him and said he couldn't do anything and he was going to get deafer and there might come a time when he would be totally deaf. And then when he was grown up another doctor offered to improve the situation but Edison refused, because he said he liked living in his laboratory without outside noises distracting him, and he was used to it."

I said, "That is fascinating." Rachel smiled proudly, as if she had made the story up herself, which, given my ignorance, she might have done. "Could he hear anything at all?"

"Yes," she replied. "He wasn't totally deaf; part of the time he could hear if people talked loud. When he was old he could read his wife's lips but it was easier for her to tap Morse code into his hand. He was married twice."

"Which wife tapped?" asked Miranda.

"The second. He taught her Morse code and asked her to marry him in Morse code and she tapped back yes."

I was growing ecstatic over this memorable information.

"Also," Rachel went on, "when he was about six or seven he went to this small school run by a man and his wife, and it was very crowded. They had kids of all different ages and didn't have much time to talk to each kid alone. He came home one day after three months and said to his mother, 'My teachers say that I'm addled.' So his mother took him and went to the school and she said to the teachers, 'This boy is smarter than you are.' Which in Edison's case was true. After that he never went back to school. His mother taught him and he taught himself and he was reading college books when he was about ten or nine. But he wasn't good at math."

"What is 'addled'?" asked Miranda.

"Confused," said Rachel. "Like you don't know what is going on."

"Did you learn anything else important about Edison?" Harry asked hopefully.

"No. I don't know. I don't remember." She stood up. "I'm finished. You can have that if you want it." She pointed to the remains on her plate.

Harry looked disturbed as he slid Rachel's plate toward him.

"Miranda," I said, lest she feel overlooked, "you'll never guess what nice thing happened to me on the way home from work."

"You caught the double-decker bus," she promptly replied.

The End of an Era
JAMES TATE

When your address book starts to fall apart
you know it's the end of an era.
When the dead or lost determine your days
then it should be decided that this is
the end of an era. Buy yourself some new shirts,
it can't hurt. Let a perfect stranger
cut your hair, what do you care? The newspapers

can't think up any new headlines. Call it
the end of an era just to get something going,
to get people thinking, to at least consider
abandoning the plan. Suddenly it *feels*
like the end of an era, like something you don't
have to say goodbye to, it's just gone.
It's not like a pet getting run over, that's

a specific pain and it will fall into place—
the street, the traffic, the odds. When
an era ends, nobody decides anything,
a terrible ooze accumulates, and a private, unspoken
nausea takes over. We awake to how wrong
everything has become, our best dishes
mean nothing, and, still alone, we cry:

"I want to break out of the Grief Motel!
I want to kick out the windows of the Grief Motel!"

Life is a muscular, tear-wrenching thing
at the end of an era.

Cooley and Kedney
PETER N. NELSON

Cooley Fitzgerald, who always carried his camera focused at infinity, died on September third, 1968, with his lens cap on, when the private plane he was flying in tried to make an emergency landing on a narrow highway only a mile and a half short of the Cedar Rapids, Iowa airport and hit the fourteenth car of a Rock Island Line freight train headed for Keokuk carrying, as it so happened, pigs. It was the most unusual thing ever to occur within a mile and a half of the Cedar Rapids airport, and remained the most unusual thing until, six years later, a small herd of dairy cows spontaneously combusted, or so the farmer who lived just down the road from the main terminal turn-off claimed, though he was widely thought to be dumb as a stick, in great need of insurance money, and irrationally religious. Still, there were the charred remains to consider. Nevertheless, Cooley's death was unquestionably more tragic. Not only did the hogs, once marketed in Chicago, represent a substantial profit for their owners, but the train derailed and traffic was blocked for hours, and that caused a problem, because the airplane Cooley had been flying in hit the side of the train opposite the closest hospital, which Cooley reached too late, the ambulance wasting forty minutes round trip in detour around the airport, too late and later, certainly, than it could have been, had everything been perfect. But then, had everything been perfect, the plane would have had more fuel, or the people who planned the airport would have put it a mile and a half closer to the site of the crash, which would have been a mile and a half farther from the religious dairy farmer, lessening the noise from the Ozark and United jetliners, which would have meant his cows would have been more contented and given more milk, and he wouldn't have had to torch them. If, in fact, he torched them. But life is not perfect like that—it is perfect in some other way, and if anybody could have, Cooley would have understood.

The real tragedy was that Cooley Fitzgerald died with his lens cap on, because he stayed reasonably lucid and capable of taking pictures up until the last moment, which came only a few moments before the surgeons entered the operating room, dripping at the elbows. The ambulance attendants and nurses all, to the best of their recollections, remember a critical patient pointing and clicking his camera at them, but unfortunately, nobody noticed that the lens cap had not been removed, nor had Cooley, who certainly cannot be faulted, under the circumstances, for committing the cardinal sin all photographers cringe at the thought of. There are conceivably few things as distracting as an imminent one-hundred-and-fifty mph collision with a Rock Island Line freight train. Still, it's a shame, because, had his pictures turned out, it would have been exactly the kind of photo essay he would have been thrilled to die for. He'd said often that the second best subject he could think of, when people were innocent enough to ask him what *subjects* he'd thought best to photograph, would be his own death. He'd said, just as often, and usually in the same breath, that the most exciting subject would have been his birth, and every time he said that, his voice seemed to dissolve in what listeners thought a discernible and sincere mist of regret.

On a brighter note, at the time of his death, the best series of photographs he'd ever taken was having the greatest success he'd ever known, though it must be made clear Cooley "F-stop" Fitzgerald did not think in terms of *best* or *greatest* or *success*, all of which was precisely why his fellow professionals considered him a genius. It is reasonable to ask, what good does success do a dead man? The answer most frequently given, and most often correct, is, none, but in Cooley's case, a great deal, because the degree to which he was dead corresponded in direct ratio to the degree to which his photographs succeeded, and not in the figurative *an artist is immortalized by his work* sense. The sense was quite literal, keeping in mind that his heart had stopped, his brain had ceased to function, and that his body temperature, in the morgue, had dropped to a cool thirty-five degrees Fahrenheit. As they laid him in the ground, his $1950.00 Hasselblad 500cm with $2499.00 500 Tele-Tessar 8.0t lens poised on his chest, his stiff shutterfinger posed at the ready, all at his request, his third choice of burial, there were in existence twenty-eight eight-by-ten black and white stills, dry-mounted and arranged chronologically in a portfolio, and one Polaroid color snapshot, upon which his life depended.

Kedney Bassett stood at the side of Cooley "F-stop" Fitzgerald's grave, weeping. She was the most gorgeous woman at the funeral, though the competition was weak. She was five-foot-two, 104 pounds, and had very thin hair the color of oak and difficult to wash in anything but very gentle shampoos. She preferred Dr. Castille's Natural Peppermint Shampoo, which made her, in addition, the most fragrant woman at the funeral, again, her stiffest challenge coming from Cooley's mother, who wore Tabu. There were five or six of Kedney's closest friends, and there were a couple of Cooley's friends from the Art Department, in which he taught a course in Photo Media, the days he wasn't off practicing his art. There was a minister, and there were Cooley's father and three brothers, and there was a poet who taught in the Iowa Writers' Workshop, an amateur photographer, friend of Cooley's and Kedney's instructor. As he stood opposite Kedney at the grave, he was thinking that with Cooley gone, he stood a chance with Kedney. He stood no chance, and never would. Kedney was Cooley's fiancée, though he had not known at the time of his death that she was.

Kedney wept. She had not wept for years, somehow, had thought, as people who have *been through too much* quite often think, that she had been rendered by life incapable of tears. She wished someone would come up to her, put his or her arms around her, and whisper soothingly, "Cry harder, it's not that good," but instead, they all tried to get her to stop, and to stop feeling again was not what she wanted. She was overcome by the usual griefs—loss, guilt, the assassination of love, especially that—but she was also overcome by irony. Cooley had hit the hog car within seconds of the moment, the very moment, Kedney Bassett had decided to marry him. Of course. She had been considering the idea for a long time, though he'd never proposed, and thought against it until the day before he left in the ill-fated Beechcraft to go cover the Democratic National Convention in Chicago for *Life* magazine, he proposed, in the form of the portfolio of twenty-eight black and white prints. They were not actually a proposal, though it was clear they were a proposal. She'd spent the two weeks Cooley had been gone looking at them, and decided she would marry him. She did not know then, naturally, that he would die, or that, at his funeral, after he died, his life would depend on them.

Before explaining the photographs or the nature of how Cooley Fitzgerald took photographs—his genius—it should be explained that he was a rather bizarre, frightening man who could leap from serenity to outrage in an instant, or disappear for days without warning, and sometimes, return unable to say exactly where he'd been or why. It should be explained as well that Kedney, beyond being the most gorgeous and fragrant woman at the funeral, was the least pregnant. Of all the women at the funeral, and more than most women in general, Kedney took great contraceptive precautions, and took children, especially the ones she might have, very seriously. Once, she and Cooley had joked that he ought to have some of his sperm frozen and then have a vasectomy, so that they could make love as much as they wanted to whenever they wanted to, and he could still father children when the time came, wherever the time came, and by whomever the time came to. There was another woman at the funeral, whom nobody knew, who had had a hysterectomy, and who was therefore not even in the competition to see who could be the least pregnant. The woman was a Mrs. Holmgren, the same woman who had originally called the ambulance which hadn't gotten Cooley to the hospital in time, a farmwife down the road whose husband, six years in the future, would burn his cows. After her hysterectomy, however it connects, she began to enjoy going to funerals.

The services ended and the mourners began to amble listlessly toward their cars, pausing to ask Kedney if she needed a ride, which she said she didn't, preferring to walk. With all the writers and poets in town, it was a celebrated cemetery, mapped and traversed in song and story. Poets probably frequented the cemetery more than fiction writers, it seemed to Kedney, summoned by uncomfortable notions that, being poets, they ought to think more about death, or drawn there by the innate morbidity of introspective people battered by bowling alleys, laundromats, and pizza places. The sky was more than three-quarters cloud, the wind more than gentle, and Kedney was glad she'd worn a windbreaker, though it was still officially summer. She noticed that in the very uppermost branches of an elm tree, the leaves were beginning to pale, signaling a premature autumn.

Kedney walked to a monument more often mentioned in Iowa City graveyard poetry than anything, the notorious Black Angel. It was a fifteen-foot-tall looming statue, wings outstretched, the whole thing leaning precariously, it seemed, over some poor woman's remains, the original white marble oxidized black before sunrise the very night the poor woman was interred because, as legend has it, her husband was betraying her memory and fornicating with her sister at the time. As legend has it. Legend, Kedney thought, can keep it.

Kedney's grief was real, so she left the cemetery, which offered up nothing but clichés. She went home and tried to play the piano but started to cry and had to stop. She tried to read, but started to cry and had to stop. She could not put her feelings into words. She missed Cooley. She couldn't conceive of not being able to see him again. A great love had risen up inside her, and she now had no way to release it. At the same time, she was afraid she would release it—that she would forget who Cooley was.

Kedney began to tremble, and felt a very real tightness in her chest, as if her heart were a clenched fist. She felt a tingling in her hands and feet, and then muscle cramps, her fingers twisting into gnarled, awful forms. She slowed her breathing, and her hands relaxed. She walked rapidly home, got in her car, and drove to a small motel outside of Dubuque, where she trembled and chain-smoked and stared out the window for six days.

She had left the photographs in Iowa City because she didn't think she could bear to look at them, for fear of what they might do to her and remind her of, but returned from Dubuque after she'd realized, biting into a French fry at Erdl's Burgers on Kerper Boulevard, that now she could not bear not to look at them. On the same fry, she also realized she was done, done being nuts.

Cooley "F-stop" Fitzgerald was a genius because he was the first Zen photographer. If he'd had a motto, though he had no motto, it would have been "To take a perfect picture—first make yourself perfect, then take a picture." In the same way that a Zen Master hits the target every time he releases an arrow because he does not aim the arrow but lets the arrow become part of the target and then find itself, Cooley's photographs were wonderful because he did not interfere with *the wonderful*. He knew, simply because it was his nature to know, when he was in the right relationship to a photographic occasion, the right angle, and he was always receptive. He opened his perception the way he opened his shutter. He loved Kedney the same way, not forcing his love on her, but simply "putting it in front of the camera of her heart," or so he had phrased it once, not as good with words as with a lens. He never, never, in his life, took a photograph of himself, and so every photograph he'd ever taken was more personal and had more of *the man behind the camera* in it than any of his contemporaries had in theirs. All the photographs he'd left Kedney were of Kedney, taken at moments when she was in a perfect state to be photographed. They revealed him to her, and more amazing, they revealed her to herself, not in the *am I that ugly?* sense, the way some photographs do, but in the sense of showing her who she really was all along, and who she could be, in her best state. That is, by being a perfect photographer, Cooley made his subjects perfect, or captured only the perfect in them—that in effect, he could make a rock say cheese and steal the souls of parking ramps.

It was complicated to explain, so Cooley seldom tried, nor did he think about it much, because it was easy enough to show, which his photographs always did, and when he showed Kedney the pictures he'd taken of her, she knew how much and how long he could love her.

Cooley loved photographs that expressed or implied the condition of the photographer at and after the click of the shutter. An example might be a picture of an attack dog in midair, about to rip Cooley's throat out, frozen in the moment before ripping it. One of the pictures Cooley took at the Democratic Convention became very famous for the same sort of anticipatory reason: it was a picture taken at about ten o'clock at night of a crowd of demonstrators being held back by an arm-locked cordon of National Guardsmen, and in the middle of the crowd, the only demonstrator wearing a white shirt—a brilliantly lit white shirt—was giving Cooley the finger. The young man had also shouted "fuck you, cocksucker!" at Cooley, and there were some who swore they could hear the man's voice off the print, and some who would say the photograph *epitomized the spirit of the sixties,* this picture taken a few days before Cooley died.

Ten days after he died and a week after the funeral, Kedney returned from her lost weekend in Dubuque, which has its share of them, to examine the portfolio Cooley had left her. The neighbor's dog snarled at her as she got out of her car on the last hot day of summer. Her landlord had taken in her mail and laid it on the newel post, letters of condolence from her friends, one from her mother, from Cooley's parents, from her grandmother, the usual bills, the unusual bills from the hospital, three envelopes from small literary magazines which she opened immediately, the contents informing her she was rejected from each, a local shopping guide, and a free sample of the latest in tampax technology. Her apartment was hot, the air dusty. She watered her plants, made a pitcher of lemonade, and sat down on the couch with the album.

There was a picture of her typing, taken from behind, in which the light of the fluorescent lamp over the typewriter made her thin pepperminty hair affect the halo she always felt was there when she was writing a good poem. There were four pictures showing how in love with Cooley she'd looked before she'd started to worry that he was too bizarre and threatening, three of them showing, in her eyes and mouth, how worrying had hurt her face. There was a picture of her in a yellow rain slicker telling a little boy he should go inside because he was getting wet. There was one of her trying to portray the syllable "butt" in a game of charades. Two of her sleeping, one with a good dream, one with a bad dream which was about to wake her up, but which also gave the sense she knew and was comforted by the knowledge that Cooley would be there to hold her when she woke. The photographs, toward the end of the album, the most recent ones, seemed to Kedney to evidence that, unaware of it at the time, she'd been falling back in love with Cooley. One showed her fishing, sitting in a boat with a borrowed pole in her hand and an old felt fedora on her head, and you could tell from the picture she was about to catch a nice walleye. One showed her in the bathtub just after having flung a handful of Mr. Bubble bubbles at Cooley. One, taken in Minneapolis, Cooley's home, showed her in a restaurant they'd eaten at the first time they'd gone to visit his parents. It was called The Skyroom, located at the top of a downtown department store where 2000 shoppers at a time could dine off the menu or opt for the Zip Lunch from the salad bar, crunching croutons, exploding cherry tomatoes between their molars, and watching fashion shows of local-label clothing. The restaurant meant something to Cooley because it was where his mother always took him and his brothers each year at Christmas, where the boys would all fight with each other and behave badly, and where Cooley had had his first clubhouse sandwich, and numerous subsequent clubhouse sandwiches because ordering anything else seemed inappropriate. It was a picture of Kedney with her mouth full of bacon, turkey, bread, tomatoes, lettuce, mayonnaise, salt, and pepper, and it was all oozing out between her teeth, and she was holding the sandwich in her hand for the camera to see, and there was the smell of hairspray and Iced Blue Secret in the air, and in the background, out the window, from twelve stories up, the layout of South Minneapolis where Cooley had roamed far and wide as a boy on a bicycle—in short, it was a picture of Kedney in exactly the right place at exactly the right time doing exactly the right thing because she was being exactly who she was. She began to cry a little, just a little, under control, to think that after all the men she'd gone through who had tried to get her to love them, and done all the sweet and charming things it took to *win* her love, Cooley had been the first man to *let* her love him, and now, as the old story goes, she thought, *his plane hit a train full of swine and he was gone.* She even laughed a little, sadly.

She went to her bulletin board, returning with the only picture of Cooley she had. She'd borrowed a friend's Polaroid Swinger and taken it. It looked exactly like him, but when she'd shown it to him, after waiting the required thirty seconds, the chemistry then not being what it is now, he'd looked at it and said, "Bean, that's really you." He called her Bean, for Kedney Bean. He was right. The picture of him had been her, Swinger in hand on one end of a teeter-totter at City Park on the Fourth of July. She understood.

Kedney poured another glass of lemonade and wondered what sort of poems she'd write about Cooley, what elegies. She started opening the letters. Her grandmother wrote:

Dear Kedney,

I just wanted to send you a little note to tell you your old grandmother loves you, for whatever that's worth. When Odell died I know all my friends tried to comfort me with words and none of it helped much, so I know there's not much I can say to help you, but I wanted to tell you that even though Odell passed on, in some ways I don't feel I've lost him at all. Having children helped and I see him in your mother and her brothers all the time, but even so when you live with someone and love him he can't be taken from you just because he's died. That must sound odd. I know Mary never really understood your "live-in" (is that what they call it?) situation with your Mister Fitzgerald, but please try to understand and forgive her. I believe you must have loved him very much and to tell you the truth I never gave a hoot if you were married or not and I told Mary so but she has her ideas.

It hurt a great deal to lose Odell but after a while he became a warm memory, like an egg inside my ribs that would never need to hatch. I hope the same thing can happen for you, and God will help you too. You don't have to write me back if you don't want to, but if you want to

get away and need a place to stay, I would be glad to clear the packages off the bed in the guest room for you. We all love you and are with you in your sorrow.
  Love,
  Grandma Bethel

P.S. I forgot to thank you for the cigars. They were very good. How did your Mister Fitzgerald ever be allowed to go to Cuba? He must have been very special. We'll talk later.

There were four letters from Kedney's friends, each of which told her to thank god she had his pictures, that always the good die young, and all offered her a place to stay, as if competing for the privilege; but she was truly moved by how much they cared. Her mother wrote:

Dearest Kedney,

Your father and I are deeply sorrowed by your friend's death, and we want you to know you can come home any time you want to, though they're wallpapering your room right now (sample enclosed) so you'll have to either sleep in one of the twin beds in Cheryl's room or stay with your father. I don't have many words I feel will comfort you. Death is never easy to understand, especially that of a loved one, and I hope you believe me when I say I know you loved Cooley. Can the past be forgotten? I love you and support you as much as I can. Maybe I love you too much some times. Marvin has been in Montreal for two weeks, but I talked to him on the phone, and I'm sure he will write to you soon. Take care, and trust that time will heal the pain. I'm sure it will. I love you.

  Mary

> *P.S. I hope you like the wallpaper—your room will be ready if you ever need it, though I'm thinking of converting it into an office the times you're away.*

Kedney wanted to dislike the wallpaper but liked it against her will because her mother had always had, she had to admit, if little else, good taste. Cooley's mother wrote to say that she and Cooley's father were fine, that the estate had been taken care of, Cooley having died as any Zen Master should, intestate, and they hoped Kedney would use the camera equipment they were sure Cooley would have wanted her to have, to complete the record of her life that he'd begun. They thought she was a fine girl, a special girl. Cooley's mother said Cooley talked to her about his "Bean" all the time, and, his mother said, "you can rest assured that I believe, at the time of his death, you were the most important thing in my son's life, and his father and I both thank you for being that." Kedney loved Cooley's family, including his younger brothers, who had helped her move Cooley's things out of their apartment before the funeral, fighting over his shirts and sweaters, joking and holding Kedney when she needed it, which was often. The letter ended:

> *Please come and visit any time. Minneapolis is beautiful in the fall, and we'll show you the lakes, which you didn't really get a chance to see. They are full of ducks. And please, please, keep in touch. We can see why Cooley loved you, and we love you too. Our deepest regret is that you two didn't get married and have children, or damnit, just have children, married or not. We hope you will continue to let us think of you as a daughter-in-law. Cooley once said to me, and I thought it odd, but then, I guess he could be a little odd, couldn't he, "Mom, sometimes I just wish I could make myself small enough to crawl inside Kedney and live there forever." Please, Kedney, let him live there. He's small enough now. We*

love you and hope you are alright. If you need anything at all, please let us know.

Much love,
Corey and Mike

Kedney found herself crying again, her face folding in on itself, both for the hopeless loss of it all and for the kindness that seemed to be flooding the space left by Cooley's death.

Kedney blew her nose and sorted through the remaining envelopes, a phone bill, a gas and electric bill, something from *Newsweek,* a letter from the hospital Cooley had been brought to, no doubt a form condolence, Kedney thought, and something from the Hillman Lab, University Hospitals, right in Iowa City. When she opened the letter from the Cedar Rapids hospital Cooley had died in, Kedney's heart began to beat rapidly, for in it was a note and also a smaller envelope, on which was written, in Cooley's own handwriting, "Bean." She took a deep breath, and set the papers aside, opening her gas bill, which came to $5.47, opening her phone bill, which amounted to $47.93 due largely to all the long-distance phone calls to Cooley in Chicago. *Newsweek* had been nice enough to drop a note saying they were making her a special offer as a college student, and just to make sure she read it all over a second time, but she could not calm the throbbing in her chest, and she feared cracking a rib from it, so she dropped the letters and went grocery shopping, buying two boxes of Bisquick even though she had half a box at home and didn't use the stuff much anyway. She drove around. She drove around some more. She came home to face what she concluded was a deathbed letter from Cooley. It was. She read the accompanying message first. It said:

Dear Mrs. Kidney,

Excuse my english for there are many things I cannot say or know how to but I must write you for Mr Cooleys sake who asked me too. We are good doctors and do all we can but I am very sorry he did not make it I have seen others die here or before in Saigon and I can convince you he did not die of very painful injuries he looked happy. He had also some moments of alertfulness to write you the letter I enclose also and gave me your adress and told me this I should send to you. Please do not think he died without thinking of you it was only one minute or more before he died after finishing what I also send. Even for nurses death is hard be please happy in time. There is Viet Nam saying I remember which says "ask the grave, it says 'life' ". I have help translating this. Maybe it helps.

> *Your friend Mai Duc Bui*
> *Cedar Rapids General*

Kedney poured two inches of warm lemonade and melted ice cubes into the wastebasket and filled the glass from a bottle of akvavit Cooley's brother Pat had left her in the refrigerator. It was a strong Scandinavian liquor that tasted like Ry Crisps and it was just what Kedney needed. She added ice, and felt prepared to read Cooley's letter.

> *Dear Bean,*
> *They tell me*

and then the handwriting, Cooley's, changed to the hesitant scratches of Mai Bui. It continued:

> *that I probably will die they don't tell me underline tell but I know period Bean I love you. By the time you received this you probably received letters from friends and wool wishers saying they love you too. Feel loved even by me after this is over with it is actually quite interesting and though Id have to admit I hope to survive quite understandably Im sure Im not at all apprehensive about this really, I hope the pictures turn out. Bean I have*

to tell you Ive not always lived as securely in the present as I might have lead you to believe Ive done something Im unsure I should tell you about but haven't the time to give the old ternatives the required consideration they deserve. So I put the problem in your hand. and trust you will do the right thing that is comma the right thing for you. Please feel under no old bligation to me because I love you two much to interfere in your life or allow it to go in any direction except that it desires. I will cut this short because I can no longer see anything. Dramatic underline dramatic arent I? If you really truely love me contact the Hillman lab at the University Hospital and give them my name if you are at all uncertain or dotfull please please I stress ignore this. Curiosity will lead to unwanted responsability. I warn you be sure of yourself first even then do what's best for you for your life underline your period. And take your time, please for me. Im sorry Im getting tired. Please send my endpromptoo stinografer here a big bowkay of you know whats I don;t think she knows who I mean she is sweet. I love you more than anything Ive ever loved period. As a group we dying men dont lie. What a group Im joining I hope I meet Abrohan Lincoln. How odd to think this is the last thing I'll ever say to you take care of yourself always I will miss you I love you if it is possible I will see you again we shall see wont we I love you.

    Cooley

ps let Sam have first shot at these pictures it their any good at all give the money

I am sorry he said no more. Your friend Mai Duc Bui. I am sorry I spell nothing good he said okay.

Kedney did not hesitate to open the letter from the Hillman Lab. It contained an invoice, itemizing $13.00 for liquid nitrogen, plus a $2.00 service charge, plus tax, coming to a total of $15.45. The letterhead read *Hillman Fertility/Urology Laboratories, University Hospitals, University of Iowa.* The bottom of the statement read, "Paid—storage and maintenance—acct. #s-424-q—7/1/68–8/30/68."

Kedney dialed the number of the lab and discovered, conversing with Dr. Fallon, who somehow could convey his bedside manner over the phone, that Cooley had deposited one hundred milliliters of sperm—an amount, if every sperm were given its egg, enough to repopulate the world eighteen times over, certainly enough for a nice sized family—in the hospital sperm bank over a period of two weeks the previous May, which had been when they'd joked about his vasectomy, and the time he'd taken the picture of her in her rain slicker with the little boy. Another picture, taken in May, showed her with her shirt off one sunny morning at breakfast, because it was a nice day, when she'd jokingly put drops of milk on each nipple, and then had cupped her small breasts toward the camera, pursing her lips. There was a bowl of Wheaties, Breakfast of Champions, in the near foreground, the photographer's meal. Had children and motherhood, Kedney wondered, been on Cooley's mind that May? And, there was a picture of her posed by the Black Angel in the cemetery, which in the hands of anybody but Cooley "F-stop" Fitzgerald was a shot that would have been, and always has been, in Iowa City, about the tritest thing you could do to photo-emulsion, but Cooley had been lying on his back on the granite coverplate and looking up at the towering angel, trying to feel dead, when Kedney had leaned over him and said "Aren't you cold?" "Only on the outside," he'd said, and clicked the shutter, locking into place the grey May rainy sky, the looming Angel, and the interposed Kedney, closer and equal in size to the Angel. It was a picture of mortality.

"And," Dr. Fallon added, "at your husband's request, made through the attendant nurse, we extracted a postmortem supplement of semen from the vas deferens and epididymis which, I should tell you, is much more viable than the sperm he had frozen last spring. The newer sperm has only been kept two weeks at minus eighty centigrade. My guess is it's roughly seventy-five percent resuscitative, whereas the older stuff is, ahh, much colder and will, when revived, be slower and less purposeful."

"Purposeful?" Kedney said, draining the last of the akvavit and noticing that she was slurring her words slightly. "Well I don't suppose I'd want to be impregnated by any shiftless loafer of a sperm."

"Well, it's more that to keep it longer we take it down to minus one-ninety-six centigrade and store it in liquid nitrogen. That'll keep it viable for up to ten years, or at least so far that's as long as we've been successful. Really, it plateaus at roughly fifty to sixty percent efficacy for nine years, but after that it drops off. We've had very little success after nine years."

"So," she said, "it's not exactly now or never, but now would be better, is that what you're saying?"

"That's a reasonably accurate statement, I should think, yes," Dr. Fallon said.

"Well, ahh, just what do I have to do, I mean, how is impregnation achieved?" she said, staring at a picture of herself in a baseball cap, the sun setting behind her, highway streetlamps coming on in the distance, the droning crowd below sitting quietly in anticipation, two out, sixth inning, Quillici on first, Oliva on second, and Harmon Killebrew at bat, Red Sox leading 4−1, her cheeks bulging from a mouth stuffed with hot dog.

"It's actually a surprisingly simple procedure," Dr. Fallon said. "The sperm is allowed to thaw to room temperature, and when it's done, caffeine is added, and then the mixture is spread on a cervical cap, quite like a diaphragm and inserted the same way. You could really do it in your own living room, though we don't recommend it."

"Caffeine?" Kedney said, "like a cup of coffee and then off to work?"

"Well, in fact," Dr. Fallon said, "the chemical function is

identical. Caffeine has been found to boost the resurrectivity, as it's called, up to 150 percent. Sperm are remarkably tenacious, even so, the extra get up and go helps a great deal. Mrs. Fitzgerald? Are you there?"

"I'm sorry," Kedney said, "yes, I am. I hope you forgive me, Doctor, but this is all rather a lot. This is the first I've heard, to tell you the truth."

"Oh my," Dr. Fallon said.

"Yes," Kedney said, "oh my."

"Hmmm. Mrs. Fitzgerald, as your husband's doctor I suggest you give the idea of raising a child fatherless some thought, and there's no hurry, but if you do choose to inseminate, your best bet would be to do it in the next month. You have nine years after that, however."

Kedney told him he'd been kind, that she'd think about it, and be in touch, and he told her that all the storage costs had been paid in advance for the duration of viability, that she would receive monthly statements, and that she need not worry about a thing, access to his sperm was restricted at Cooley's request to her, his wife.

"Did he say specifically to me, 'his wife'?" Kedney asked.

"Well, I assumed. . . ."

"We weren't married, Doctor. My last name is Bassett."

"Oh," he said. There was a short pause. "Well, I have last say, really, as his doctor, but I do think we should keep this under our hats, because I don't really know about the legality of it, and I don't know what people will think with all this Haight-Ashbury free love sort of thing going on, but I do know that this is Iowa and Iowa morality we're dealing with, and it would be a mistake to lose sight of that fact. We have a lot of churchgoers here, and Dr. Hillman goes twice each Sunday and once Monday, if you know what I mean."

"You're not Catholic, are you, Doctor?" Kedney asked.

"Hardly, I would say, more like transcendentalist, if anything in particular—why?"

"I don't know," Kedney said, "your name, it's Irish, isn't it? Cooley was Irish."

"Finnish," he said, "but in fact, it's an odd coincidence, but Cooley and I went to the same high school, years apart. My senior year, I played on a football team that went undefeated, and the string eventually went to sixty-eight games without a loss. I think that's some sort of national record. Cooley played on the team that lost. The man he was supposed to cover caught the winning pass. I kidded him once, and told him I'd only take his sperm if he promised to keep his sons out of football. That's a promise I won't hold you to, I should add."

"You're from Minneapolis," Kedney said. "I was there last summer. We went to a Twins game. Killebrew hit a home run with two on in the sixth to tie it, and another in the ninth to win it."

"He had a helluva year," Dr. Fallon said. "I remember that game. Five to four."

Kedney was staring at the leaves that had fallen from one of her plants to the floor, and she wanted to continue to stare mindlessly, so she thanked Dr. Fallon and hung up. For five minutes, she stared, wondering only what the name of her plant was.

Kedney tucked the letters and the Polaroid snapshot in the portfolio from Cooley, put the portfolio on her bookshelf and *things in perspective.* She was a twenty-six-year-old woman, a poet, with a history of love affairs that never seemed to turn out right, her propensity for failure something she sometimes blamed on her parents' bad marriage. She had had two abortions, and one wonderful live-in terrifying true deep forever love affair with a dead genius who, small enough now to live inside her, had willed her his sperm to do with as she saw fit, nor did she care for what was going on in Viet Nam, and Eugene McCarthy needed her help. That was her attempt at perspective.

Kedney Bassett went back to Dubuque for two days.

When she returned, she decided to do the only sensible thing: live her life. She could not really fathom the full implications of that, but realized that whether she chose to or not, her life would be lived by her as sure as trains would continue to haul hogs to Keokuk and she'd damned well better get used to it. She did not want, particularly, to live without Cooley, but after some time she could find no way around the fact that he was dead, she was alive, and that they had, in this way, grown apart. Cooley once said he wanted to be rich enough at his death to be able to afford to have himself stuffed, and then hire a staff of attendants to continue to place him in front of the television when his favorite shows were on, *Star Trek* or *I Spy* or *Run for Your Life*, or take him down to the local bar occasionally. His second choice was "to be skinned, cleaned, dressed, cooked, and then fed to the Johnson Administration," and then have someone tell them what they'd eaten. His regret was that he would be unable to see the expression on Robert MacNamara's face, and he said he'd will his cameras to whoever would take the picture and send him a print. But, Kedney thought, driving back from Dubuque through the gorgeous colors of autumn in Iowa, across land farmers were squeezing every last penny from every square inch of, Cooley had had to settle for his third choice of interment, and was turning blues, greens, and purples in a coffin six feet beneath and 130 yards south of the Black Angel, and there was nothing she could do about it. Except have his child. Which she preferred not to think about, just yet.

In the following years, Kedney Bassett would "go to Dubuque" often, a few times in the literal sense, reassured by the familiarity of that one plain, bare motel room where she could cohabit with her grief, whatever the cause at the time. It was nice to be able to keep it all in one room. Other times, when her life and career took her beyond a convenient drive, she "went to Dubuque" figuratively, once, for example, in 1973, waking up in a private clinic in Bloomfield Hills, Michigan, north of Detroit, gaining slowly an awareness that her mother had killed herself with an overdose of Nembutal. In the months immediately following Cooley's death, Kedney spent a good part of her time trying to contain the emotional energy she could feel storming inside her, because she would run the vacuum cleaner into the leg of a chair accidentally and burst into tears, or slip on the ice getting out of her car and burst into tears, and she was tired of bursting into tears. She took up racquetball, swatting ferociously at the ball, hoping not that it would carom properly and score a point but that it would splatter against the front wall like an ink blot. She canvassed her neighborhood for Eugene McCarthy, and watched impassively that November when the "Nixon Phenomenon" vaulted "Tricky Dicky" into office. She'd go to bed at night and long for Cooley. When Nixon waffled on his troop withdrawal promises and threatened "appropriate action" in response to any Viet Cong aggression, one of her racquetball partners, a fellow poet from Rapid City, South Dakota, named David Sundance, or who called himself David Sundance, asked her to help him organize a poetry reading against the war, and she agreed.

Kedney and David and three other members of the committee met a few times in bars, and as often as not, Kedney felt distracted and out of place, though she tried to contribute. It was her idea that they should organize a way to have students donate blood which, ultimately, would be poured out on the steps of Old Capitol, a functionless building in the middle of campus which everybody agreed symbolically represented the government even though the offices and officers of government had been relocated in Des Moines in 1857. The idea was met with enthusiasm and carried out, the big demonstration coming on April first. On May 15, 1969, Kedney handed in her thesis, entitled *Getting Warmer*, which broke basically into three sections—love poems, elegies, and antiwar poems. On the same day, rioting erupted at the People's Park in Berkeley. David Sundance had organized another, more broadly based committee, and left Kedney out of it because she continued to play racquetball, a game he'd stopped playing because of its similarity to war, but even so, Kedney participated in a *display of solidarity* with fellow student protesters in California. She still needed to play racquetball, but she was playing less frequently. She was finding a change taking place, a substitution, for the angrier she was during the day, the less sad she was at night. In June she got her M.F.A. degree, and in July she got a job at Mills College, a women's college in the MacArthur Park section of Oakland. On the first anniversary of Cooley's death, Kedney taught her first poetry workshop in blue jeans and no make-up to a class of young upper-class, well-mannered women who all wore skirts and scarves and mascara. She'd asked them to bring samples of their poetry, and they had, and eight of the poems were entitled "Life" and all the rest were about horses. Kedney drove into Chinatown for dinner that night, and as she drove, she thought of what a considerable amount of consciousness-raising she had set before her. As she tore at a bite of moo goo gai pan, she saw in the paper that Israel had shelled guerrilla sanctuaries in Lebanon. Driving home, she marveled at how different from Iowa San Francisco was, and how obvious a marvel she'd just had, but she felt compelled to measure the distance she'd come in a year, in larger terms than miles or days. When she got home, she felt calm and relaxed, and reached almost casually for the portfolio she'd only a day before placed on her brand new bookshelves, but when she pulled it out, the envelopes fell to the floor, and the one which landed on the top of the pile was the one from Cooley which said "Bean" on the outside, and it was instantly as if nothing had changed at all. The tears came suddenly, and she fell to her knees. She spent the night on the telephone.

By the second anniversary of Cooley's death, 9/3/70, Kedney was wearing her hair curly, was still the most gorgeous fragrant woman at any funeral, and had been arrested four times for demonstrating against, in order, the Cambodian incursion, Nixon in general, Kent State, and the closing of a daycare center in Berkeley. That day, Xuan Thay, North Viet Nam's chief negotiator, returned to the Paris peace talks. On September third, 1971, Kedney was seeing a man, a young and rather inept zookeeper who was constantly being bitten, stung, or clawed by something, whom Kedney felt sorry for, and because she was leaving that week for Tucson, Arizona, where she would teach a graduate poetry workshop, her first book soon to be published to much acclaim, she let that zookeeper be the first man since Cooley to sleep with her. She'd had one more arrest that year for joining a sit-in on behalf of lettuce pickers. She'd developed a kidney infection, and had had to go six months without drinking any alcohol. She'd published, as her last official act at Mills College, the school literary review, entitled *Life and Horses*, though to be fair, the poems anthologized were considerably better than they'd been initially, and she felt proud. She'd learned how to change her oil and tune her engine that year, though she was still uncertain what the "dwell" was. As the man entered her she thought of Cooley, and drove to Arizona the next day, three days earlier than planned, in a fit of self-loathing and a blue Volvo. She spent the better part of her first week in Arizona in Dubuque.

Two days before the fourth anniversary of Cooley's death, Bobby Fischer won the world chess championship. One day before, a Spanish woman in Tyler, Texas, saw the Virgin Mary breastfeed a goat in an arroyo by the first light of dawn, though no money was being made off the miracle until well after lunch. On the anniversary itself, Mark Spitz won his sixth of seven gold medals, and the Soviet Union announced that Aleksandr Solzhenitsyn would not be allowed to go to Stockholm to receive his Nobel Prize. On the evening of the fourth anniversary, Kedney looked through the album once, read the letters, looked at her snapshot of Cooley, and quietly put it all in a box which she wrapped, roped, and mailed the next day to Cooley's mother with a note expressing the wish Cooley's mother keep it, unopened, until further instruction. Kedney had hoped to become cold and callous about the photos, hoped they'd become as remote and frozen and ungraspable as an Iowa City winter seemed to a Tucson resident, which was what she intended to be and stay. She wanted them to fade past cognitive recollection but knew Cooley didn't take photographs that ever would. It was a warm desert night, and she went for a drive west of town toward the Saguaro National Monument, turning off before reaching the desert museum, parking at the mouth of Red Rock Gulch. Kedney was pleased to think the gulch was there and named before the Hopalong Cassidy movies and Roy Rogers westerns made such places seem so ludicrous and false. She walked down the sandy path, the walls climbing gently to either side, and she saw a javelina scooting up a wash, and she heard coyotes, and she made a fire from dust-dry mesquite branches, and she spent the night in Dubuque. She had to evict Cooley, as it were, because she wasn't making any money inside, had had no tenants, and while admitting to herself she'd never really shown the place around to the men who'd been attracted to her, she did not like the thought of turning thirty without the prospect of company. She'd had feelings for Cooley she'd not had since Cooley, and she wanted them back, but from someone living. It looked to her as if Cooley had to go, out on the street with rags on his feet but please, she told the sliver of a maiden moon above Red Rock Gulch, let it be let go of—let it be gone.

The day after she mailed the package to Cooley's mother, she threw out the notices from the Hillman Lab and wrote asking Dr. Fallon to have whoever was sending them stop. Two weeks after mailing the package she received a plane ticket and a note in the mail from Stanley Kunitz informing her that, as that year's judge, he had selected her manuscript, *Doubt Healer*, as the winner of the Yale Younger Poets Prize, and could she come pick it up? By the time Kedney got the card telling her Dr. Fallon was no longer at University Hospitals, but could be reached at the Dobler Clinic, University of Minnesota Hospitals, two black students had been shot at Southern University, and Kedney didn't give the card much notice. Also, she was trying as hard as she could to fall in love with a man she would marry in eight months.

On the fifth anniversary of Cooley's death, 9/3/73, Kedney sent Corey Fitzgerald a letter apologizing for not thanking her sooner for the wedding gift, an exquisite bathroom wall's worth of slabware tiles. The letter went on:

> *I wish you could have been here, but it is certainly a long drive.*
>
> *Corey—I can hardly tell you how much I appreciated staying with you after mother's funeral. I find I know no one in Detroit any more, and the house, which I always thought was empty anyway, was even emptier. I hope you will let me think of you as my mother now—we all need someone to at least think of as mothering us. Cooley took a picture of me in a cemetery once which he claimed captured the smell of my hair there. What happened at mother's (cemetery) is something I guess I understand now, but in a way never will, really. How could I love her so much underneath and hate her so much on the surface? How did I hide it from myself? The doctor called what happened "SCHIZOPHRENIC COGNITIVE DISSONANCE PSYCHOSIS." I love that kind of talk. Did they tell you, when you talked to them (when I was babbling in my rubber room) what started it?*
>
> *They say what triggers it is never important. I was standing there, listening to the minister, and where they found him I'll never know, when I saw a Hostess Twinkie wrapper blow into the grave, right into the hole itself. I saw a boy hiding behind a headstone where apparently he'd been eating his lunch—he had his lawnmower turned off. Anyway, he was peeking over the stone, watching, maybe to see if anyone had noticed the wrapper. Corey, I couldn't help it—I started thinking of mother spending eternity with a Twinkies wrapper in her grave, and I started laughing hysterically, and then apparently I really lost it, but all I remember is that it was too much, and I don't care what they say, I still think it's funny. But I'm better. Where did I get so unstable?*
>
> *I'm writing you from our new address in Georgetown,*

where we both begin teaching in only a few weeks. I will also consult, somehow—nobody seems to have answers to any of my questions—with the Library of Congress. It's no big deal, believe me. I'll find out what my job is once I do it, which is the way everything else works in this town. And Corey, this town is incredible—I've never been anywhere so exciting. Nobody, but nobody, believes the bastard when he "accepts the responsibility (for the break-in) but denies personal involvement." It's become a party joke around here, when you hear people saying, "hey baby, wanna go to bed? I'll accept the responsibility but deny personal involvement." I believe Sirica will get the tapes.

Also, our house has a breakfast nook almost exactly like yours, with unstained pine and a rather smallish French window. I am looking for a porcelain butter dish like the one you have to complete the picture, but I doubt I'll find one. What fun to actually own a house after ten years of leaky, drafty apartments with roaches and old refrigerators that shudder in the night. David is a good man, and takes good care of me, in many ways. This is not, I guess, your fairy-tale romance of everlasting passion, but I have learned it is wrong to compare the way we live to the way we'd love to live—the ideal. David and I are both intelligent people, and we love each other, and we will work it all out. I have not forgotten Cooley—I never will, but I have made room for David. I have not forgotten you either. There is a good chance I could be in Minneapolis around Christmas time for an interview. Can I stay with you? I'll let you know the poop. And speaking of poops, hello Mike, you old fart (an Irish fart, which as everybody knows is the worst kind).

I love you both. Take care.

Love, Bean
(officially Kedney Bassett Weisman)

Kedney Bassett Weisman's first real pregnancy did not go to term, spontaneously aborting without her ever the wiser in its fifth week, four days before her birthday, a kind of gift, though in truth any suspected connection would be specious. It was just as well, if such things can be just as well, because hers was an Andrea Doria of a marriage, on the rocks and sinking fast, capsized by a sheer incompatibility of detail and a realization on her part that David's Jewishness, which had at first been so new to her and what attracted her to him in the first place, was not enough to compensate for the fact that he was at heart a real prick, selfish and cruel at times, terribly insecure, and not, her therapist told her, obviously not Kedney's type. It was a depressing winter. There were long boring lines at all the gas stations, gloomy forecasts on every front, from the Economic Outlook to the Future of the Novel to the Human Prospect, and worse, in Washington, D.C., proper, where Kedney's apartment was—into which she'd moved the day Henry Aaron announced his intention to beat his career into the ground and play another year—storekeepers and janitors everywhere were keeping the lights turned off, and Washington, a town built out of little other than stone, marble, and granite, was enough of a goddamn mausoleum, Kedney thought, even with the lights turned on. For Kedney as well, it was a time of closing down, pulling in, and conserving. She taught her courses and went home, where there was no phone to answer, and no mail to bother with because after the split she felt it important that no one know where she was, and she kept her new address private. She read, and wrote, and did what the rest of the country was doing, which was watching the vivisectioning of the Nixon Presidency on the television, at the hands of a simple country lawyer on his way out and an ambitious country senator from Tennessee on his way in. She spent Christmas alone, though she tried not to make too much of a sentimental big deal about it, to herself, going to church at eight o'clock Christmas Eve, which was nice, afterwards spending two hours chatting in a restaurant with a woman from Thailand whose first name was Suaruang, whose last name sounded like "Bun-under-pot-corn," and who, no matter how much Kedney explained, couldn't understand the purpose of Santa Claus. Kedney was divorced on the third of January.

Kedney's course load lightened the next semester, which gave her more time to spend at home. In the entire month of February, she managed to produce only one line of poetry, which went: "If I were a man I would grow a beard," after which she stopped because she could think of no way to follow it. She even went out and bought a razor and a can of Rapid Shave, and shaved her face in an attempt to unblock herself, but all that resulted was a small cut which she hoped she would not have to explain to her office-mate. On April 29th, Nixon released the edited transcripts of his tapes and, politically speaking, the Frankenstein was turning on its creator, and had him pinned in the corner by the throat. Kedney spent all of August 9th, 1974 reading, and so first heard of Nixon's resignation when she read it on the cover of a local tabloid in four-inch-tall letters while waiting in the checkout line at 5:15 A.M. in an all-night A&P near the Tidal Basin where she'd gone to buy blueberries and wheatpuffs for breakfast, not because she was hungry but because as usual she couldn't sleep. When she saw the cover, her heart did somersaults, and she was as pleased as any normal person would be, that the rascal was routed. She bought a copy to read with her yogurt. Inside, on page seven, her eye was drawn to a headline in forty-eight-point Futura Bold type announcing the usual sort of sensational story such tabloids thrive on:

Herd of Cows Bursts into Flames: Investigators Baffled

Chicago. AP A Cedar Rapids Iowa farmer, Luther Holmgren, claimed Friday his herd of guernsey dairy cows, sixteen in all, caught fire and died in their enclosure on a farm just north of the Cedar Rapids airport. Said Holmgren, "I am just a sinner. God is punishing me by striking down my cows. Thank God though that they were insured. This is a blessing in disguise. The Lord works in mysterious ways."

Insurance investigators are checking into the possibility of arson. An airport official said it was doubtful an overpassing jet could have dropped fuel on the herd, and no UFO sightings were reported in the area. Six years ago, a private plane tried to make a forced landing on the highway leading to the airport, but crashed into a train that was crossing the road, killing all the passengers, and injuring livestock. Reports of other unexplained phenomena in the area are being looked into.

When Richard Nixon resigned, people rushed out to the drugstores and newsstands to buy copies of *Time* or *Newsweek*, to anchor themselves in History as it Happened. People who had been waiting and watching quit smoking the day he resigned, went on diets, began books they'd put off, started to paint their houses. Office pools were collected, backs were patted, and the Press, particularly the Washington Press, buried hatchets with each other, got in cars, drove to bars and got in the bag together, and stayed there for days. "Hippies" got haircuts, and war resisters returned from Canada, though not necessarily to turn themselves in, but certainly to celebrate.

Kedney Bassett called Iowa City the day after Nixon resigned and accepted the job she'd been hesitant to accept, a year's appointment to teach at the same Writers' Workshop she'd graduated from, offered by the same poet who'd had designs on her at Cooley's funeral, though she wasn't worried about that. She called collect from a payphone in a shopping mall, and even as she spoke, she thought she could see on the faces of all the shoppers milling about her that something had changed, that something important had ended, and even if that weren't true, she told herself, she felt something new inside her. It was, if nothing else, she told herself, a way of taking advantage of history, of letting herself be carried forward by the notion that perhaps Justice had Triumphed, that the air was clear and vibrant in the summer heat, that her lease was coming due and gas supplies were coming back to near normal, that a job she'd never tried to specify, about the war, about the condition of the world, was over in a way it wasn't necessary to articulate, and all that was clear was that she didn't have to do it anymore, could do something else. She thought now that it would be nice to be back where she'd lived with Cooley, nice to be close to Dubuque, and nice to teach a nice young bunch of nice students in a nice building just a nice ten minutes' walk from where they kept the frozen sperm she intended to impregnate herself with.

She drove first to Minneapolis, and spent the weekend with the Fitzgeralds. She sang as she drove, and thought her terrible voice was as terrible as ever. She was excited when she arrived, but did not tell the Fitzgeralds anything about the possibility of making them grandparents because it was only that—a possibility, not a certainty. She retrieved the package containing the photos, but did not open it, and told Corey it was a manuscript she'd wanted to "let ferment a while." By the time she'd reached Iowa City in her falling apart blue Volvo, Kedney had decided she would not open the package until the right moment, and she trusted she would know when that was.

She was disappointed to learn from the receptionist at the Hillman Lab that Dr. Fallon had moved, because she'd wanted to meet him, and more than disappointed when the same receptionist told her that in 1972 the Iowa legislature had passed the Downs Bill, which mandated that all sperm-bank donations be encoded by number only, and that Cooley's name was not enough. Kedney panicked, slightly, but calmed down when Dr. Fallon, who remembered her, told her long-distance that he would take care of everything.

"Yes, well, my understanding was that the law was based on genetic-engineering scares and black-market baby scandals going on in New York at the time it was passed, so the law would make sense in New York, where there isn't one, but not in Iowa, where there is, but I did warn you we're dealing with Iowans, didn't I?" Dr. Fallon said.

"You have a good memory, Doctor," Kedney said.

"An unmarried couple having children six years after one of them has died is not something I'd ordinarily forget, I would say. What I'll do is get a letter in the mail tomorrow to old Hillman, and I think you should see Dr. Semba for the actual procedure. He's a friend of mine who will understand. I'll send him a note too."

"Dr. Fallon," Kedney said, "you said once it was so easy I could do it in my own living room."

"Ahh, but I added, as I recall, that we don't recommend it, for reasons, among others, of sterilization."

"Well that's what I want, anyway. I'll be clean. Do you think I could, or would it be too much trouble, or illegal or anything? It is important to me."

"How important?"

"Very important."

"Well, Kedney," Dr. Fallon said, "I don't know if they'll let you, but I think you could do it, and home insemination is not completely without precedent. You'd need a vacuum bottle to carry it in, and a c.i.c.—cervical insemination cap—and a thermometer, some caffeine solution, and they'll measure it all out for you. But Kedney, you should know, that even under optimal conditions, we only succeed fifty or sixty percent of the time, and often try for months before hitting paydirt. Do you know when you ovulate? There's a slightly increased chance the baby will be, well, malformed or under-developed in some way, slight but real. It could take a long time, and it might not work at all, and I want to know if you're ready for that?"

"I think so," Kedney said, though to know for sure seemed impossible. But she knew what she knew, and where she'd been, and what a long time was. "I mean, Doctor, it seems to me that what I've got to lose is a good deal less than what I stand to gain."

Kedney spent the last week of August moving into a new apartment on Jefferson Street which had a kitchen, a bathroom, a living room, a bedroom, and another room with enough space for either a study or a nursery, and it should be made clear that she left her boxes of books on the floor of this room, not elsewhere. On the sixth anniversary of Cooley's death, she put in the trunk of her Volvo a suitcase with a weekend's worth of clothes in it, two fifths of Irish whiskey, her notebooks, four pens, and the portfolio Cooley had given her, still unopened. The doctor was a short Japanese man, as one might have guessed, but he did not smile as incessantly as Kedney had supposed he would. He did have a thick accent, but a Southern rather than Oriental one, having grown up in New Orleans. He spent the better part of an hour instructing Kedney—what temperature to let the sperm thaw to, when to add the caffeine, how to butter the cap, what her vaginal temperature should be, and so on. Kedney had imagined telling Dr. Semba that she was at the top of her menstrual cycle, coincidentally, and he would smile and say "velly good," but instead he said he thought that was "just jim dandy." Dr. Semba's wife/nurse assisted in the demonstration, a Vietnamese woman named Mai Bui Semba, the very same, and she remembered Cooley.

"I could not forget him, Miss Bassett. I never seen man so serene, you know, and remember he ask me if I were married. When I said no, he said I should marry Japanese man because Japanese make good cameras. Then he make joke you know and said, 'In fact, some Japanese are born cameras.' I recall laughing but not understanding."

"That was sort of how you had to take him," Kedney said.

She had time to kill, and spent that day driving leisurely along the back roads and off the main highways. She passed horse buggies carrying Mennonite and Amish people to and from wherever Mennonite and Amish people go, to each other's farms, Kedney wondered, or do they shop in real stores in town? She took pictures of them, and of anything she thought to take a picture of. She tried to take pictures Cooley's way, without trying, but she felt a little foolish and a poor imitator. She thought however that, as with the one other creative effort she intended to make that weekend, she would wait to see what developed. It was a good year for corn in Iowa, which is something like saying a good year for snow in Siberia, but it was true—the corn was six or seven feet high in places, and where the road dipped below the fields, Kedney felt as if she were driving through a tunnel of green, the sheer multiplicity of life around her like a blanket, the drive wrapping her in the rolling landscape of Eastern Iowa. She did not cross a bridge that boys weren't fishing off of, and all the dogs in the world were out and barking. The day was hot and, by late afternoon, turned overcast. Birds wheeled and swarmed in the windbreaks, and where the gambling farmers were harvesting early, purple martins followed the tractors as they unearthed or unseated insects. Like seagulls, Kedney thought, following ships out to sea for their trash. Kedney caught herself feeling very organic and fertile, and under the circumstances, let the feeling grow, so that, of course, it was raining as she drove into Dubuque, a small, dirty, smelly little town on the Mississippi River, with railroad yards and warehouses, neon signs with letters missing from them, black wires as thick as a finger strung from creosoted poles, and small motels with one car in the parking lot.

Kedney's motel had, bless its heart, not changed, save for a new Coke machine and a row of shrubs that did not look as if they were going to make it. She signed in using the name she'd always used—Anne Frank—another frightened girl trapped in a room, trying to love everything or just understand a little of it. She asked for and got room eight, her room. She threw her suitcase on the bed, and set beside it her packages, the portfolio, and the things from Dr. Semba, and then she closed and locked the door behind her and drove to Erdl's Burgers for dinner. The rain was not hard, and it appeared as if it were not going to let up. Erdl's had, in the time elapsed, closed down because Erdl, a man who if he flexed his muscles would rip his hat, had shot his wife and killed her in the arms of her lover in Galena, Illinois, Erdl now slinging hash in the kitchen of the Anamosa State Penitentiary. Kedney found another place called, simply, "Eat." She read the *Des Moines Register.* Across the horseshoe counter from her, a red-eared man was explaining how someone named Vern had been trampled by his own cows, and the red-eared man took care to emphasize that these were fat cows, not lean ones, as if, Kedney thought, it made any difference. It was warm and comfortable in the cafe. Kedney ordered a bowl of chili. The red-eared man had moved on to the topic of Luther Holmgren.

"Do you think Ford will pardon him?" a voice to her left said. She turned to face the voice, which had come from an old man whose crutches leaned against the counter beside him. Kedney's first impulse was to ask who was to be pardoned, and then she was surprised at how little she'd been keeping track of what was going on. But when she thought about it, she realized that she didn't really care one way or the other if they pardoned Nixon or not, and she was not one who felt he had suffered enough, either. On the front page of the paper, in the lower left-hand corner, it was reported that Luther Holmgren had been picked up and charged with arson in the Great Cedar Rapids Conflagration of Cows Scandal—Burgergate—with Watergate just two equal symptoms to Kedney of how terribly difficult it is to live perfectly, and people should understand. She didn't want to see Richard Nixon and Luther Holmgren crucified like Christ and Barrabas. She wanted them to be allowed to go golfing together, and help each other, and talk to each other, and work things out, but knew, laughing out loud in the Cafe Eat, that it was not to be.

"I don't know—I guess," she told the man.

"I've been in jail," the man began, but Kedney stood and paid her bill and left.

She went back to her motel, the rain a steady late-summer or early-autumn Iowa rain like rain anywhere really, but here, in the Corn State, Hog State, Farm State, Kedney thought, each raindrop a penny from heaven, an extra kernel per acre, money in the bank. It was about eleven o'clock. She opened the vacuum bottle, inside of which was what looked like a sugar cube, softening already at the edges. She set the lid aside, to let the semen thaw. Her vaginal temperature was 99.5. She was ovulating. She went into the bathroom and brushed her teeth, and when she returned, she took her clothes off and put on a red flannel nightshirt that had been Cooley's, which she'd expropriated from him and worn the first night they'd slept together and most nights thereafter. She had not worn it since he died. She lay on the bed and opened the package. She read the letter from her mother, who was dead now. Had she told her mother she'd really liked the wallpaper? Yes, she had, but it was no comfort. She missed her mother. She read the letter from her grandmother, who was still alive, and decided to write her the next day, and to send some cigars. She read the note from Mai Duc Bui, whose English was much improved now that she was happily married. She read Cooley's mother's letter, and planned to drive to Minneapolis soon, maybe the following week. She saved Cooley's letter for last. She'd never been able to evict him from inside her. Even when she'd tried to toss him out on his ear, she'd felt his presence, looking in the window, not asking to come in, just interested, looking and loving her. She was sure she had really loved him, as he'd asked her to be sure, and she'd taken her time, as he'd asked, and she was now giving Cooley, who had lived, with one precaution, without expectations or designs beyond the present, a future. She hoped he'd met Abe Lincoln. She checked the temperature of the sperm, but it was still cold.

She looked for the snapshot of Cooley, but couldn't find it anywhere, nor could she understand how she could have lost the only picture of him she could ever show her child. She thought back to Tucson, was sure she'd put it in the package, but then she realized she didn't really need it, and was not so angry or upset. She looked at the pictures of her and saw him in each. A picture of her daydreaming while sliding a piece of Juicy Fruit in her mouth with the foil still on it. The rain slicker photo, the milked nipples photo, a montage of lakes and sandwiches and dreams. There was a picture he had taken of her when they'd both had the flu, and had lain together in bed for a week, blowing each other's noses, taking medicine, and embracing toward health. A shot of her from far away, through a telephoto lens, taken as she'd been walking toward their house, the July sun setting splendidly behind her, her straw summer hat under her arm, an ice-cream cone in her hand, a dog at her feet looking at the cone, a child approaching rapidly from behind her on a tricycle. And simple portraits of her face, her twenty-six-year-old face. It was smooth. It was without blemishes, skin happy in forgetting the pain of junior high acne and senior high pregnancy, eyes unaware of what they would see, the police at Berkeley, the televised news of the Tet Offensive, the faces of men she couldn't see beyond the shadows of—but—in the photographs they were only twenty-six-year-old eyes adoring with all the love they could muster the man behind the camera. Kedney Bassett was thirty-two years old now. Cooley Fitzgerald had been twenty-nine when his plane crashed.

The sperm was at room temperature. Kedney tasted it, but thought that it somehow did not taste the same, and then remembered that it had been cut with ten percent glycerine for freezing. She added the caffeine, and waited the five minutes she'd been instructed to wait. She smeared the sperm on the cap with a sterile swab, inserted it over her cervix, tucked it in place, and turned out the lights, pulling the covers up to her chin. There was the sound of trucks passing the motel, going to Chicago or Omaha, the drone of diesel engines and the sibilance of tires on wet pavement. And there was the sound of the rain on the roof, steady and reliable. Kedney began to masturbate, slowly, and in ten minutes, she began to come.

Richard Nixon would sulk in blue suits about the grounds of San Clemente for a few years, sell the place, and move to New York. Luther Holmgren's insurance company dropped its case when Luther dropped his claim; his wife wanted to give the cows funerals. Dr. Fallon went to Sacramento, Henry Aaron retired in '76 with 755 slammers, Killebrew in '77 with 573.

Dr. Semba and Mai stayed in Iowa City, and Cooley's parents retired to Tucson, where Kedney occasionally visited them.

Kedney Bassett was to give them two grandchildren by artificially inseminating herself with Cooley "F-stop" Fitzgerald's sperm, the first a boy, Cooley, the second a girl, Bethel. Kedney would write a book which would be one of the finalists, but not the winner, of the National Book Award, the year Cooley Jr. turned six. The title of the book would be *I Never Went Back to Dubuque*. Cooley had perfection in him, and he brought it out in Kedney. The children were, of course, like all children, perfect.

Immediately after her orgasm, though Dr. Fallon would later assure her it was quite impossible, Kedney knew for a fact she was pregnant, and she fell warmly into a better sleep than she'd known in years—the best night's sleep since the night before the 1968 Democratic Convention in Chicago when Cooley had put his hand on her cheek, brushed her hair back, and said, "Sleep, Bean, I'll be back in two weeks."

Ghosts

JACK GILBERT

I heard a noise this morning and found two old men
leaning on the wall of my vineyard looking out
over the fields, silent. Went back to my desk
until somebody raised the trapdoor on the well.
It was the one with the cane looking down in.
But I was annoyed when the door rattled where
the grain and wine are. Went to the kitchen window
and stared at him. He said something in Greek.
I lifted my hand to ask what he was doing. Softly
he explained about growing up out here long ago.

That now they were making a little walk among
the old places. Silently telling it with his hands.
He made a final small gesture, rubbing the side
of the first finger against the second slightly.
I think it meant how much he felt about being there.
We smiled. I saw he was almost blind.
Later my bucket banged and I saw the heavier one
pulling up water. He cleaned the mule's basin
carefully with his hand. Put back the stone
for the doves to stand on, and poured in fresh water.
Stayed there feeling the old letters cut in the marble.
I watched them go slowly down the lane and out of sight.
They did not look back. I listened as I typed
for the dogs to tell me which farms they went to next.
But the dogs stayed silent all the way down the valley.

In Umbria

JACK GILBERT

Once upon a time I was sitting outside the cafe
watching twilight in Umbria when a girl came
from the bakery with the bread her mother wanted
and did not know what to do. Already bewildered
by being thirteen and just that summer a woman.
Now had to walk right by the American man.
But she did great. Went past and around the corner
with style, not noticing me. Almost perfect.
At the last second could not resist darting a look
down at her new breasts. Often I go back
to that dip of her head when people talk to me
about this one or that one of the great beauties.

Alma in the Dark
LINDA GREGG

She reaches over and puts a hand on his hipbone
and presses. He turns softly away and she makes
his shape against the back, her arm around
the waist covering his unguarded stomach.
He does not wake. Her heart in its nest
sings foolishly. It is awake and happy
and useless at this time. Saying dumb things
like *The stone house is firm*
or *The almond tree is blown around in the wind.*

Everything Else You Can Get You Take
ROBERT DANA

Blue fields. Great white
bison of cloud lugging their
easy humps. It's that kind
of day.
      Hay and panic grass
combed into rolling windrows.
Minstrel-faced sheep. A few
head of cross-bred Charlies.

No place we ever imagined
we'd be. No sea's edge
where a low wave sputters,
ignites like a fuse, and races
hissing along the shore.

No thin, viral mist fizzing
the windshield, gorges rising
grey as China in the rain.

Only this long roll of
space where day-lilies
leap any breaks in the fences,
flooding down ditches, orange
against the many colors of green,
—only the jingle and ring of
morning crickets in the dew.

Don't ask how long we've
been here, or why we stayed.
You fall in love with
a climate. Everything else
you can get you take.

From Commerce to the Capitol: Montgomery, Alabama
ANDREW HUDGINS

Despite the heat that stammers in the street
each day at noon I leave my desk and walk
the route the marchers took. I windowshop,
waste time, and use my whole lunch hour to stroll
this via dolorosa in the heat-drugged noon—
the kind of heat that might make you recall
Nat Turner skinned and rendered into grease
if you shared my cheap liberal guilt for sins
before your time. I hold it dear. I know
if I had lived in 1861

I would have fought in butternut, not blue,
and never known I'd sinned: Nat Turner skinned
for doing what I like to think I'd do
if I were him. The fierce blast furnace heat
of summer loosens my tight neck, grown stiff
from air conditioning.
                        Outside the door
an old black man, weight forward on his cane,
taps down the steaming asphalt. Before the war
half-naked coffles were paraded to
Court Square, where Mary Chesnut gasped—"seasick"—
to see a bright mulatto woman sold.
Draped in red silk, she flirted with the crowd.
I'm sure the poor thing knew who'd purchase her,
said Mrs. Chesnut, who plopped on a stool
to discipline her thoughts. Today I saw,
in that same square, three black girls toe loose tar,
then throw it at each other's bright new dress
to see if it would stick. I'll bet those girls
caught hell when they got home, their dresses smudged
with tar. I can't recall: Was it three girls,
or four, blown up in church in Birmingham?
The legendary buses rumble down the street
and past the Dexter Baptist Church,
where Reverend King preached when he lived in town—
a town somehow more his than mine, despite
my memory of standing outside Belk's
and watching, fascinated, a black man cook
six eggs on his Dodge Dart. Because I'd watched,
he gave me one with flecks of dark blue paint
stuck on the yolk. My mother slapped my hand.
I dropped the egg. Then, when I tried to say
I'm sorry, Mother grabbed my wrist and marched
me to the car.
                The uphill walk past banks
and courts, past shops, and past the Feed and Seed
gets sweat to running down my back. My white

shirt clings like mustard plaster to my back.
Before I reach Goat Hill, I'm drenched. My neck
loosens. Atop its pole, the stars-and-bars,
too heavy for the breeze, hangs listlessly.

Once, standing where Jeff Davis took his oath,
I saw the crippled governor wheeled into
the Capitol. He shrank into his chair,
so wizened with paralysis he looked
incurable, face white as schoolroom paste,
hair black as just-paved road. He's fatter now.
He courts black votes, and life is calmer than
when Muslims shot whites on this street, and calmer
than when the Klan blew up Judge Johnson's house,
or Martin Luther King's. It could be worse.
It could be Birmingham. It could be Selma.
It could be Philadelphia, Mississippi.

Two months before she died my grandmother
remembered when I'd sassed her as a child,
and at the dinner table in midbite,
leaned over, struck the grown man on the mouth,
and if I hadn't said *I'm sorry*—fast!—
she would have gone for me again. My aunt,
from laughing, choked on a piece of cherry pie.
But I'm not sure. I'm just Christian enough
to think each sin taints every one of us,
a harsh philosophy that doesn't seem
to get me very far—just to the Capitol
each day at lunch, walking the heat-stunned street.
On my way back, I buy a large cheeseburger
and eat it at my desk on company time.
Slowly unsticking from my skin, the shirt
peels loose and dries. Outside, on Commerce Street,
heat builds till four or five, then breaks, some days,
in thunderclouds that pound across the river—
bruise-colored clouds unburdening themselves

of rain that's almost body temperature.
I work late. Till it stops. When I drive home,
the tempered heat feels cool. The streets are hushed.
The sky's as blue as Billie Holiday.

Elegy for Cello and Piano
DONALD JUSTICE

The Bestor papers have come down to me.
I would imagine, though, they're destined for
The quiet archival twilight of some library.
Meanwhile, I have been sorting through the scores.
The one I linger over is the last,
The "Elegy." I seem to see the notes
Flying above the staff like flags of mourning;
And I can hear the sounds the notes intend.
(Some duo of the mind produces them,
Without error, ghost-music materializing;
Faintly, of course, like whispers overheard.)
And then? I might work up the piano part,
Not that it matters. Where is there a cellist
This side of the causeway? And who plays Bestor now?

This time of day I listen to the surf
Myself; I listen to it from my terrace.
The sun eases its way down through the palms,
Scattering colors—a bit of orange, some blues.
Do you know that painting of Bonnard's, *The Terrace*?
It shows a water pitcher blossom-ready
And a woman who bends down to the doomed blossoms—
One of the fates, in orange—and then the sea
With its own streaks of orange, harmonious.

It used to hang in the Phillips near the Steinway.
Can anyone call back now the web of sound
The piano and the cello wove together
In the same Phillips not too long ago?
The three plucked final chords—someone might still
Recall, if not the chords, then the effect
They made—as if the air were troubled somehow.
As if . . . but everything there is is that.
The cello had one phrase, an early phrase,
That does stay with me. (It may be mixed by now
With Bonnard's colors.) A brief rush upward, then
A brief subsiding. Can it be abstract?—
As Stravinsky said it must be to be music.
But what if a phrase *could* represent a thought—
Or feeling, should I say?—without existence
Apart from the score where someone catches it:

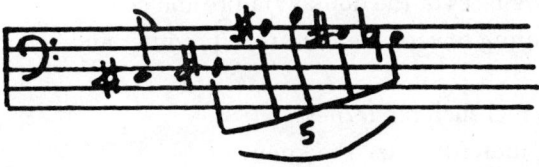

Inhale, exhale: a drawn-out gasp or sigh.
Falling asleep, I hear it. It is just there.
I don't say what it means. And I agree
It's sentimental to suppose my friend
Survives in just this fragment, this tone-row
A hundred people halfway heard one Sunday
And one of them no more than half remembers.
The hard early years of study, those still,
Sequestered mornings in the studio,
The perfect ear, the technique, the great gift
All have come down to this one ghostly phrase.
And soon nobody will recall the sound
These six notes made once or that there were six.

Hear the gulls. That's our local music.
I like it myself; and, as you can see,
Our sunset-maker studied with Bonnard.

In the Basilica of San Francesco
LAURIE SHECK

In the quiet chamber that holds us
like a kind of moonlit night, we see them gathered
without rancor, these animals staring with great tenderness,
witnessing the birth of Christ.
Giotto has left them here;
the mild attentive faces of the donkey, lamb, and cow,
their heads inclining toward the blue-robed mother and her
    child.
Having come to feel such tenderness
there is nothing more they need to know.
Far behind them, a single pallid tree
fans its branches out in all directions,
deep into the mother sky. How frail it looks,
and yet it seems as if it's rooted there forever,
each golden leaf completely still,
small eye-shaped mirrors hanging in the silence,
covered with fine dust. And the lambs
look wholly past themselves, so calmly,
onto the massive rock that is the world. . . .
But the moment is frozen,
the tenderness kept without effort,
the thrall of birth and newness blanketing
each creature, spidering them in.
It is as if they had not yet woken.
As if a strange unearthly music lulled them,

satiate and pure. But how soon the spell
must be broken, and the years accumulate their meanings,
and the child cry out beyond solace
as his mother turns, in her sorrow, toward the window,
the flayed leaves churning, twisting downward
in a tattered slowness, the wind dragging
its great trap across the ground.
And the father, too, will sigh with tiredness,
and the donkey tug his master's cart up the steep hills,
while flies clot near his eyes
and whip marks scar his skin. And yet,
as we look into this world brought to life
by Giotto's hand, it seems the donkey's eyes
must still hold kindness, they are so deeply kind,
no matter the knowledge of affliction burning in his body,
no matter the weariness, the meekness,
as he pulls the farmer's cart over rocks
and thorny vines, pressing hard into the forest's
haunted promise, deep into the mangled beauty of the world.

The Trail

TIM MCGINNIS

*At seventeen, he had already read Nietzsche, at forty
he still read fairy tales and the Czech Boy Scout Magazine*
—Ernst Pawel, The Nightmare of Reason: A Life of
Franz Kafka

August 2. I chafe at the tyranny of the buddy system. Why should I be concerned about the fate of Herr N.? Our afternoon swims in Lake Sudenfalles make me yearn for liberation. This afternoon our patrol leader reprimanded me, "Work on your trudgen, Kafka!"

August 3. Tonight, Herr N. crouches in the corner of our tent. I stare at him malignantly as he gnaws on an onion. Herr N. also keeps stale pretzel rods in his haversack. He smells like a stable boy and constantly fails inspection. I am smarting with unhappiness. Soon the whole camp will be talking about the two imbeciles in our tent.

August 4. I continue to sleep fitfully. I wake in a cold sweat and rack my brains trying to remember how to purify drinking water. Slowly, sleep returns. Then the pain-wracking anxiety dream begins. My two hard-earned merit badges, bugling and insect lore, consume themselves on my sash. Another recurrent nightmare: My father's stern voice bellowing at me from the window as I leave for a troop meeting, "Stay away from woodworking!"

August 5. This morning, at mail call, I tear open a letter from Prague with dread. Father is upset with me again. He found out that I played a field mouse in the camp play.

August 6. Today Schnassvogel demagnetized my compass. The big hike is just four days away. However, nothing seems to upset Herr N. He shows me his prized possession, a tattered piece of shed snakeskin. N. thinks that old socks make good kindling. I take pains not to be seen with him when we police the area after breakfast.

August 7. A scout is brave, that cannot be argued, but the others don't have to answer to *my father*.

August 8. I make a checklist for the big hike.
    toothbrush
    matches in tin box
    ground sheet
    flashlight
    poncho

eating kit
   notes for "The Great Wall of China"

August 9. My heart aches for my fellow scouts. I hunger for brotherhood, anything to escape the forlorn, mad life of a second-class scout. But no amount of compassion can compel me to practice mouth-to-mouth resuscitation on Herr N. I watch him carefully as his dull eyes glaze over during our discussion of the Morse Code.

August 10. I tremble, because in a few days, my father will want to know where the Big Dipper is located. And what of the swimming merit badge he wants me to earn? Was this a test devised by Sisyphus himself? How can they expect me to inflate my trousers while treading water? Herr Scoutmaster barks at me: "Tie a half-hitch, Kafka." But all I want to do is read Kleist on my cot. That, too, is nearly impossible as Herr N. babbles constantly about the sweeping changes he is planning for his ant farm.

August 11. I neglect to practice my surface dive. My axmanship suffers. A mounting repulsion toward these endless hike checklists. The hike is tomorrow. Scoutmaster Werrmann has just delivered his talk on the universal distress signal. I don't know if I could bring myself to shout for help three times. How can a plight so intimate be reported on such a public scale?

August 12. The hike begins. At first, all is merry and full of good fellowship. We sing "Edelweiss" and talk about ham radio operation. Then a harsh-faced patrol leader tells us to recognize roots and tubers. The chickweed at lunch was inedible. It looked fine in the *Scout Handbook*. The heat in this remote valley begins to take its toll. The regimentation is appalling. Werrmann strides back toward the end of the column. "Let's go, Kafka, you're lagging behind."
   Later, as we ford the stream at the foot of the highlands,

Werrmann tightens the slide of my scout neckerchief until I'm choking beet red in the face. "Wear your uniform properly," he snarls. "We don't want word of this kind of behavior getting back to Prague."

I decide to escape. Werrmann returns to the front where Herr N. plies two tenderfoots with off-brand soda crackers. I dawdle for a second, fiddling with the laces on my hiking boots, and then dive headfirst into a briar patch. My throat fills with screams but I dare not loose them. Scratched and bedraggled, I wander in the darkening woods. Without a compass, I try to keep two landmarks in a straight line in front of me. But I know I am circling.

August 13. Will they send a search party? Perhaps, but only after I have ruined the family name. I can't bring myself to use the universal distress signal. I can hear the scout authorities discussing my disappearance. "Look here, men, Franz was not mentally awake. He was not clean, thrifty, and reverent. Only these cold nights will prevent him from having heat stroke."

August 14. I am condemned forever to walk this trail, endlessly demonstrating the scout handclasp with myself until they unclench my fist after my last moments on earth.

Wonderland

C. S. GODSHALK

When the room was like this, in the dark, with only the window letting in moonlight and the white blanket looming up pale and square, anything could be in it. Anyone. Merle could be curled up on the day bed grinding his teeth, his small knees jammed into his chest. He was. She could be rolling over on the big fold-out couch, snoring lightly, or just there. She wasn't. But in the night Paulie was never completely sure. He let this uncertainty fold over him, the dreamy possibility of his mother's presence in the room would roll up under his chin, and he would sleep.

In the morning it was just himself and Merle, but it was all right because in the morning he was energetic and there were things to do fast. Juice and cereal and Bugs Bunny vitamins and hot milk heated in the little pot on the good burner and the pot run full of water right away so he could clean it out easily when they got back. Then rinsing and stacking the dishes in the sink and smoothing out the beds. He got Merle's jacket and hat and gave him the fifty cents. He had made her fill out the form saying they needed lunch for fifty cents and not a dollar like the other kids only a lot of the other kids had the same form.

Sometimes, when he first woke up but didn't open his eyes, knowing she'd be nowhere in the room, he would panic. He'd decide then to tell them, he'd yell to them all off the backstairs of the apartment and down the halls of Our Lady of the Snows, that she had left. "What kind of a mother is she!" they would cry. "A Whore! A Drunk!" and he would rush into their arms, into all their arms. But it would be Peg holding him, smiling with her cigarette and that stretched pink and silver sweater, looking nothing like anybody's mother, and a tremendous ache would fill his chest. That's when he dropped an arm off the bed and groped for his sneakers. He knew if they were there, exactly as he left them, side by side with the toes perfectly even, it would be all right and he could get up.

He poured the milk out of the pot over two bowls of Cap'n Crunch while Merle's headless form stumbled out of the bathroom. Paulie reached out with his free hand and yanked at the little boy's shirt until the large grey eyes appeared, the shirt still hitched on the nose, the face of a baby robber.

"Did you go to the bathroom? Did you DO anything?" The small boy looked up gravely, his red cheeks almost comical under Paulie's long pale chin. Despite their differences, the children shared a wide mouth and straight, almost broomlike reddish hair. "That bed damn well better be dry!" Paulie said.

After the dishes, Paulie took the plastic watering can from under the sink and watered all the plants. Then he shoved Merle's arms into a leather jacket and zipped up both their jackets, checked for the key in his breast pocket, and slammed the door. That part of the day was finished right. Outside, down the rickety backstairs, they stepped carefully over the brilliant bits of ice, beneath Nudorf's underwear lifting flat and frozen in the sunlight, midhigh to the peeling bottle of Meyer's Rum shooting its tremendous cap and stars off the billboard into the bright blue sky.

The house itself listed. It looked like all the other broken-down three deckers in East Boston, except it was tilted slightly forward so that, they had discovered, a marble rolled on their bathroom floor on the second floor would continue out across the linoleum, slowly increasing speed, making a little leap over the TV wire, over the kitchen door jamb and out the back door, dropping in little crystal slaps down the twenty-seven steps, staying in the depression in the middle of each, before it fell backward off the twenty-seventh step and clanked on the trash cans.

They had told Peg about the marble. Paulie told her exactly how it would go but she just shoved him away, holding her cigarette inside the cup of her hand the way she did when she touched them. Later she came out on the back porch with her fake fur jacket over her robe and grabbed Paulie's neck and steered him back inside to the bathroom and smacked a marble in his hand. She shuffled back out to the porch and yelled "Go!" and he squatted and let the marble go, he didn't push it, he just let it roll away, and it passed her dirty pink slippers and started to bounce and she leaned over the wooden rail and watched it hop down below her until the final chink on the can and she said "Holy shit!" with that smile. She wasn't drunk then and she wasn't sober. She was in between and she was nice.

That was the week before she left. He got back from school

with Merle and there was a box of cream-filled cupcakes on the dinette. On top of the box was a long envelope with magic marker writing. The magic marker was still there with its top off. She never put the tops back on and they always got dry. "Paulie" it said on the envelope "I'm going away for awhile" and he closed his eyes. "I'm going on a trip. You're almost twelve. That's no baby! Make sure Merle eats and don't take any crap. If you need me, *a real emergency*, go up to Nudorf and use this number." It was the number of the new guy from Texas. Mitch. "Uncle" Mitch. Inside the envelope were eight twenty dollar bills and a piece of yellow paper. "Use this slow" it said on the paper. "I'll be back before it's gone, or I'll send your father." A bright set of her lips was pressed into the paper.

"Fuck her" he said in a high, choked voice. He ripped open the cupcakes and shoved them at Merle. Merle pushed a cupcake into his mouth and backed away.

"Fuck her!" Paulie said again and the little boy started to cry. Chocolate squeezed out of the sides of his mouth and onto his shirt. "Fuck her!" Paulie screamed, and Merle moaned, a slow bright circle of water surrounding his darkened pants as if the tears were too much for the eyes alone to discharge.

"You pig!" Paulie said. "You little pig!" Merle began to wail and Paulie shoved him into a chair and stared at him savagely until he was quiet. Then he went over and dumped out the twenty dollar bills. He took one and folded it up and shoved it deep in his breast pocket and he stuffed the rest in a jar and put it way in back of the freezer part of the refrigerator. He took the envelope and tore it into bits and dropped them in the trash. "We're not calling her" he said, pulling off the small boy's shoes and socks and pants and wrapping him around with a dishtowel. "Ever."

He decided the first thing to do, despite the cash in the jar, was to get a job. He went to Foodland the next afternoon and applied for a job bagging. He was younger than the other bag boys, but he was tall and acted polite and they didn't hassle him. At first it was only for Saturday, but by the next week they told him he could come every day after school. Between Foodland and Peg's cash, he figured they could last for quite awhile.

Except for the nights, which Merle screwed up, it was better than it had been. They got to school on time. The place looked good. They ate right. "If anybody asks" Paulie said to Merle repeatedly "Old man Nudorf, Sister Cecilia, *anybody*, Peg's outa town. Say we got our aunt to cook and do stuff. Say Peg sends us postcards."

"Where?" Merle suddenly brightened.

"Where what?"

"Where are the postcards?" the child's eyes shone even more. "I want to see 'em!"

"There ARE no postcards, you little shit. Pay attention!" Merle looked at him blankly. He started to rock, as if a light breeze had entered the room. "Now" Paulie said again. "What are you going to say if someone asks—like Sister Cecilia?"

"What?"

"What are YOU going to say?" Paulie's fingers dug into the small arm. "YOU say—'my aunt is staying with us and cooks and stuff. My mother will be BACK SOON!'"

"She will?" Merle cried in pain.

Paulie let go of his arm and sunk into the yellow chair. "Yeah" he said blackly. They had gone eleven days, though, and nobody asked. When Nudorf finally squared them off on the stairs, putting down his bag of soda bottles and drilling into them with small, colorless eyes, they both wet their lips. "Where's your mother?" the old man said, and before Paulie could jerk back he grabbed a pinch of white cheek. "Jesus, you two look nice!" Nudorf's eyebrows raised like little hats. "She must have run outa booze in there and had nothing to do but polish you up!" He bent over and heaved the bottles against his chest and pushed past. They watched his galoshes push up under the dirty coat, disappearing and reappearing like pedals, until the old man vanished around the bend of stair and sky.

Our Lady of the Snows elementary school was a huge yellow building set between the church on one side and the convent and rectory on the other. Our Lady herself stood in yellow stucco in front of the church, balancing her bare feet on a little globe. Merle waited here for Paulie each day because the second grade always got out before the seventh. He stood in front of Our Lady while the buses pulled up and hundreds of kids rushed out and around him and then he held on to the gate so as not to be pushed out of place. Eventually he'd see Paulie's purple ski hat bouncing through the crowd.

Paulie would push up his collar and they'd walk together to Foodland. Sometimes Angel Ruiz would join them. Ruiz was smaller and older than Paulie. He looked like a monkey with dark, skinny arms and a wide mouth. He was always happy looking. He'd shuffle up fast in his stupid little jacket, the small shoulders twitching back and forth, his sneakers bouncing.

Ruiz was the only one Paulie told about Peg. "No shit!" he said smiling "Wow, if my old lady took off I'd grow some fucking wings or something!" He reversed to a moonwalk. Ruiz could moonwalk for blocks. "But why Foodland? I mean FOODLAND!" he slapped his forehead and rocked back drunkenly. "My old lady puts you on a roof, two hours you make fifty bucks. Just have to 'look'! Just tell 'em who's going down the street. FOODLAND!" Ruiz stumbled backwards again, laughing.

"Your old lady" Paulie said, shoving Merle forward. "How long is she going to do that thing with the string? A guy whistles in the alley—down comes Rosita's string with the stuff. I mean EVERYBODY sees it. What does she need a guy on the roof for?" Paulie had sat on the roof with Ruiz once or twice. The last time it was freezing, and they sat there watching the street and fooling with the steam coming out of their mouths. Suddenly Ruiz jumped up and began a little break routine on the ledge, jiving fast, before Paulie yanked him back down on the tar. "Ruiz is crazy" he said to Merle later. "Don't hang around with him unless I'm there."

Usually Ruiz left them at Dean Street, but this time he went all the way to Foodland. He hung around inside for awhile, then he slipped some gum into his jeans and did a fancy move on the electric eye mat and waved good-bye without turning back.

The day after Paulie told him about Peg, Ruiz came to the apartment. He had a big bag, full of Fritos and Sprite and Spanish stuff in cans. He said he could get more if Paulie needed it. At home, Paulie knew, Ruiz ate strangely. There'd be nothing for days and then Rosita would have fifty people over and there would be meat and bananas, big cooked bananas, beans and beer and guys in beautiful tight shirts. Only now Rosita's parties were small. Ruiz suddenly had real money because of these parties. He did his first trick with two guys she had up there over Christmas. "You gotta get out of there" Paulie said when he told him. "Yeah" Ruiz smiled softly. "Next week I'm going to Miami."

After Ruiz left Foodland, Paulie put on the yellow jacket and took Merle to the receiving area in back of produce. He sat him on a box between other boxes and gave him some old comics and told him not to move. Most of the time he wouldn't. He sat there turning the pages, rubbing his feet together. The first day Paulie told the assistant manager that he had to watch Merle sometimes after school and the guy said "No way," but when he passed the small boy sitting with the comic books a few days later, he shrugged and walked away. Merle ate stuff in back of Foodland, but he was careful. Paulie told him not to take anything out of the store that wasn't in his stomach and he didn't.

Going home, they wouldn't talk for blocks. They'd walk through the alley behind the store, down and over the MTA tracks and up the small embankment toward the fading light in the west. Sometimes Paulie would pretend she was there waiting for them in the gold armchair, and the pale yellow light became part of the vast chair, her reddish hair spread out above, her wide lips smiling over the bank of clouds like something floating on a movie screen. Once the light spread out in a dappled band and he saw her suddenly in her leopard kerchief the way she was that one time she came to school. She came for the Christmas play and she stood in the hallway with her fur jacket and her hair high and puffy under the leopard kerchief. She was the only adult there and she looked somehow saved when she saw him. "Paulie! Where do I go?" He was walking in a line of boys and he just kept in line as they passed her. "Home" he spat.

"What? Whatya mean?" she cried. "You said ten o'clock!" but he kept going. "I'm EARLY!" she screamed, rushing after him and yanking him around so that the kids in back bunched up and then walked around them, staring. "Ten o'clock yesterday" he said with venom, then pushed past. At the end of the hallway he glanced back and she was still standing there in that stupid kerchief, her hands dangling dead out of the jacket. He flung the image from his mind and twisted round to look for Merle. The small, pinched face pushed all sorrow from his heart.

By the time they turned onto their street the sun had usually disappeared, but Nudorf's laundry still caught the high lemon color, waving to them like bright cardboard cutouts of himself. The top of the huge billboard bottle glinted too in the yellow air, and they knew they were home.

One time, starting up the stairs, Paulie stopped. "What's that?" he asked, and Merle slipped a small brown ball into his pocket.

"A kiwi."

"I told you NOT to take stuff out of the store!"

"I didn't take it. I was LOOKING at them and Lifson gave me one.

"They're green inside" Merle said more quietly "like green jelly."

"Open it."

"No."

"Why not, for Christ's sake! I want to see. It'll get rotten like that other crap you stashed away."

"So what."

The boys climbed the stairs silently, the higher windows blinding them in the last iridescence. "You're saving it for her!" Paulie said suddenly. "You dumb jerk! That's what you're doing! All that stuff! The dried-up Fritos, those cupcakes! You're saving them for her!" Merle pressed his baby lips together and looked away.

"Christ" Paulie said.

Inside he hung the two jackets on doorknobs and looked around. It still surprised him to get in and find everything so quiet and neat. The lousy smell was gone, the cigarette butts pushed into food were gone, her makeup all over the place was gone. She always wore makeup and she never put any of it away. He liked her best in the morning when her eyes were plain and they didn't jump out of her face like they did later. She'd start with a tube of light brown stuff and then build on it. A few times she put this stuff on Merle after she hit him. Once on his arm where Kenny had pressed it. She was nice after times like that, sometimes for days. She tried to put the brown stuff on him one time, over a split cheek, but he shoved her off.

At night the two of them usually had cereal and then watched TV in their pajamas which Paulie already took twice to the laundromat with their other stuff. Sometimes they had tuna because for some reason Peg had four years' supply of tuna in the kitchen, or like this night, Paulie fried up pork chops with Wonderbread on the side, which was their favorite. He set the pink formica table with two folded pieces of toilet paper and put the small snake plant in the middle of it and two forks and two knives. The snake plant looked good in the middle of the table, its sharp thick spikes pointing upward, dark green with no brown like when she took care of it. All the plants looked good. The big one with the ribbon and the pink foil looked great. Uncle Mitch brought it. Uncles were always bringing stuff. Crap. One day before Christmas she told him Uncle Phil was bringing them both Big Wheels and he told her she could shove Uncle Phil and all the other uncles up her ass, but that's what she did anyway, and that's when she opened his cheek with her hair dryer.

Paulie liked the plants. He got a small box of Vitagrow from Foodland and used it carefully after reading the directions several times. "You don't use too much of this stuff or you burn the roots" he said to Merle. And he watered them regularly, but not too much. "She drowned half of 'em and dried up the rest" he said.

He checked the mail each day before he dropped it in a big shopping bag. There was one tremendous, oversized postcard that came from her the second week. It was a big monkey waving from the side of a skyscraper and it was all bent around the edges. "Hi guys!" it said. "Say hi to Kenny. Be good!" It was surrounded by a frame of xs and another pair of Peg's lips in the center. Kenny, she told Paulie a few years back, was his father. He might have been too, because she didn't call him Uncle Kenny and she didn't seem to like him very much. He was a pale guy who always looked like he wanted to be somewhere else. Kenny didn't seem to see Paulie when he was around. Merle's father was another guy. His name was Merle and Peg named Merle after him, but it didn't do much good because it turned out the guy hated the name. Somehow Peg must have asked Kenny to keep an eye on them. This made Paulie laugh.

On Fridays Paulie dumped out the shopping bag and sorted the mail. He did this when Peg was there too, because she wasn't too good with mail. He separated what was junk, what was important—like Boston Edison—what bills could be forgotten forever practically, and what could be forgotten for a long time. Rent could wait because Peg paid that more or less on time so Nudorf wouldn't hassle him for probably a month. The phone was no problem because it was gone. Peg flung it at the guy who came from New England Telephone to take it out. She switched her cigarette to her mouth and actually ripped it off the kitchen wall and flung it at this guy's chest, and she was a small lady. She'd do terrific stuff like that sometimes. Paulie asked Merle in bed one night if he remembered the phone guy, but Merle was asleep.

By the third week in February, there was one twenty left in the jar. Paulie walked around with the Edison bill in his jacket because he felt somehow if he had it on him, they couldn't use it. He knew this was ridiculous, but he still did it. At night he would wake up and see the long envelope, the one he had torn up, he would see it in front of his eyes, but he couldn't see the phone number written on it. That postcard came from New York anyway, not Texas, so who knew where the hell she was. There were other times when he came home and he was positive she had called. She had called Nudorf upstairs. Once he got back from the deli and Merle was in front of the TV which was on very loud the way he liked it when Paulie left him alone, and Paulie asked him.

"Did she call?"

"Who?" Merle's eyes stayed glued on the tube.

"Wonder Woman."

"Yeah."

"She DID! Christ! She DID!"

"What?"

"Did Mr. Nudorf come down?"

"No—I think—no."

"Merle!" Paulie pulled him up from the floor brutally and his head hit the side of the TV and he began to scream. In the night, on the rare occasions when Nudorf's phone rang upstairs, Paulie listened breathlessly to the old man's weight creaking over the floor. He'd wait for him to cross over to the door and start down the stairs. "Paulie!" Nudorf would shout outside their door. "Your mother is on the phone! Hey!" But he didn't.

Merle was the real problem. He wet the bed all the time now, and not just wet. The apartment smelled. Paulie kept him home from school a lot and stayed home too. He bought some postcards and wrote on them and gave them to Merle. "She sent them" he said. "She's coming back soon."

"You sent them" Merle said in a queer voice.

One night, when he made a particularly disgusting mess of his bed, Paulie hit him. He hit him hard, and Merle was quiet for a long time. He seemed all right, there was no mark, but he just wouldn't talk or anything, so Paulie finally picked him up and put him in his own bed and got in with him. He wrapped his legs around him and they slept like that and Merle was all right and didn't do anything. But when they got up the next morning, he made a mess on the floor. Paulie didn't clean it up. He got a ball point and a piece of paper from his looseleaf and he sat down and began to write. He wrote to CHATTERS at the Boston Globe. He read CHATTERS sometimes when Peg got the paper. He read it usually after Garfield and the ads for the topless bars. People wrote to CHATTERS with their problems, and other people—regular people—wrote the answers.

"Dear Chatters" he wrote "I have a small boy who wets the bed all the time and now it's more than just wetting. What do you recommend? I don't want to hit him or anything like that. Is there another mother out there with the same problem who has stopped her child from doing this? If you are the one, please answer." He signed it "Big Boy." People always signed their CHATTERS letters with funny or weird names. He mailed it right away and then he waited two days and checked a Globe at Soviero's deli, but "Big Boy" wasn't in yet. "Double Virgo" asked how to clean smudges off burnished copper. "Crazed Mom" asked how to stop spanking her four year old daughter. "Lamp Lady" asked if someone had the directions for a doll lamp. No "Big Boy."

He thought of asking Ruiz about Merle because, as crazy as Ruiz was, he sometimes gave strangely good advice. He checked for the narrow back with the black and yellow jacket in social studies, but the seat was empty. This was not unusual, half the time Ruiz never showed up. Just before recess, Sister Bonaventure, the principal, came into the classroom and put her hands together so that the big white sleeves fell back like wings and she waited until everyone was quiet. "I'm sorry, boys and girls" she said, and her big ugly face looked sorry. "We've learned that Angel Ruiz has had a terrible accident. Last night he fell off the roof of his home. He died this morning at Children's Hospital." One or two children giggled softly. "We must pray for his family, for his poor parents." Paulie saw

Ruiz pass before him smiling, rotating like a wheel in the darkness, and he could not find air anywhere in the room.

"Where is he now?" Merle asked that night. "In a box" Paulie said tonelessly. "Tomorrow they'll cover the box with flowers. They'll put it in the ground and fifty people will come and eat."

The entire class went to the funeral Mass. Rosita was there with a black hat resting like an elbow over her eyes. She was swaying sideways on a smaller darker man. "At least you didn't get him" Paulie thought savagely, and at that moment Rosita looked up and he had never seen such a sad face in all his life.

In the night Paulie balled up Ruiz and Merle, Peg and the Edison bill and Rosita, he balled up all of it and he punched it until it was hard like a rock and he flung it to the back of his skull. He decided, wildly, to clean the apartment. On Saturday he shoved Merle into his jacket and hat and gloves and put him in front of the TV and then opened all the windows and the cold air rushed in. He worked hard, scrubbing and cleaning, and when he was finished he closed all the windows and took Merle's stuff off and looked around. The place looked and smelled much better, but there was still something. The stuff on the doorknobs looked the worst. At Our Lady of the Snows they had hooks, a long line of brass hooks for coats which Paulie admired, and also rough plastic mats at the side doors where you could scrape your shoes before going inside.

The hooks were easy. He just slipped them inside his jacket at DeVito's hardware and glided toward the door so they didn't chink together. At the door he picked up a bright green rectangle of sharp plastic grass and walked out. He walked fast, waiting for a heavy weight on his shoulder to spin him around. He was ready for it, his chest filled with air, ready to tell them everything, but nobody stopped him.

Back home he made Merle hold the hooks one by one as he pounded a nail through the hole in each one. Merle winced each time, but his small hand remained steady. After three hooks were up, the door flew open and Nudorf stood with his hands clenched, bouncing over his slippers. "You wanna bring the whole god damn place down!" he cried. "I got two pictures off the wall already! Cut it out! Where's your mother?"

Merle stared at him, his mouth open wetly. Paulie riveted his eyes on the nail and went on hammering furiously and when he was done he flipped the hammer on the yellow chair.

"Get them coats!" he ordered Merle. He turned his eyes on the old man. "Did you wipe your feet?" he asked contemptuously. "That's what the green mat's for! I shouldn't have to tell you that!"

Nudorf found himself scraping his slippers, and then turned round vacantly and went out the doorway. "Close the door!" Paulie commanded, but he was already shuffling up the stairs in confusion.

Paulie worried after he left. The old guy would go upstairs and think about it, he knew, think about just the two of them being there in the apartment. He decided to go up right away and tell him about the aunt.

Upstairs Nudorf opened the door and put out his hand and pulled Paulie in by his shirt. This had never happened before and Paulie was afraid. Inside, the old man let go of him and sank into a chair. Except for the light over a table and the chair, the room was dark. It was cramped with huge furniture and the air smelled like Nudorf, only stronger.

"Paulie" the watery eyes blinked up. "She's gone, ain't she?"

"I've got to go" Paulie said. "My aunt's coming. She doesn't like me to leave Merle alone."

"How long have you been doing this?" the watery eyes swelled open. "HOW have you been doing this?" Paulie slipped back out of the light, and Nudorf was silent. For a moment the old man seemed to forget him. He picked up a spoon that had been buried in some mush and then slowly let it go. Paulie walked around touching things lightly. In the little kitchen there were a lot of large soda bottles lined up behind the sink. Lemon soda.

"What do you do with all the lemon soda?"

Nudorf jerked up, shifting toward the voice. "It goes down

easy. I got problems here" he pointed to his stomach. Paulie lifted the dank curtain over the sink and looked out. The bottle of rum looked different from up here. You could see the four spotlights that went on at night and the huge dry flakes peeling off the top. He dropped the curtain and continued walking around, running his hand over the heavy furniture, keeping out of Nudorf's range.

"It's okay" Nudorf said suddenly. "I was a man at twelve! I was an old man at seventeen! Now" he pushed away the mush "I'm a baby. You'll be all right. Better off in fact!"

Paulie fingered things while Nudorf talked. Nothing in the whole place was worth two cents. He pulled out a drawer and Nudorf stopped talking, his eyes bright with panic. "What's that! What've you got!" Paulie withdrew his hand silently. Inside the drawer he could see loose toothpicks and a photo. It was of a tan boy about his own age in a too small jacket with his arms stiffly at his sides.

"This your kid?"

"Yes. No. It's me, I think." Nudorf started to get up and Paulie slipped out the door. The air in the rancid hallway was like a breath of spring.

"You and your brother" Nudorf cried, sticking his head out the door. "I saw you crossing the tracks. Don't do that! In the snow you can't hear so good. Snow does something funny to the sound!" but Paulie had slipped down the stairs.

Inside Merle was asleep on the floor in front of the TV. Paulie took his blanket off the bed and tucked it around him and sat down and looked at the tube. A lady and two kids were smiling at a very shiny floor. It was extremely shiny, like a mirror. He looked down at the pitted linoleum between his sneakers and rolled away into the couch. He curved his arms and legs around one of the stiff pillows, kicking off his sneakers, and clung softly to what he knew was a spinning ball, with the water not falling off, with fishes hanging in it, bright sunlight on the other side, revolving fast, nothing falling off ever, he clung with his curled toes, clung to the vast cheek, the red hair lifted behind, the cigarette cupped away somewhere out in the universe.

In the morning it was abnormally quiet. It was Sunday, but that wasn't it. The room was filled with a soft luminescence. Paulie got up and shut off the TV and the lamp, but the soft brightness remained. Merle was still asleep on the floor, soaking in the sweet smell of urine. Paulie covered him with the damp blanket and got his own sneakers on quietly and then his jacket and opened the back door. The dazzling whiteness made him wince. He stood there blind in the fiery dazzle, cracking his eyes now and then until the backstairs materialized in a sparkling spiral. He made a first step, plucking his foot back out and inspecting the perfect blue imprint. Below the cars extended in softly glistening humps all the way to the end of the street. It made him suddenly happy. He threw a snowball at her once, she was standing where he was now, looking down, and he threw a fistful of snow and her eyelashes were suddenly full of snow. "Wonderland!" she said, laughing.

At the bottom of the stairs he began to walk slowly through the quiet brilliance. It was too early for traffic on the side streets. Nothing moved. In a short time he reached the overpass where the sidewalk ducked into a tunnel and the world turned abruptly black. Cars reverberated overhead and when he emerged in front of Soviero's deli, the snow was already grey and used.

The Sunday Globe was big and he couldn't thumb through it fast enough to check CHATTERS without Soviero bitching at him, so he bought it. Outside he cradled the heavy Globe and a box of doughnut holes in both arms and the change stuck inside his glove. There was a dollar thirty-four left. "In a dollar thirty-four" he thought with a strange twist to his lips "she would be back. Or a dollar thirty-three. She said before it was gone." He jerked the glove off with his teeth and flung the money away. After walking a few yards he stopped, his eyes burning, and went back. He sunk to his knees and began poking through the small, circular tunnels made by the change, then kicked the slush violently from side to side.

There was traffic on their street when he turned the corner, several black rectangles appeared where cars had been removed, and something else. His eyes narrowed, scanning back and forth over the street for what he had seen, over the buildings and the line of parked cars, and there it was, the fender of the deep red Camaro. It sat in front of the snow filled vacant lot. Mitch's car. He walked up and put his hand tentatively on the windshield, tracing the screaming eagle decal beneath the glass. On the bumper it said "Cowboys make better lovers." Inside there were several packs of cigarettes on the front seat, her cigarettes. He shifted the Globe and the doughnut holes and looked up at the house and the blank second story porch, still like the others, but not like the others because behind it she was kissing and rocking Merle, and Mitch had his filthy head in the frig searching for a beer. He sat down on the stoop by the car and leaned back. The blueness beyond the roofs seemed to fall away from his eyes, as if gravity reversed and he could fall up, up, as soon as he let go. He ached to see her, to collapse against her. He knew, in a moment, he would. He would get up and walk the hundred yards and climb the stairs and throw open the door and that would be that. But he just sat there.

    A green truck idled a few doors down, the driver leaning on his horn for a car sliding sideways out of a parking space and the sound reverberating cruelly in the wet air. Across the street a boy in a big parka was playing with a little girl of about three. It looked like they were playing hide and seek in front of the stoop. Paulie watched the boy hold both the little girl's hands and spin around. Her eyes were closed and then she would continue to spin around alone, smiling with her arms out, and the boy would dart fast behind a car or the stoop and the little girl would look round and round and not see him and call him and then begin to cry. He would wait until she looked afraid and started to cry desperately, and then he would pop out and she would stop crying and look happy almost immediately and they would start to play again. After awhile he would sneak quickly behind another car and she'd call him and start to cry again. Paulie watched as both were repeated again and again, the little girl's joy, desolation, joy, as she continued to play, having too short a memory for despair, or too long for joy. He continued to watch, amazed.

We Are Americans Now, We Live in the Tundra
MARILYN CHIN

Today in hazy San Francisco, I face seaward
Toward China, a giant begonia—

Pink, fragrant, bitten
By verdigris and insects. I sing her

A blues song; even a Chinese girl gets the blues,
Her reticence is black and blue.

Let's sing about the extinct
Bengal tigers, about giant Pandas—

"Ling Ling loves Xing Xing . . . yet,
We will not mate. We are

Not impotent, we are important.
We blame the environment, we blame the zoo!"

What shall we plant for the future?
Bamboo, sasagrass, coconut palms? No!

legumes, wheat, maize, old swines
To milk the new.

We are Americans now, we live in the tundra
Of the logical, a sea of cities, a wood of cars.

Farewell my ancestors:
Hirsute Taoists, failed scholars, farewell

My wetnurse who feared and loathed the Catholics,
Who called out:

> Now that the half-men have occupied Canton
> Hide your daughters, lock your doors!

Reading Aquinas
MICHAEL HEFFERNAN

Maybe what Thomas means when he says grace
is its own prerequisite, or words to that effect,
has something to do with these sweet tides of joy
one feels now and then in the bottom of the breast
while crossing the street against the light
or watching children at play or cats copulating
or birds leaving the branches quivering under them
and the stillness of the branches afterwards.
Maybe it's times like these that Thomas means,
though I'm in doubt on this and other issues,
including the one correlative idea
about how the Divine Essence cannot be known
to a person who is still in the body, except

"in dreams or alienations of the senses,"
which is a truly wonderful consideration
coming from a corpulent 13th-century Dominican—
and grace again is an explicit component here:
"the images in the imagination are divinely formed,"
involving "the infusion of gratuitous light,"
Thomas having elsewhere carefully explained
how it takes grace to prepare oneself for grace,
as in that sudden shower one afternoon last summer,
like a sparkling airy essence of divine light,
I found a portly African in a Hawaiian shirt
baptizing himself in the street and marveling:
"I couldn't help myself! This rain is exquisite!"—
the two of us finally standing face to face,
one of us an angel in a shirt of flowers,
the other blessed as he could be because of that.

Amazing
LAURA JENSEN

I was myself, the tattered who can.
The sky autumn, the fog
standing down in the pool of bay.

Far up, many stories,
your desperate flag was waving,
signaling for rescue.
But only polishing the inside
of the sliding door.
You came outside
in your white uniform.

And all of us were watching
from far below—a lady
with a permanent, an older lady
with a red umbrella
against the sun, myself
who just mailed two letters. You became

amazing, a gyration
of the psyche. You were cleaning,
so many stories above us,
and it was not your house.
It became like a circus,
you were flying from the trapeze
and it was not your house.

If it is your house
and you wear the uniform
only to clean
then my poem is meaningless,
then uniforms know no respect
in this town, then your psyche
performs something dangerous
to us, to our country
of women and poets, something
aberrant and cruel.

No one could be so cruel to a poet.
You were performing, walking
a tightwire of the mind,
raising cleaning to its rightful
elevation, polishing
the windows, so many stories
above us, when it was not your house.

East Grandville School
SANDRA NELSON

A narrow two story red brick house
that looked like it expected company.
When we puked, they put dust on it
sweeping it into a pan.
Indoor toilets, cool and dim
with stone floors and walls that shouted
to everyone exactly what you were doing.
Teachers were old fat ladies. Miss Ehlert
would take her teeth out after lunch to rest them.
Her chair had a big seat and a bad smell.
The basement took turns,
being the auditorium, gym, and lunchroom, corn,
we ate corn and soft peas with warm milk;
all rotten potatoes and two prunes, carrots
cut in tiny squares, old, older, oldest spinach,
white and brown pudding, igloo rice piles,
gravy every day, we were the lucky ones.
Every fifth child born in the world is Chinese.
Our family is lucky to have only four kids.
Volks and Gessells each had six children.
Neither Rosy or Janie was Chinese because God
made them Catholic instead.
We made the world out of play dough. The land
was green, mountains brown, and all water
blue. Baghdad, Mozambique,
rubber, diamonds, chinchilla, steel,
all with printed names. Flies,
we caught a lot of flies, or if a dog got in
that was good, or if your nose
bled giant red spots on the *Weekly Reader*.
I see you've been picking it again.
Miss Ehlert had to go to the hospital

to have her toe cut off 'cause it made
one of her legs too fat. Everyone wrote
her sick letters.
We were shot by the nurses, polio,
TB you had a scab as big as a nickel.
Nurses took Darlene away before summer
because of her scab. Sandy
ate all the paste again. I will not eat
art supplies. With huge round brushes
we painted a green stripe for the earth,
near the top a blue one for the sky. The sun,
one fourth of a lemon pie, always upper left.
Snow was a rain of white mice, puffy and big.
We liked to make red mittens and coats.
Robert Davis was my square dance mate.
When it came time to swing your partner,
we went real fast and then let go. Wow.
On days when we played ball, they gave us
soft balls so big like you couldn't see or something.
Thock, plump, bop, then the strings hung out,
so you threw it by its tongue,
till it was a hairball. You had to sing
about ducks, beavers, bees, dogs, and rowboats;
teapots and tulips, courting frogs,
and purple mountain magic trees.
Diane was extra fat and her hands cracked,
flaking away from eczema. She wore three sweaters
because she had a chest and knew where babies
came from. We listened, but knew we didn't come
from down there. You were lucky
if you were adopted. The blue sky rolled
down like a shade touching the green earth. The sun
traded corners and cooled in a tree. You could paint
a person behind a person. More people
fit in your pictures so
they gave you more colors.

In the Workshop after I Read My Poem Aloud

DON COLBURN

All at once everyone in the room says
nothing. They continue doing this and I begin to know
it is not because they are dumb. Finally

the guy from the Bay Area who wears his chapbook
on his sleeve says he likes the poem a lot
but can't really say why and silence

starts all over until someone says she only has
a couple of teeny suggestions such as taking out
the first three stanzas along with

all modifiers except "slippery" and "delicious"
in the remaining four lines. A guy who
hasn't said a word in three days says

he too likes the poem but wonders why
it was written and since I don't know either
and don't even know if I should

I'm grateful there's a rule
I can't say anything now. Somebody
I think it's the shrink from Seattle

says the emotion is not earned and I wonder
when is it ever. The woman on my left
who just had a prose poem in *Green Thumbs & Geoducks*

says the opening stanza is unbelievable
and vindication comes for a sweet moment
until I realize she means unbelievable.

But I have my defenders too and the MFA from Iowa
the one who thinks the you is an I
and the they a we and the then a now

wants to praise the way the essential nihilism
of the poem's occasion serves to undermine
the formality of its diction. Just like your comment

I say to myself. Another admires the zenlike polarity
of the final image despite the mildly bathetic
symbolism of sheep droppings and he loves how

the three clichés in the penultimate stanza
are rescued by the brazen self-exploiting risk.
The teacher asks what about the last line

and the guy with the chapbook volunteers it suits
the poem's unambitious purpose though he has to admit
it could be worded somewhat differently.

The Battle of Manila

LAURA KALPAKIAN

The iceman brought me to that day, woke me, I mean. He usually brought me two, but this day he didn't bring me nothing, just woke me where I sat on the porch having my dream when he knocked on the rail and said, "Afternoon, Mrs. Dance, I come to collect."

I lifted one eye at him, hardly able to see him at all in the glare of his white uniform and the sunlight shuddering in and out of the foxtails in the yard and the heat baking down in waves underneath the tin roof. I asked him what I owed.

"Two dollars thirty-five, same as ever, Mrs. Dance."

"You're robbing me same as ever," I say, but I got up and went in the house, that dog sniffing at my heels and got my coin purse off the piano where I always keep it between all the pictures and took it back out. "The ice melts too fast in this heat," I say. "Maybe you better bring me an extra cake. I need some for the icebox and some to cool off."

He looks strange for a minute, scratches a pimple on his chin, and asks if I got his note, the one he left with the last delivery. "It was the last delivery, Mrs. Dance, the very last one. No more ice no more. No more iceboxes. Everyone in St. Elmo's got refrigerators nowadays and they don't need no ice."

"I got an icebox," I tell him.

He counts me back my change. "Well you get one of your boys to buy you a refrigerator, why don't you? Will and Archie are making good money. They can buy you a refrigerator. Why, some of them fridges have little freezers up top and you can make your own ice." He tips his hat and starts to leave me, to fight his way back up through the foxtails to where I know the fence is and after that, the sidewalk and the icewagon. I hear the squeal of the gate before I call out after him. "What day is it?"

"Tuesday, like ever, Mrs. Dance. I always come—used to come—on Tuesday."

"What Tuesday?" I holler.

"Tuesday the 17th of August," he cries back.

"But what's the year?"

Over the chug of the ice wagon, he shouts, "It's 1948, Mrs. Dance, and everyone has a refrigerator and don't need no more ice."

And that's how the iceman brought me to and I knew time was passing and it was years since the Luzon campaign and the battle of Manila Bay.

I go back inside, dog at my heels and put the coin purse back up top of the piano between the picture of my son Will and Mrs. Will and their children, and my son Archie and Mrs. Archie and their children. They're twins, Will and Archie and they had joined up the Navy together and they was at Pearl Harbor when the Japs blowed it up, but they wasn't neither of them killed or even injured when it happened. But this whole house might just as well have been atop the Arizona that day because my husband Hank had the radio on and my youngest Ben was reading the funny paper and I was fixing breakfast when the news of Pearl Harbor come on. Ben drops the paper and screams. I drop the dishes and scream and peed my pants, but Hank, he did not scream. He gasps and moans out the bitterest note I ever heard, a long ragged groan and then a sharp, high one and he crumples over, falls forward out of his chair to the floor. He had a heart attack and died in Ben's arms. The only victim of Pearl Harbor to be living in California.

They give Hank a veteran's funeral, not for his being the first California victim of the second war, but for having fought in the first. Hank had joined up in May, 1917, even though he was a married man and didn't have to go. He said he hated the Hun and owed it to his country. So his country owed it to him to bury him and they did. Hank's no sooner in the grave than Ben's telling me how he hates the Japs and owes it to his country to quit school and join up. I said: Will and Archie will save the world, you stay home with me till they call you. They'll call you soon enough. You're only eighteen. I told him that and Connie told him that and between us we kept him in St. Elmo till after high school graduation, but then he joins up to be like his brothers. He joins the Army to be different from them.

But Ben wasn't like his brothers. They both lived and come home and got married and had families and now, just like the ice man said, they're doing real well. Will's manager of the St. Elmo Feed and Seed and he can't string two words together without he talks about diversifying and expansion and hard goods and profit. Archie, he goes to law school. Good thing Hank was already dead because Hank hated lawyers. Hank was a union man. Hank loved the union the way some folks love God or baseball. But Archie's a lawyer and him and his family live over in the new part of town and they even got a television set. They want me to come over and watch their television set, but I say no, I'll just stay here and watch my old dog and whatever flies come to roost and the honeysuckle when it cares to flower. Now, though, I know I'll have to call Archie and Will and say something about a refrigerator because I can't live without ice. I go in and check the icebox and the cake has got another day, maybe more, so I can wait to phone. I chip me off some ice and go back out to the porch and my dream.

It's a new dream. Not real new, but since Christmas, maybe, or some holiday like that. Before, I only dreamed of Ben little, running up these steps and falling and hurting his knee and his little arms around my neck while I carry him into the house and wash the blood and mud off him, my lips against his sweet cheek. Or little Ben in the bathwater taking the suds from his hair and putting them on his chin and saying to me, ho ho ho, like he was Santy Claus. Or little Ben all dressed up to be a pirate on Halloween and coming into the kitchen where I am making popcorn balls, coming up behind me and saying "Boo!" and scaring me out of my wits. But in this new dream, I am in the middle of the amphibious assault on Manila Bay. The fighting is going on all around me, but it don't notice me and I don't pay no mind to the shocks and shells, the blast and shriek all around while I am looking for my son. I am in my old dress like the one I got on now and my old green checked apron that's wore through here and there and I kneel in the mud beside a body I know is Ben. I pull him into my lap and turn him over slowly. The first few times I have this dream, that's all I do: just kneel and turn him over, glad to see his face is only muddy, no blood or nothing. I am glad they have not shot up his face. But lately in my dream I find fresh water from somewheres and I bathe that mud from his face and I am so happy that with the mud washed off, it is still perfect.

Maybe Ben didn't die in the mud, but that's the way I dream it, so that's how it is, even if that ain't how it was. I rock on this porch and suck on the ice and wait for the dream to come get me, even though I can hear the dog snuffling and kids' voices somewheres, kids up to no good, no doubt, and the foxtails rasping against one another and the weight of this honeysuckle vine sagging down on the porch and pretty soon I don't hear no kids or dog, nor nothing but the fighting going on all around me in Manila Bay and I scrape the mud from my son's beautiful young face, his nice tanned skin and fine mouth, his sandy colored hair and I bathe his closed eyes with fresh water. I kiss his eyes.

After a time the sun squints under that tin roof and lights up my eyelids bright and I know it's time to quit the dream and go in and get supper for me and this old dog. I heave my bones out of the rocker and the dog follows me to the kitchen. I don't worry about losing the dream. It will come back and it don't scare me in the least because I know it means I have accepted Ben's death and God's will and I am not fighting God any longer.

Ben's death near killed me. They said I was wild with grief. They said they couldn't figure it because I had took Hank's death so well. Well, of course I did. Hank and me, we had our good times, we had our family and our laughs and our cries and a few beers after the boys were abed, our days on this porch, our nights in that old bed for near twenty-five years and always, even in the worst of the Depression, Hank always had work with the railroad and our boys never knew the cramp of hunger in the gut. Me and Hank, we had all of that, but Ben was only twenty-two. Ben had nothing unless you count that slut Connie, which I don't.

I didn't always think she was a slut. I used to like her. A pretty girl. Plump and pink and blue-eyed and mad for Ben. She set her cap for him and she went after him and if Connie Frett had been my daughter, I'd have tanned her hide before I'd let her run after a boy like that, but she got him. They was in love and they couldn't keep their eyes off one another—or their hands neither is my guess. After Ben died I kept watch on Connie Frett, hoping I'd see her sprout a big belly, but I told myself it wouldn't be Ben's baby anyway. He had been gone too long. But Connie was a good girl in her way and after Ben died, she couldn't do enough for me. She was over here all the time, like we had to be together because we was the only ones who loved Ben that much. I shared her grief, but I couldn't let her share mine. She and me, we'd come out on this porch in the evenings and sit on the steps together and I'd say, thank you for cooking supper, Connie, and for cleaning up, or thank you for sweeping the porch and dusting up the place, Connie. And then she'd put her head in my lap and weep and I'd pat her back. We'd stay that way for a long time, but I couldn't let her share my grief. That was all my very own.

After a while she quit coming over so regular and folks said Connie was coming out of it and wasn't that good and I said, yes it was. They said the war was over and the boys all home and wasn't that good and I said yes. But I got lonely after Connie quit coming and it was just me and Ben and this old dog left here and no more Connie flinging herself into my lap, sobbing her eyes out and needing me.

Then one night, I get a knock on my door and it's Connie Frett. She looks real pretty with a gardenia in her hair and a yellow cotton dress on. She leans down and pats this old dog and then she smiles up at me and says: Hi Manila.

That's my lawful name, Manila. I was born the same time Admirable Dewey took Manila Bay, when we whipped them Spanish and showed them what real Americans was made of. My mother told me folks was mad with victory and she could hear my father telling Dr. Tipton that he was going to name me Admirable Dewey and that the doctor pointed out that no girl could go around St. Elmo being called Admirable Dewey. It was the doctor suggested Manila and everyone agreed that was just the perfect name for a baby girl.

I said: What brings you by, Connie? I took two Coca-Colas out of the icebox and we sat on the front porch step, her pink arm next to my brown one, her yellow dress next to my green checked apron and the smell of her gardenia washing over us. She told me she was getting married in a week and she didn't want me hearing it from nobody else. "I'm marrying Michael Kehoe. He fought in Europe and he's home now. He was on the football team with Ben. Maybe you remember him, Manila."

"I don't remember no one but the quarterback."

"Ben was the quarterback."

"I know."

"Ben and Mike Kehoe were very good friends, Manila. They loved cars and football. They were a lot alike."

"No one was like Ben."

"No," she says, slow, pulling the word out taut, like bread dough till it frays and tatters in the middle. "I thought I would die when Ben died. I wanted to die." Connie swallows hard. I hear it. "If I couldn't die, then I wanted to grieve for him my whole life. But I can't."

"Who says you should?" I ask, swilling my Coca-Cola.

"I'm young," she goes on. "I love Michael Kehoe, not like I loved Ben, but I love him and I'm going to marry him and be a good wife to him."

"You never deserved Ben anyway," I say, hating myself, but saying it just the same. "You were a slut."

Connie stood and handed me back the Coke bottle. She brushed off the seat of her yellow dress and started to walk down the path to the gate which you could see in them days because the foxtails hadn't yet growed over it. She gets halfway to the gate and she calls back, sad-like, "I guess Ben is all yours now, Manila."

I don't say nothing. I stay where I am and keep hold on the dog so he don't go after her. I want to ask Connie if she had ever made love with my boy Ben. I'd like to know he had a girl's love before he died. That isn't so much to ask. But I don't say nothing. I just sit here on the step and watch her yellow dress go out of the gate when you could still see the gate because the foxtails hadn't growed over it yet.

"I can't have the new fridge delivered, Ma, until you get these foxtails cut down." That's what Archie says to me, standing on the front porch, popping sweat and I tell him he wouldn't be so hot if he didn't wear vests and wool suits in summer. He laughs. He says, "Ma, that's part of my job. Who ever heard of a lawyer in overalls?"

"A mule in a party dress is still a mule."

"Yes, well, what about these foxtails? Let me send a boy over here to cut them down. Hell, Ma, I'll do it myself if you'd let me, but I'm telling you, they won't deliver the fridge until they can get through the yard."

"Then you do it," I tell him. "Only don't wear no suit."

So Archie and Will both come over and cut down my nice foxtails and pretty soon some men come into my kitchen and push the icebox in the corner and puff and huff and bring in a refrigerator and plug it in. I tell them: all I want is some ice. They show me these little trays that you put fresh water in and put them in the freezer and wait a long time and you get ice.

Real nice ice and lots of it. Enough for my Coca-Cola and some for me to drop down my dress and a square or two for the dog so's we can come out here on the porch and rock and let my dream come back to me: the mud of Manila Bay soaking over my skirt and up my knees as I kneel with Ben in my arms and the battle shrieking around us, guns booming and men screaming and mud. Me with my fresh water bathing Ben's beautiful young face, his hair, opening the collar of his uniform and washing the mud from his neck. I pull him tighter into my arms and put my weathered cheek against his perfect one.

Then one day, sometime later, I know it must have been later because my dream wasn't new anymore, but an old dream, I was sitting on the porch, in summer. Anyway, it was hot. I was having my dream when I hear voices and I think it's the soldiers in the battle and I think it's strange I can hear them at last, but it's not soldiers and pretty soon I know it. Other voices. Calling at me. *Manila Dance has ants in her pants . . . Manila Dance has ants* I come to and the dog is barking and snarling and I smell the smoke from the battle all around me. The dog don't leave my side, but sniffs and squeals and looks up at me and barks when I say, "Holy Frijole, they've set us afire!" The smoke was thick everywhere now, but I couldn't see no flames, just a curtain of smoke and that awful chant to cut through it *Manila Dance has ants in her*

Me and the dog run into the house. He must have run under a bed, but I go straight to the piano and snatch all Ben's pictures off, the one in his football uniform and holding his helmet, his graduation picture and the other one of him when he joined up the Army, so smart looking and beautiful. Then I grab the wedding picture of me and Hank and my coin purse with all my money. I pull off my green apron and make a bag of it and throw the picture in and I see I got room for the pictures of Will and Archie when they was little, before Ben came along. I tie it all up quick and make a run for the kitchen and the back door. I can see flames in the service porch and burnt my hand on the back doorknob and I could see the wringer washing machine starting to pop and crackle with the heat, so I run back to Ben's bedroom, but the window is locked. I break it with my elbow and throw my pictures out and call for the dog and he comes bounding and we leap out, me getting a long jagged cut down my leg which I don't notice just then because I hear sirens coming from all directions, blasting and blaring through the smoke. By the time me and the dog have got to the street, the fire department has got their hoses pumping and spraying the house and drowning the yard, fighting their way in the front door through the smoke. I stay as close by the house as they'll let me. I see the blood pouring out my leg. I kneel there and hold my dog and my pictures and I think: this is how it was in my dream, the smoke and ash and soot and blood, the mud, even, of Manila Bay.

Me and the dog have to stay with Will and Mrs. Will and their three children that night and Archie comes over, growling and snarling about how the police have already caught the little bastards that done it and how Archie is going to see they get their little bastard asses locked up for good and always.

But it didn't happen that way. Me and Will and Archie sat in court and listened to the judge rap them boys' little knuckles a few times and say they was never to come near my place again. Then he turns it on the parents and gives them a lot of ragging about their children being a menace to the public safety and how their children was their responsibility and then he says Case Dismissed. Just then one of the little bastards' fathers stands up and says to the Judge, "While you're at it, Your Honor, why don't you do something about her?" (He points to me.) "I ask you, is she responsible? Is anyone who lives in a fire trap and a pig sty and never comes out, who looses her dog on little children, isn't she a menace to the public safety? That woman is crazy, Your Honor, and a threat to property! She's forcing us all out of the neighborhood! She's crazy and she ought to be locked up for good and always!"

"Stuff it where the sun don't shine!" I yell, but then Will gets hold of my arm and marches me out of the courtroom and tells me for Chrissake to shut up.

He drives me to his house, a new one with a lot of other new ones all around it and skinny little trees in front and a pool out back. We all sit by the pool and drink lemonade. (Mrs. Will don't allow no Coca-Cola in her house. She says it will rot nails and just think what it will do to your teeth and brains.) They say they want me to come and live with them. Which I say no. Then Archie and Mrs. Archie drive up and come out to the pool too. They say: Why don't we get you a nice apartment, Ma? You don't need that big house anymore, living all by yourself. The yard is just too much for you. There's lots of nice apartments in St. Elmo nowadays, new ones. You could have neighbors and live close to shopping and not have Shirley do your shopping for you.

"I never asked Mrs. Will to do nothing for me," I tell them. "She just does it and she won't never take no for an answer. I'm not moving. Hank bought that house and that's where he lived till he died and that's where I'll live till I die."

Will says: "The house is ruint now, Ma."

"It's just blacked up a little from the smoke and the service porch gone, that's all. No more washing machine. I don't wash too much anyway."

Archie says: "Ma, fifty years ago Guadalupe Street might have been a good neighborhood, even twenty or thirty years ago, but it's just not anymore. That man was right, Ma. All the nice people are moving out."

"What do I care? I don't have no dealings with the neighbors and once the foxtails grow back, I don't even have to see them. Why, once them foxtails grow back, I could live next door to the White House and not see President Roosevelt."

"Roosevelt?" says Mrs. Archie with a little gag. "Roosevelt's dead, Mom. Roosevelt's been dead for ten years. Eisenhower's the president now."

"Eisenhower's the general."

They all look from one to the other. They tell me about how the general got to be the President. Then they go back to talking about the apartment I should live in and neighbors and shopping, but I don't have to hear it. I crunch on my ice and it fills up my ears. I drink my lemonade, wishing I had a Coke and wondering how it could be that so much time had passed since they quit delivering the ice and wondering if my refrigerator still worked and how long it would take the foxtails to grow back and if I could bear to sit on the porch till they did.

They all shout and snuffle at me, but the next day I get Mrs. Will to drive me back to my own house. I won't let her come in. I am glad to be rid of her. Of all of them. A week at Will's is like a year and a half anywhere else. Maybe I been there longer than a week. My house still stinks of smoke, but the wet's almost all dried up, everything except the couch and the chair: they are still wet and they are starting to smell. The television set don't work either.

I tell the dog, let's get to work. First thing is to open all the windows and get the smell of battle out. Then I undo the knot on my green apron and take my pictures out and use the apron to give the piano a nice dust up, to get the ash and cinders off. The wood is all buckled up, but I don't play anyhow. It was always Ben like to thump the piano and grin at Connie Frett while she swooned alongside him. The pictures I left on the piano, they got wet, but not burnt and that's all I really care about anyway.

First I put my wedding picture back up and then I put the one of Will and Archie when they was little. I look at it. I move it so it sits between the one of Will and Mrs. Will, and their family and the one of Archie and Mrs. Archie and their family. Look at that, will you? Will and Archie are getting old! I wonder why I never noticed it in the flesh. Then I say to myself: Manila, it's because you never much look at them in the flesh. But I think on them now, think on them hard, on what they look like now. Will's hair is all pepper and salt and he's got one more chin than God gave him. Archie's hair clings alongside his ears, but it has deserted the top of his head and Archie has a paunch. Will and Archie never was no beauties (and their children ditto and their wives the same), but I had never before noticed that they are getting old.

I reach down and pick up Ben's pictures and set them on the piano, first the football one and then high school graduation and then Ben in his uniform. I touch his beautiful young face. Ben will never grow old, Ben will never be bald or have a paunch or gray hair. Everyone else will change, but not Ben. I pick up the uniform picture and press it to me, but I have to sit down at the piano bench because I get dizzy when I think how it's been ten years since Roosevelt died, since all the boys come home. I get weak when I think how pretty soon everyone will forget all about the boys that didn't come home. No one will remember them. They won't have no children to look like them. The dead don't have no law offices with their names on shingles, don't have their pictures in the paper cutting ribbons for new stores. The boys that didn't come home don't have friends and families and boys of their own who will go to high school and court girls in yellow cotton dresses with gardenias in their hair. Ben won't have none of that. Ever. I hold Ben's picture but I won't cry because I have accepted his death and God's will. I hear a voice come into my ear, steady as the drone of a gnat. *Ben has you, Manila. You're all Ben's got, Manila. Ben and you will live in this house till you die.* I start to cry then and the dog comes over and rubs against my bandaged leg. He thinks I am crying for Ben's death, but I have accepted Ben's death. I am crying because Ben won't have no life. I am crying because I am all the life Ben has and he deserves better than me. I am crying because I know when I die, Ben will die too. He will stay forever young and beautiful and die when I do and no one will ever know he once lived. No one will remember how he filled my arms with his baby body, how he said ho ho ho in the bathwater and Boo at Halloween, that he brought in the newspaper or teased me for the cherries on my hat, that he grinned at Connie Frett while he sat on this piano bench. I slide to the floor with the dog. I cry into his dog smell and promise Ben that when I die they'll put Ben's name on the stone too. Ben don't have no stone in St. Elmo. Ben's buried in the Philippines, but he won't die till I do. Ben Dance 1923–1945, Manila Dance, 1898 to whenever she dies. Ben and Manila, they died together, knee deep in the mud and blood and smoke and stink of battle, the last battle of Manila, the one they fought in St. Elmo, California.

The dog died first. He was old and he just went peaceful in his sleep, but I couldn't lift him so I waited until Mrs. Will come with my groceries and then I told her the dog died and she said she would call Will at the Home Center.

"The what?" I say.

"Sit down, Mom, and relax and I'll make you a cup of coffee." While she's making the coffee, she goes on about how there ain't no Feed and Seed anymore, but the St. Elmo Home Center which carries everything for the Do-It-Yourselfer. She leaves me in the kitchen with the coffee and I hear her go into the living room and dial the phone and tell Will how he better bring the Home Center truck for the dog, how he better do it fast because she don't know exactly when the dog died. Then she waits for a bit and adds that I might go round the bend if I see the Humane Society truck. I wonder what bend she's talking about since I never leave this house.

Mrs. Will comes back in the kitchen and pours herself a cup of coffee and sits at the table with me and starts to gab like she always does about her kids and what fine things they're doing. Like I could care. I can't even keep their names straight, or which one's got foil all over his teeth and which ones don't. I am wondering what I will do without that old dog. I never liked him and he was mangy and ugly, but we got on and he was a good watch dog. He always heard the kids nosing about the place and he'd snarl and take after them till he got too old. He was mangy, but he was useful. And in the middle of my thinking about the dog, I hear Mrs. Will say something about Connie.

"Connie? Connie Frett? Ben's girlfriend?"

"Connie Kehoe, Mom. She came into the Home Center the other day with her husband and we had a real nice chat. She's got three kids now, a boy and two little girls. Mike's going to relight the kitchen for her, fluorescent light, the latest thing, and they've just poured a new patio too.

"Connie asked after you, Mom. She was real concerned, you living here all by yourself in this bad neighborhood. She said she read in the newspaper about the fire. I told her how we've been trying to get you to move for years now and how stubborn you are." Mrs. Will stopped there like I am supposed to laugh or apologize or say how nice that was. I wipe my nose with my hand. "Connie says she keeps meaning to come over and see you one day, but with all those kids, she just can't—"

"I don't want to see her or no one. You tell her. You tell her she better not come around Guadalupe Street, not her, or no one else. Bad enough I have to jaw and pass the time of day with the meter reader and the mailman, though I don't get no mail no more, just stuff for occupant. I don't even get no bills anymore, come to think of it. I can't remember the last time I got a bill or anything with my real name on it. Manila Dance. I miss the ice man."

Mrs. Will pats my hand and says that was because all my bills now went to Will and Archie and they pay them and wasn't I lucky to have two such fine sons.

"I got three sons," I tell her. "Three and don't you forget it. Don't none of you forget Ben just because he's dead and you're not."

"I didn't mean it like that, Mom. I'm sure if Ben had lived—"

But I get up and go to the fridge for a Coke because I can't stand to hear it from her lips, what Ben might have done if he'd lived. He didn't live. He didn't grow old and fat like Will or fat and bald like Archie. Ben died in Manila Bay. Ben lives in Manila Dance. And then I heard Connie Frett's voice float back to me, past all the years and foxtails, *I guess Ben is all yours now, Manila.* And I thought: she knew it, even then, that little slut of a girl, she knew what would happen to Ben and I did not.

I go to the sink and wash my face and Mrs. Will says she's real sorry about the dog.

Then one day in the spring, they all come over, all the grandchildren and Will and Archie and their wives all dressed up and they brung me a cake and a puppy and told me Happy Birthday. They told me I was sixty and they got me this dog for my birthday. They said his name was Lucky.

I hated the little bastard. He peed on everything and got under my feet and was always climbing up on the bed like it was his. I kicked him off, but he always come back and pretty soon I got so's I couldn't remember the other dog that much and I sort of liked this frisky one, but I told him he wasn't getting nothing special from me and he'd have to earn his keep just like the old one done.

One morning I wake up to hear him barking like a sonofabitch. I put on my robe and open the door so he can go out and pee, but he tears up through the foxtails and then I hear an "Ooof! Ouch! Help! Call off this damn dog! Ow!"

I wait a little, maybe count to ten. Maybe twelve. Then I call the dog off. I go out to this bimbo and ask him what he's doing in my yard. He points to the sign he has just hammered in amongst the foxtails, just about buried in foxtails and right next to the fence. It says:

PUBLIC NOTICE

These premises constitute a public hazard. They will be cleared within thirty (30) days of the date hereon in accordance with Civic Code #452-12-J, Article 5. The owners of title shall clear said property or be fined appropriate to Property Code 21569.

I say: "What the hell does that mean?"
He says: "It means you clean up this pigsty, lady, or they're going to cart you off to the funny farm."
I make like I am going to let go of the dog. He leaves.
Archie come over that night and he says the sign don't mean that exactly. Archie says the City of St. Elmo was very concerned for the fire hazard my house and yard presented. I said there wouldn't be no fire, nor no hazard as long as no bastard brats torched my place, but Archie says that's all five years ago now and that this summer's been especially hot and dry and that the city was afraid that if a passer-by flicked his cigarette into my foxtails, the whole neighborhood would go up in flames. He said of course I wouldn't want that on my conscience.
I said I didn't give a good goddamn. I didn't know any of my neighbors and anyway, they was all a long ways from my house. "Least I got a real yard," I told Archie. "One half acre of real yard, not like that postage stamp with a pool you call your back yard."
Archie started to go on about the city some more, but I watch the electric light gleaming off the top of his head. He don't have no hair there at all anymore. Is Archie just about the same age Hank was when he died? Is he? He don't look like Hank. Hank always had hair. Maybe Archie looks like me,

but I reach up top of my head and I got hair too and then I remember that I don't know what I look like anymore so how could I know who Archie looks like? My face swims up to Archie's for a closer look, but all I can tell for certain is that Archie don't look like Ben. Ben is still twenty-two and in the mud and I start to tell Archie about my old dream, about how it was scaring me now because even though I had accepted Ben's death and God's will, I was scared, too scared to go on with my dream where I have got Ben's shirt unbuttoned, open, but I can't do nothing more. What if I get his shirt off and find him all bloody and blasted? No, God, please God, no, don't let his flesh be shredded before my eyes. What if I get my son's shirt off his shoulders and back and find he don't have no back, no shoulders, no body that's not bloodied into pulp? Oh, Archie, what if the mud turns red? I can't remember where Ben took the bullets, Archie, or how it was he died at all except for Manila Bay and I . . .

"Now, Ma, let me call the doctor, Ma. Please. Better yet, let me take you to the hospital. They can help you, Ma. Really. They can help you get along with other people. Just a little stay at the hospital, that's all you need. Just to get away from this house and stay where the doctors can help you forget the past and get on with your life."

Well what could I do but laugh out loud? I laughed so hard that dog jumped up and waved its little black tail like I was about to throw him a bone and when I was through laughing, I said, "The first person who comes here to cut them weeds gets shot. And the first doctor who comes near me, he gets shot too. My life is getting on just fine, Archie Dance, without no doctors and without no hospitals and your life is getting on too, Archie, and if you once looked in the mirror you'd see it. You're old, Archie. You're old and fat and you won't never be young and beautiful again."

Archie took his hat off the table and jammed it on his bald head. He said: "That's the way it happens to the living, Ma."

I told him to save it for the jury and leave me be.

They come to cut the foxtails and just like I promised, I holler out the window that I have a shotgun and I am about to blow them to bits. I didn't have no gun, but it sounded good.

The guy hollers back that he was leaving, but that he'd be back with a court order signed by my own son, Judge Archibald Dance.

I turned to the little dog and I said, "Just imagine Archie being a judge and never telling me." The little dog looked at me funny and that's when I thought maybe Archie had told me. I went to the piano and asked Ben what he thought of Archie being a judge and Ben give me his old boyish grin and said this was our foxtail foxhole, our fortress and wouldn't no one get in, judge or no judge. I laughed and turned Ben's picture so he could see the TV. We like the game shows and cartoons best of all. I eat my lunch with Sheriff Sam and the Cartoon Corral.

I must have fell asleep because there was something else on the TV, the picture sputtering up and down when I woke to the sound of a knock on my door. The dog woke up too. (He never was as good a watchdog as the old one.) I go to the door and there stands this blonde kid, pink and pale and kind of fat, his blue eyes big with fright. He keeps licking his lips. He says: "I'm Danny Kehoe." He looks over his shoulder. "My mother's down the walk, there, just outside the gate."

I say: "Tell it to the marines. I don't want any."

"My mother, Connie Kehoe, she wants to know if you want me to cut your grass. You talk to her."

He makes like he's going to call her, but I say, real quick, I say, "No, I don't want to see her." I stare at this boy and I can see Connie Frett all over him, but the foxtails are so nice and high that I can't see Connie down at the gate. The boy is thirteen or fourteen, maybe, fat like Connie was when she first set her cap for Ben. I say: "I don't have no grass and I like the foxtails just as they are."

He looks like he wants to run or pee his pants, but he licks his lips again and says, "My mother said I was to do for you whatever might need doing here. She says I'm to do it for you and your boy."

"For Ben?" I say. "For Ben?"

"I don't know his name."

"For Ben," I say again and this time I smile.

Twice a month that boy come. I wouldn't let him touch the foxtails, but he cleared off the tumbleweeds and picked up the trash and cleared away the last of the wreck from the fire, the wringer washer and a mattress I had thrown out too. He said he didn't think there'd be another war and I didn't have to save my tin cans no more and if I got rid of them, maybe I wouldn't have so much mice. He said, if I wanted the mice, he'd leave the cans be. I let him use Ben's little red wagon to gather them cans all up and put them in bags and take them out to the street so the trashmen could come and get them. He said the trash people come Monday on Guadalupe Street and when he come on Saturday, he'd put my trash out. Those Saturdays he didn't come, the trash don't go out. Then one day he shows up hauling a bright trash can, so shiny it makes you blink and he says he got it at the Home Center, that Will give it to him. Connie's boy trimmed back the honeysuckle so it didn't weigh so heavy on the tin roof over the porch, then he put some props alongside the railings and said he would fix the raingutters, but then he looked at them and they were too rotted to fix. He even fixed the window in Ben's room, the one I'd put my elbow through escaping from the fire. I always just stuffed newspapers there to keep out the wind and cold and animals, but he fixed it up with glass and he said Will told him he could have whatever he needed to fix my place up. Danny said since Will was giving away, why not some new raingutters? I said: Why not? Then Danny said: "I'll do the raingutters, Manila, and then I'll trim the foxtails."

While Connie's boy was working I'd remember how Connie used to moon about this yard waiting for Ben to finish his chores so he could take her to the matinee and then out for a soda. When Connie's boy finished up his chores, me and him always had a Coke if it was hot, or coffee if it was cold. He liked his coffee just the way Ben did, with sugar and milk and lots of it. I started having Mrs. Will buy more sugar and milk and asked for some cookies too. Danny said Oreos were his favorite.

One afternoon while we was having coffee, Danny flips on the TV Archie got me after the fire. Danny asks me what's wrong with it. Nothing, I tell him. It works fine. Danny says I'd get a lot more channels if I'd let him put an aerial up, but I didn't know what that was. He said it was no never mind and he'd get it from Will at the Home Center. Even though the next day was Sunday, Danny come back over and he spends the whole afternoon on the roof handing me down wire and calling back and forth while we slid the wire in the window and he used some little pliers to diddle the back of the TV. Then, up he goes again, back on the roof and tells me to holler when the picture is the best. "Just imagine," I said when he come back down, "just imagine all that was going on TV all the time and I never got nothing but Channel 11 and Channel 13."

"Now you can watch the football games, Manila," Danny said, but I told him I hadn't been to a football game since Ben graduated from high school and he said they had them on TV now and you could watch football and not leave the comfort of your own home.

After that, Danny'd come earlier and stay later and watch the football games with me. He explained the game. I didn't get it, but I pretended I did. I asked a lot of questions because it was so nice to hear a boy talk about football like Ben used to do. One day Danny asked me why I didn't get some beer so I put it on my list for Mrs. Will and she near puked when she read it. Next thing I know I got Archie in my living room ragging on me about buying beer for minors.

"There's no minors in St. Elmo," I tell him. "St. Elmo's a railroad town."

Archie's face rumples up like a baked potato. "Ma," he says, "we are all very pleased at what Danny Kehoe has been able to do for you. We are very pleased that you will let him help out around here and you ought to know that I have offered both him and Connie money and they won't take it."

"Money for what?"

"There's been a great transformation in you and in this place in the last two years, Ma."

"Years?" I say, "*two years?*"

"But if he is going to ask you to buy beer for him, I must tell him to quit coming, it's against the law and—"

"Don't you dare, Archie Dance! Don't you dare! What's it to you, Mr. Judge Dance, if I have a couple of beers? I'm not buying it for Danny. I'm buying it for me and Ben. We like a beer now and then and who are you to tell us we can't have one?"

So a six pack of beer come with the groceries, but only once a month. Mrs. Will said that was all I needed. I didn't like the beer as much as I like Coke, but it was nice to have a beer with Danny while we watched football after he done the chores. He even painted the porch and the smell come all over the house. I breathed it in. Ben painted the porch once, just before he joined up.

One afternoon I hear a knock and I go to the door and it's Danny and he's wearing a gorilla mask. Scared the living Be-Jesus out of me. He has a sack of candy in his hand. "It's Halloween, Manila," says Danny, lifting his mask. "And I think I'll just sit here this year and hand out the candy and keep trouble away. We don't want any trouble like last year when those kids broke your window, do we?"

"There's no beer, Danny," I tell him. "We drunk it all up."

"Well, I'll stay here and hold down the fort and you go to Garcia's and get us a six pack."

"I couldn't."

"Sure you could, Manila. Garcia's store is just down the street three blocks. This side. You can't miss it."

"No." I start to back away, but Danny comes up to me and I see that he's taller than me. I come to the same place on Danny that I used to come to on Ben. Danny is still pink and blonde like Connie but he's not fat anymore. He's tall.

He takes my old coat off the hook and helps me into it.

"What's Halloween without a few beers, Manila? Don't worry, I'll fight off the troops."

That's what I said to Garcia (or whoever it was behind the till). I said: What's Halloween without a few beers? And Garcia says *Si Si* and rolled his eyes toward heaven. He says: Very happy to help you, Manila and I say: How'd you know my name? And he says: Everyone knows you, Manila. You are the crazy lady of Guadalupe Street. Crazy Manila, our lady of Guadalupe.

I squint at Garcia and at one or two others squatting on their haunches near the counter. I say: Boo!

We had a good laugh over that and I go back with the beer. When the kids come to the door, I say: Boo! while Danny stands behind me in his gorilla mask handing out the candy and them kids don't know whether to laugh or run or blubber. We don't get no little kids. Just big ones and when Danny tells them no funny stuff this year, they look at one another and say: Funny stuff? Funny stuff? Oh, I laughed over and over and when Danny left, I told him that was the best Halloween since Ben was a pirate and I was sorry it wouldn't come around again for another year.

After that I went to Garcia's pretty often for beer and maybe twice a week besides, just to get some little thing, some animal crackers for the dog and a box of Cheez-its for me, a bar of Palmolive. Mrs. Will would ask where I got these little things when she brung my regular groceries and I told her I bought them myself. She said that was very good. She said Danny and Garcia were good for me. She said I was getting better. I told her I wasn't sick.

Still, I might have been getting better, but it certainly didn't have nothing to do with Danny or Garcia. It was my dream that was making me happy. I didn't have the dream so often now, but when I did, I could peel Ben's shirt from his shoulders, from his arms, and back and not find no blood nor blasted flesh. He hadn't been shot to bits anywhere. He was still whole and perfect. I washed the mud off him and pulled him into my arms and put his head against my shoulder and held him, my cheek pressed close to his hair, and sang. And sometimes, even though the mud stayed in my dream, the battle didn't. All I could hear was myself singing, no shriek and blast, no groans of others dying, no shot and shell, just my singing to Ben. And when I'd wake, I'd go in to the piano and look at Ben and it made me happy to know that he hadn't been bloodied up and blown apart, that he was still perfect and young and nothing could ever touch him. And I was happy for me too because me and Ben, we had a good life together and he needed me and I was always here for him.

Danny asked me about him once and I showed him Ben's picture on the piano. Danny said Connie told him they'd been friends in high school. "You wouldn't recognize the place anymore, Manila."

"What place?" I asked, all ready to tell him more about Ben.

"St. Elmo High. They got a new auditorium now and a Senior Quad and a new cafeteria and they're fixing up the boys' gym with a new wing. Mom says she doesn't recognize it, except for some of the old teachers." He winks at me. "Some of them are just about as old as you can get and still draw breath."

"You think they might remember Ben?"

"Hell, Manila, they remember Moses. Anyway, you ought to come to my graduation and see the old place."

"I haven't been to a graduation since Ben's."

"Then you come to mine. I'll see you get an invite."

I went to the St. Elmo High graduation, but not because of Danny. One of Archie's boys was Valedictorian of the Class of 1965. I listened to the speeches, but I was looking for Danny amongst the 700 up there. "Seven hundred," I said to Mrs. Archie. "Just imagine St. Elmo High so big they have 700 graduates."

"There's two other high schools too, you know, Mom," she whispers.

"There is? They got 700 too?"

"Hush, Mom. Here comes Ronald. It's Ronald's turn to speak."

I tried to remember how many had graduated with me, but I couldn't even remember my graduating at all. But Ben's, I could remember that. How many graduated with the Class of 1942? They didn't have no auditorium in those days. They had the graduation on the grass out front of the school. Hotter than hell it was. I remember the cherries on my hat clacking when I clapped for the speeches they give, lots of talk about the vile Japs who snuck up and bombed Pearl Harbor and who beat General MacArthur out of the Philippines and everyone that day was talking about the war and the great destiny these boys was going off to and how they would fight in the name of freedom and give their lives and sacred honor and I clapped like everyone else. But I didn't believe it. I didn't believe a word of it. I didn't believe it for a minute that Ben would die in the mud at Manila. Not Ben Dance. Ben's life lay all before him. *Yes, all three years of it.*

"Stop it, Mom. Stop. Archie, do something with her."

"Hand me a handkerchief. Hush, Ma. We want to hear Ronald. Hush, dammit, Ma, hush!"

"Archie, do something!"

The next thing I know we are out of the auditorium and standing by a drinking fountain and Archie wets down the handkerchief and mops my face and says he knew they shouldn't have brung me.

There was a war after Danny's graduation too. Sometimes I watched it on TV now that I get a lot of stations. Danny joined up the Army, but he told me not to worry. He said they would send him to Germany where he could drink all the beer he wanted. I told him Germany was the enemy, same as the Japs. Danny said, "Not this time, Manila. The Germans and Japs are our friends now."

"Not my friends."

"It's the gooks who are the enemy now. Gooks for enemies. Gooks for allies. Can't tell the difference anymore."

"Where are they fighting?"

"In Vietnam."

"Is that close to Manila?"

"Hell no, you don't have to worry. You're safe here in St. Elmo."

They sent Danny to Manila and he sent me a lot of postcards which I taped to the piano. He wrote on them he thought I'd like to see the city I was named for. It looked pretty and green and tropical and moist and not at all like St. Elmo which is dry and dusty and brown except for two weeks in the winter when it floods.

St. Elmo is dry and dusty and brown as leather, I wrote in my first letter in a thousand years. I didn't have no pen, just the stub of a pencil I use for my grocery list and the paper Mrs. Will leaves me to write on. I found an envelope back of my bureau and I wrote out Danny's name and his address which was just a lot of numbers mainly. Course I don't have no stamps so I put on my coat to walk to the post office, the one near my house, or what I remember near my house, but there was a parking lot and a Sav-On drug there and no one ever heard of a post office. I thought I probably turned the wrong way and I would just go back, but I turned the wrong way again, and maybe again after that, because I couldn't find my house, couldn't find nothing, only the Dairy Queen and 7-11, the Lotus Blossom and Jolly Burger and Quik Photo and cars. Lots of cars. Cars everywhere. How could St. Elmo be so big and bright and ugly and have so much noise? No more oleanders and the palms all so tall I couldn't see the tops. I hang onto my letter like it is Danny's hand, but there is no one to lead me and I am loster and loster in St. Elmo where I have lived my whole life.

A girl finds me in the dark, a Jap girl wearing a shirt that says Lotus Blossom and she wants to know what I am doing by the dumpster where it is so dark and cold. I push my face into the dark of my hands till my hands light up bright with flashing lights whirling around, red and blue and dizzy. A policeman comes up. I hear leather creak and squeal when he kneels down, before I hear his voice asking where I live. He takes hold my hand, the one with the letter, but I tell him that letter is mine and he gives me back my hand and takes my elbow to stand me up. Where do you live, he says again and again. Where do you live, old lady? I tell him I am our crazy lady of Guadalupe Street. He puts me in the car where there is a lot of squawking and squealing. He drives to the Dairy Queen and tells me to wait. He comes back with a hamburger in a little white bag and a Coke. I drink the Coke all up before we get to the police station.

Pretty soon I see Archie. All the police say: Sorry, Your Honor, we didn't know she was your mother.

Archie says: I commend you all for the care you've taken of her.

The police all seem to line up and open doors for us as bald Archie leads me out to his big black car. He says he is taking me home with him. He says he has moved and how he lives up in the hills and out of the smog. I pull my coat around me. "I don't care where you live now," I tell him. "I don't want to go home with you. I want to go home with me. Take me to my house. And mail this letter on the way."

"Who could you be writing to, Ma?"

"I have a friend in Manila," I tell him. "That's where Ben died, you know."

"I know Ben died, Ma, but you don't."

I am glad to see he turns the car around, but I don't say nothing more till we get to my house and the little dog is glad to see me. Archie walks in and turns on all the lights. Then he says: "You ever pull a stunt like that again, Ma, and I swear, I'll have you committed. I should have had you committed years and years ago. This is a warning. You better heed me or it's the state hospital for you. The loony bin, Ma. You understand? The funny farm."

After that I put stamps on my shopping list for Mrs. Will. I quit going to Garcia's. (Though one New Year's Garcia brung me some tamales which I thanked him for, but they were too weird for me. I fed them to the dog who farted all night.) The foxtails started growing back up and I thought: I'll just wait for Danny to get back from Manila before I cut them, but a long time must have passed because they grew up over the fence again and Will and Archie come over with their boys and they spend one whole day cutting them down and not taking no for an answer. The paint chipped off the porch Danny painted and the raingutter fell off again and when Halloween came around, I didn't say Boo to no one. I sat in the dark, in the corner between the piano and the wall, holding my picture of Ben and hoping them kids would go away and not set fire to my house again.

I waited for the mailman to bring me some more postcards from Manila, but Danny didn't send no more. One or two letters, scribbled so bad it looked like I might have wrote them. No pictures. In my letter I said: Please send me some more picture postcards for my piano. Then Danny wrote me a letter. He said there wasn't no postcards where he was now, only heat and rain and mud.

"Mud?" I said to the dog. "Mud?" I held on to the porch rail and stood up slow. *Mud?* I felt my heart quicken and thud in my breast, hard thuds like dirt clods flying and spraying in my eyes and mouth. I got to my bed and the dog followed and loaded his old bones on the bed at my feet to keep them warm, but the rest of me was cold. I lay there and I wondered if I was going to die. I prayed to God I wouldn't die, prayed not for me, but for Ben. Ben was still too young to die and I am all that keeps him alive. Keeping him alive is my life, but it's hard on you, this living for and loving the dead, it's hard, harder because you can't love death. You have to hate the death while you love the dead and keeping them alive is hard for an old woman like me. I tried to think how old I was, but give it up and went back to praying, praying like hell that God would spare me and God would spare Danny too because I knew I didn't have enough life in me to go on living for Ben and Danny too.

The next morning I was real glad to find myself alive. The dog and me, just as we were, me still dressed, so that saved time and I got up and made us some coffee and told the dog it was going to be a hot one today. We go out on our porch, but before noon the smog comes creeping up underneath the tin roof and the honeysuckle vine and sticking its little yellow fingers in my eyes. I have to go inside and watch Sesame Street till it cools off, but it don't seem to. I take the dog back out and hose him down and hose me down too and then we drip dry on the porch till it was time for cartoons and a couple Cokes. After cartoons it's the news. I listen for word of Manila Bay, but there's nothing, so I turned off the TV and said to the dog: Suppertime. He don't even get up and pad after me. He is getting real old.

I go into the kitchen, but it's too hot to fire up the stove, even for a can of beans, so I get another Coke out of the fridge and some ice and an extra ice cube for the dog. I run ice over my face and neck and then drop it in my glass, pour the Coke and I'm taking the dog's ice in to him when I hear the gate squeal. The dog starts up. We go to the screen door and watch the foxtails swish and whisper like they do when so much as a cat prowls through them, but this is no cat. I can see a body moving through them. It's too late for the mailman and then I see it's a woman's body, but it's not Mrs. Will or Mrs. Archie because the dog starts to growl. I squint into the sun, lowering itself into the foxtails, lighting them up like a thousand torches, flickering in the desert wind. And then I see it's Connie Frett. Connie Frett or someone like her.

Someone pink and puffy and fat. No yellow dress. No gardenia in the hair. The hair is gray and short and the woman is gray and short and fat, but underneath all that I know it's Connie Frett, though she don't say anything. She just comes up to the porch and we sit down together. I ask her the question, the one I wanted to ask all those years ago before her yellow dress disappeared up the walk. "Did you make love with him, Connie?" I ask. "Did he have that much? Did he know a girl's love?"

"Yes. He had that much. I loved him."

"I didn't mean what I said, Connie, about your not deserving him. Calling you a slut. I don't know why I said such a mean thing. I'm sorry. I apologize." I start to wonder how long ago it was, but Connie lowers her head into my lap and I know it doesn't matter, the years, the time. There isn't any years or time, there's only living and dying and laughing and grieving and you keep doing them over and over like the seasons. "You keep living and dying and laughing and grieving," I tell Connie, "but the one thing you don't do, not more than once anyway, is forget. If you once forget, then you have forgot forever and for all time."

"He's only missing in action, Manila. He might come back. Don't you think?" Connie raises up her fat, tear-stained face, the lips chewed raw with grief. "Of course."

"He might," I say. "There might be someone we don't know about, Connie, someone who finds him in the mud, lying there, face down in the mud and maybe, probably, they turn him over. They bathe his face and eyes and unbutton his shirt and wash the mud off his chest and his shoulders and they find he isn't bloody or mangled at all. Just stunned, Connie. That's all. He's just stunned and he's not dead. Someone will touch his eyes, kiss them, and he'll open his eyes and smile, Connie."

"Yes," says Connie, laying her graying head back in my lap. "He's stunned and separated from the rest of his unit, but he's not dead, is he, Manila?"

"No."

"Tell me again, Manila. Tell me how it happens."

I stroke her hair and back. My grief is not my own anymore. I hold her and tell her over and over about the battle for Manila and the mud and finding the body and how someone will lift Danny from the mud, bathe his face, and find he isn't bloody in the least, just muddy and how when the mud is washed off, he is still perfect and young and beautiful. I tell how she will pull him into her arms and hold him against her shoulder, sing maybe. I tell how he will smile, how he will know the touch even if he don't know the person. I hold Connie Frett and I tell her over and over and we stay on the porch till it's long past dark and the dry red moon rises slow in the night sky.

R for Rosemary
GERALD STERN

I heard a fluttering—just inside the door
of my *casita*; it was inside a bush,
a kind of pine, a kind of blue rosemary,
and since I saw two doves wandering under
my window yesterday and over my stones
I thought there had to be a mourning dove—
or two of them—puffed up and asleep,
living inside that bush, one of them frightened
by my loud steps. But I will know them later
by their sweet smell, whether they stretch their necks
or stick their chests out, getting ready to soar,
for they have made the mistake of living in rosemary
and they are spies for now and carry the stench
of betrayal on them. I could have reached inside
and heard them scream and watched the bushes shudder
with terror, but I let them go. More
and more I do that. Why did I wait so long
to let them have their darkness? I rub the leaves
under my chin and over my wrists. I know
the smell will last. I crawl up under my window
and try my keys. I'll have to pull the blinds
and close the curtains, those doves are so rotten; they are
such eavesdroppers. We listen to each other
through the glass, we preen in our mirrors; their cooing
is absurd, it is the noisy sound
of Codex International; I know
the tapping, I know the turning of the head;
and it is odd to watch them stretch a wire
between their beaks and under my windowsill,
then walk off unaffected. I put powder
over my shoes. I know that trick. I called it
blue rosemary because of the flowers, I should have
called it lavender; it was my color

when I was a boy; there were *two* doves; we wandered
from bush to bush, it was a disease of the spine
that took the other one; she was a dove. If I
spend year after year explaining it is because
I was left without her. I have a sprig
of the dried-up plant, the leaves and the flowers have mixed,
the color is greenish-blue, almost an olive;
it has some weight, the woody part is heavy,
it is itself a kind of flattened tree;
it is a bookmark; it is a perfumed wing.

The Nineties

Saul and Patsy Are Pregnant

CHARLES BAXTER

A smell of spilled gasoline: when Saul opened his eyes, he was still strapped in behind his lap-and-shoulder belt, but the car he sat in was upside down and in a field of some sort. The Chevy's headlights illuminated a sky of dirt, and, in the distance, a tree growing downward from that same sky. Perhaps he had awakened out of sleep into another dream. "Patsy?" he said, turning with difficulty toward his wife, strapped in on the passenger side, her hair hanging down from her scalp, but, from Saul's perspective, standing up. She was still sleeping; she was always a sound sleeper; she could sleep upside down and was doing so now. The car's radio was playing Ray Charles's "Unchain My Heart," and Saul said, "You know, I've always liked that song." His voice was thick from beer and cigarettes, and he knew from the smell of the beer that this was no dream because he had never been able to imagine concrete details like that. No: he had fallen asleep at the wheel, driven off the road, and rolled the car. Here he was now. A thought passed through him, in an unpleasant slow-motion way, that the car was tilted and that the ignition was still on; he switched it off and felt intelligent for three seconds, until the lap belt began to hurt him and he felt stupid again. No ignition, no Ray Charles. His mind, often anxiety prone, was moving slowly down a dark narrow alleyway cluttered with alcohol, fatigue, and the first onset of shock. Probably the car would blow up, and the only satisfaction his mother would receive from this accident would come years from now, when she would tell people, when they were all through reminiscing about Saul, "I *told* him not to drink. I told him about drinking and driving. But he never listened to me. Never."

"Patsy." He reached out and gave her a little shake.

"What?"

"Wake up. I rolled the car. Patsy, we've got to get out of here."

"Why?"

"Because we have to. Patsy, we're not at home. We're in the car. And we're upside down. Come on, honey, wake up. Please. This is serious."

"I am awake." She blinked, twisted her head, then looked calm. Her opal earring glittered in the light of the dashboard. The earring made Saul think of stability and a possible future life, if only he would normalize himself. Patsy smiled. Saul thought that this smile had something to do with guardian angels who, judging from the evidence, flew invisibly around her head, beaming down benevolence. "Well," she said, turning to look at him carefully, "are you all right?"

"Yes, yes. I'm not hurt at all."

"Good. Well. Neither am I." She reached up for the ceiling. "This isn't fun. Did *you* do this, Saul?"

"Yes, I did. How do we get out of here?"

"Let's see," she said, speaking calmly, in her usual tone. "What I think you do is, you release your seat belt, stick your arms straight up, then lower yourself slowly so you don't break your neck. Then you crawl out the window, the higher one. That would be yours."

"Okay." He held his arm up, then unfastened the clasp and felt himself dropping onto the car's ceiling. He pulled himself toward the side window. When he was outside, he leaned over, back in, and extended his hand to Patsy to help her out.

As she was emerging through the window, she was smiling. "Haven't you ever rolled a car before, Saul? I have. Or one of my boyfriends did, years ago." She was breathing rapidly. She dragged herself out, dusted her jeans, and strolled a few feet beyond the car's tire tracks in the mud, as if nothing much had happened. "Beautiful night," she said. "Look at those stars."

"Jeez, Patsy," Saul said, jumping down close to where she stood, "this is no time for being cosmic." Then he gazed up. She was right: the sky was pillowed with stars. She took his hand.

"Are you really okay?" she asked. "My God, feel that. You're shaking like a leaf. You must be in shock." She wrapped her arms around him and held him for half a minute. "There," she said, "now that's better."

"We could have died," Saul said, his mouth dry.

"But we didn't."

"We *could* have."

"All right. Yes. I know. You can die in your sleep. You can die watching television." She watched him in the dark. "I wish I had been driving. It's so warm, a spring night, I think I would have been singing along to the radio. 'Unchain My Heart'—I would have been singing along to Ray Charles and we'd be home by now." She leaned over. "Smell the soil? It's loamy. You know, Saul, you should turn the car's headlights off."

"Patsy, the car is *wrecked*! Look at it."

"Don't be silly." She studied the car with equanimity, one hand raised to her face, the other hand cradling her elbow. Patsy's equanimity was otherworldly and constant. Her psychic economy, combined with her beauty and persistent unexplainable interest in Saul, was the cause of his love for her; he loved her desperately and addictively. He had loved her this way before they were married, and it was still the same now. "Saul, that car is fine. We might be driving it tomorrow. The roof will have a dent, that's all. The car turned over slowly and softly. It's hardly hurt. What we have to do now is get to a house and call someone to help us. We could walk across this field, or we could just take the road back to Mad Dog's." Mad Dog was the host of the party they had come from. He was a high school gym teacher whose real name was Howard Bettermine. He looked, in fact, like a dog, but not a mad dog, as he thought, but a healthy and sober golden retriever.

"Patsy, I can't think. My brain has seized up."

"Well," she said, taking his hand, "I happen to like these stars, and that looks like a nice field, and I'd rather stay away from highway fourteen this time of night, what with the drunks on the road, and all." She gave him a tug on his sleeve, and he almost fell. "There you are," she said. "Come on."

As Saul walked across the field, hearing the slurp of his shoes in the spring mud, he saw the red blinking light of a radio tower in the distance, the only remotely friendly sight anywhere beneath the horizon. The fact that he was here at all was a sign, he thought, that his life was disordered, abandoned to chaos among Midwesterners, connoisseurs of violence and piety. He smelled manure, and somewhere behind him he thought he heard the predatory wing of a bat or an owl.

Sick of cities, Saul had come to the Midwest two years before from Baltimore as a high school history teacher, believing that he was a missionary of some new kind, bringing education and the higher enlightenments to rural, benighted adolescents, but somehow the conversion had gone the other way, and now he was acting like them: getting drunk, falling asleep, rolling his car. It was the sort of accident Christians had. He felt obscurely that he had given up personal complexity and become simple. He was like those girls who worked in the drugstore arranging greeting cards. They were so straightforward that two seconds before they did anything, like give change, you could see every gesture coming. He was becoming like that. As a personality, Saul had once prided himself on being interesting, almost byzantine, a challenge to any therapist. But he had lately joined the school bowling league and couldn't seem to concentrate on Schopenhauer on those days when, at odds and ashamed of himself, he took the battered Signet Classic down from the shelf and glowered at the incomprehensible lines he had highlighted with yellow magic marker in college. When he did understand, the philosopher no longer seemed profound, but merely a disappointed idealist with a bad prose style.

"Saul?"

"What?"

"I've been talking to you. Didn't you hear me?"

"Guess not. I was lost in thought." He stumbled against a bush. He couldn't see much, and he reached out for Patsy's hand. "I was thinking about girls in drugstores and Schopenhauer and the reasons why we ever came to this place."

"Oh. That. If you had been listening to me, you wouldn't have stumbled into that bush. That's what I was warning you about."

"Thanks. Where are we?"

"We're going down into this little gully, and when we get up on the other side, we'll be right near that farmhouse. What's the matter?"

He turned around and saw, across the field, the headlights of his car shining on the upturned dirt; he saw the Chevy's four tires facing the air; and he thought of his new jovial recklessness and of how he had almost killed himself and his wife. He said nothing because he was beginning to feel soul-sick, a state of spiritual dizziness. He was possessed by disequilibrium; he felt the urge to giggle, and was horrified by himself. He had a sudden marionette feeling.

"Saul! You're drifting off again. What is it this time?"

"Puppets."

"Puppets?"

"Yeah. You know: the way they don't have a center of gravity. The way they look. . . ."

"Watch out for that stump."

He saw it in time to avoid it. "Patsy, how do you live in the world? This is a serious question."

"Stop it, Saul. You've been to a party. You're tired. Don't get metaphysical. It's two in the morning. You live in the world by knocking on the door of that farmhouse, that's what you do. You ring the doorbell."

They walked up past a shed whose flaking red door was hanging open, and they crossed the pitted driveway onto a small front yard with an evenly mowed lawn. A tire swing, pendulating slowly, hung down from a tree branch. Saul couldn't see much of the house in the dark, but as they crossed the driveway, kicking a few stones, they heard the bark of a dog from inside the house, a low bark from a big dog: a farm dog.

"Anti-Semites," Saul said.

"Just ring the bell."

After a moment, the porch light went on, yellow, probably a

bug light, Saul thought; and then under the oddly colored glare a very young woman appeared, pale blond hair and skin, very pretty, but under the effect of the bulb, looking a bit jaundiced. With her fists she was rubbing her eyes with sleepiness. She wore a bathrobe decorated with huge blue flowers. Saul and Patsy explained themselves and their predicament—Saul was sure he had seen this young woman before—and she invited them in to use the phone. When they entered, the dog—old, with a gray muzzle—growled from under a living room table but did not bother to get up. After Patsy and the woman, whose name was Anne, began talking, it developed that they had met before in the insurance office where Patsy worked as a secretary. They leaned toward each other. Their voices quickly rose in the transfiguration of friendliness as they disappeared into the kitchen. They seemed suddenly chipper and cheery to Saul, as if a new party had started. He had the impression that women enjoyed being friendly, whereas for men it was an effort; at least it was an effort for *him*. He heard Patsy dialing a number on a rotary phone, laughing and whispering as she did so.

He was left alone in the living room. Having nothing else to do, he looked around: high ceilings and elaborate wainscoting, lamps, table, rug, dog, calendar, the usual crucifix on the wall above the TV. There was something about the room that bothered him, and it took a moment before he knew what it was. It felt like a museum of earlier American feelings. Not a single ironic sentence had ever been spoken here. Everything in the room was sincere, everything except himself. In the midst of all this Midwestern earnestness, he was the one thing wrong. What was he doing here? What was he doing anywhere? He was accustomed to asking himself such questions.

"Mr. Bernstein?"

Saul turned around and saw the man of the house, who at first glance still seemed to be a boy, standing at the bottom of the stairs. He had his arms crossed, and he wore a sleepy but alert look on his face. He had on boxer shorts and a T-shirt, and Saul recognized, underneath the brown hair and the beard, a student from last year, Emory . . . something. Emory McPhee. That was it. A good-looking, solid kid. He had married this woman, Anne, last year, both of them barely eighteen years old, and moved out here. That was it. That was who they were. Saul had heard that Emory had become a housepainter.

"Emory," Saul said. The boy was stocky—he had played varsity football starting in his sophomore year—and he looked at Saul now with pleased curiosity. "Emory, my wife and I have had an accident, over there, on the other side of your field."

"What kind of accident, Mr. Bernstein?"

"We drove off the road." Saul waited, his hands in his pockets. Then he said the rest of it. "The car turned over on us."

"Wow," Emory said. "You're lucky you weren't hurt. That's amazing. Good thing it wasn't worse."

"Well, yes, but the car was going slow." Saul always sounded stupid to himself late at night. The boy's bland blue-eyed gaze stayed on him now, not moving, genial but inquisitorial, and Saul thought of all the people who had hated school, never liked even a minute of it, and had had a low-level suspicion toward teachers for the rest of their lives. They voted down millages. They didn't even like to buy pencils.

"How did you go off the road?"

"I fell asleep, Emory. We'd been to a party and I fell asleep at the wheel. Never happened to me before."

"Wow," Emory said again, but slowly this time, with no real surprise in his voice. He shrugged his shoulders, then bent down as if he were doing calisthenics. Saul knew that his own breath smelled of beer, so there was no point in going into that. "Do you want a cup of coffee? I'd offer you a beer, but we don't have it."

Saul tried to smile, an effort. "I don't think so, Emory, not tonight." He looked down at the floor, at his socks—he had taken off his muddy shoes—and saw an ashtray filled with cigarette butts. "But I would like a cigarette, if you could spare one."

"Sure." The boy reached down and offered the pack in

Saul's direction. "Didn't know you smoked. Didn't know you had any vices at all."

They exchanged a look. "I'm like everybody else," Saul said. "Sometimes the right thing just gets loose from me and I don't do it." He picked up a book of matches. He would have to watch his sentences: that one hadn't made any sense. On the outside of the matchbook was an advertisement.

SECRETS

OF THE

UNIVERSE

*** see inside ***

Saul put the matchbook into his pocket, after lighting up.

"Were you drunk?" the boy said suddenly.

"No, I don't think so."

"Teachers shouldn't drink," Emory said. "That's my belief."

"Well, maybe not."

Saul inhaled from the cigarette, and Emory came closer toward him and sat down on the floor. He gave off the smell of turpentine; he had flecks of white paint in his hair. He rubbed at his beard again. "Do you remember me from school?"

Saul leaned back. He tried to think. "Sure, of course I do. You sat in the back and you played with a ballpoint pen. You used to sketch the other kids in the class. Once when we were doing the First World War, you said it didn't make any sense no matter how much you read about it. I remember your report on the League of Nations. You stared out the window a lot. You sat near Anne in my class and you passed notes to her."

"I didn't think you'd remember that much." Emory whistled toward the dog, who thumped his tail and waddled over toward Emory's lap. "I wasn't very good. I thought it was a waste of time, no offense. I wanted to get married, that's all. I wanted to get married to Anne, and I wanted to be outside, not cooped up, doing something, making a living, earning money. The thing is, I'm different now." He stood up, as if he were about to demonstrate how different he had become or had thought of something important to say.

"How are you different?"

"I'm real happy," Emory said, looking toward the kitchen. "I bet you don't believe that. I bet you think: here's this kid and his wife, out here, ignorant as a couple of plain pigs, and how could they be happy? But it's weird. You can't tell about anything." He was looking away from Saul. "Schools tell you that people like me aren't supposed to be happy or . . . what's that word you used in class all the time? 'Fulfilled'? We're not supposed to be that. But we're doing okay. But then I'm not trying to tell you anything."

"I know, Emory. I know that." Saul raised his hand to his scalp and touched his bald spot.

"Hell," Emory said, apparently building up steam, "you could work all your life to be as happy as Anne and me, and you might not do it. People . . . they try to be happy. They work at it. But it doesn't always take." He laughed. "I shouldn't be talking to you this way, Mr. Bernstein, and I wouldn't be, except it's the middle of the night, and I'm saying stuff. You know, I respected you. But now here you are, smelling of beer, and I remember the grades you gave me, all those D's, like you thought I'd never do anything in life except fail. But you can't hurt me now because I'm not in school anymore. So I apologize. See, I apologize for messing up in school and I forgive you for flunking me out."

Emory held out his hand, and Saul stood up and took it, thinking that he might be making a mistake.

"You shouldn't flunk people out of school," Emory said, "if you're going to get drunk and roll cars."

Saul held on to Emory's hand and tried to grip hard and diligently in return. "I didn't get drunk, Emory. I fell asleep. And you didn't flunk out. You dropped out."

Emory released his hand. "Well, I don't care," he said. "I was sleeping when you came to our door. I don't go to parties anymore because I have to get up and work. I sleep because I'm married and working. I can't see anything outside that."

Saul suddenly wanted Patsy back in this room, so that they could go. Who the hell did this boy think he was, anyway?

"Well, none of this is anything," Emory said at last. "I don't blame you for anything at all. Maybe you did me a favor. I had to do something in my life, so I got my mom and dad to buy us this farm, which we're paying them back for every month, every dollar and cent, even though we aren't farming it. But we might. I'm reading up on horticulture." He pronounced the word carefully and proudly. "You want to sleep on the floor, you can, or on the sofa there. And there's a spare bed upstairs, you want it."

"Sorry about the bother," Saul said.

"No trouble."

"I appreciate this."

"Forget it." Emory patted the dog.

"But thanks."

"Sure."

The two men looked at each other for a moment, and Saul had one of his momentary envy-shocks: he looked at this man, this boy—he couldn't decide which he was—his hair standing up, and he thought: whatever else he is, this kid is real. Emory was living in the real; Saul felt himself floating up out of the unreal and rapidly sinking back into it, the lagoon of self-consciousness and irony.

In a kind of desperation, Saul looked up at the wall, where someone had hung a picture of a horse with a woman beside it, drawn in pencil, and framed in a cheap dime-store frame. The woman was probably Anne. She looked approximately like her. "Nice picture."

"I drew it."

"You have real talent, Emory," Saul said, insincerely examining the details. "You could be an artist."

"I *am* an artist," Emory said, staring at his old teacher. He picked at a scab on his calf. He turned his back to Saul. "I could draw from when I was a kid." A baby's cry came from upstairs. Emory looked at the ceiling, then exhaled.

"What kind of horse is that?" Saul asked, in what he vowed

silently would be his final effort at politeness this evening. "Is that any kind of horse in particular?"

Emory was going back up the stairs. Then he faced Saul. "Every horse is some horse in particular, Mr. Bernstein. There aren't any horses in general. You can sleep there on the sofa if you want to. Good night."

"Good night."

Whatever happened to the God of the Old Testament, Saul wondered, looking at Emory's house, the God that had chosen Israel above the other nations? Why had He allowed this scene to take place and why had He allowed Emory McPhee, this dropout, to make him feel like a putz? The Red Sea had not parted for Saul in a long time; he felt he had about as much clout with God as, perhaps, a sparrow did. The whole evening was a joke at Saul's expense. He heard God laughing, a sound like surf on rocks.

When Patsy and Anne came out of the kitchen, announcing that an all-night towing service was on its way and would probably have the car turned over and running in about half an hour, Saul smiled as if everything would be as fine as they claimed. Anne and Patsy were laughing. The flowers on Anne's bathrobe were laughing. God was, even now, laughing and enjoying the joke. Feeling like a zombie, and not laughing himself, but wearing the smile of the classically undead, Saul hooked his hand into Patsy's and went back outside. Some nights, he knew, had a way of not ending. This was one.

"How was Emory?" Patsy asked.

"Emory? Oh, Emory was fine," Saul told her.

On the days following, Saul began to be obsessed with happiness, an unhealthy obsession, but he couldn't get rid of it. His feelings had always been the city of dreadful night. He was ball-and-chained to his emotions. On some days the obsession weighed him down so heavily that he could not get out of bed to go to work without groaning and reaching for his hair, as if to drag himself up bodily for the working day.

Prior to his accident and his meeting with Emory McPhee,

Saul had managed to forget about happiness, a state that had once bothered him for its general inaccessibility. He loved Patsy; that he knew. Now he believed that compared to others he was actually and truly unhappy, especially since his mind insisted on thinking about the problem, poring over it, ragging him on and on. It was like the discontent of adolescence, the discontent with situations, but this was larger, the discontent with being itself, a psychic itch with nowhere to scratch. This was like Schopenhauer arriving at the door with a big suitcase, settling down for a long stay in the brain.

Patsy wasn't ordinary for many reasons but also because she loved Saul. Nevertheless, she was happy. Early in the summer he stole glances at her as she turned the pansies over in their pots, tamping them out, and planting them in the flowerbeds near the front walk. Blue sky, aggressive sun. She was barefoot, because she liked to go barefoot in the summer—her tomboy side—and she was squatting down in her shorts, wearing one of Saul's old flannel shirts flecked with dirt, and the sleeves rolled up to the elbows. Her brown hair fell backward down her shoulders. From the front window he watched her and studied her hands, those slender fingers doing their work. Helplessly, his eyes took in the clothed outlines of his wife. He was hers. That was that. She liked being a woman. She liked it in a way that, Saul now knew, he himself did not like being a man. There was the guilt, for one thing, for the manly hobbies of war and the thoroughgoing destruction of the earth. Patriarchy, carnage, rape, pleasurable bloodletting and bloodsport: Saul would admit a gender responsibility for all these, if anyone asked him, though no one ever did.

Patsy wiped her forehead with the back of her hand, saw Saul, and waved at him, turning her head slightly, tilting it, as she did whenever she caught sight of him. She smiled, a smile he had gladly given his life away for, a look of radiant intelligence. She was into the real, too; she didn't ponder it, she just planted flowers, if that was what she wanted to do. Beyond her was the driveway, and their Chevrolet with its bashed-in roof.

Saul turned from the window—it was Saturday morning—and tried to think for a moment of what he wanted to do. Taking a Detroit Tigers cap off the front hall hat rack, he went outside and with great care put it, from behind and unannounced, on Patsy's head. "Save you from sunburn," he said, when she turned around and looked at him. "Save you from heatstroke."

"I want a motorcycle," Patsy said. "I've been thinking about it. We don't need another car, but I want a motorcycle. I always have. Women *can* ride motorcycles, Saul, don't deny it. Oh. And another thing." She dropped one hand into the dirt and balanced herself on it. "This morning I was trying to think of where the Cayuse Indians lived, and I couldn't remember, and we don't have an encyclopedia to check. We need that." She put her hand over her eyes, to shade them. "Saul, why are you looking like that? Are you in a state?"

"No, I'm not in a state."

"A motorcycle would do wonders for *both* of us, Saul. A small one, not one of those hogs. Do you like my petunias? Should I have some purple over there? Maybe this is too much red and white. What would you think of some dianthus right there?" She pointed with her trowel. "Or maybe some sweet william?"

"Sure, sure." He didn't know what either variety looked like. Flowers seemed so irrelevant to everything. He looked down at her bare feet.

"Where *did* the Cayuse Indians live, Saul?"

"Oregon, I think."

"What do you think about a motorcycle? For little trips into town."

"Sounds okay. They aren't exactly safe, you know. People get killed on motorcycles."

"Those people aren't careful. I'll be careful. I'll wear a helmet. I just want to do it. Imagine a girl—me—on one of those machines. Makes you feel good, doesn't it? A motorcycle girl in Michigan. The car's silly for small trips. Besides, I want to visit my friends in town."

It was true: Patsy already had many friends around Five

Oaks. She belonged here, but she always seemed to belong anywhere. Now she stood up, dropping her trowel, and put her feet on Saul's shoes and leaned herself into him. The visor of her cap bumped into his forehead. But she embraced him for only a moment. "Want to help, Saul? Give me a hand putting the rest of these flowers in? And what do you say to some dianthus over there?"

"Not right now, Patsy. I don't think so."

"What's the matter?"

"I don't know."

"You *are* in a state."

"I guess I might be."

"What is it this time? Our recent brush with death? The McPhees?"

"What about the McPhees?" he asked. She had probably guessed.

"Well, they were so cute, the two of them. So sweet. And so young, too. And I know you, Saul, and I know what you thought. You thought: what have these two got that I don't have?"

She had guessed. She usually did. He stepped backward. "Yes," he said, "you're right. What *do* they have? And why don't I have it? I'm happy with *you*, but I—"

"—You can't be like them because you can't, Saul. You fret. That's your hobby. It's how you stay occupied. You've heard about spots? About how a person can't change them? Well, I *like* your spots. I like how you're a professional worrier. And you always know about things like the Cayuse Indians. I'm not like that. And I don't want to be married to somebody like me. I'd put myself to sleep. But you're perfect. You're an early warning system. You bark and growl at life. You're my dog. You do see that, don't you?"

"Yes." He nodded.

After he had kissed her, and returned to the house, he took the matchbook he had pocketed at the McPhees' up to his study. At his desk, with a pair of scissors, he cut off the flap of the matches, filled in his name and address, and wrote a check for six dollars to the Wisdom Foundation, located at a post office box number in Cincinnati, Ohio. Just to make sure, he enclosed a letter.

> *Dear Sirs,*
> *Enclosed please find a check for six dollars for your SECRETS OF THE UNIVERSE. Also included is my name and address, written on the back of this book of matches. You will also find them typed at the bottom of this letter. Thank you. I look forward, very much, to reading the secrets.*
> *Sincerely,*
> *Saul Bernstein*

He examined the letter, wondering if the last sentence might not be too ironic, too . . . something. But he decided to leave it there. He took the letter, carefully stamped—he put commemorative stamps on all his important mail—out to the mailbox, and lifted the little red flag.

He thought: I am no longer a serious person. My grandfather read the Torah, my father read Spinoza and Heine and books on immunology, and here I am, writing off for this.

On his trips into town, Saul began to take the long route, past the McPhees' house, slowing down when he was close to their yard. Each time that he found himself within a mile of their farm, he felt his stomach knotting up in anxiety and sick curiosity. He felt himself twisting the coils of something like envy, but not envy, not exactly. Driving past, at evening, he occasionally saw them out in the yard, Emory mowing or clipping, their baby strapped to his back, Anne up on a ladder doing something to the windows, or out in the garden like Patsy, planting. They could have been anybody, except that, for Saul, they gave off a disturbing aura of unreflective happiness.

The road was far enough away from their house and the flaking shed so that they wouldn't see him; his car was just another car. But on a particular Friday, in early June, after work, he drove past their property and saw Emory in the front yard, in the gold twilight, pushing his wife, who was sitting in the swing. Emory, the ex–football player, had on his face (through Saul's binoculars) a solemnly contented expression. The baby was in a stroller close by. His wife was in a white T-shirt and jeans, and Emory himself was wearing jeans but no shirt. She was probably proud of her breasts and he was probably proud of his shoulders. Anne held on to the ropes of the swing. Her hair flew up as she rose, and Saul, who took this all in in a few seconds, could hear her cries of delight from his car. Taking his surreptitious glances, he almost drove off the road again. Of course they were children, he knew that, and that wasn't it. They gave off a terrible glow. They had the blank glow of angels.

They lived smack in the middle of reality and never gave it a minute's thought. They'd never felt like actors. They'd never been sick with irony. The long tunnel of their thoughts had never swallowed them. They'd never had restless sleepless nights, the urgent wordless unexplainable wrestling matches with the shadowy bands of soul-thieves.

God damn it, Saul thought. Everybody gets to be happy except me. Saul heard Anne's cries. The sun was sweating all over his forehead. He felt faint, and Jewish, as usual. He turned on the radio. It happened to be tuned to a religious station and some choir was singing "When Jesus Wept."

"It's your play, Saul."
"I know, I know."
"What's the matter? You got some bad letters?"
"The worst. The worst letters I've ever had."
"You always say that. You whine and complain. You're such a whiner, Saul, you even whine in bed. You were complaining that time just before you spelled out 'axiom' over that triple word score and got all those points last winter. You do this act when we play Scrabble and then you always beat me." Patsy was sitting cross-legged in her chair, as she liked to do, with a

root beer bottle positioned against her instep, as she arranged and rearranged the letters on her slate.

Saul examined the board. The only word he could think of spelling out was "paint," but the word made him think of Emory McPhee. The hand of fate again, playing tricks on him. Glancing down at the words on the board, he thought he saw that same hand at work, spelling out some invisible story.

           DEER
            O
            U
     MOONBEAM
      U   T   I
ROAR   LUST
    KEY   D
     Y

Saul always treated Scrabble boards as if they were fortune-telling equipment, with the order creating a narrative. Patsy had started with "moon," and he had added "beam" onto it. When she hung a "mild" from the moonbeam, he spiced it up with "lust," but she had replied to his interest in sex with "murky," hanging the word from that same moonbeam. "Mild" and "murky" came close to how he felt. His mother, Delia, had said so on the phone yesterday. "Saul, darling," she said, "you're sounding rather *dark* and *mysterious* lately. What's gotten into you?" He had not told her about the accident. She would have been alarmed and would have stayed alarmed for several months. She was a fierce mother, always had been. "I'm okay, Ma," he had said. "I'm just working some things through."

"You're leaving Five Oaks?" she asked hopefully.

"No, Ma," he had said. "This town suits me."

"All that mud, Saulie," she had said, dubious as always about the soil. "All those farms," she added vaguely. "You didn't have a *seder* this year, did you?"

"No, Ma. I told you we didn't."

"You didn't open the door for Elijah? When you were a little boy you loved to do that. When it came time in the service, you always ran for the front door and held it open and you—"

"—Saul," Patsy said. "Wake up." She shook him. "You're woolgathering."

"Just thinking about my mother," he said. He looked up at Patsy. "What are all those deer doing on our Scrabble board?" he asked. "Give me a swig of your root beer."

She handed it to him. He appreciated the golden color of the fine hairs on her arm in the lamplight. "I think I saw some, as a matter of fact," she said. "I thought I saw, what would you call it, a herd of deer, far in back, beyond our property line, a few nights ago. If you ever go back up to the roof, honey, give a look around. You might see them."

"Right, right." He couldn't put all five of his letters for "paint" on the Scrabble board. He removed the *t*. Pain. He held the four letters for pain in his hand, and he added them to the final *t* in "lust."

"Funny how 'pain' and 'lust' give you 'paint,'" Patsy said. "Sort of makes me think of the McPhees and the heady smell of turpentine."

They glanced at each other, and he tried to smile. A fly was buzzing around the bulb in the lamp. He was thinking of Patsy's new blue motorcycle out back, shiny and powerful and dangerous to ride. The salesman had said it could go from zero to fifty in less than six seconds. The hand of fate was ready to give him a good slapping around. It had announced itself. Saul felt a groan coming on. He looked at Patsy with helpless love.

"Oh, Saul," she said. She clambered into his lap. "You always get this way during these games. You always do." He saw her smiling in the reflection of his love for her. "You're so cute," she said, then kissed him a long time.

At ten minutes past three o'clock, he rose out of bed, half to get a glass of water and half to look out the back window. When he did, he saw them: just about where Patsy said they would be, far in the distance, beyond their property line, a herd of deer, silently passing. He ran downstairs in his underwear and went out through the unlocked back door as quietly as he could. He stood in the yard in the June night, the crickets sounding, the moon dimly outlined behind a thin cloud in the shape of a scimitar. In this gauzy light, the deer, about eight of them, distant animal forms, walked across his neighbor's field into a stand of woods. He found himself transfixed with the mystery and beauty of it. Hunting animals suddenly made no sense to him. He went back to bed. "I saw the deer," he said. He didn't know if Patsy was asleep. During the summer she wore Saul's T-shirts to bed, and that was all; her arms were crossed on her chest like a Crusader. "I saw the deer," he said again, and, awake or asleep, she nodded.

Two days later, the letter containing the secrets of the universe came from the Wisdom Foundation in Cincinnati. Saul sat down on the front stoop and tore the letter open. It was six pages long and had been printed out by a computer, with Saul's name inserted here and there.

> *Dear Mr. Bernstein,*
> *Nothing is settled. Everything is still possible. Your thoughts are both yours and someone else's. Sometimes we say hello to the world and then good-bye, but that is not the end and we say hello again. God is love, **Mr. Bernstein** , denying it only makes us unhappy. Riches are mere appearances. **Our thoughts are more real than hammers and nails.** We can make others believe us, **Mr. Bernstein** , if the truth is in us. Buddha and Jesus the Christ and Mohammed agreed about just about everything. Causing pain to others only prolongs our own pain. A free and open heart is the best thing. Live simply. Don't pretend to know something you don't have a clue about. You may feel as if you are headed toward some terrible fate, **Mr. Bernstein** , but that may not come to pass. You can avoid it. **Throw your bad thoughts into the mental wastebasket.** There is a right way and a wrong*

way to dispose of bad thoughts. Everything about the universe worth knowing is known. What is not known about the universe is not worth knowing. Follow these steps. Remember that trees will always be with us, mice will always be with us, mosquitoes will always be with us. Therefore, avoid mental cleanliness. Never start a sentence with the words, "What if everybody...."

It went on for several more pages. Saul liked the letter. It sounded like his other grandfather, Isaac, the pious atheist, an exuberant man much given to laughter at appropriate and inappropriate moments, who offered advice as he passed out candy bars and halvah to his grandchildren. This letter, from the Wisdom Foundation, was signed by someone named Giovanni d'Amato.

Saul looked up. For a moment the terrifying banality of the landscape seemed to dissolve into geometrical patterns of color and light. Taken by surprise, he felt the habitual weight on his heart lifting, as if by pulleys, or, better yet, birds of the spirit sent by direct mail from Giovanni d'Amato. He decided to test this happiness and got into the dented car.

He drove toward the McPhees'. The dust on the dirt road whirled up behind him. He thought he would be able to stand their middle-American happiness. Besides, Emory was probably working. No: it was Saturday. They would both be home. He would just drive by and that would be that. So what if they were happy, these dropouts from school? He was happy, too. He would test his temporary happiness against theirs.

The trees rushed past the car in a kind of chaotic blur.

He pressed down on the accelerator. A solitary cloud—wandering and thick with moisture—straying overhead but not blocking the sun, let down a minute's worth of vagrant rainbowed shower on Saul's car. The water droplets, growing larger, actually bounced on the car's hood. He turned on the wipers, causing the dust to streak in perfect protractor curves. The rain made Saul's car smell like a nursery of newborn vegetation. He felt the car drive over something. He hoped it wasn't an animal, one of those anonymous rodents like mice and chipmunks that squealed and died and disappeared.

Ahead and to the left was the McPhees'.

As usual, it looked like something out of an American genre painting, the kind of second-rate canvas hidden in the back of most museums near the elevators. Happiness lives in such houses, where people like Saul had never been permitted. In the bright standing sunshine its midwestern gothic acute angles pointed up straight toward heaven, a place where there had been a land rush for centuries and all the stakes had been claimed. Standing there in the bright theatrical sun—the rain had gone off on its way—the house seemed to know something, to be an answer ending with an exclamation point.

Saul crept past the front driveway. His window was open, and, except for the engine, there was no sound: no dog barking. And no sign, either, of Anne or Emory or their baby, at least out here. Nothing on the front porch, nothing in the yard. He *could* stop and say hello. That was permitted. He could thank them for their help two weeks ago. He hadn't done that. Emory's pickup was in the driveway, so they were at home; happy people don't go much of anywhere anyway, Saul thought, backing his car up and parking halfway in on the driveway.

When he reached the backyard, Saul saw a flash of white, on legs, bounding at the far distances of the McPhees' field into the woods. From this distance it looked like nothing he knew, a trick of the eye. Turning, he saw Anne McPhee sitting in a lawn chair, reading the morning paper, a glass of lemonade nearby, their baby in the crib in the shade of the house, and Emory, some distance away, in a hammock, reading the sports section. Both of them held up their newspapers so that their view of him was blocked.

Quietly he crossed their back lawn, then stood in the middle, between them. Emory turned the pages of his paper, then put it down and closed his eyes. Anne went on reading. Saul stood quietly. Only the baby saw him. Saul reached down and picked out of the lawn a sprig of grass. Anne McPhee coughed. The baby was rattling one of its crib toys.

He waited for a minute, then walked back to his car. Anne and Emory had not seen him, and he felt like a prowler, a spy from God. He felt literally now what he had once felt metaphorically: that he was invisible.

When he was almost home, he remembered, or thought he remembered, that Anne McPhee had been sunning herself and had not been wearing a blouse or a bra. Or was he now imagining this? He couldn't be sure.

Patsy nudged him in the middle of the night. "I know what it is," she said.

"What?"

"What's bothering you."

He waited. "What? What is it?"

"You're like men. You're a man and you're like them. You want to be everything. You want to have endless endless potential. But then you grow up. And you're one thing. Your body is, anyway. It's trapped in *this* life. You have to say goodbye to the dreams of everything."

"Dreams of everything."

"Yes." She rolled over and made designs on his chest with her fingers. "Don't pretend that you don't understand. You want to be an astronaut and a Don Juan and Elvis and Einstein."

"No. I want to be Magic Johnson."

"Whatever. But you want to be all those people. You want to be a whole roomful of people, Saul. That's kid stuff." She let her head drop so that her hair brushed against him.

"What about you?"

"Me? I don't want to be anything else," she said sleepily, beginning to rub his back. "I don't have to be a great person. I just want to do a little of this and a little of that."

"What's wrong with ambitions?" he asked. "You could be great at something."

Her hand moved into his hair, tickling him. "Being great is

too tiring, Saul, and it's boring. Look at the great ambition people. They're wrecking the earth, aren't they. They're leaving it in bits and scraps." She concentrated on him in the dark. "Saul," she said.

"Your diaphragm's not in."

"I know."

"But."

"So?"

"Well, what if?"

"What if? You'd be a father, that's what if." She had turned him so that she was right up against him, her breasts pressing him, challenging him.

"No," he said. He drew back. "Not yet. Let me figure this out on my own. There'd be no future."

"For the baby?"

"No. For me." He waited, trying to figure out how to say this. "I'd have to be one person forever. Does that make sense?"

"From you, it does." She pulled herself slightly away from him. They rearranged themselves.

The following Saturday he drove into Five Oaks for a haircut. When his hair was so long that it made the back of his neck itch, he went to Harold, the barber, and had it trimmed back. Harold was a pale, slightly bland-looking Lutheran, a terrible barber with a nice disposition who was in the same bowling league with Saul and who sometimes practiced basketball at the same times that Saul did. Many of the men in Five Oaks looked slightly peculiar and asymmetrical, thanks to Harold. The last time Saul had come in, Harold had been deep in a conversation with a woman who was accusing him of things; Saul couldn't tell exactly what Harold was being accused of, but it sounded like a lovers' quarrel, and Saul liked that. Anyone else's troubles diminished his.

By coincidence, the same woman as before was back again in the barbershop with her son, whose hair Harold was cutting when Saul rang the bell over the door when he entered. To pass the time and achieve a moment's invisibility, he picked up a newspaper from the next chair over and read the morning's headlines.

Shots Fired at Holbein Reactor
Iranian Terrorists Suspected

Shielded by his paper, Saul heard the woman whispering directions to Harold, and Harold's faint, exasperated, "Louise, I can do this." Saul pretended to read the article; the shots, as it turned out, had been harmless. Even though there had been no damage, some sort of investigation was going on. Saul thought Iranians could do better than this.

There was more whispering, which Saul tried not to hear. After the woman had paid for her son's haircut and left, Saul sat himself down in Harold's chair.

"Hey, Saul," Harold said, covering him with the white cloth. "You always come in when she does. How do you do that?"

"Beats me. Her name Louise?"

"That's right. The usual trim, Saul?"

"The usual. Harold, this time try to keep it the same length on both sides, okay?"

"I try, Saul. It's just that your hair's so curly."

"Right, right." Saul saw his reflection in the mirror and closed his eyes. He felt like asking Harold, the Lutheran, a moral question. "Harold," he said, "do you ever wonder where your thoughts come from? I mean, do we own our thoughts, or do they come from somewhere else, or what? For example, you can't always control your thoughts or your impulses, can you? So, whose thoughts are those, anyway, the ones you can't control? And another thing. Are you happy? Be honest."

The scissors stopped clipping. "Gosh, Saul, are you okay? What drugs have you been taking lately?"

"No drugs. Just tell me: are your thoughts always yours? That's what I need to know."

The barber looked into the mirror opposite them. Saul saw Harold's plain features. "All right," Harold said. "I'll answer your question." Then, with what Saul took to be great sadness, the barber said, "I don't have many thoughts. And when I do, they're all mine."

"Okay," Saul said. "I'm sorry. I was just asking." He tried to slump down in his chair, but the barber said, "Sit up straight, Saul." Saul did.

Days later, Saul is asleep. He knows this. He knows he is asleep next to Patsy. He knows it is night, that cradle of dreams, but the earth's mad companion, the moon, is shining stainless steel beams across the bed, and Saul is dreaming of being in a car that cannot stop rolling over, an endless flip of metal, and this time Patsy is not belted in, and something horrible must be happening to her, judging from the blur of her head. She is being hurt terribly thanks to the way he has driven the car, the mad way, the un-American way, and now she is walking across a bridge made of moonlight, and she falls. The door, Saul's door, is being kept open for Elijah, but Elijah does not come in. How will we recognize him? Saul's mind is not in Saul's head; it is above him, above his yarmulke, above his prayer shawl, his tallith. Patsy is hurt, she lies in a ditch. Deer and doubt mix with the murky roar of mild lust on the Scrabble board. And here, behind the barber chair, is Giovanni d'Amato, sage of Cincinnati, saying, "You shouldn't flunk people out of school if you're going to get drunk and roll cars." Saul, the child, is speaking to Saul the grown-up: "You'll never figure it out," and when Saul the adult asks, "What?" the child says, "Adulthood. Any of it." And then he says, "Saul, you're pregnant."

Saul woke and looked over at Patsy, still sleeping. He groaned audibly with relief that she hadn't been hurt. What an annoying dream. He had never even owned a tallith. After putting on his shirt, jeans, and boots, he went downstairs, and, taking the keys off the kitchen table, stepped outside.

The motorcycle felt quiet and powerful underneath him as he accelerated down Whitefeather Road. He had driven a motorcycle briefly in college—until a small embarrassing accident—and the process all came back to him now. This one, Patsy's new machine, painted pink and blue, 250 cc's, was easy to shift, and the machine gave him the impression that he was floating, or better yet, was flowing down the archways of dark stunted Michigan trees. His eyes watered, and bugs hit him in the face as he speeded up. He felt the rear wheel slip on the dirt. He didn't know what he was doing out here and he didn't care.

He turned left onto highway fourteen, and then County Road H, also dirt, and he downshifted, feeling the tight, close gears meshing, and he let the clutch out, slowing him down. On the road the cycle's headlight was like a cone, leading him forward, away from himself, toward something more inviting and dangerous. In the grip of spiritual longing, a person goes anywhere, traveling over the speed limit. The night was warm, but none of the summer stars was visible. Behind the clouds the stars were even now rushing away in the infinity of expanding space. Saul felt like an astral body himself. He too would rush away into emptiness. In the green light of the speedometer he saw that he was doing a respectable fifty. Up ahead the wintry white eyes of a possum glanced toward him before the animal scurried into the high grass near the road. Saul wanted to be lost but knew he could not be. He knew exactly where he was: fields, forest, fields. He knew each one, and he knew whom they belonged to, he had been here that long.

And of course he knew where he was going: he was headed toward the McPhees', that house of happiness, that castle of light, where everyone, man woman and child, would be sleeping soundly, the sleep of the happy and just and thoughtless. Saul felt blank, gripped by obsession, simultaneously vacant and full of shame.

He looked at his watch. It was past midnight. Their house would be dark.

But it was not. On the road beyond their driveway, Saul slowed down and then shut off the engine, holding on tightly to the handlebars as he stared, like the prowler he was, toward the second floor windows, from which sounds emerged. From where he was spying, Saul could see Anne sitting in a rocking chair by the window with their baby. The baby was crying, screaming; Saul could hear it from the road. And, in the background, back and forth, Saul could see Emory McPhee pacing, the all-night walk of the helpless father. An infant with colic, a rocking mother, a pacing father, screams of infant misery, and now the two of them, Anne and Emory, beginning to shout at each other over what to do.

Saul turned his motorcycle around, pushed it down the road, then started the engine. He felt better. He could have gone to their front door and welcomed them as the official greeter of ordinary disharmony. *I was always just as real as they were,* Saul thought. *I always was.*

On the left the broken fences bordering the farmland quavered up and down and seemed to start bouncing, visually, as he accelerated. The lines on the telephone poles jumped nervously as he passed them until they had the rapid and nervous movements of pens on graph paper marking an erratic heartbeat. Rain—he hadn't known it was going to rain, no one had told him—began falling, getting into his eyes and falling with cold precision on the backs of his hands. He felt the cloth of his shirt getting soaked and sticking to his shoulders. The rain was persistent and serious. He felt the tires of Patsy's motorcycle slipping on the mud, nudging the rear end of the bike off, slightly, thoughtfully, toward the left side. Then the road joined up with the highway, where the traction improved, but the rain was falling more heavily now, soaking him so he could hardly see. He came to a bridge, slowed the bike, and huddled in its shelter for a moment, until the rain seemed to let up, and he set out again. Accelerate, clutch, shift. He wanted to get home to Patsy. He wanted to dry his hair and get into bed next to her. He couldn't think of anything else he wanted.

A few hundred feet from his own driveway, he looked through the rain, only a drizzle now, and he saw, looking back at him, their eyes lit by his headlamp, the deer he had seen before, closer now, crossing his yard. They stood there, on his property. But this time, there was another, a last deer, one he hadn't seen before, behind the others, slightly smaller, as if reduced somehow. It was an albino. In the darkness and rain it moved in a haze of whiteness. Seeing it, Saul thought: Oh my God, I'm about to die. The deer had stopped, momentarily frozen in the light. The albino's eyes—it was a doe—were pink, and its fur was as white as linen. The animal flicked its tail, nervously hypnotized. Its terrible pink eyes, blank as stars at the center, stared at him. Saul turned off the engine and the headlight. Now, in the dark, two brown deer bounded toward the west, but the albino stood still, staring in Saul's direction, a purposeful stare. He gripped the handlebars so hard that his forearms began to knot into a cramp. The animal was a sign of some kind, he was sure—only a fool would think otherwise—and he felt a moment of dread pass through his body as the deer now turned her eyes away from his and began to walk off into the night. He saw her disappear behind a maple tree in his backyard, but he couldn't follow her beyond that. He was trembling now. Shivering spasms began at his wet shoulders and passed down his chest toward his legs. The dread he had felt before was turning rapidly into pure spiritual fright, alternating waves of chill and heat rushing up and down his body. He remembered to get off the road. He pushed the motorcycle into the garage, kicking down its stand, and by the time he had crossed the yard and had reached the back door, he felt that he knew one thing, which was that he would not despise his own life. He had been told not to. The rain picked up again and sprayed into him as the wind carried it. In his mind's eye he saw the deer looking back at him. He had been judged, and the judgment was that he, Saul, was only and always himself, now and onward into infinity. His boots were wet. They stank of wet leather. Outside the back door, on the lawn, he took the boots off, then his wet shirt and his jeans. It occurred to him to stand there naked. With no clothes on he stood in the rain and the dark, and he fell to his knees. He wasn't praying. He didn't know what he was doing. Something was filling him up. It felt like the spirit, but the spirit of what, he didn't know. He lay down on the grass. One sob tore through him, and then it was over.

He felt like getting up and running out into the field in back of the house, but he knew he couldn't break through his self-consciousness enough to do that. In the rain, which no longer felt cold, he sensed that he was entering a condition that had nothing to do with happiness because it was so far beyond it. All he was sure about was that he was empty before and now was filled, filled with both fullness and emptiness. These emotions didn't quite make sense, but he didn't care. The emptiness was sweet; he could live with it. He hurried into the house and dried off his hair in the dark downstairs bathroom. Quickly he toweled himself down and then rushed up the stairs. There was a secret, after all. In fact there were probably a lot of secrets, but there was one he now knew.

He entered their bedroom. Rain fingernailed against the window glass. Patsy lay in bed in almost complete darkness, wearing one of Saul's T-shirts. Her arms were up above her head. He could see that she was watching him.

"Where were you?"

"I went for a ride on your motorcycle. I couldn't sleep."

"Saul, it's raining. Why are you naked?"

"It's raining now. Not when I started."

"Why are you standing there? You don't have any clothes on."

"I saw something. I can't tell you. I think I'm not supposed to tell you what I saw. It was an animal. It was a private animal. Patsy, I took off my clothes and lay down on the lawn in the rain, and it didn't feel weird, it felt like just what I should do."

"Saul, what is this about?"

"I'm not sure."

"Try. Try to say."

"I think I'm pregnant."

"What does that mean?"

"I think it means that whoever I am, I'm not alone with myself."

"I don't understand that."

"I know."

"Come to bed, Saul. Get in under the sheet."

He climbed in and put his leg over hers.

"I can't quite get used to you," she said. "You're quite a mess of metaphors, Saul, you know that."

"Yes."

"A man being pregnant." She put her hand familiarly on his thigh. "I wonder what that means."

"It's a feeling, Patsy. It's a secret. Men have secrets, too."

"I never said they didn't. They love secrets. They have lodges and secret societies and stuff—the Fraternal Order of Moose."

"Can we make love now, right this minute? Because I love you. I love you like crazy."

"I love you, too, Saul. What if you make *me* pregnant? It could happen. What if I get knocked up? Is it all right now?"

"Yeah. What's the problem?"

"What will we say, for example?"

"We'll say, 'Saul and Patsy are pregnant.'"

"Oh sure we will."

"Okay, we won't say it." He had thrown the sheet back and was kissing the backs of her knees.

"Are you crying? Your face is wet."

"Yes."

"But you're being so jokey."

"That's how I handle it."

"Why are you crying?"

"Because. . . ." He wanted to get this right. "Because there are signs and wonders. What can I tell you? It's all a feeling. In the morning, I'll deny I said this."

She was kissing him now, but she stopped, as if thinking about his recent sentences. "You *want* to make me pregnant, too, don't you?"

"Yes."

"So you're not alone in this."

"That's right."

"One more little ambassador from the present to the future. That's what you want."

"Sort of." He moved up and took her fingers one by one into his mouth and bit them tenderly. Patsy had started to hum. She was humming "Unchain My Heart." Then she opened her mouth and sang quietly, "Unchain my heart, and set me free."

"I'll try, Patsy."

"Yes." They often talked while they made love. A moment later, she said, "This won't solve anything. There'll be tears. People—babies—you know how they cry."

"Yes." And even now Saul felt as though he heard someone wailing softly in the next room. Still he continued. Then he had a thought.

"Patsy," he said, "the window. We should stand by the window."

"Why?"

"To try it." He disentangled himself from her, stood, and brought her over to the window. He opened it so that droplets of rain blew in over them. "Now," he said. There was a bit of lightning, and he lifted her to him. She held on, her arms clasped behind his neck. He felt as though a thousand eyes, but not human eyes, were looking in on them with tender indifference. They were and were not interested. They would and would not care. They would and would not love them. Finally they would turn away, as they tended to turn away from all human things, in time. Saul felt Patsy begin to tremble, a slight shivering along her back, a rising in tension before release. More rain came in, warm June rain on his arm. He felt Patsy's mouth on his curls, the ones recently cut by Harold; she was panting, and so was he, and for a split-second, he understood it all. He understood everything, the secret of the universe. After an instant, he lost it. Having lost the secret, forgotten it, he felt the usual onset of the ordinary, of everything else, with Patsy around him, the two of them in their own familiar rhythms. He would not admit to anyone that he had known the secret of the universe for a split-second. That part of his life was hidden away and would always be: the part that makes a person draw in the breath quickly, in surprise, and stare at the curtains in the morning, upon awakening.

Peelings

MARY SWANDER

Sister, pull the curtain.
No, not for the bedpan,
but to scoot your chair closer.
You've been so good, here every day,
I hesitate to ask more, but tonight the question
plays over and over: how much longer?
Oh, wouldn't it be nice to be in our little house
in Vence where we open the windows out to the meadow
filled with poppies and tangerine trees? Orange.
I lie hour after hour, staring at the lightbulb
in that lamp over the bed, then everything seems rimmed
in peelings—the intercom, the nurses' caps, the strings
that tie this gown around my neck. I'm encased in
this room and if I could pull away the rind of this illness,
it's been so long, I wonder what might be left underneath.
My skin. No one can understand the pain of being touched.
Or not. The problem: not even a rash to show the staff
bustling in at 6 A.M. Disappointing, I'm sure, for the interns.
And difficult for any visitor to believe that I'm not
just grieving for some lost love I met last summer
on the beach. But when anything—object, cloth,
or hand—comes in contact, the beehive stirs,
then stings from my hairline down to my toes.

For months, you know, I slept in my clothes,
the thought of a dress brushing over my back too much.
The buzzing began in my ears even before I'd lie down,
then it'd come of its own with each toss or turn.
I'd wake up burning. The flames rising.
This little bell became my trail to the outside world.
Remember that trip to Tibet when we bought it
at the monastery, the monks' chants echoing down the valley?
I'd ring and you'd come to calm my screams and bring
a glass of water. We had no idea what was the matter,
and all the money Mother and Father left us
couldn't find a cause or cure. "Normal. Nothing unusual
shows up here. We could do further tests, but I suggest
you go home, rest, and try to eliminate stress."
Bells of Chartres, the Seville Cathedral,
Bell of St. Patrick's Will, harness bells
tinkling through the Moscow snow. I'd imagine myself
wrapped in a blanket of ice and dream of those monks
controlling their body temperature by breathing.
On the freezing mountain tops. Out, in.
I became a buoy at sea and most steered clear,
not knowing what to do, to say, thinking all along
I must be cracked. But we kept searching and you,
my dear, never let me drift. We tried a dry climate
and moved to the Texas desert, but there
the bees became scorpions and brown recluse spiders
eating holes through my pores. Here, the doctors
are trying to dig down and uncover the seed
of the problem and have a hunch it may be
in my own mouth: mercury poisoning from the
dental amalgam. Tomorrow all my fillings will be
replaced with porcelain. My tongue moves from
side to side tolling the hours until it's time,
while outside the window over the lake, the sun
is a cinder. This morning while you were sleeping,
there was a code across the hall. I don't know
the details but through the door I saw

the swarms of teams, heard the elevator ding
when they rolled her away on the stretcher.
Sister, tonight I'll try to tolerate a sheet.
Let's pull it up toward my chin and then
I'd like you to cup your hands near my face,
ever so lightly, gently, as if you were reaching out
to pluck a piece of fruit ripe from a limb.

Long, Disconsolate Lines

JANE COOPER

in memory of Shirley Eliason Haupt

Because it is a gray day but not snowy, because traffic grinds
   by outside,
because I woke myself crying help! to no other in my bed and
   no god,
because I am in confusion about god,
because the tree out there with its gray, bare limbs is shaped
   like a lyre,
but it is only January, nothing plays it, no lacerating March
   sleet,
no thrum of returning rain,
because its arms are empty of buds and even of protective
   snow,
I am in confusion, words harbor in my throat, I hear not one
   confident tune,
and however long I draw out this sentence
it will not arrive at any truth.

It's true my friend died in September and I have not yet
   begun to mourn.

Overnight, without warning, the good adversary knocked at her door,
the one she so often portrayed
as a cloud-filled drop out of the cave's mouth, crumpled dark of an old garden chair. . . .
But a lyre-shaped tree? yes, a lyre-shaped tree. It's true that at twenty-four
in the dripping, raw Iowa woods
she sketched just such a tree, and I saw it, fell in love with its half-heard lament
as if my friend, in her pristine skin, already thrashed by the storm-blows ahead,
had folded herself around them,
as if she gave up nothing, as if she sang.

Midwestern Villanelle

ROBIN BEHN

Lately, where my body ends, yours begins.
Or so I keep thinking, although you are far.
It's hard to say, sometimes, just what has been.

To reconstruct the feeling of it, give me some men
—all strangers, please—to synchronize the bar
stools' twirling: when the one called *me* winds down you begin

to stir the afternoon. A fifth of gin,
too, please, to symbolize how clear we were
each to each. I know just what has been

between us; it still is. My body here, lupine,
hungry to hear you say how far
it is to where this wanting ends and you begin

the drive back over red, real miles again.
Come back: Galesburg, known for trains, Star-
lite Motel where giant neon lips flash *What's Been*

Can Be Again. There's a compass in
your body. My open legs? Your two-point star
that lights up where our one body ends. Or else begins:
beneficent, hard to hold, just what's always been.

One Continuous Substance
ALBERT GOLDBARTH

A small boy and a slant of morning light
both exit the last dark trees of this forest, though
the boy is gone in an instant. Not

the light: it travels its famous 186,000 miles per second
to be this still gold bar
on the floor of the darkness. I suppose

that from the universe's point of view
we do the same: a small boy and an old man
being one continuous substance.

We were making love when the phone rang
saying my father was dead, and the sun
kept touching you, there, and there, where I'd been.

Across These Landscapes of Early Darkness
DIONISIO D. MARTÍNEZ

He is learning to play the elegant songs
again. By ear. By heart. He is picking

up a signal from America, a faint humming,
a plea. He doesn't understand it. The elegant

music will suffice for the moment. This
time he will listen for the diesels slicing

the fog as they come up each morning,
their headlights leaving trails like a

photograph's version of life. There is elegance
in this, too. But there is more. A sense

of decorum as motif for a whole generation.
He is learning to live in style again. Here's

the suit for the nights when all
the stars are out and closer than usual

and some tradition says that you must count them.
Here's the pale shirt with no purpose.

Here are all the pointed shoes, all
the hats, the ties with the wrong patterns.

It is no one else's style. This makes it
more solid somehow, more durable. This

makes him happy. He hasn't laughed this
hard in years. He is picking up signals from

countries where the last transmission
took place light years ago. This is how

he learns about light years and how time
equals distance and distance is a kind

of salvation. He wants to come to America,
home of the faint signal, land of stolen

elegance. By now he has caught on
to the way we package someone else's tradition,

the way we price each package. These days
he is in the market for a new tradition.

It is all so obvious—the way we manufacture
our legacies. We are not the best of

thieves. Our music is always holding something
back, always looking for its source. He is

willing—at last—to take us as we are.
He runs to catch up, but by the time he manages

to get his hands on the essence of a song,
the song itself is light years from his hands.

Dove

STANLEY PLUMLY

Shapes as a series of edges, each edge
a wave exhausted yet extended just
enough until the shoulder is complete,
or the leaf or the chair, which is flying,
which, if we weren't flying too, we could see—
it is a beautiful shoulder, either
elegant or useful, like a calla
lily or cello or a mountain road,
it is a big, flat-handed, star-point oak,
and a rocker, elder, utterly still.
Shapes as the sunlight serial in light,
the sadness of the blur in the picture,
bend of the wing, the white wing-bars, white
edges that at any distance become
integral to the losses of objects
wasting into the air like grain above
the harvest, like the close-up once I saw
of the type hitting the paper like a
hammer, exploding on the high desert
proving-ground of the page in such a way
that dust along the outline of the ink
rose in a shadow of fine dead powder.
The way touching would be fingerprinted
if the flesh could somehow hold the fracture.
Waves of heat, waves of the river rising
from the river, the rainbow edges like
those lines in earth drawn with sticks that will be
straight but not in this life, love, nor money.

Both Definitions of Save

ALBERT GOLDBARTH

1. YIDDISH

> *Hand me a relic, I'll treat it up right.*
> *Grandma, Grandma, rub it in* schmaltz.
> *Yes hand me a relic, I'll treat it up right.*
> *Anubis, pack it in natron salts.*

*

Another nostalgic vignette with a grandmother canning—in this case, Nettie. It's 1960. I'm twelve. She has one year to live. You'd never guess it: her hair done up in a durable Old World bun, her hands in their finicky repetitions. Everything's sure and fluid; the gnarls and florets she's pickling in viscous brine are one with the movement that lifts and deposits them. A garnet peel of beet, an inbunched clump of cauliflower, slices, slices: cameos and medallions. She incorporates a flicked taste into her rhythm.

She hums some mouthful Old World mutter-of-a-song, and this scene is so seamlessly one piece that, finally, these twisted and whiskery vegetable nibbles can't be told apart from, *are*, the Yiddish on her tongue.

It takes her back. I'm only twelve, and maybe not the sharpest twelve at that, but I can see the wings and gutturals of her song reverse the current, take that kitchen and its passenger and soften all of their borders by fifty-some years. She touches the locket around her neck—a curl of his hair inside. She might be waiting to hear him fumble open the door, it's evening, he's home from a twelve-hour hell-day of ghetto peddling, eager to rest in her flesh . . .

I know: this has an overlush and suspect glow, I can't help it. William Kittredge says that "back deep in the misty past there is this land inhabited by dreams and passions, and you love it . . . you want it to be all perfection, bronzed in your memory like baby shoes." Canned. Sugary and canned. That's nostalgia—a marmalade.

Was she quarrelsome, ever? Did she meddle? Oh yes. Could she whine? Was she stubborn? Intuitively did she know how to slip it between the ribs and twist, and then coo guilefully for forgiveness? Of course.

But time has saved a saying from the rubble of her people: *Alleh kalles zaynen sheyn, alleh meyssim zaynen frum.*—All brides are beautiful, all the dead are holy.

*

Donkey pizzle! he thinks at his rival, *worm turd!* Then he burbles his heavy lips in frustration. Oh he wants this drawing by Seghers, really just a sketch not even the size of a varnish rag, but done by one of the great impassioned masters of Dutch art (now, alas, discredited in an age of taste for daintier fare than Seghers of the wild, winding lines . . .). "One hundred florins."

"One hundred and ten." Some fey young bidder, in a beaver-collared suit of bottle green, is baiting him higher by tens, and more for a lazy afternoon's game than for any understanding of the life behind the drawing. That's the prickle of it: this fellow would rather pay florins than homage.

So, "One hundred and—" Rembrandt is about to say "twenty" but why continue dancing stupid little two-step boxes with this irksome heifer? He's brought two hundred florins in his purse. The only other bidder had dropped out at eighty. "One hundred and sixty florins."

There's that half-a-breath of stillness in the warehouse. Clearly Beaver Collar is done; he fingers a wiffley dismissive gesture through the air in front of his nose, as if to say he'll be competitive, yes, but not *foolish* . . . "Well bid," the auctioneer sings on the brink of disbelief, "well bid by master Rembrandt van Rijn of the most discerning eye . . ." and then a maundering trail of oilier compliments, as if in fear the sale might otherwise never become official.

But Rembrandt has shut off his ears. He isn't in the warehouse, and the warehouse isn't in Amsterdam or anywhere on God's Earth. There's just this one aspatial burning bridge of vision between his eyes and the drawing, he owns it, he can enter it, he could wander its charcoal lanes all day, could stretch his hand and rest it on a charcoal railing Seghers sketched, and when he lifted it off, he'd see his whole palm colored charcoal . . .

In the essay "On Collecting," Jed Perl admits and details "the grubbiness of the collector's life. Breakage, exaggerated or inaccurate descriptions, boredom, petty betrayals, overspending, regret," and of course "the terms of the marketplace."

But he also reports a small talk by Sam Wagstaff ("probably the most interesting photography collector in America"), a talk that was "a deeply serious defense of collecting, a kind of ethics of collecting. Collectors, Wagstaff argued, often labor to preserve aspects of the past—ephemeral publications, marginal works of art—when these things are headed for the trash bin, overlooked by the traditional custodians of culture . . . Wagstaff's collector was a kind of odd man out, conservationist of the man-made past, and Wagstaff's remarks took a trajectory that made collecting seem a strangely pure, clean pursuit."

I'm not claiming this sufficiently explains each minuscule classified ad in an antiques newsletter's swatch of back pages: someone's seeking "Nazi daggers & other SS paraphernalia," someone (I'm not inventing this) is in need of "old rubber enema bags w/nozzle, for private collection," someone "PAYING TOP DOLLAR FOR 1920'S LADIES IRON HAIR CRIMPERS!!!"

But who *wouldn't* care to dawdle in the lavishdom of that five-story rose-brick house on Sint Antoniebreestraat? Charles L. Mee, Jr., gives a sense of the wonderful jumble amassed by the later 1630s, worth quoting in full:

"Among many other things he had a little painting of a pastry cook by Adriaen Brouwer, a still life of food by Brouwer, a candlelight scene by Lievens, a moonlight scene by Lievens, a raising of Lazarus by Lievens, a hermit by Lievens, a plaster cast of two naked children, a landscape by

Hercules Seghers, some small houses by Seghers, a wooded landscape by Seghers, a Tobias by Pieter Lastman, a small ox by Lastman, a portrait head by the great Raphael of Urbino, a mirror in an ebony frame, a marble wine-cooling bucket, a walnut table, a copper kettle, an embroidered tablecloth, an oak stand, some rare Venetian glass, a Chinese bowl filled with minerals, a small backgammon board, a large lump of white coral, an East Indian basket, a bird of paradise, a marble ink stand, a bin filled with thirty-three antique hand weapons and wind instruments, a bin of sixty Indian hand weapons, arrows, javelins and bows, a bin of thirteen bamboo wind instruments, a harp, a Turkish bow, seventeen hands and arms cast from life, a collection of antlers, four crossbows and footbows, five antique helmets and shields, a satyr's head with horns, a large sea plant, seven stringed instruments, a giant's head (a giant's head?), skins of both a lion and a lioness, a painting by Raphael, a book of prints by Lucas van Leyden, 'the precious book' by Andrea Mantegna, a book of prints by the elder Brueghel, a book of prints by Raphael, a book of prints by Tempesta, a book of prints by Cranach, a book with almost all the work of Titian, a book of portraits by Rubens and others, a book full of the work of Michelangelo, a book of erotica by Raphael and others, a book of Roman architecture, baskets full of prints by Rubens, Jacob Jordaens, and Titian, a book of woodcuts by Albrecht Dürer, a painting by Frans Hals, a pistol, an ornamented iron shield, a cabinet full of medals, a Turkish powder horn, a collection of shells, another of coral, forty-seven specimens of land and sea animals, a Moor's head cast from life, an East Indian sewing box, several walking sticks . . ."

Now he jingles the forty florins left in his purse, and won't head home without the sea monster cleverly sewn together from the taxidermied carcasses of a monkey and a shark.

*

The question isn't one of ownership, but stewardship—enabling separate objects, maybe even separate *moments*, to travel inviolate for a stretch, untouched by Time.

Isn't that my attempt? I'm twelve: I'm sprawled in the living room, forcing my gaze from a comic book page to watch her flurry of easy expertise at the lineup of Mason jars, half-listening to the Yiddish warble under her breath.

And: I'm forty-two, I'm looking and I'm listening back at the same.

Between those poles-of-me, a charge of preservative arcs, in which I hold her, soak her fully in it, make of her a collected thing.

The size of a saint on a dashboard: Grandma Nettie Pickling in Kitchenlight.

*

Held static by these various amperes and saccharines, historicized, that scene reoccurs unchanged when I want, its details clear through thirty years of episodes that otherwise grow astigmatically jagged or erode at their edges grain by grain.

The comic book is the current *Green Lantern* (number 3, December 1960; he was my favorite superhero then, with his "power ring" and his "emerald oath": I'll tell you about him later).

Her song is a bittersweet undulation, de-DAH, de-DAH, de-de-de-DAH, oi-YOY, the last a plaintive phrase stretched thin to nearly breaking: *mine liebe, mine liebe,* my love, my love. The light is the light of late afternoon, and it denses itself in tufts of her hair that have unsprung from the bun as if a blossoming of memories are escaping her head, on fire.

In the basement below us, my father, her son, is "doing the books," as he called it, sitting hopelessly over a ledger of accounts that, opened, seemed to me to be about the size of a refrigerator, and just as cold: an oblong you could enter and have the door lock on you. Once a month, that happens to my father. He goes to take a quick look at the rent and grocery holding, and we need to drag him out hours later, back into the land of the human.

The basement is where we've stored ill-fitting clothes and miscellaneous linens, where the dog pouts overnight, with his bowls of liverish mush and water, with his "pissy post" surrounded by fanned-out newspaper. Here, in a corner, my father positioned a desk and a thrift shop pea-green file cabinet. This is where he comes to corrugate his forehead over the angst of household expenditure.

I know it doesn't sound pretty but, if I think of its loss, a sticky affection sludges through my system. I love the aisles in old-fashioned office supply shops. Here, I'll find similar ledgers; when I lightly run my fingers over the deep-imprinted mottling of their fake black leather covers, or when I look at the stacks of spools of paper tape of the kind he'd use in his clunker Neolithic "adding machine," punching numbers clumsily in with his forefinger, I can feel the profound emotion—the raw, familial *caring*—that kept him in place at that desk until the job was done. And I can't help but feel, gawking through some sleek new CompuCenter with its blipping "electronic money management programming/entertainment monitors" ready to forcibly cure me of a barbaric dependence on paper clips or a sentimental attachment to those docile flocks of "jumbo" erasers the pink of bubble gum . . . I can't help fear, Luddite me, that replacing the world of Frieda Garfunkle's Paper Goods & Office Notions with these *très* trim temples of hi-tech engineering means replacing, too, the simple generosities and ritual perseverance with which he safely saw our house through choppy fiscal waters, down there with the tape of the adding machine unspooling entry by entry into the night like a captain's log.

It's the same willful application of love I'll see through the cracked-open bathroom door when he's testing her pee for diabetes, dropping the tablet into that richly amber vial and waiting for its alchemical play of color change—this, twice a week. Or helping her with her antiquated buttonhook shoes. (Could she be belligerent, *noodg, noodg, noodg?*—oh yes.) Or helping her, long past the days of her need for vanity, unwrap the equally antiquated iron hair crimper, heating it, curling the last sad skimplets of gray. I remember the smell of singed hair floating over her folding-bed.

Amol iz geven un haynt iz nito.—Once it was; today, no more.

2. THE THEORY OF HAWTHORNE'S NOTEBOOKS

"Something like this happens, it's crazy—then *everything's* crazy."

I'm silent at my end of the 750 miles; the phone line fills with pinprick crackles.

Craig tries clarifying his grief: "I mean, we were together *fifteen years*," and he goes on (and on—I'm paying) to talk about missing the sharing, or helping Gaylene pack up for the move to her own apartment, "I still talk to her, do you know that?—to an empty space that follows me around." The day before, I'd phoned Gaylene. She'd said, "It hurts inside, like twigs are snapping all of the time. I'll start some smart rejoinder at a conference, and: *snap*, and then I'm just staring ahead with waterfall eyes like a loony-toon." I've known them for ten of those fifteen years, two people as snugly hinged as the wings of a diptych. Now this. It *is* crazy.

"Then," he says, "dividing up the collections!" These were the signs of their love, toy taj mahals by which their hearts' ineffable whoop-de-do was made visible.

Miniature books (the giantmost four-postage-stamps size), each scouted out indefatigably with a strictness of passion that matched the passion that fashioned those thumbnail marbled endpapers. 1920s and '30s Mexican handcarved carousel horses (seven, madly champing along one wall of their second-story apartment); they were chanced-on in the early days when even pinchpenny graduate students might corral these eternally fiery-maned lime and coral beauties. And (convened beneath the Big Top patiently over a decade of crosscountry hunting) one entire set of inchling Schoenhut circus figurines from three generations ago, not only the clowns, the trapezists, and dancing bears, etc., but the tents, the banners, the cages and feed troughs, the comet-painted center ring—the giraffe and the zebu, *everything*.

"Albert, listen"—I've called Craig up from a roadside telephone booth in the middle of Nowhere, Oklahoma: of course I'm going to listen—"we're nearly forty, even now we care about each other's feelings, we're civilized human beings, and there we were at four in the morning, back in the alley, howling the living piss out of our systems, fighting over the ringmaster. Over the goddamn three-inch ringmaster.

"Gaylene was going to punch me one, I could read it in her musculature, but halfway there she turned it into the crack of an invisible whip, see?—*she* was the ringmaster, I was down on my knees in the glass and the burger wrappers, I was an animal being tamed, and then *I* was the ringmaster, she was on her back . . . The only saving grace is, nobody called the police. It's *crazy*."

These are the people whose friends consult them regularly for reasoned advice. This is the couple that sleeps like spoons.

"Last night . . . I thought if only I could find *some* sensible thing to hold to, *anything*. So I looked in the newspaper." Over the roll of dustbowl wind, I hear the soft rattle of *Daily Clarion* pages, the clearing of stagey phlegm.

" 'In London, a pedestrian was killed last night when an unknown assailant threw a turnip at him from a passing car. Also hospitalized was a woman who suffered severe stomach injuries after being hit by a cabbage. London police'—blah blah blah."

Page-turn. "Stamford, Connecticut. 'Tattoo artist Spider Webb has opened a Bra Museum, exhibiting *100 Years of Brassieres*, including a tinfoil bra, a Plexiglas bra, and a cockroach bra.' Then he's quoted."

Page-turn. Voice is going watery now. " 'A 21-year-old Phoenix woman was sentenced to jail for leaving her 18-month-old daughter locked in a closet for eight days, when' *get this*" (his voice is only the thinnest gurgle) " 'she went to the hospital to have another baby . . .'

"It was all like some system for *amplifying* the craziness I was feeling. Albert, really: what kind of a cosmos *is* this?"

*

The answer from the start of Hawthorne's *American Notebooks* is: the cosmos is clear, and calm, and considered in partite, in language equally clear and calm.

"A walk down to the Juniper. The shore of the coves strewn with bunches of seaweed, driven in by recent winds. Eel-grass, rolled and bundled up, and entangled with it,—large marine vegetables, of an olive color, with round, slender, snake-like stalks, four or five feet long, and nearly two feet broad: these are the herbage of the deep sea."

These are the book's first words, from June of 1835; its entries continue for eighteen years, and not once is the great task flinched from: looking the world in the eye, and then finding the words for its sharpest delineation.

"The village, viewed from the top of a hill . . . It is amusing to see all the distributed property of the aristocracy and commonality, the various and conflicting interests of the town, the loves and hates, compressed into a space which the eye takes in completely as the arrangement of a tea-table." That same day, he writes of "the one-armed soap-maker, Lawyer H———, [who] wears an iron hook," and, later, he bothers to note, "The green is deeper in consequence of the recent rain."

He's always ready to capture Nature: sunsets, tidelines, rainstorms, flocks and swarms, "and an enormous eel . . . truly he had the taste of the whole river in his flesh, with a very prominent flavor of mud." But really *all* of the things of this world are made space for. "A withered, yellow, sodden, dead-alive looking woman,—an opium eater." "Objects on a wharf—a huge pile of cotton bales, from a New Orleans ship, twenty or thirty feet high, as high as a house. Barrels of molasses . . . casks of linseed oil . . . iron in bars . . . Long Wharf is devoted to ponderous, evil-smelling, inelegant necessities of life."

And there's another world, also accommodated. As naturally as noting afternoon's lengthening shadows or fall's first russets, Hawthorne writes that "the spells of witches have the power of producing meats and viands," that "when we shall be endowed with our spiritual bodies, I think that they will be so constituted that we may send thoughts and feelings any distance in no time at all." For every update on a sunrise, there's some awestruck traipse through a landscape forever in haze, a "body possessed by two different spirits," "a book of magic," "a phantom," "a prophecy."

It reminds me of random paging through a huge volume of Rembrandt's unprejudiced eye. Here, Christ preaches, backed by an angle of sunlight as substantial as a newel-post. There, a woman brusquely raises her orchidy underskirts, to squat to piss. The angel appears to Abraham. A rat-killer peddles his service.

The many worlds are one world, finally; Hawthorne can't draw the line. He says, "I have observed that butterflies—very broad-winged and magnificent butterflies—frequently come on board of the salt-ship, where I am at work, where there are no flowers nor any green thing. I cannot account for them, unless they are the lovely fantasies of the mind."

*

I called Gaylene from a town that consisted, it seemed, of a gas pump, the pump attendant, and two thin chickens that looked as if for years they'd been used to wipe dipsticks. One half-hour down the highway, I called Craig. A man *should* worry, at the frailty of strong friends. Even their casualness disturbed me, it was something like a teapot beat out from battleship plating: its origin couldn't be hidden. Yes, I've promised them both at their separate numbers, I'll call again that afternoon, from Austin, Texas. A few minutes later, I pass an overturned crew-car of tar, which had spread to be a black circle about the size of a major resort hotel swimming pool—and even so, the landscape I'm driving through dwindles it to a demitasse serving.

I live in Wichita, Kansas, now. For ten years, though, I lived in Austin; when I left (at the end of one of those enervating bouts of post-divorce-carouse-*cum*-depression) I left near thirty cartons of miscellaneous books, old mail, and papers in

Jim Magnuson's keeping stored in the UT English Department's lock room.

"They want to make it a lounge now, buddy." And so I was coaxing the Dodge Colt south through Oklahoma, past the beckoning exit for GENE AUTRY, past the A/A rhyme scheme exit sign for the brother cities WAYNE PAYNE, through the ironed-flat plains of that state, in a bad August lull where the heat sets up shop in your marrow and deals its product from there, down memory lane, up caffeine rushes, eventually past my favorite Dallas exit sign, CAMP WISDOM RD.

I could have used some of its wares. I only vaguely remembered what dead notes and doodads were hodgepodged into those cartons, and I'd done without them smartly enough for two good Wichita years. I should have had Jim order them hauled to the dump.

Except I *couldn't* have, of course. They'd been mine and the ghosts of my fingerprints eddied, countless tiny weathermaps of storms, above them yet. They'd been mine, and they called, and I hearkened. I came with fresh flat boxes and tape, to redo it all fitted to my car. Ten hours there, ten back. An idiot's errand. I couldn't let go.

*

"Three-pronged steel forks . . ." "The soul . . ." What Hawthorne's notebooks do is give us such a rich collection from this *olla-podrida* planet of ours, the craziest elements fit. Rembrandt's *oeuvre*, the same.

"The thing is, you and Gaylene, your story is just one page, and you're stuck on it, reading it over and over. That's what your psyche needs to do now, read it over and over. Maybe another extraneous paragraph or three drift in from . . . a newspaper, say; but not enough to give you a sense of the whole collected *shmeer*.

"But later, a day, a year, who-knows-when, *later*—you'll read the big picture. Your own page won't seem so crazy, believe me."

Back in my divorce days, Craig would call up three, four times a night, delivering similar pep talks. So: I'm phoning him from Austin.

Louis Simpson has a poem that starts

> The first time I saw a pawnshop
> I thought, Sheer insanity.
> A revolver lying next to a camera,
> violins hanging in the air like hams . . .

but eight lines later he's come to see the Theory of Hawthorne's Notebooks; he tells us, "Each has its place in the universe."

*

But Craig is little comforted by my theory, as it turns out. "Albert, listen: I want my unhappiness *over*, I don't need to hear that it has its own niche in the Scheme of Things." Well, maybe. But it was my best shot.

"Late last night I couldn't sleep, my arm kept stretching into her space in the bed, like extending it up-to-the-elbow into an alternate dimension.

"Just to take my mind off everything, I whammoed *They Saved Hitler's Brain* into the VCR. You remember."

I remember. Years ago, when I was sore in need of cheering up, we watched it: a '63 Z-level piece of schlockola that (wouldn't you know it?) by now has attracted its own "cult following."

Edited from footage shot in the Philippines (we *think*) and in America (though neither looks to have been aware, when the cameras were rolling, that it was made for wedding with the other), and with a car crash "borrowed" from *Thunder Road*, the plot is incoherent; but as I recall, a scientist's beautiful daughter and stalwart son-in-law (the love interest) somehow adventure through "Mandoras," a Latin American banana republic, saving civilized life from a band of retired Nazis who own the head of Adolf Hitler, and hatch big plans for finding *der Führer* another body and taking over the world with stockpiled canisters of nerve gas. A book on spliced-tripe cinema puts the title character's contribution this way: "Through it all, the brain of 'Mr. H.' (as he is respectfully known) is represented by a gooey, waxed face poured into a pickle jar and hooked up to bubbling, crackling, hissing life-support systems." Got it?

"Albert, get this: I wouldn't tell anyone else: but I was worn so ragged that when the dewy-eyed glances that passed for a love scene started, I began sobbing, dry sobbing, right there in my underwear. That's right, you heard me.

"Seriously sobbing."

*

Gaylene says: "Maybe it was 5 A.M. Did he tell you? I got the circus. Big deal. But you should see how we battled about it.

"I sat down in front of it, thinking it might help me forget. I *willed* myself, my whole self, to be just the size of my eyes. Do I have a screw loose, or what? And then I walked through the midway.

"I thought—how can I say this?—I thought I'd talk to my favorite ones. The clown with the pompom cap who juggled oranges and tenpins. The woman who does ballet on the rump of a galloping horse. The lion tamer. I even heard the calliope music. OOMpahpah, OOMpahpah. But all of them: I'd bought them with Craig, they each had a story. Who we had to haggle with, what cobwebby corner of what slopped shop we rooted through, where we were in our lives then. Whole summers, in some cases, fish fries and walking the pier.

"It rose up from each of the figures, gradually, this foggy twin. Do you see what I'm saying? The majorette couldn't twirl her baton without this hurtful majorette-out-of-fog coming up behind her.

"And a me-of-fog, and a him-of-fog . . . Anyway," pulling herself together, "by that time it was morning. I dressed and left for work."

*

Hawthorne is filled with ghosts.

In groups or singly, claiming a protagonist's share of attention or simply weaving between the lines like old smoke in a pillow, black-hatted, primly bonneted, dour, they bow in sacerdotal greeting from the past, they accuse, they won't be polished off the brass like any common smudges, they mist at the window, they well up the throat and brandy won't help, they linger. On some pages, walking the streets of Concord or Salem means walking through ghosts as heavy as opera drapes.

A classically imagined one: "A ghost seen by moonlight; when the moon was out, it would shine and melt through the airy substance of the ghost, as through a cloud." What might he have done with a later, westward sensibility? Ghosts of disenfranchised Sioux and Comanche, ghosts of passenger pigeons flocking as thick as a pudding, showing visibly, as moisture on the cheeks.

In every culture there's some version of the tale where the monkey is trapped—his fist in the cookie jar, robbing it overmuch, is too full, and he can't slip out. But he won't give up even one cookie. *He* thinks it's the *jar* that won't let go.

Every ghost has a jar that keeps him here.

We see them at night; or on damp and bleary days, rain making gray twill of the air. *Let go*, they're saying, *let go of us*.

There's a promise from three generations back that needs mending; there's an unopened trunk; there's an axe; there's a locket. *Let go-o-o-o-o of us.*

3. LANGUAGE LESSONS

Fun yidishe reyd ken men zikh nit opvashn in tsen vassern.
—Ten waters will not cleanse you of Jewish talk.

*

My grandmother took an H (it meant *heart*: she'd have to be checked); they started to lead her away. The enormous receiving room was a brutal assault of confusion: clamor, tangles of lines, you didn't know for what, but ahead a woman was crying out *No, no, no,* like a child. Close to fifty immigrants sprawled in a corner in different degrees of lassitude. A girl about eight, with a shaved scalp, played with a filthy rag; you could see dull welts, from scratching, lined her cranium, as if she were some kind of medical chart.

"By the basket at the window," my grandfather said. These were his first words since they'd been sent to this line an hour before. The total of all the words he'd spoken since docking early that morning couldn't have been much more than three times that. They'd learned, on the long way over, to hold such luxuries as speech, or even obvious shows of affection, in reserve. It was a faith: that their affection wasn't dead, but in abeyance.

Now she wanted to weep at his brief and sudden Yiddish. A hunger for more of it washed through her, she wanted him shouting it at these *fershlooginer* men and women in their soiled green uniform jackets, she thought if he stopped speaking Yiddish right now, he'd be dropping the one frayed rope that still attached them at all to the world she was born in.

*

In 1881, Alexander III pursued what Irving Howe calls "a steady anti-Jewish policy"—this is a translation of what was often a drunk footsoldier ripping intestines out of a freshly savaged sixteen-year-old girl, and waving them overhead for a trophy. "The *shtetl* began to empty a portion of its youth into the slums of Warsaw, Vilna, Lodz, Minsk, Bialystok . . ." and, eventually, New York.

Once just a word for the hellish section below deck, *steerage* has come to mean, for my grandparents' people, the whole of transition experience: homeless, hungry, cut, and stunned, and then the narrow oilstained stairway down to a hard dark shelf, for being stored like sacks of coal above where the stirring-screws trembled twenty-four hours. "Someone above me vomited straight upon my head . . ." ". . . the babies throwing up even their mother's milk . . ." ". . . in their berths in a stupor, from breathing air whose oxygen has been mostly replaced by foul gases."

The language went with. "It was the word that counted most. Yiddish culture was a culture of speech, and its God a God who spoke . . . Neither set nor formalized, always in rapid process of growth and dissolution, Yiddish . . . acquired an international scope, borrowing freely from almost every European language . . . intimately reflecting the travail of wandering, exile."

It's not singular to the Jewish tradition, of course, that *naming* it *causes* it to be (in the Mayan *Popol Vuh*, for instance, "the first word" precedes "the face of the earth"). "Let there be light," and everything hierarchically follows, out of this ur-nanosecond utterance. When Adam names the animals on Eden's plains, he specifies that general creation: *kudu, dodo, cassowary, tapir, lemur, axolotl, emu, kiwi, kodiak, koala, narwhal, dog, lamb, snake,* and *angelfish*. Noah repeats this original naming at the gangplank, checking them off by twos. They're herded aboard, the crowded and terrifying journey begins, and then they're brusquely disembarked, wobbly and needing to start the world anew.

My grandparents knew this concept as The Diaspora. The clouds broke and they landed at Ellis Island. They had one paper satchel of clothes, some Yiddish proverbs, and their names.

*

What he meant, she understood, was "We won't leave this room until we both meet at the basket, then we'll leave together." She shook her head *no*: "Under that picture of ships." The basket might disappear, a picture hung up was a safer bet. She'd learned, the last few years, to make these swift decisions in favor of a half-degree's greater assurance. He was too worn even to wink at her savvy modification. Then, led to her line, she was lost inside another hundred just like her.

The picture was of two faint-sepia steamships, ironing out

some sepia waves. He waited patiently, crumpling his hat, then carefully shaping it back again. To left and right, vast numbers of even newer arrivals were being processed. They fixed 5,000 a day as the official number, but some days the truth was closer to 15,000. People were being questioned, for retardation. In one room, he knew, he'd been there, a medic was lining up the men and "doing" their asses as casually and quickly as if sorting mail; he only jerked his glove in the dish of disinfectant each ninth or tenth case.

"*Oyyy* . . ." A woman, in line to have her eyelid creased back. (The eye disease trachoma caused more than half of all the medical detentions.) Where was Nettie? Women out of sight were whimpering. He tried to listen but none of the words in the air made sense, and most of what he heard as "talking" shaded off, immediately, into noise.

Now Nettie's arm was folded lightly in his, from nowhere it seemed, from out of the barracks dinge, and by her face he knew she'd passed whatever arcane cardiac gauntlet was required. Without a word, they walked to the outside rail and breathed New York over the water. She looked back: of course, the basket was gone. Did she have the right wall?—even the sepia ships had disappeared.

They were off: the hawsers whipped up, the ferry bucked. What did he see, with his okayed eyes, and his okayed wife beside him? Not much, fog was low, you couldn't see three feet ahead. The harbor reeked, and the ferry chopped through it with equal pungency: feta cheese in splotchy wheels, old mattress ticking, sausage in hogbowel casings, tins of greasy feathers, sheaves of leather, wrinkled dried fruits knotted up in a kerchief, babies' bottomrags.

They docked. Somewhere he'd lost his hat. The dockworkers' voices, more strange than the gulls'.

Then they were at "the Pig Market," Hester near Ludlow. The streets were . . . you see? They didn't have the words.

A welter of pushcarts sorted the little late-afternoon light: peaches a penny a quart, alarm clocks, cucumbers floating in milk tubs, watch it buddy, faster, kapow, by the hundred, whores, look move it, wagons hauling the Christian proselytizers, a boy not over twelve distributing cards with the whores' addresses, neckties straightened just *so*, that's my place mac, cracked eggs, the boxing match this, hey sugar, the boxing match that, beneath these new American angels: pigeons, gray and mean.

Says Irving Howe, "The density of the Tenth Ward . . . shortly after the turn of the century was greater than most of the worst sections of Bombay." And, "The first English expressions that struck my foreign ear as I walked through the ghetto that day . . . were 'sharrap' (shut up) and 'garrarrahere' (get out of here). It took me a little while to learn that the English tongue was not restricted to these two terms."

They rested near the scissorsman, his grindstone throwing off sparks. Nettie sat on their single satchel. She wished he hadn't lost his hat, the way his hair was thinning. She knew how he could be about that. *Draikop*, she told herself, "silly head." How *much* had they lost, this last year, and here she was worrying over a hat.

"They gots some help for greenhorns." He'd put down a scissors to motion across the street, then he repeated his statement in Yiddish—a *landsman*! Was she *tzedráyt*, insane? She wanted to reach at his lips and catch it all leaving, as if they might be tiny birds.

"They'll get us rooms? A job?" My grandfather knew of such agencies, even had some names folded into his pocket; still, in the midst of the tumult, this news appeared incredible.

"Sure. Now, please . . ." (switch to English) "I dun't gots da time." And back to the turning wheel.

That evening, as boarders in a tenement flat, they each unscrewed a door and set it on two low fish-smelling crates, and so had side-by-side beds in a room where four other people already snored. The room was dim, but she could see one sleeper's upturned cheek was fissured with scars; they were thin, as if maybe a knife. My grandfather tied a string from his leg to the satchel.

Whispering.

"What's Sarah doing back home, do you think?"

He thought. "I don't know." Silence. "This is our home."

"It was some day, yah?"

"Yes. This ice with the flavor in, it was good."

"But still, it was some day."

"Yes."

"Sarah must be closing up the shop by now, with the new goods."

"I said I don't know."

"I only . . ."

Harsh: "I-said-I-don't-know."

(Already the trouble was starting. In that dim room you could still see it coming.)

Silence.

Then, making light of his ire: "Ah, why don't I sharrap."

They held hands, slab to slab. When it was clear that their roommates would sleep through a *pogrom* he slurred her a lullabye in his late-night after-some-vodka voice of the old days, *Netteleh, Netteleh, zing mir a lideleh*, tracing tightening circles over her breasts. But he fell into sleep the first, a weary man on the fidgeting end of a string.

She couldn't sleep, there was this plank inside her as stiff as the door beneath. She walked the two flights down to the stoop, too weary herself to feel caution. For a while she only stared with passive fixity at the scraps of moving moonlight on a trickle of filth in the gutter across the way. She started singing then, a childhood tune in a lightheaded hush, *Mama makes with the tea for me, Papa makes with the honey, When I grow up I'll dance all day, And buy white lace with my money.*

A street dog trotted up and forthrightly rested its head in her lap. It was ragged and, from what she could tell in the half-dark, seemed to be the color of a wen. She stroked its snout.

"Dat's a pretty song, lady."

"Yah, yah, pretty. Pretty-schmitty. From a long time back."

"Dun't be so cynical, kiddo. A voice like yours, like a lark on da ving, troo' da fields—*hoo*! You could rule dis crapped-up vorld."

"So show me this lark. So show me this field, Mr. Big Shot Dog."

"Vell . . . howzabout I show you da crapped-up vorld part? I gots mit plenty of dat."

"From that, I don't need seeing no more."

"Oh, like it or not, you gonna, *tsahtskaleh*. Up and down, morn to moon, vork and a liddle more vork. May as vell face it down mit your tail up, dat's vhat us dogs say. Look, I come by sometime, I show you around."

"Yah, sure, why not?"

"Mr. Loner Dog, Mr. Boner Dog, Mr. Howler mit Growler mit Groaner Dog—dat's me. You'll *zing* me some more? A *lideleh*?"

"Yah, yah."

"Okay by me. So tell me: you ain't puzzled, a dog should be talking like dis here to you?"

"First, *hoont*, you're a dream. The second, you make me more sense in my head than any talk yet in America."

"Fletterer. Go back now. Go, sleep by him."

"Yah, sleep . . ."

sleep . . .

(joking:) "Garrarrahere."

*

It was a mongrel.

It razzed the fatcat boys, it blatted out its ass, it danced in circles with God for a partner, it boozed and it shmoozed and it prayed all night in the coal cellar under the buttery light of a few thumbs of tallow—this Yiddish.

It resourcefully lopes into History, from the basin of the Moselle and the banks of the Rhine, around 1100, a quadru-hybrid: Rabbinic Hebrew, Old French, Old Italian, and Middle High German, a language in search of a saint and an all-night poker game, this Yiddish, this mongrel, this backstreet patch-work creature, suspect, coupling in the alley crannies, thieving, lean and wry and rolling a phlegm in its throat as rich as sperm-whale oil. Somewhere in between the blazing gates of Heaven and the backstage door of a burlesque joint, its *oy* and *ich* are bickering, dickering, giving a *yoohoo* out the window, scented with a breathy mishmash of lox and *kasha* and stomach bile.

Over five hundred Yiddish words have officially crossed into *Webster's*. From the earliest days, the New York ghetto was home to a flexible "Yinglish." Say one affluent week you scrounge an extra nickel or two, you saunter to the soda parlor. Restauranting, foreign to a *shtetl* Jew, "is spreading every day," the *Jewish Forward* reported in 1903. You take the missus's arm, you go for a double dip: *oysesn*, "out-eating."

But language lags. The trolleys swoosh their first fierce time before your greenhorn eyes, with the confusing force of Ezekiel's roil of wheels, and the words for it don't catch up for a while.

Our sense of the future *requires* that wait, Bronowski says. Once input flashes whambang into the brain, it enters a period of "reflection, during which different lines of action are played through and tested." Memory, which Bronowski defines as "the storing of signals in some symbolic form, so that they may be used to revive our senses in the future," is possible only "if the initial response . . . is delayed long enough to separate some abstract marker and fix it in the brain. This is basically a linguistic mechanism."

In this way, language and memory enable—in some sense, even may *be*—each other. William Gass: "I remember—I contain a past—partly because my friends and family allow me to repeat and polish my tales." In a Louis Simpson poem, "Profession of Faith," the speaker understands that a memory of his wife "in the garden . . . reaching up, pulling a branch," and of a purely fictional figure spectrally "floating in mid-air" really are equivalent: "The things we see and the things we imagine, / afterwards, when you think about them, / are equally composed of words. / / It is the words we use, finally, / that matter, if anything does."

Gass again: "To *know* is to possess words . . . we name incessantly, conserving achievements and customs, and countries that no longer exist."

She stands in the kitchen, preserving. Light goes sea-green in the Mason jars, the smell of brine pinches the air. Or she's not there at all, no, she's humming her Yiddish ditties and it's 1911, her hair is an inky plait to her waist, his lips are idly jittering over the small of her back as she's singing for him, a low, slow, soulful version of a village tune they'd do together reining the wagon up to its rail at Sarah's shop for tannery goods, and then she'd invite them for sweet tea, with the samovar winking the lees of the sun off its sloped copper shoulders, an heirloom, she insisted, from the grandmother she most missed . . .

conserving countries that no longer exist

4. BUNDLES

They paid for a one-room apartment by now, a crate that nightly floated them over the *dreck* and commotion. Both of them worked, though hers was part-time seamstressing for a shopfront two or three removes from the major garment district mayhem. And, in slack times, she could bring her baskets of rough cloth home: they'd play that she was a lady of leisure.

"Shit!" She'd pricked her thumb. She didn't so much learn the word, as have it simply seep into her from the streets, an ineradicable brown dye streaking her standard lessonbook English. He tried to, but couldn't, drum home its difference from her other, native imprecation, "Feh!" and in time it replaced the earlier word completely. Once, when they were having an argument: "Can it!" she blurted, no less surprised than he was, "Baloney!"

But nothing stopped Mr. *Hoont* from visiting. Loneliness could summon him, or wearying toil; she suffered both, and through her hazed half-wakefulness, he'd gradually materialize, always with a harmless leer or with made-up news from the Old Country, Yasha was doing this now, Sarah that. At these times, English shinnied out the room's one window and down the drainpipe. Yiddish filled the room then, every sentence like a burning-red bouquet set into a milkglass vase, until the space around her was roses and fire.

And my grandfather?—he had his own companion, not a dog, a *dybbuk*, a spirit, a streetwise guy in a slanting derby. Anyway, that's what the voice was like. It hovered outside the window some nights while she was asleep, it hovered there as if on a cloud of streetstink-and-squabble. *Forget the pack*, it told him. *You can leave it all behind you, guy. It's easy, just trust me. Let go-o-o-o-o of it* . . .

About the pack:

"In the cities of the North," says Howe, "during the years of industrial expansion, peddling was backbreaking and soul-destroying work." He quotes Morris Witcowsky on his merchandise pack: ". . . weighed about a hundred and twenty pounds, eighty pounds strapped to the back and a forty-pound 'balancer' in the front." Then you walked, you climbed, the tenement stairs of the ghetto blurring to one enormous treadmill. Knock. Who is it? DryYYY GooOOOoods. Get out of here you show your hook-nose face again I'll kick your ass clear back to Roosia. Twelve hours a day of this, until at the end the pack was the brain, the rider, and you were its well-whipped beast.

"You want a *bisseleh* ice cream?" he asked her.

"No, but I come with." She set down the sewing—a yellow strip of buttonholes in a basket of strips of buttonholes. "Maybe just for the air, yes? Some fresh air."

He was silent.

The light in their single room was often lost halfway to the floor, so giving it the thick look of an aquarium of ill-kept water. Even with the window opened, the feeling was often one of uncut murk.

"It would be nice, the fresh air."

"I *heard* you, Nettie!" He spoke, though, in the direction of the pack. It filled one corner. There was a night when she woke, he was snoring exhausted beside her, and she thought she saw it twitch in the gloom, then grow in front of her eyes.

Too much was new, "the way people walked, the rhythms

of the streets, the division of the day into strict units of time, the disposal of waste, the relations among members of the family, the exchange of goods and money." And Howe continues, "That symptoms of social dislocation and even pathology should have appeared under the extreme circumstances in which the early Jewish immigrants lived seems unavoidable."

Gangs were common, especially gangs of pickpockets, "grifters," and up to 30 percent of all delinquents brought before the Children's Court of New York in 1906 were Jewish. On some streets—Allen, Rivington, Stanton, Delancey—prostitution flourished. "Dancing academies" trained young girls and recruited pimps, "cadets." The Yiddish term for "whore," of course, a *nahfkie* or a *koorveh*, long preceded the wave to America; and still, for some, it's surprising to see such obviously Jewish names appearing on lists of offenders: "Lena Blum, Ida Katz, Sadie Feldman . . ." They squatted on stoops, exhibited thighs that bulged like overripe bries. Some knitted, some chewed Russian sunflower seeds, they squeezed their breasts with rude duck honkings. And here, the famous hoodlums—Legs Diamond, Little Kishky, Spanish Johnny, all Jews—concocted their apprenticeship swindles.

Husbands abandoned their families. Pressures and temptations were extraordinary, after all. Of requests for financial relief made to United Hebrew Charities in 1903 and 1904, 10 to 15 percent came from deserted women; by 1911, a National Desertion Bureau had been established. For years, the most popular features of the Yiddish newspaper the *Forward* were the "Bintel Brief" (the "Bundle of Letters"), where readers wrote in with their crises, and the "Gallery of Missing Husbands," where, as a typical instance, Bessie Cohen would be "looking for Nathan Cohen my husband, an umbrella peddler, 22 years old, the little finger of his right hand is bent. He abandoned me and a five-month-old baby in great need. I offer $25 . . ."

The *dybbuk* was busy. *Let go-o-o-o-o of it . . .*

The air down in the streets *was* fresher, marginally. The great machine-tinged winds of the elevated's passing clatter quivered those dense heated blocks of aroma that rested above their designated pushcarts: fish spillings, hardening butter, mushbodied cabbages. A broomstick-and-tincan game of baseball hogged one corner. On Allen Street, the girls yoohooed and flashed their ankles in playful scissoring kicks.

"No, Nettie. We go down some other way."

"Yes, hokay." She'd been distracted by the ragtag game of ball, the ganglier older players, and one befuddled six-or-seven-year-old who was waddling about with a sopping pantsful—for a while now, she'd been thinking of children. But then: "Oh, wait. It's Lena. *Leeena!*"

"Nettie." A tug. His hand like a mastiff at her black sleeve. "Wait, it's Lena. Lena!"

Halfway down Allen, Lena crossed her meaty calves and waved back.

"You know such a woman?" The pack had been heavy all day with a thousand weights, and now this.

"This is Lena," she said, beginning to sense the enormity of the situation, what she'd started in crossing a social boundary for companionship's sake, her English beginning to stumble under the stress, "from Cracow. *Nu?* She *geb* me butter, to her I *geb* salt." Something in his look. "She makes my friend." You traded butter for salt, back then, and there, it made you a friend. Prouder in repetition, and as if the naked fact of it undid a net of lesser considerations, "She makes my friend."

This extra weight, this thousandth-and-one. He felt his eyes grime over with some emotion he had no word for, not in any of his languages.

"Come, Nettie. We go now." The el rattled past; this close, they both could feel shiverings inside their bodies like dishes and ewers precariously shelved.

"We go down Allen Street, yes? It would be short. To say hello Lena. Salt I give her, is all. For the pickled herring."

"You do not know such women."

"I have eyes, I see things. *You* know such women."

Then he called her a name.

In the wake of the el, the silence became like a third party standing there with them.

"I think you go back, for the pack," she said. "In it you put your clothes and your *chuchik* for the cigarettes and your knife." She paused. "You will not no more live inside my house." She'd never before said anything so softly, and by this he knew its sincerity.

He was gone that night.

She stepped in the space where the pack had been. Its absence ordered the room around it, as definitely as its presence had. "Shit! Shit!" and she pulled her hair. Then she fell to the floor and was weeping into her basket of cloths, she wept now for the first time since he'd shouldered his belongings and stepped through the door. Her eyes poured it lavishly out, she imagined the basket spilling it onto the boards. Her last thought, right before sleep: that Lena could come for this bundle of salt now, could borrow as much as she wanted.

*

The monster came flying.

It missed his head by inches, unstitching apart in midair, the shark half falling gracelessly into a puddle on the after-rain clay, but the monkey half continuing in a high arc, with its stuffing showering out of its undone bottom, and a swag of dirty linen trailing out of the same, snapping like a pennant.

"No! And no! And no!" Hendrickje was screaming at him from where she stood in the doorway, each deep-throated *no* volleyed into the lane with the angry strength she'd given to pitching the curio.

Rembrandt shuffled there, speechless, angry in turn (the 200 florins was *his* commission, not hers) and shamed (but wasn't it true she'd been counting each carrot these days, each seam in a hem, and what could he expect when she returned from the market with fishtails for the broth because anything savorier was beyond their meager means this week, and waiting for her in the hush of the parlor, on a teak base, was Mathilde, as he'd taken to calling his purchase, Mathilde wearing an overturned tulip on her head to crown her "Queen of the Deep" . . .) and then angry again, no not at Hendrickje posing with her hands on her aproned hips in classic pique, and not with himself, but simply with circumstance, that had brought them together, and then had brought them to this. He gingerly lifted the shark-half, shrugged at its lumpishness, sighed once (histrionically: she was watching, still), then turned and shambled off. He'd snugged Mathilde's wet netherpart under one arm, and a sketchbook under the other.

Somewhere in between the house on the Rozengracht (for this is where he lived now, having lost the earlier showplace-of-a-dwelling) and the synagogue (for that was his destination) he let go the ratty remnant of shark; he couldn't even remember where or how.

But the sketchbook he gripped as if it would float him over these recently troubled waters. The sketchbook was where he would stay for the afternoon, until he was healed of ire and guilt. He eased himself up to the shadow-side of a pillar (they didn't all like being sketched, these Sons of David), unwrapped a stick of charcoal, and let the nimbleness that lived in his fingers run free. "Going Jewing," a neighbor of his had derisively termed it. Alright then, he was. The faces here were creased and hurt and determined in ways he'd never seen in any other Amsterdam face, though sometimes they reminded him, crazily enough, of an unworldly gaunt-cheeked bearded look he'd seen in certain fish at the market he privately thought of as "High Priest fish."

". . . no other Amsterdam painter did as many portraits of Jews as Rembrandt. One scholar has guessed that about a fifth of Rembrandt's portraits of men are Jews—this at a time when the Jews represented perhaps one percent of the population of Amsterdam. This would fit with the general impression that Rembrandt gives of a temperament moved more by personal warmth than by ideology." [Charles L. Mee, Jr.]

Some of his friends were Sephardic Jews, educated, assimilated denizens of the cultural life. But today, at the synagogue, Rembrandt is sketching furiously at the faces of Ashkenazim, newly arrived from Poland: the women in shawls and slipping wigs, the men in tunics concocted of grain sacks tied by rope at the waist, and their faces!—inward-looking, ethereal, and yet tuberlike faces! One is cantankering with a compatriot now, and he places a finger alongside his nose, for every point of logic he scores . . .

Because I'm trying to write of how and why we save things over time, I'll quote what Kenneth Clark says, "He had always loved painting Jews: he saw in them repositories of ancient wisdom and an unchanging faith."

. . . and almost as quickly, a finger in charcoal takes shape alongside a charcoal nose.

5. ZAMLERS

"Because I'm trying to write of how and why we save things over time," I wrote, and meant both definitions of *save*: "to collect" and "to rescue."

"The word for it is *hemshekh*," Aaron Lansky says, " 'continuity.' " Lansky sweeps an open hand at 700,000 Yiddish-language books on the floor of a renovated paper factory in Holyoke, Massachusetts; there are 200,000 more in the National Yiddish Book Center's primary office, and six or seven hundred donated volumes a week are still received. "This is from the world Hitler tried to destroy."

In 1980, when Lansky was twenty-four, he founded the Center with earnings from a summer of migrant blueberry picking in Maine. The Center consisted of a government-surplus typewriter and a picnic table. Ten years later, Lansky heads a network of 100 volunteer *zamlers* ("collectors") and 8,000 dues-paying members. Not all of the titles are warehoused; some already have "been returned to circulation, restored to the life of books" for readers in Brooklyn, Thailand, Guam, or Tokyo. "As native speakers pass on, the books become the sole access to the last thousand years of Jewish history."

It's as if he lives in a sentence, at exactly the inky atom of a sentence, where the word *razed* puns into *raised*. "They're giving up a library," Lansky says of his typical elderly Jewish donors; for them "it's like a moment of transition."

"They're giving up the library before they die. So they often cry and tell stories."

*

Time loves a book—to fox its pages in lovely rust, tea, sepia, and fecal starclusters; to brittle it; to riddle it with pinwidth insect labyrinths; to fade, chip, buckle, cockle, scrape, and in general tick eternity away by units of wholesale decomposition; Time loves to suck a book as clean as a chicken wingbone.

A. D. Baynes-Cope's *Caring for Books and Documents* reads like the opening speech of a five-star general to his troops in time of war. He is stern, and exact, and his epaulets flash like artillery in the parade-ground sun as he tells his ranks, "We know what books and documents are made of, and how these materials can be expected to behave in various climatic conditions, what their enemies are and how to outwit them." The foe is legion. "Light is an enemy of books . . . Heat can also be an enemy of books . . . Indirectly windows are an enemy of books . . . Fire and flood are obviously major enemies." The ugly truth is, "every solid, liquid or gaseous object in this universe is a chemical or a mixture of chemicals" and so of course is suspect of constant attack.

Cats are enemies, and the fleas on the cats are enemies, and the microbes on the fleas are eager to swirl across a library's spines in garish fungal sargassos. "Indeed, the enemies may be internal"—a book's own traitorous acids can eat it into oblivion, like a man's heart's being lapped by that man's own bile. Need it even be said that "we can include human beings as an enemy of books through sins of omission and commission"?

There is no question but that the war must be fought. But Baynes-Cope refuses to euphemize the privations that await us: "Time, thought, trouble and money must be expended." For instance, if insect damage is merely hinted at, "the treatment must be designed to cope with the likelihood that all four stages of insect growth—egg, larva, pupa and insect—are present. Even if only one book is affected, those books on that shelf, and the ones above, below, and backing onto it, must be examined thoroughly, preferably out of doors, and the infected books brushed with a soft paint-brush or gently with a vacuum cleaner fitted with a softish baluster brush"; the latter "is a little fierce but the suck can be reduced by drilling a few 1/4 or 3/8 in. (6mm or 9mm) holes in the tubing." Bats require yet greater effort. Sniffing for dampness earns its own dense paragraph of instruction. Never let the size of the battlefront mislead you into underestimating the toil required: "the problems of producing a safe climate in a single case may be more difficult than those for a single room."

Is it worth it, this endless seriocomic operatic clash of the forces of Entropy and Conservation? The answer is wholly serious. Aaron Lansky recounts his first book-gathering mission, to an eighty-seven-year-old man named Temmelman, in Atlantic City: Lansky arrives at noon, to find the man in his apartment building's lobby. "I hope you haven't been waiting long."

"Oh I been here since seven this morning, young man. I diddin want I should miss you."

Every volume has its history. "You know, my wife and I . . . this book we bought in 1925, yes! We went without lunch for a week we should be able to afford it."

*

Everybody's saving, from cereal boxtops to souls.

Imagine standing in the restorer's lab as the first dabbed fraction of night in *The Night Watch* cleans back into the patchily almondine daylight of Rembrandt's palette. Banning Cocq, Van Ruytenburgh, Vischer, Engelen, Kemp, and the rest of the musketeers are gridded-*nth*-of-an-inch-by-*nth* revisioned, as the very molecular bonding of midnight breaks, swabs off, and clears the fine-crazed stage for an intricate play of the effects of sun on their faces and antique costumery. That room must have been an enormous held breath.

Reviving hither, regilding yon, the World Monuments Fund is endlessly busy—fifty restoration projects in fifteen countries. Sculpture on the portal of the Collegiate Church in Toro, Spain . . . Diego Rivera murals in Mexico City . . . Easter Island . . . Angkor Wat . . . One current project is the Château de Commarque, which sits on a cave of wall engravings and paintings 20,000 years old: a leaping horse, a profiled human head, and so many obvious male and female symbols that prehistorians call the cave "the sex shop." Hubert de Commarque: "Our lives are a bit lost today because we have lost the knowledge of the earth, of the sky . . . That is what I want most from this work—to give to the people that connection that's been lost."

For some, the glory days of burlesque—the legendary plumed glitter-queens and their retinues. For some, the lone orchid pressed in an album; its oils have long past stained the paper around it translucent, a wimple of spectral sheen.

*

"It's history. It's art. It's culture. It's dying."—On page 24 of this issue of *Amtrak Express*, the Lighthouse Preservation Society asks for your help to "Keep It Shining." Page 9, the Save the Manatee Club suggests you "ask about our 'Adopt a Manatee' program." Who *wouldn't* want to halt their extinction? Seal-bodied hippos is what they look like, a ton of seagrass-munching rotundity. Only 1,200 or so remain in U.S. waters. The California condor needs saving, and our culture may never again see the like of the smokily peignoir-petaled bodies of 1940s Vargas-style pinup art. Fountain pens. Cuspidors. Bauhaus.

Someone's brushing crumbs of dirt from between two tiny marble toes. That's all: two tiny marble toes, unattached to anything. The brush is correspondingly tiny, and softer than a cosmetician's rouge brush. What is it about the Past? We're down on our knees at two of its toes, and it's beautiful, the way the veins in the marble simulate veins in the flesh. Send in your money. Help save the toes. They'll be photographed, labeled, and wrapped in seven layers of cotton and styrofoam sheeting. Somewhere: marble legs and a torso (where, though?). Somewhere: marble wings.

*

Angels. Since 1976, Joyce Berg has collected 8,366 figurines of angels. One sits with its legs crossed, reading a book, and looks like a seven-year-old on the potty. A somberly religious one raises its fingers in ritual benediction. Angels in crystal, in wood, in ceramic. One, in clay, is carrying a halo on its head like a balanced doughnut. One is clearly a cat, in a celadon ballerina's getup. Lowell Berg says, "She writes down where she bought it, when, what she paid, whether the clerk was bald; you know, all the important stuff."

George Logue owns fifty working two-ton Caterpillar tractors (including—his most prized—a 1932 diesel model), arranged like a pasturing herd on his family farm. Ken Soderbeck: a dozen antique fire trucks (including the 1912 Knox piston pumper) with subsidiary uniforms, equipment, and Tisch and Ike, his two dalmations. Tom Bates: 30,000 soda and beer cans, amassed in his and his sister Ginnie's Museum of Beverage Containers and Advertising. Jim Hambrick: wowee! an assemblage of Superman figures, banks, comic books, board games, pinbacks, clocks, etc., 40,000 superitems large.

Whenever I'm glum these days, I go to this photo in which Bob Malkin sits amid the icons of his passion. "It's all I thought about. I'd go to flea markets before dawn with a flashlight." He collects giantdom—oversize advertising memorabilia. Here, he's perched in a chair that diminishes him to a two-year-old's size, though a two-year-old in a business suit and tie. One foot rests on top of a shoe (a natty wingtip brogue) with the bulk of a motor scooter; the other foot's in a gym shoe you could coddle a papoose inside of spaciously. There's a birdbath-diametered coffee cup, a pocket watch like one of a sixteen-wheeler's tires, a telephone you could straddle for a carnival ride, and Malkin's wearing this silly grin sized perfectly for his face, and signing a legal pad, roughly of loveseat-length, with the Fountain Pen of the Gods.

*

"Pull in here." And doughty Kit Hathaway did—a comic book shop we were passing by chance in Saratoga. I was his guest for two days surrounding a reading I gave at Union College and, stout heart, he was striving mightily to cater to my trashorama needs. You never know what you'll find in a back bin of yellowing paper. Not Kit, not two customers browsing T-shirts, or the clerk heard the clarion blasting through my cochlea. But there it was, from thirty years back, exactly as I remembered: *Green Lantern* number 3, December 1960.

As you may know, Green Lantern is "really" Hal Jordan, test pilot for the Ferris Aircraft Company in Coast City. One day, a trainer plane he was testing lifted into the air mysteriously and was guided to where a spaceship lay crashed in the desert. Summoned inside, Hal met the dying extraterrestrial Abin Sur (bald, angle-browed, and jellybean-red), who with his final words decreed Hal Jordan his successor as this sector-of-the-universe's "Green Lantern." He had the costume prepared, and the power ring, and he taught Hal Jordan the sacred Oath Against Evil that must be recited when recharging the ring at the Power Lamp every twenty-four hours. Through the ring, green psychic energy made the leap to solidity, and many is the ne'er-do-well who found himself in the midst, say, of a bank heist lifted by limousine-sized green tongs, then slammed by a man-high green hand efficiently into a green cage, and then whisked on a flying green platter straight to the calaboose. The Oath was stirring: In brightest day, in blackest night, / No evil shall escape my sight! / Let those who worship evil's might / Beware my power, Green Lantern's light!

That's the genesis story I must be referring to here, in *GL* number 3, on page 2 of "Green Lantern's Mail Chute": *Dear Editor: I think* Green Lantern *is one of the most exciting and different action magazines on the market today. However, I was disappointed when half of the exciting lead story, "Planet of*

Doomed Men," was devoted to Green Lantern's origin, which already had been printed in the first issue. Albert Goldbarth, Chicago Ill.

I plunked down thirty dollars for what was once a ten-cent comic book and left the shop whistling.

My First Published Work.

. . .

> *it is not what a thing is*
> *but what you feel about it that counts.*
> — Louis Simpson

*

I'm twelve, I look up from reading that page—or I look up from my writing about my reading that page, it really doesn't matter—and see her working in light the kitchen curtains texture. Fussing at all of those jars mechanically. Her mind in a circle of othertime.

And when I see my father, in this same replaying retrospective scene, he's always down at that desk, embattled by numbers, the spiral of tape from the adding machine having frozen his pose, and me, and Grandma Nettie, and by extension every mote of 1960—like a watchspring having frozen the hands of its watch, or like the coiled soul of a wind-up toy having frozen its colorful body into a single gesture forever.

In that block of stalled chronology, she's stopped to touch the locket at her throat. The counter is rowed with crocks of cucumbers canopically floating. I see it as if a bolt of green power has leaped from between my hands and, charged with all of the voltage of human wishing, has zapped this picture permanent. Lascaux won't fade, Hal Jordan won't fail, the diabetes won't eat her away.

6. KISHEF FOR THE SWIGMAN

In six months he hadn't uttered a word of Yiddish. And the words he'd learned—! A clown is a "joey." A fistfight with the locals is a "clem." Here he'd learned "cunt," and that his cigarettes were "coffin nails." He was called a "razorback" or "roustabout"—he'd help the elephant push their handful of gaudy, gewgawed wagons out of the backroads mire. Godiva said he could work up to joey one day, but when? Godiva in her bareback rider's flouncing tutu. Godiva was a "star."

"Hey, mac": it had happened this simply. "Think you can handle a hammer?" So he'd pitched in, on that first day nearly half-a-year back, as they hoisted the canvas, guying-out its violently flapping sides. It was a sixteen-pound sledgehammer—it was, as he'd learn to say here, "no picnic"—but, as he sweated his *kishkes* out, he sweated out everything bitter inside, that horseradish taste on his tongue, he sweated away the last dust of the pack and its prisoning ghetto world: he couldn't have been farther away, here with The Human Cannonball, and Mad Marie the Mule-Faced Girl, and the uric tang from the one sad tiger's groin-shag weaving around its wagon as palpably as the one sad anaconda might.

"Your name?" the ringmaster had asked. And he'd said "*Vhat?*" in his accented English in response, not expecting the question, and intuiting immediately that a new life required a new appellation, that he would need to keep a line between the two people he was, and yet he hadn't had the time to think this over. "Walt?" said the ringmaster, "Walter?" So he'd been put on the payroll that way. *Walter* was entered alongside Barko the Ape Man, and Lisette, and Hi-Step Hank, and Wonder-O.

And there was Godiva. Her hair was gold and ringleted, as perfect as torquing in some machine. She shamelessly worked her butt when she walked. He'd seen her bend with her ass in the air, a spangled tutu framing it; she'd uncork a bottle of wine between her knees. His first day there, she threw him the look. But he was careful. He was new, a Jew to boot, and far from home. He hadn't imagined it, though—the second day, a look. One night he drank too much. When? he asked her. He even fell to his knees. Not yet, she told him. She fingered a ringlet. Later, when he'd proved himself, when he moved up in rank and they made him a joey. This was probably true, he reasoned. There were three clowns and she granted her favors to two of them. (The other was Mad Marie's.)

For now, his primary duty was catering to Professor Oink the Educated Pig. A pig!—if he wanted to turn from the world of the rabbis, he'd certainly managed. He also hauled the wagons, as I said, and watered Jumbo, and did a bit of whatever ball-busting and ego-eroding drifter's labor was required. But lately Professor Oink, who added, subtracted, and told the future, was a special draw, and so was provided with special attention.

My grandfather brushed him and hand-fed him cabbage, and just before showtime wiped the shit he'd been rolling in from his flanks and rump. It never failed: every showtime, shit. A few weeks into this assignment, and it was the moment he thought of his wife most tenderly. *Shit, shit, shit,* he heard her clumsily saying, and smiled. He thought of her often. He sent money every week, no note but money (all he earned, in fact). She'd be seamstressing, he knew. He felt the needle in his heart.

But always, Godiva was there. And always, something new was happening. Sheriffs were running them out of the county. Hellfire preachers, with burning crosses and monkeys dressed up like devils, would join forces with them for a town or two. The tiger, Bengali, escaped once and they found him on top of a wagon of hay bales, terrified: a yapping dog about the size of a handkerchief was streaking about the wheels. It was a shabby excuse of a circus; the one-time parakeet-green of its handbills and banners had faded to a color that looked coughed-up. But they attracted crowds, in back-bend towns where funerals and shotgun weddings were usually the only diversion. One day, flies and itch and nothing else. The next day, TOOT-TOOT-TOOT, hey, the circus!

And he had a plan. He was learning magic. Canchak the Great had quit the show, in Salliesburg. The story included the mayor, the mayor's wife, and the circus's dancing bear, and no one agreed on the details, but the following morning the bear and the mayor remained, while the other two featured participants disappeared into the moonlight.

No matter: now there was clearly an opening. He practiced in secret. The day was hot, and everybody else was sprawled in the relative cool of the wagons. He was sitting in the shade of a stunted maple, alongside Professor Oink. Tell me, pig, pick a card. Okay, now wait, you see here? look—*your card!* But Oink, from a line of professionals, was singularly unimpressed.

*

And Nettie?

She didn't need him. She could buy her grapneled chicken legs without his help, she'd even finagled a new (used) feather mattress. Once a week, the envelopes arrived in care of the Jewish Women's Organization, and every week she slipped the twelve dollars into a celluloid whatnot box, refusing to spend it, to be so demeaned—and with the emptied envelopes she lined the birdcage. *Pisher'l*, that was the bird: Little Pisser.

"*Nu?* He's a bum, a no-goodnik."

"Yah, yah, Lena."

"*Yah* you say, but you don't *listen*. He's a bum, *a shandel un a charpeh.*" A shame and disgrace. "Now you say it."

"*Lena . . .*"

My grandmother chopped in the kitchen—or what saved space in the room, by the red-and-white-check oilcloth's declaration, became the "kitchen." He'd been gone six months and she'd moved, though leaving a message behind, with the new address. She was happy here, some days she hummed to the onions, *mine liebe, mine liebe*; once Lena unexpectedly knocked and found her dancing in circles, with a shirtwaist from her basket of work. This new room had sun; it filled the window, making gilded Russian domes of the onions. In one corner Pisher'l, himself the shape of a gold note, sang and dipped to his dish of gold seeds.

Irving Howe: "Never having regarded herself as part of a spiritual elite, she did not suffer so wrenching a drop in status and self-regard as her husband. She was a practical person, she had mouths to feed, and, by and large, she saw to it that they were fed."

And "large" is the word. At night, without the sun, and while Pisher'l balled up into sleep, she wept—she rubbed her burgeoning tummy, slowly, singing, *mine liebe, mine liebe,* as if its thickening fetal waters could broadcast her longing and reach him, like a shortwave set.

In the dismalest stretches, she wouldn't doze for days. Nor would she admit to Lena the visceral toll of the garment shop—where now, on her own, she needed to spend some full days. Of 25,000 Jews employed on the East Side in 1890, more than 12,000 were garment workers. By 1899 the growth of the industry, "measured by number of workers and value of product, was two or three times as rapid as the average for all industries." But by 1911, the standard female garment worker nonetheless earned under ten dollars a week.

The shops were ill-lit, poorly ventilated, and some shops supplied a single toilet for up to 85 workers that "passed odors directly into the work space." The gas lighting leaked. The hand-operated pressing irons caused curvature of the spine. Not infrequently, managers hinted for "favors" from the girls. The shopowners often were fellow Jews—that stinks especially, that stinks like a sweatshop toilet late in the shift, in August. By her sixth month, my grandmother couldn't even squeeze behind her machine without a painful intake of breath.

"What *you* do, Lena—is easy?"

"Not so easy, no. They come, these *shloomps*, they don't know if their breath is like a *chazzer's tuchus*" (a swine's ass) "but their head is filled with the *shtup shtup shtup*, so *nu?*" She shrugged. "So I get filled with the *shtup shtup shtup* a *bissel* mineself. But I tell you, Nettie, I don't got no *troggedik pupik*" (pregnant belly-button) "and every night with the crying *oy g'vald!* for a bum like this what he leaves you, a tramp he is!"

"Lena . . ."

"A tramp he is, a *shmootz*, say it!"

But the more the censorious Lena inveighed, the less sure my grandmother grew.

Sometimes she'd stop her chopping to listen—some foot on the stair. On certain days she'd think she could hear a hand along the banister. She remembered those hands.

Every day was piecework and onions. Every night, the feather mattress (such luxury!) that she started to wish was a door set hard on two wood crates with his set by it, touching.

And if then, when she returned to the knife and the vegetable row of work to be done, she didn't hum but under her breath she called the onions "*Tz'drayt-en-kopf! Meshoogeneh!*" like curse words, I can understand. Crazy-in-head! Dummy! Crying, losing track, and dicing the light itself. "*Nar ainer!*" You fool, you! (Him? Herself?) *You-Stupid! My-Fault! Shit-Shit-Shit!* Or more directly—for this was his name—*Albert.*

. . . like a shortwave set . . .

*

Names, and their powers. Names, and their link to the named.

The names of scalawags, by their occupations, in England in Elizabeth's time: a prigman, a ruffler, a whip-jack, a queer-bird, a doxie, a palliard, a tinkard, a kinchin mort, a gyle hather, a nunquam, a dummerer, a demander for glimmer, a bawdy basket, an apple-squire, a scrippet, a nip, a troll hazard of trace. My grandfather, then, was a swigman: "A swigman goeth with a pedlar's pack."

In his study *Jewish Magic and Superstition*, Joshua Trachtenberg says: "The essential character of things and of men resides in their names. Therefore to know a name is to be privy to the secret of its owner's being, and master of his fate . . . To know the name of a man is to exercise power. One Hebrew text says 'his name is his soul.'"

Even the angels hearkened when they were called. "To set them to work the magician must know the *names* of these angels, for the name was the controlling factor." For instance: "I command you, Haniel, and Hasdiel, and Zadkiel, by these names, to do *(thus and thus),*" and so were they summoned: Benevolence, Grace, and Mercy.

She'd saved a wisp of hair from his brush, and twisted it into a locket. If she slept at all, she slept clutching this.

*

Here is how it happened.

Women filled his dreams, his head was a candle-lit *bagnio.* Sometimes Nettie's face; sometimes Godiva's. He was embarrassed to wake in front of the other workers, bulging.

Over time, the face was more and more Nettie's. What, what, what to do? "Here." Hi-Step Hank handed over the bottle. "You look like yesterday's bearshit." This was true. This was also, my grandfather knew, an enormous expression of friendship—in terms of its primary roustabout medium, hooch.

So he was drunk that night, approaching Godiva's wagon. Not *too* drunk—voices stopped him. He stood behind a pyramid of water barrels. She'd been drinking too, and Hap the joey.

"Fuck you, mister."

"Fuck you, *sister.* Fuck you and your momma and your momma's momma, with a dry tent pole, and fuck that grunting asshole you make the googoo eyes at."

"You're crazy, you know that? A lard-brain." When she laughed to show disdain, it ran a rich, theatrical scale.

"I ain't blind, we none of us are. You know who."

"The kikey? Oh."

"C'mere." Then there was a minute of urgent breath-sound and nebulous wriggle. When she spoke again, it tumbled quick and emotionally pitched to perfection, as if she'd practiced this set-speech in her own head many times already.

"I like you, Hap. I like to suck you, I like to feel your grubby little fingers spreading my crack. Do you know why?" —she didn't wait—"All day I stand in my cherub outfit and twirl on a white horse for the Jesus-drooling citizens of Clean Ass, Kansas, and when they applaud they lift me out of the ring to the Throne of God Himself, and God Himself admires me up on one pink toe and praises my perfection." You could tell, she was posing herself all the while.

"At night I need to get myself filthy, to balance it. You're my filth, Hap. You're my animal-stud-fucking-filth. And on the day I think the kikey man can handle the job"—she posed again, to emphasize what *the job* was—"he can be my filth too."

"Oh yeah? Well you're—" But he was gone, my grandfather. He didn't need Hap the joey's retort.

Godiva knew something was wrong, when she woke. Through booze-haze she could hear the usual fracas, the bear, the calliope practice . . . something else, though, a terrible wail. She wrapped up in a chenille robe and strode outside. Professor Oink was strung up in back of her wagon, by his aft trotters. He was making one hell of an unacademic squeal. Someone, whoever the lunatic was that did it, had fastened her spangled tutu around him.

*

But there's another version.

My grandfather woke, so late that even The Great Gambooni was passed out now, making the thrum of a snare drum in his throat.

Come here . . . It was fuzzy outside, and fuzzy inside my grandfather's head. The damn pig seemed to be calling him, that was crazy of course, but after all it was a circus. *Come here* . . . He started in that direction.

Wait . . . Another voice. A dog had gently clipped a loose fold of pajama-leg in its teeth. Then it let go, and spoke again. *Come mit me.*

"Who are you?"

I'm a hoont, you can't see? Then: *Who are you?*

"My name is Walter."

Come mit me, Albert. Come, follow mit me.

*

A foot on the stair. A hand on the banister.

*

They have too much of anger and healing for us to consider nakedly. I leave them for now on the feather mattress, his first night back. I only want to quote from the *Zohar*, a Jewish mystical text of the *Kabbalah*. It tells us that when a man journeys, his "heavenly wife" is with him all that while— a spirit-form of his matrimonial union remains continuous, and "he is now male and female in the country, as he was male and female in the town." When a man returns from journeying, "it is his duty, once back home, to give his wife pleasure, inasmuch as she it was who obtained for him the heavenly union."

He strokes her taut hill-of-a-belly.

Oi-YOY, mine liebe, mine liebe.

*

Downstairs, on the table where Mathilde the Queen of the Ocean Deeps once held court, they'd left a loonily piled Ararat of Hendrickje's underthings. Moonlight through the room's huge windows dappled over it, silver and shadowy blue.

Upstairs, he unfolded himself from the musty cup of her arm. She'd sleep if a meteor hit the garden, now, in the after-exhaustion of sex and a flagon of wine. She always slept well, after reconciliation. He watched her, a moment: here, the moonlight lay like a rosin around her, a malt.

Then he slipped to the studio. There were candles enough. Sleep beckoned him too, but wooing him more imploringly than that was a face from his sketchbook. With the canvas sized from last week, he could start it into oils tonight, while the burning was on him. A Jewess's face—it had broken out of a small complacence of faces by the tumult of emotions it wore. And this excited him, thinking the paint would soon be human skin, and then the skin would be that mixspot where a woman's acquiescence meets her hard determination, now a tittle of indigo, gray, red, thickly squiggled salmon . . . particularizing the chisel-edge of light along her nape and then into the tassels of hair below one ear, and over the jaw set slightly off-center in thought...

Preserving this one face—doleful, triumphant, whatever—as best he can, and while he can, while it still isn't doused from his system.

*

She turned. The half-moon lit her face and would have made it timelessly lovely, except an upright from the fire escape flung one long bar of shadow across her.

"I think we will call him the name of Ervin."

"Yes, a good name." He sighed, immensely. "Such a day, Nettie...!"

"Such a life."

"Yes." Then he paused, he was ashamed. "With this *kaddishel*"—this baby boy—"he'll be here soon..."

"Or a girl, yah. Then Hannah we call her."

"... but the money, I don't have this. From a circus, they don't give the money so much. A place to be, peoples you talk with, yes; but the money, no. So..." he halted, he'd never failed this way.

She opened her second-hand steamer trunk and withdrew the celluloid whatnot box. Twelve dollars a week, six months—it was a fortune, 288 dollars.

"Nettie! How do you make this for us, from nothing?"

"*Kishef*," she told him—magic.

*

"It isn't always a happy ending, is it?" Gaylene has exhibited, for my histrionic oohing, every porcelain nixie, 1920s bakelite bangle, and near-mint first-edition Oz series title in her apartment. We've even played with the Schoenhut figurines, doing seal noise (ROWK! ROWK!), tiger-&-lion growl, crowd hubbahubba. But what we can't do is conjure Craig, and what *I* can't do is love her enough in the way I do love her to make that not matter.

Later, I visit Craig. He's getting along, he says. We knock

back some beers on the building's crumbling balcony, then a few more beers. He isn't getting along, he says then. What went wrong? Didn't they *try* hard?

It's a rhetorical question; no one tried harder. We sit there in silence, surrounded by the kit-kat clocks with moving eyes, the toby mugs, the inkwells and quills, the frog and ostrich and bulldog and Martian and porcupine rubber squeeze-me toys, the turn-of-the-century printer's type, the cowboy lamps, the vastly tasteless selection of lime-green naugahyde.

They'd saved everything imaginable *except* Hitler's brain; and their marriage.

7. POSTSCRIPT: THE FINAL ENTRY

I was still in Oklahoma when I exited: some dried-out, moon-cratered place. Its squalid version of an oasis was a makeshift dump where broken boxspring mattresses and shattered toilets, unsaveable and long past any compromise with use or sensibility, wavered like bad TV reception, in the upshaft heat of decay. I pulled alongside it, into its swimming stink. Austin was science-fiction distance south of me; Wichita, north.

This wasn't the plan, of course. I couldn't have done it, *planned*. But I unloaded the trunk, the back seat, and the U-Haul mini-hitch with a swift efficiency that normally only preparedness could account for. Thirty cartons of lousy job and soured marriage, with the scarab-green and iridescent blackberry sheen of compost-flies already in exploratory orbits.

I could have *flown* the Dodge Colt home, it felt so light.

*

You need to know when to let go. Otherwise . . .

Jeanmarie, a friend, has a story. Her grandmother's died and the family holds a traditional nightlong keening and tippling Catholic/Irish wake. Everyone slobbering piteously, getting juiced, emitting great shaken-out moans from the heartcore, throwing themselves across the open coffin as if with *suttee* in mind, and in general wreaking very grievous and merry prefunereal havoc.

"Some time before sunup my grandfather lifted her corpse from the coffin and started dancing, *ballroom dancing*, around the room. They couldn't pry him away from her, maybe they half didn't want to. He couldn't let go of her. Dancing. His hand at the small of her back." Dancing around the room until the candles burned down as flat as wax coins.

*

In 1656, the court ordered Rembrandt's holdings catalogued for sale. He was deeply in debt, and this euphemistic *cessio bonorum*, a "surrender of goods," replaced the harsher official declaration of bankruptcy saved for the truly fraudulent. Everything went—the gold helmets, the walrus-tusk carvings, everything. The inventory taker from the Chamber of Insolvent Estates compiled 363 separate entries.

Kenneth Clark says, "It is usually supposed that the sale of all these precious possessions was a great blow to him. But who can tell?" (Mee seconds this uncertainty: "There is no way to know how Rembrandt was feeling during all this.") Then Clark philosophizes, "There is a point at which possessions become a burden: they are exhilarating to buy, but a nuisance to look after. What if moths had got into the fur caps, and the Japanese armour had rusted, and pupils had spilt turpentine on his Marcantonio engravings and poisoned his pet monkey (which one of them actually did). The grandest and calmest of all his self-portraits was done in the year of his sale."

He's ruminating out of the frame—but inwardly, at the same time—with a kind of understanding resignation, and this somehow doesn't negate, but deepens, poignantizes, the natural big-bodied majesty.

*

In Lewis Hyde's insightful study *The Gift*, he tells us, "A gift is a thing we do not get by our own efforts. We cannot buy it; we cannot acquire it through an act of will. It is bestowed upon us." In a sense, my finding *Green Lantern* number 3 is such a gift, hoped-for but unarrangeable, surely a moment of grace in which the cosmos let me open up Time and take a step retrograde into it; and the thirty dollars is not so much the price of a commodity, as the necessary clearing-away of a space where serendipity occurs. No matter what a comics price guide says, there is no market value for such an occasion; it exists in its own green atemporal shimmer.

Hyde continues, "Thus we rightly speak of 'talent' as a 'gift,' for although a talent can be perfected through an effort of the will, no effort in the world can cause its initial appearance. Mozart, composing on the harpsichord at the age of four, had a gift." And Rembrandt stretches his arm on the table, rests his head in its bend, and sighs his way at last into a fitful slumber, under the half-complete painting. This is where we take our leave of him.

"Moreover, a gift that cannot be given away ceases to be a gift. The spirit of a gift is kept alive by its constant donation. May Sarton writes: 'The gift turned inward, unable to be given, becomes a heavy burden, even sometimes a kind of poison. It is as though the flow of life were locked up.' It is the talent which is not in use that is lost or atrophies, and to bestow one of our creations is the surest way to invoke the next. Bestowal creates that empty place into which new energy may flow. The alternative is petrifaction, writer's block, 'the flow of life backed up.'"

For any ongoing, then, there needs to be an equal emptying-out: the tile mosaic must leave the artist's studio for the gallery; the lover must carry his knit wool keepsake into battle; the High Gods must look down with a gaze that meets the burnt offering wafting up on a chargray plume of sacrifice-smoke.

This is one of the ancientmost wars: a page of Yiddish, fixing the years and their passions against disappearance; and the man with the match, who needs to get on with the thousand-and-one tugs of living.

*

This is the final entry in Nathaniel Hawthorne's *American Notebooks*: "I burned great heaps of old letters, and other papers, a little while ago, preparatory to going to England. Among them were hundreds of ————'s letters. The world has no more such, and now they are all dust and ashes. What a trustful guardian of secret matters is fire! What should we do without fire and death?"

Note
Transliteration from the Yiddish, both individual words and mannerisms of phrasing, is not entirely consistent throughout the text, the better to account for the flexible and adaptive qualities of the language, and the confusion of the early immigrant experience. Some guiding spirits have helped me considerably. In addition to the poems of Louis Simpson, they are: William Kittredge, *Owning It All*; Jed Perl, "On Collecting"; Charles L. Mee, Jr., *Rembrandt's Portrait*; Irving Howe, *World of Our Fathers*; William Gass, *Habitations of the Word*; Jacob Bronowski, *A Sense of the Future*; Daniel Benjamin (on Aaron Lansky), "Preserving the Printed Word"; Joshua Trachtenberg, *Jewish Magic and Superstition*; Kenneth Clark, *An Introduction to Rembrandt*; and Lewis Hyde, *The Gift*. There are some small instances when material quoted from these texts is rearranged for purposes of rhythm or concision.

Waiting for Lesser Duckweed:
On a Proposal of Issa's
SANDRA MCPHERSON

December, a weekday,
no one else crossing
    (by way of the wet path)

the bird sanctuary's yellow
spongy bottomland,
    no duckweed

any longer willow-green—
for now, the almost smoldering
    gas-lacy water says,

it's down making turions.
The way to be introduced to it
    is first

to meet nothing. In rain,
a thin microscope-specimen rain.
    One raises a face

to flooded sketchlike
territories of trees,
    sepia, seeping;

to blunt, upward bluffs of ivy,
bared poison oak;
    a soaking place,

fed by springs and floods,
shallow water table
    strained by willows.

In spring, in a more forward month,
yellow-red willow-bud husks
   will sharpen the trail,

their old pen tips,
oleo-spot gulls' beaks,
   brighten the flat brown pond,

and a man with a knife,
whack, whack,
   righthanded down the path,

will kill new twigs too new
yet to be woody.
   But there's

no duckweed until the summer
when finally where a creek
   swims in,

   there's duckweed
barely tugging
the moss-strandy bottom,

   wheatcolored
seed-shrimps
touring in and around

   the barbless roots,
hyaline drag-lines,
where a mud-smooth leech adjusts

   and tows
the duckweed a bit.
Some places it bunches,

    simple but chained,
a soft hauberk on the stream.
Some places it wrinkles,

    a basilisk's back.
It is utterly simple
and multiple.

    It is floating,
one of many rafts.
The water here is cold,

    fresh, still
and hard. Ovals, ovals.
"Let's take the duckweed way

    to clouds,"
said Issa. Let's take it
when it comes to us,

    its leaf
not called a leaf,
diameter for which there is no term

    but green;
let's follow
the least weed up

    to nimbuses
however many
steps it takes,

    late in the day's
rootless endurance
to make much progress

the duckweed way.
Let us grow and wane
with this ideal, the way

  it keeps the single petal
of its bloom confidential
in a hollow on its side.

> *Lemna minor*
>
> *with thanks to Lucien Stryk,
> who translated*

Dominion
DEBRA HINES

In the half of the shell
that had not fallen away,

angled like the palmiers in the bakery,
they could see the skinned elbow of the wing.

It showed enough blood to attract ants,
the ants, smaller than anything

about the bird, with its heart
looming.

The husband turned to his wife.
"I should kill it."

With his foot held above the heartbeat,
as if he were taking a step,

the husband hesitated.
The wife used the toe of her sandal

to scrape the bird from the sidewalk
to the grass.

She swiveled the ball of her foot
hard into the ground.

After they heard the crunching shell,
the wife pressed her foot farther into the grass.

The husband pulled her away
from where she stooped to look.

He felt ill, suddenly, and said so.
"Maybe I was wrong," the wife said.

The husband replied, "To be eaten slowly
by ants, no matter what size you are,

no matter how young and pink,
can't be pleasant."

They laughed.
The wife pushed the husband forward

and fell against him.
He leaned back his head and laughed.

The wife gave him another push,
then ran ahead and grabbed his hand.

He tripped and fell against her.
She pretended to fall, then fell.

Walking toward the bakery, they talked of
business and how much work

they could expect in the next few months;
of the fifteen-year mortgage instead of thirty;

of how old their first child would be
when the second was born.

Numberless

HEATHER MCHUGH

By law of rod
and cone, the closer it gets
the darker it looks. You look

benighted. I can hardly make out
elbow, lobe, or nape, and once
we go into the whole

conundrum, it's by blind
feel, slowly summing
something's curve, some verb's
becoming, wound up where the room and all
its things are gone: the lampshade,
doorknob, chair—they've gone inside—
they've faded into eyelid, nipple, hip,
it isn't long before the world,
the world itself is gone

inside us, where an appetite is
humming, thumping, damp, and then
there's only inside left to lose, and then

that too is lost, all's
lost

in a drench, a
din, of
downfall,
voltage poured away
in brilliant paralyzing pulse . . .

Then four walls,

seven windows
reappear. Our shoes
show up, right where we left them, glasses
poised beside the bed, which led us into
such an indistinction: it now pulls apart
into the two of us, meiotic aftermath . . .
There is a ticking, there's
a cooling off. Come to my senses, I can see
nine inches from my face
the watched wrists fallen
on a pillow, side by side:
attached to different
beings in time:

one is a bracket of lidded silvers, fast asleep;
the other's open, strapped with hide . . .

Journey One
RADCLIFFE SQUIRES

Motion, oh tidal Adam, was the temptation
That eased you from your luminous arbor.
Now, what you adore are the adornments of motion.
The carapace of athletes. The shell of chariots. The skin
Of a ship wherein we crawl in the sea's crawl among those
Who, when they lock another's eyes, feel themselves
Become the gazing sea water—and look away fearful
Of becoming the other's death.
But they do not say, "Assassin and saviour fall through
The eyes of the other."

We sashay in the jelly of the trough.
We glide toward the wave-crest where we behold
The meerschaum petals of the sea falling
In that other sky beneath us, and while
We hang there, the drive-shaft shudders
As the screw tastes air, and the smell
Of angina unnerves the engine room.
But we do not as we again glide downward sing,
"We are the sons who fell through each other's arms."

In the glittering calms we draw down the sun
Like a blister in the astrolabe to show we are
Stretched here in the same burning azimuth.
But we do not say, "We are the strange brothers,
Stalled in motion. We are the comets
Whose burning bodies trail darkness."

The Envoy
RADCLIFFE SQUIRES

If I touch a certain place on
My leg I am a child again
Wading a cold mountain stream.
No water clearer, but to the parallactic eye none
Less certain. Sunlight scatters like orange peel
Over the surface. In the depths a molten swell
Lifts rags of sand. Water beads
Skitter in dimples about
Legs which trail away like flat
Long underwear toward the mere blue blur of feet.

Then I see something bitterly white push
From the bank mud through scarlet tree roots, pause,
Then move again slowly out toward
Me. If a serpent it is faceless; if a worm it is wide
As my wrist. It moves beyond my leg, not quite
Touching me, then the tip curls back and for
A moment nuzzles the calf. Colder than space
The touch is nevertheless a kiss
In which there is no wish to possess—
Only some antique courtesy, as though
Cold were sending an envoy to Warm
To tell him some of the customs of snow
And learn some of what it means to burn.

Another Elegy

DONALD HALL

in memory of William Trout

O God! thought I, that madest kynde,
Shal I noon other weyes dye?
Wher Joves woll me stellyfye,
Or what thing may this sygnifye?...
 —*Geoffrey Chaucer*, House of Fame

The task and potential greatness of mortals reside in their
ability to produce things which are at home in everlastingness.
—*Hannah Arendt*, The Human Condition

Both one and many; in the brown baked features
The eyes of a familiar compound ghost...
 —*T. S. Eliot*, "Little Gidding"

It rained all night on the remaining elms. April soaked
through night loam into sleep. This morning, rain delays
above drenched earth. Whitethroated sparrows shake
wet from their feathers, singing in the oak, while fog
snags like lambswool on Kearsarge. The Blackwater River
runs high. The blacksnake budges in his hole, resurrecting
from winter's coma.
 Now green will start from stubble
and horned pout fatten. By the pond, pussywillows
will labor awake to trudge from darkness and cold
through April's creaking gate.
 Bill Trout remains
fixed in a long box where we left him, a dozen years ago.

•

July, nineteen-sixty: Three friends with their families
visited Bill at his Maine cabin secluded among scrub pines—
setting up tents, joking, frying pickerel in cool dusk.

Only Bill was divorced, drinking all night, living alone
on his shabby acre. Drunk the whole week, he recited
Milton's syllables of lament, interrupting our argument,
told Nazarene parables, and wept for his friends
and their children. While the rest of us dove from a dock
or played badminton with our wives, Bill paced
muttering, smoking his Lucky Strikes. Later the rest
divorced and paced.
      We fished the river for horned pout,
Bill standing with a joint by the dam, watching the warm
water thick with fish, black bodies packed, flapping
and contending to breathe. Dropping hooks without bait
we pulled up the horny, loricate fish, then flipped them
on grass to shrivel, as we watched and joked, old
friends together. Continually sloshed, Bill proclaimed
that life was shit, death was shit—even *shit* was *shit*.

•

Idaho made him, Pocatello of hobos and freightyards—
clangor of iron, fetor of coalsmoke. With his brothers
he listened for the Mountain Bluebird as he dropped worms
into the Snake River, harvesting catfish for a Saturday
supper in the 1930s.
     Two Sisters of the Sacred Heart
cossetted him when he strayed from the boys' flock
to scan the unchanging dactyls of Ovid. Landowska set out
the Goldberg Variations on a hand-wound Victrola.
When he was fifteen he stayed home from fishing to number
feet that promenaded to a Union Pacific tune, ABAB
pentameters. At the University his teacher the disappointed
novelist nodded his head—in admiration, envy, and pity—
while Bill sat late at a yellow dormitory desk, daydreaming
that his poems lifted through night sky to become stars
fixed in heaven, as Keats's poems rose from Hampstead
lanes and talks with Hunt and Haydon.
        When he considered

the cloth, Bill saw himself martyred. The ambition
of priest and poet!—innocent; and brainless as a shark.

•

Sculptors make models for touch; singers raise voices
to the possible voice; basketball players improvise
humors of levitation. They jump, carve, and sing in plain
air as we do dreaming.
                         Because emblems of every calling
measure its aspiration, the basketball player shoots
three hundred freethrows before breakfast; the mezzo
exists in service to the sound she makes, without eating
or loving except for song, selfish and selfless together;
the novice imagines herself healing a dozen Calcuttas
as Mother Teresa smiles from a gold cloud, and violates
holiness by her daydream of holiness.
                                         Bill Trout
woke up, the best mornings of his life—without debilities
of hangover, without pills or panic—to practice joy
at four o'clock dawn: to test words, to break them down
and build again, patient to construct immovable objects
of art by the pains of intelligent attention—remaining
alert or awake to nightmare.
                              But the maker of bronzes
dies decapitated in the carwreck; the whitefaced mimic
dozes tied to the wheelchair; the saint babbles and drools;
carcinoma refines chemist, farmer, wino, professor, poet,
imbecile, and banker into a passion of three nerves
and a feeding tube.
                    At the Bayside Hospice Bill's body
heaved as it worked for air; IVs dripped; bloody phlegm
boiled from the hole punched like a grommet in his throat.

•

Another fisherman writes me: "A man's death is his own;
you take Bill's death away, for public tears." I remember
Bill depressed, drinking double Manhattans straight-up,

taunting himself: "Compassion's flack! Elmer Gantry
of Guggenheim grief!" In Coleridge's *Notebooks*,
he underlined: "Poetry—excites us to artificial feelings—
callous to real ones."
                        Commonly Bill recited, from John 14,
"I go to make a place," then shrugged and sang the Wobbly
hymn, "You'll Eat Pie in the Sky Bye and Bye—When
   You Die."
After reciting Thomas Hardy, he went on to mimick Oliver.

Two years after the Maine summer, he worked for SNCC
in Alabama, in a cadre of Christians and Jews, beaten bloody
and jailed, declaiming Amos as gospel of anger and love.

Angry he married again; loving he wrote "Selma with
   Hellfire."

A decade after, as we sat late in a bare Port Townsend room,
bossily I reminded him to eat the wax-paper'd hamburger
cooling by his ashtray. Bill delivered a line, in his voice
as lush as an old Shakespearean's: "Ohhhh . . . to think
of the mornings I've waked with a cold cheeseburger
   beside me!"

He walked into water and out again; he woke in the drunktank
heaving; he trembled after electroshock; he made the poems.

•

If ambition is innocent, nevertheless it impairs those
it possesses, not to mention their irretrievable children.

In the interstices of alcohol and woe, Bill vibrated
awake to a room that surged, shook, and altered shape.
He secreted vowel-honey in images dangling from
   prepositions;
he praised survival.
                  When he finished his sojourn

at McLean, where Very and Lowell had paced before him;
when Margaret left him, removing their daughter, and Bill
declared bankruptcy; when he was unable for five years
to take Communion—he drank two Guggenheims and
   snorted
an NEA. He quoted Amos: ". . . as if a man fled from a lion
and a bear met him."
                       From his house in Oakland, USIS
flew him to Prague, then home to detox. Once I visited him
just back from drying-out, shuffling from chair to table
like a ninety-year-old, shaking as he tried to light
his Lucky, barely able to speak.
                       Then in middle-age
he fell in love again. He listened again to Chaucer
and recited Spencer's refrain as he stood by the Thames,
holding his Hindu love by the hand, or walking arm in arm
by a lake where Wordsworth walked;
                               or, happy in Delhi,
reading the Gita, he breathed each morning India's fetid
exhausted air, filling his notebook in warm dawn
as parrots flashed and his throat opened with gold
vowels, line after beautiful line, all the last summer.

•

The week before he died he handed me a clutch of poems.
Speechless, syllables occluded in his throat, he raised
a yellow pad and wrote, "That's it." Eyes protruded
from bone sockets; neck-cords strained; trunk heaved
as he looked for his love who gazed out the window
of the room, bare except for a crucifix, downward to the Bay
and the brown edges of March.
                         After he died Reba gave me
his Modern Library Dickinson, in which editors corrected
the poet's lines. I imagine Bill in Eugene, penciling,
neat in the margin, restorations of Amherst.
                               Each year
his death grows older. Outside this house, past Kearsarge

changing from pink and lavender through blue and white
to green, public language ridicules "eager pursuit of honor."

Do I tell lies? "... in middle-age he fell in love ..."
Did he never again tremble from chair to table? At night
Bill delivered his imagination and study to *Laverne
and Shirley*, laughing when a laughtrack bullied him
to laugh—while Reba groaned an incredulous Bengali
    groan—
in order not to drink.
                      Yet again he walked in a blue
robe in detox, love's anguish and anger walking beside him.

•

It is twelve Aprils since we buried him. Now dissertation-
salt preserves *The Collected Poems of William Trout*
like Lenin. Here is another elegy in the tradition
of mourning and envy, love and self-love—as another
    morning
delivers rain on the fishbone leaves of the rotted year.
Again I measure the poems Bill Trout left on the shore
of his scattery life: quatrains that scrubbed Pocatello
clean, numbers of nightmare and magic, late songs in love
with Reba and vowels—his lifelines that hooked and landed
himself and his own for his book.
                      But if a new fixed star
resurrects Bill's words who labored and excelled, not even
Chaucer's or Ovid's accomplishment— "Joves woll me
    stellyfye"—
will revise electrodes, jail, and death at fifty.
Bill Trout is incorrigible, like the recidivist blacksnake,
sparrow, and high water that turn and return in April's
versions—cycles of the same, fish making fish—
                                  "unless,"
Bill dying, shrivelled and absolved, wrote on a yellow
pad: "Jesus who walked from the tomb has made us a place."

Work

YUSEF KOMUNYAKAA

I won't look at her.
My body's been one
Solid motion from sunrise,
Leaning into the lawnmower's
Roar through pine needles
& crabgrass. Tiger-colored
Bumblebees nudge pale blossoms
Till they sway like silent bells
Calling. But I won't look.
Her husband's outside Oxford,
Mississippi, bidding on miles
Of timber. I wonder if he's buying
Faulkner's ghost, if he might run
Into Colonel Sartoris
Along some dusty road.
Their teenage daughter & son sped off
An hour ago in a red Corvette
For the tennis courts,
& the cook, Roberta,
Only works a half day
Saturdays. This antebellum house
Looms behind oak & pine
Like a secret, as quail
Flash through branches.
I won't look at her. Nude
On a hammock among elephant ears
& ferns, a pitcher of lemonade
Sweating like our skin.
Afternoon burns on the pool
Till everything's blue,
Till I hear Johnny Mathis
Beside her like a whisper.
I work all the quick hooks

Of light, the same unbroken
Rhythm my father taught me
Years ago: *Always give
A man a good day's labor.*
I won't look. The engine
Pulls me like a dare.
Scent of honeysuckle
Sings black sap through mystery,
Taboo, law, creed, what kills
A fire that is its own heart
Burning open the mouth.
But I won't look
At the insinuation of buds
Tipped with cinnabar.
I'm here, as if I never left,
Stopped in this garden,
Drawn to some Lotus-eater. Pollen
Explodes, but I only smell
Gasoline & oil on my hands,
& can't say why there's this bed
Of crushed narcissus
As if gods wrestled here.

The Adulterers

KENNETH MASON

Gwen Forester passed away on July 8 at her home in Spartanburg. "Mrs. Pug," as she was affectionately known to three generations of Tremont boys, was the widow of former Athletic Director William "Pug" Forester. She served as School Postmistress from the time of his death in 1962 until her retirement in 1976.

   Tremont Academy Alumni News, Fall 1991

I was thirteen years old and a third-former at the Tremont Academy for Boys when I happened to glance over at Mr. Forester's table one Sunday night at supper and see Mrs. Forester send an anguished look over her soup spoon to Mr. Potter, buttering his roll three tables away. Their two gazes embraced longingly in midair; then Mrs. Forester turned to say something to Mr. Forester, and Mr. Potter turned to say something to Peewee Welch. I recognized that look; I'd seen it lots of times in the movies my mother and I used to go to during the years she was a widow in Tremont, before she married my stepfather and moved to Chicago. It was the way Irene Dunne looked at John Boles in *Back Street*, the way George Brent looked at Ruth Chatterton in *The Crash*, the way Adolphe Menjou looked at Barbara Stanwyck in *Forbidden*. I looked back at Mrs. Forester. As though she felt my eyes on her, she suddenly stared straight at me, even though I was at Mr. Barry's table, nowhere near Mr. Potter's. She smiled at me. She was always catching me looking at her, and she always smiled at me when she did. I smiled back. I liked Mrs. Forester. She looked like Claudette Colbert in *The Sign of the Cross*. I wasn't surprised she was committing adultery; it was a mystery to me why she had married Mr. Forester in the first place.

Mr. Forester looked like Charles Laughton in *The Island of Lost Souls*. He parted his hair in the middle; his eyes only opened halfway. He was six-foot-two and weighed two hundred and thirty pounds. He got his nickname, Pug, when he was an all-Conference guard for Clemson in 1928. He had been on the Olympic shot-put team the same year. In addition to coaching football and basketball, Mr. Forester taught manual training and was in charge of the Nature Club's overnight camping trips up Bald Mountain.

Henry Potter was hall master for the third form. He looked like Leslie Howard in *The Scarlet Pimpernel*. He wore black shirts with a white knit tie. He had played on the Princeton tennis team. He taught third and fourth form English, and he coached dramatics, one play each semester. He was such a good director that each spring a special performance of the commencement play was given for the public at the Imperial Theater in Tremont. When my older brother Ron starred in *Journey's End* his fifth form year, the *Tremont Citizen-Times* reviewed the play and said the production was of professional caliber. They said the same thing last year about *Androcles and the Lion*, in which I had played Lavinia.

Mr. Potter lived in two rooms at the west end of the third floor of Larkin Hall. Mr. and Mrs. Forester lived in the married master's apartment at the opposite end of the same floor. There was a door from the hall into their living room, but it was always locked; their apartment had its own entrance from private stairs from the ground floor. The only time the Foresters unlocked their door to the hall was on Thursday nights, when Mrs. Forester invited the boys on the third floor to come in their bathrobes for a glass of milk and a cookie before bed. Once, when Mr. Potter was away, Mr. Forester opened the door and shouted at the boys to quiet down. There were twenty third-formers on the third floor; we could make a lot of noise, especially when we all came piling in at 5 P.M. after athletics, or 9 P.M. after study hall. My room was right next to the Foresters' apartment. I could never host an after-lights gripe session because the Foresters would hear it if they were in their living room; I knew, because I could hear them when they had company. Another thing wrong with my room was it was the farthest from the can.

I wasn't the only person who didn't think Mr. Forester was the right man for Mrs. Forester; my mother didn't either. Actually, Mom wouldn't have approved of anybody Mrs. Forester married because she thought eighteen was too young for a girl to get married, especially a bright girl like Gwen Malone who had gone to Chatham Hall and who should have gone on to college. It also didn't help that Mr. Forester wasn't from Tremont and Mom didn't know who his people were. She knew Gwen Malone because Mr. Malone had the big insurance agency in Tremont and had handled the insurance payments after my father died. Gwen's older sister Dorothy used to babysit when Ron and I were little, and both girls had helped at the house the summer Mom came out of mourning, serving at two garden parties she gave. I was only six that year, but I never forgot how much fun it was helping the pretty Malone sisters fold napkins and put out place cards before the party started.

After Ron was boarding at the Academy, Mrs. Forester would always come over to talk to Mom and me when we came out for a basketball game or a play Ron was in. I could still call her Gwen then, but Ron had to call her Mrs. Forester because she was a faculty wife. The year I entered first form, when Mom drove Ron and me out for the first day of school, I saw Gwen and yelled "Hi, Gwen!" out the car window. "Mrs. Forester, you dope," Ron said, giving me a poke. "I forgot," I said. "Well, don't forget again or you'll get stuck five points," Ron said. When Mrs. Forester came to the car to talk to Mom while Ron and I were unloading our stuff, she smiled at me and said, "How are you, Randy? I'm so glad to see you. If you ever need anything after your mother moves to Chicago, you let me know, you hear?" "Yes, Mrs. Forester," I said.

Gwen Forester wore her black hair in a short straight bob with bangs over her forehead, just like some of the girls from St. Genevieve-of-the-Pines who came out to school for dances. She dressed more like those girls than a faculty wife too: sweaters and skirts and saddle shoes, and a ribbon in her hair. For dinner she always wore a dress to the dining room, and on Saturday nights she sometimes wore a green silk dress dotted with hundreds of tiny pink buds; it buttoned up the back and had billowy sleeves and a pleated skirt and a little leather belt around the middle. Sometimes she wore it with a silk scarf around her shoulders, the same pale pink as the buds on her dress. That was my favorite. I thought she was beautiful when she was Gwen Malone and I was helping her set the outdoor tables for Mom's garden parties, but I thought she was even more beautiful as Mrs. William "Pug" Forester, even though I wished she had married somebody else. I wasn't the only one who thought she was beautiful. At the commencement dance more seniors danced with her than any other faculty wife, and she danced with them just like their dates did, doing all the dips and twirls as though she were a student herself. Actually, she was twenty-four years old the year I was in third form, and I remember Mom's saying it was strange Gwen didn't have any children yet, Pug being such a big outdoorsman and all.

At vesper service after supper, I began remembering things about Mrs. Forester and Mr. Potter I never would have remembered if I hadn't seen them exchange their look at dinner. Just last Friday, two days before, I'd passed the two of them talking so intently as they walked back to Larkin from play rehearsal they hadn't even noticed me, so I didn't say hello. Mrs. Forester was wardrobe mistress for the Dramatic Society, but why did she go to play practice every day when there was nothing for her to do until dress rehearsal night? I remembered something else, too: the afternoon I'd been stuck twenty points and sent to my room early from athletics for talking back to Mr. Hunt at junior football practice. As I passed Mr. Potter's room at the top of the third floor landing, I heard Mrs. Forester's voice inside, and when I got to my own room at the end of the hall I looked back just in time to see that Mr. Potter had come out into the hall to see who it was and was just turning back into his room. I closed my door and lay on my bed, trying not to cry, I was so sore about being stuck and losing my Wednesday free afternoons for three weeks. A few minutes later I heard footsteps, and Mrs. Forester's door open and close. It hadn't meant anything to me then, but now, thinking about it during vespers, I would have bet anything they had been holding hands and kissing in Mr. Potter's room when I went by.

After Christmas vacation Mr. Potter gave me a copy of *Whistling in the Dark*, the play he had selected for the winter term, and told me I was to play the female lead, Toby Van-Buren. Rehearsals began in February. The first week the cast just sat in a circle on the stage, reading their parts from their scripts. The second week we walked around the stage trying to say our lines from memory. From the third week on, the two boys playing girls had to wear girls' jumpers over their clothes and high-heeled shoes at every rehearsal; this was so we'd be used to them by opening night and not spoil our entrance by falling on our faces. The Dramatic Society's wardrobe had inherited a fair number of girls' shoes through the years, but none of them fit me comfortably, so Mrs. Forester had to take me to town on Wednesday free afternoon to buy a pair of high-heeled shoes just for me. I didn't mind; I'd been stuck so many points I would have been on the sidewalk sweeping crew otherwise.

Mrs. Forester said she'd have to decide what dress I was going to wear before she bought the shoes. After lunch on Wednesday she took me up the private stairway to her apartment, led me into her bedroom, opened the closet door, took out two dresses, and laid them on one of the twin beds. I undressed to my underwear. She put a brown wool dress on me; it had long tight sleeves and buttoned high on the throat.

"What do you think?"

"It scratches."

"Really? It's nicely lined."

"It scratches my arms and neck. Can we try another?"

"Of course. You're the star. We have to please the star. Just turn around for a minute and let me see the back."

"I'm not the star. Ben Moody's the star."

"You're both stars. Ben's the leading man, you're the leading lady."

"I'd rather play Wally. Wally gets all the laughs."

"You'll get those parts later, after you're older. Your brother started in girls' roles. Remember him in *The Dover Road*?"

"Sure. He played Eustacia. He wore Mom's velvet evening dress and got make-up all over it. She was sore."

"I wish you liked this, Randy. It fits you so nicely."

"It's too tight. And it scratches."

"All right, we'll take it off. What about this?" She slipped a black sleeveless dress over my head, then made me put on a funny little jacket that barely reached my belly button.

"Won't do," she said. "Too sophisticated."

"You mean too ugly."

"It would be more polite, Mr. Jeffries, if you kept your comments on my wardrobe to yourself."

"I mean ugly on me. On you it would be very haute monde."

"Haute monde! My goodness, don't we have an impressive vocabulary. And aren't we fresh. Did I hear you got stuck twenty points again for talking back?"

"It wasn't fair. I didn't talk back. I really didn't. I just asked Mr. Havighurst if he was really sure——"

"I don't want to get into it, Randolph. Here, let's put this on."

It was the green silk dress she wore at Saturday night dinners. It slipped down over my arms and shoulders and thighs like a cool breeze on a hot summer day. The skirt settled over my hips just where it was supposed to. My arms floated in air in the wide, billowy sleeves. She began buttoning the back; I buttoned the sleeves at my wrists without waiting for her to tell me to. I fastened the leather belt against my stomach. I wiggled my hips and shoulders to make the silk brush against my body again.

"Boy, does that ever feel smooth," I said.

"It's silk. I'm not sure I can let you wear this. It does look nice, though. You'd have to be very careful with it."

"You mean not get make-up on it."

"I mean no clowning around in it, like dancing around backstage with the skirt over your head to prove you're not really a girl. You boys think that's very funny, but it isn't; it's disgusting."

"I won't do that any more. I promise."

When I played Lavinia in *Androcles and the Lion* the year before, they dressed me in a white toga with a rope around the middle; I didn't even have to practice high heels during rehearsals, because Lavinia wore sandals. All they did to make me a girl was put a wig on my head and a padded brassiere on my chest. It wasn't anything like wearing a soft silk dress with a soft round neck that just nestled against your throat, and wide weightless sleeves that made you feel you could float through the air if you wanted to.

"If I let you wear this you've got to promise me you'll be

very careful with it, you understand? Especially the buttons in the back. Never try to take it off without me, you understand?"

"I'll be careful. Can I see what I look like?"

"Oh, Randy, I'm sorry, of course you can. Here, come look."

"Boy, do I look dumb," I said in front of the mirror. But I didn't feel dumb. I felt vibrant, alive, special. I wished her phone would ring and she would have to answer it and talk for a long time while I just stood there in her silk dress, the sleeves billowing around my arms, the little leather belt holding the dress tight against my stomach, the skirt shimmering along my thighs. She could be on the phone all day and I wouldn't care; I'd be happy just standing there in her dress, as long as she wanted me to.

"I'm going to need an awful lot of padding you know where."

"Yes, Mr. Smarty, that will all be taken care of. And a necklace, I think. Maybe Mrs. Havighurst will lend us her pearls. If I don't tell her who they're for, of course."

"You think she's mad at me too?"

"Don't you imagine? After the way you insulted her husband?"

"I didn't insult him. That wasn't a fair stick. All I did was ask—"

"We're taking this off now. You unbutton the sleeves, Randolph. Do it carefully."

"This young man is playing a part in a school play and we need a pair of black pumps. Medium heels. Your lowest price."

The salesman at Pollock's looked like Peter Lorre in *The Man Who Knew Too Much*. He had pasty skin and shifty eyes, he was very short, and his name was Freddy Bourne. He leered up at me as though he were measuring the foot of the half-man half-woman from the sideshow at the Ringling Brothers circus. Mrs. Forester had brought a pair of silk stockings in her purse; I had taken off my own shoes and stockings and put her silk ones on up to my ankles. The first two pairs of shoes pinched my toes, but maybe that was the way all girls' shoes fit. Mrs. Forester asked Freddy Bourne what he thought. He smiled at her the way Uriah Heep smiled at Madge Evans in *David Copperfield* and said he didn't know, it was the first time he'd ever tried to fit girls' shoes on a boy. Mrs. Forester said try the next size. Freddy Bourne came back with only one pair. I walked down the aisle in them, ignoring the smirk on his face. They're OK, I said. I sat down, gave Mrs. Forester her silk stockings back, put my own shoes and stockings back on, and followed her to the sales desk. Freddy Bourne gave Mrs. Forester her change and handed the shoe box to me. "Y'all come back and see us now, y'hear?" he said, giving us another Uriah Heep as he held the door. I gave him one back that would have dropped the original Heep to his knees, added the old Italian finger behind Mrs. Forester's back the way Ron had showed me at Christmas, then sauntered down the sidewalk at Mrs. Forester's side.

"I want to congratulate you, Randolph," Mrs. Forester said as we walked to her car. "I saw the way that silly man looked at you. You were a perfect gentleman through the whole thing."

I didn't answer. I was imagining what it would be like if I were Mrs. Forester's daughter instead of just a boy in a play at school. Freddy Bourne would have treated me with deference, smiling instead of smirking, happy to kneel down to feel my toe in the shoe. We'd have made him bring out dozens of pairs before deciding, and afterwards we'd have gone into Eckerd's for a chocolate marshmallow sundae instead of just heading back to the car. Mrs. Forester would have been holding my hand as we walked in, the way mothers always hold their daughters' hands when they take them shopping, pulling them along behind them to the next rack or counter. We would have sat in a booth and put our packages down beside us and let our coats slide off our shoulders behind us while we looked at the list. We would have stayed an hour at least, talking about movies and clothes, and gossiping about the masters' wives at the Academy. On the way out we'd have bought Silver Screen magazine and I'd be reading juicy bits to her about

Norma Shearer and Robert Taylor in the car now on the way home. What a wonderful life it would be to be Mrs. Forester's daughter, I thought, until it occurred to me that if I were Mrs. Forester's daughter, Mr. Forester would be my father, at which point my reverie spiraled toward earth like a German Fokker in *Dawn Patrol*, smoke pouring from its tail, blood trickling out the side of its doomed pilot's mouth.

"How did you and Mr. Forester meet?" I asked as we drove back to school. "He's not from Tremont."

"Dorothy introduced us. She had a boyfriend who went to Clemson, and he invited her for homecoming, and she said how about arranging a date for my baby sister."

"And your date turned out to be Mr. Forester."

"Oh no, Pug would never have had a blind date. He was the big man on the campus. My date turned out to be a very nice freshman who started to write to me after, and then the next spring invited me to the prom. I accepted, and that's when I met Pug, at the prom."

"What happened to the fellow who invited you the first time? The one who wrote to you."

"I don't know. I'm sure he found another girl. He was very nice."

"Maybe he died of a broken heart."

"There wouldn't be somebody in this car making fun of me, would there?"

"I'm not making fun. That's what I would have done."

She looked over at me. I looked down at my hands. "Why, thank you, Randolph, I take that as a real sincere compliment. Thank you very much."

After a moment I said, "Do you think Mr. Potter will ever get married?"

"I don't know, what do you think?"

"I'm surprised some girl hasn't snagged him already, he's such a good dresser. And tennis player."

"Yes, I'm surprised too. He's certainly very handsome, don't you think?"

"I suppose. Except he doesn't have a very good build. Of course you wouldn't know that, but we see him in the shower every morning, and—"

"That will do, Randolph," she said sternly. We drove in silence for a few minutes; then she looked over at me and shook her head. "You really are a caution today, Randy. I can't imagine what's got into you."

Toward the end of the winter term it seemed to me Mrs. Forester was getting reckless. She began going into Mr. Potter's room, coming out of her apartment right onto our floor to leave a note on his desk, or return a book of his she'd borrowed, or drop off a plate of sugar cookies. Once she surprised Conner and MacLean with no clothes on; they had to go tearing into the nearest room and close the door until she had passed, then run back to their own rooms before she came back. Practically every time she spotted Mr. Potter she'd act as though she'd just thought of something she needed to tell him. "Oh, Henry," she'd say, and call him over to her, or go over to where he was. It was getting to the point where the poor man couldn't go anywhere without her swooping down on him to ask him a question, or walk along with him to Mayberry or the post office. I couldn't stand it; she was making a fool of herself. I asked Bill Batty if he ever noticed how Mrs. Forester was always saying, "Oh, Henry." Batty said yes, he did notice it.

Batty's room was three down the hall from mine, and he was one of the stage hands for *Whistling in the Dark*. We started looking at each other and rolling our eyes every time we heard Mrs. Forester say "Oh, Henry." The week of dress rehearsal we happened to be two of the eight third-formers assigned to the Foresters' table. Dress rehearsal was to be Friday night, school performance Saturday night. On Tuesday we were getting up from our chairs after lunch when Mrs. Forester called, "Oh, Henry." We rolled our eyes and walked down to the canteen together. In addition to my usual ice cream sandwich, I bought an Oh Henry bar.

Batty caught on right away. "Where you going to put it?"

"Under her napkin at dinner," I said.

"What, her napkin sitting on top of an Oh Henry bar when she walks in? It'll be too obvious. Everyone will see it."

"Just the wrapper, underneath. No one will see it except her."

"Do you think she'll get the message?"

"She'd better get it," I said.

I got to the dining hall early for dinner. There was a five-minute buzzer and a one-minute buzzer. I walked casually toward the Foresters' table after the first buzzer. I looked around; nobody was paying any attention to me. I slipped the candy wrapper under Mrs. Forester's napkin, then strolled idly over to the wall and studied the photo of the 1912 football team behind Dean Coughlan's table until the one-minute buzzer rang and everyone started filing in.

We all bowed our heads while the Dean said grace. After grace I looked at Bill Batty, sitting two seats to the left of Mr. Forester. Batty rolled his eyes expectantly. Mrs. Forester was sitting on Mr. Forester's right. I was four seats away from her, almost in the middle of the table. The waiters started coming out of the kitchen with soup tureens on their trays. The Foresters' waiter put a tureen with a ladle and ten soup plates in front of Mr. Forester. He picked up his napkin. We all picked up our napkins. I saw the Oh Henry wrapper fall into Mrs. Forester's lap. She picked it up and looked at it for a moment, smiling expectantly, like a little girl finding a party surprise. I suddenly felt sick. I looked at Batty; he was staring at Mrs. Forester, his mouth open. I looked back at Mrs. Forester; she was showing the wrapper to her husband, her face still so innocent of its malevolent mission I wanted to cry. Mr. Forester put the soup ladle down and took the candy wrapper from her.

"What's this?"

"It was under my napkin."

Mr. Forester studied the wrapper for a second, then crushed it angrily in his hand and put it in his pocket. He started ladling the soup, passing the first plate to her. She looked at me and smiled. I smiled weakly back, my cheeks on fire, then sat riveted in despair as she read in my guilty countenance the message the wrapper was meant to convey and the identity of the person who sent it. *You?* her stricken eyes asked, you of all people? I wanted to look away, but her gaze held me. Finally she had to pass some soup. I found a spot just past Pug's left shoulder and stared at it. I could see Batty giving me the eye; I ignored it. All I could think of was ways to die. I saw myself hanging by the neck from a rafter. I saw myself leaping off the railroad trestle. I imagined myself in the electric chair, hood over my face, Pat O'Brien reading the last rites, executioner's hand on the switch. Hurry, I begged, please hurry and throw the switch. But there was no switch; dinner went on and on. When the bell finally rang I was the first person in the dining hall on my feet.

"Wait, Randolph."

She said it in a normal tone of voice while one hundred and fifty boys were standing up and pushing their chairs back into place; she could have whispered it and I would still have heard it.

Mr. Forester stood up. She remained seated. "I'm going for a walk," he said.

She didn't look at him. "Fine," she said.

Mr. Forester stared at her for a moment, then turned and walked stiffly toward the door. Mrs. Forester motioned to me to come to her.

"We're going to my apartment, Randolph. I want to try on your dress for the play again."

"What about study hall?"

"I'll see that you get a late slip. Come with me."

We walked wordlessly up the stairs to her apartment. She led me into her bedroom.

"Take your clothes off," she said.

I stripped to my shorts.

"Raise your arms," she said.

It was the brown wool dress.

"I'm not wearing the green one?"

"It's too delicate. You might tear it."

"I wouldn't tear it. I'd be very, very careful. I promise."

"This is a better dress for the part. Here, let me button the throat. Turn around. It fits you absolutely perfectly."

"I hate this dress. It's too tight. It scratches my neck. Why can't I wear the other one?"

"Because I've decided you're wearing this one."

"Does it have to be so tight at the neck? Can't I leave the top button unfastened?"

"No you may not. It isn't that tight. Don't be such a complainer."

"I hate this dress." I began to cry. "I hate you."

"Yes, I know you do. You proved that tonight."

"For God's sake, Gwen, have you got that boy in a dress again?" It was Pug from the living room.

"I thought you were going for a walk," she said. "Write Randolph a late slip for study hall, will you?"

I started pulling the dress over my head. "All right, Randolph, don't rip it. Another ten seconds won't kill you."

"What's the matter," Pug called, "you girls having a spat?"

"Everything's fine. Randolph just had a little temper tantrum is all."

"I didn't have a temper tantrum."

She closed the bedroom door. "You're talking back, Randolph. Do you want to get stuck twenty points?"

"Go ahead and stick me twenty points. Stick me forty points. Stick me four hundred points. I didn't have a temper tantrum."

"Watch your tone, Randolph, or you're going to find yourself in real trouble. Now put your clothes on and go to study hall."

I put my clothes on. She opened the bedroom door and closed it behind me. I started down the stairs.

"Wait a minute, Jeffries, you've forgotten your late slip," Pug said. I turned around. Pug handed me the late slip, then pulled the crumpled Oh Henry wrapper from his pocket and put it in my hand.

"Now listen to me, son. It's time you stopped acting like a little kid. You're not Ron Jeffries's baby brother any more. You're going to be a fourth-former in a few months. Start acting like it."

I went down the stairs and started down the path to Mayberry. Four more days, I told myself: I had to let her put her ugly wool dress on me for dress rehearsal Friday night and the school performance Saturday night. After that I'd never play a girl's part again for the rest of my life. She'd never catch me looking at her in the dining room again for the rest of my life either.

Mom decided I shouldn't come to Chicago for the ten-day spring break the second week of April because things were a little hard for my stepfather right now and it was an awful lot of money to spend on train fare for just a few days at home. I didn't mind; Ron wasn't going home for the break at Carolina, and it wasn't any fun at home anymore without Ron. Several other kids were also staying: Diggory Penn from England, Miguel Quesada from Cuba, the Baxter brothers, who were on scholarship and whose folks everybody knew were poor, and three seniors who were having trouble with their grades and were getting special tutoring during the break. Most of the married faculty stayed; most of the bachelors, like Mr. Potter, went home.

With only three tables in the dining room, Mrs. Forester and I were often at the same table. It wasn't a problem; we had been unfailingly if stiffly courteous to one another since the play, which everybody said had been brilliantly acted. Mr. Potter told me I had done an outstanding job. Mrs. Forester also complimented me; on both nights, as she was helping me get out of her dress, she said, "You were excellent, Randolph. I'm proud of you." The way she said it I knew it was Randolph Jeffries the actor she was complimenting, not Randolph Jeffries the human being. I said thank you very much, Mrs.

Forester, in a voice just as mechanical as hers had been, thanking Mrs. Forester the theater critic, not the Mrs. Forester I had once loved.

On the Monday afternoon before the Wednesday morning school started again, I was practicing fast starts and stops on my roller skates on the cement walk near the entrance to the Foresters' apartment when I saw her watching me through the glass in the ground-floor door. I sat down on the walk and pretended to adjust the straps on my skates. She opened the door and came out.

"Hi, Randy."

"Hi."

"You didn't feel like going on Pug's hike today?"

"I felt like skating."

"Isn't it lonesome, skating all by yourself?"

"I'm not lonesome. I'm practicing starts and stops."

"You want to come for tea and cookies this afternoon? Just you and me?"

"What time?"

"When you finish practicing."

"I'm finished now."

"All right, come now then."

I took off my skates and started up the stairs after her. Halfway up the first flight she turned and put out her hand. I took it, and she led me by the hand up the remaining flight-and-a-half to her apartment. It was all I could do not to jump on the stairs and shout, so much happiness suddenly erupted inside me. At the top I left my skates on the landing and followed her into her kitchen.

"You clear the coffee table in the living room, Randy. The cups and saucers are in that cabinet. The sugar bowl's over there. There's cream in the little pitcher in the icebox. Use the tray on the counter."

I arranged everything neatly on the coffee table. Going back to the kitchen I paused at the bedroom door, leaned the tray against the wall, tiptoed in, and opened the door to her closet. Her green dress was there, on the end, next to the wall.

"Oh, Randy." She was watching me from the bedroom door. "It was mean of me not to let you wear it."

"It's all right. What I did was mean too."

"Do you want to put it on again?"

"You mean now?"

"If you want to."

"For tea?"

"Of course, for tea. We'll pretend you're Toby VanBuren come for tea. It'll be our own private play."

I stripped to my shorts and raised my arms. She let the cool soft silk shimmer across my shoulders and down my arms and thighs. I buttoned the sleeves. She started buttoning the back.

"I sure could use some padding you know where."

"You want a padded bra?"

"Go all the way over to the wardrobe?"

"No, silly, I have one here."

She took a padded bra out of the dresser, unbuttoned my back, slipped my arms in the bra, fastened it, and began re-buttoning the dress.

"Why have you got a padded bra? You don't need a padded bra."

"If you don't mind, Mr. Jeffries, there are some questions gentlemen don't ask ladies. Now look at yourself. Aren't you beautiful?"

"I need a wig. And high-heel shoes."

"Shall we get in the car and go see your friend at Pollock's?"

"Peter Lorre? Thanks just the same. Can I stay barefoot?"

"Yes, leave those dirty shoes off. And I've got an idea, too." She took her hairbrush and brushed my hair into bangs across my forehead. "Wait," she said, "don't move." She took a pink ribbon from a drawer and tied it into a bow in the middle of my head. "Now what do you say?"

I looked into the mirror; Gwen Forester and a girl with a boy's haircut looked back at me. We were exactly the same height.

"Boy, this sure is a beautiful dress."

"Yes, it's my favorite too."

"You know what I like? When you wear it on Saturday nights with the scarf around your shoulders."

She laughed. "Oh? So you want the scarf too?"

"No, I was just saying—"

"Never mind, it's right here. How do you prefer to wear it, Miss VanBuren, over one shoulder? Over both?"

She draped the scarf over my shoulders and tied it in front. She held me at arm's length for a moment before letting me go.

"My goodness, you really do look scrumptious, Randolph," she said wistfully. "Now, shall we have our tea?"

This must be what they mean when they ask in chapel if you're at peace with your maker, I thought: I had never been so at peace as I was now, sitting next to her on the couch, breathing air scented by her skin and her hair, my skirt touching hers, our bodies separated by two scant millimeters of cloth. We talked about *Whistling in the Dark*; about the commencement play, *Leave It to Psmith*, which I wouldn't be in; about my mother, and how she liked Chicago; about my chances of making the junior basketball team next year.

"Next year you'll be playing men's roles."

"No kidding! Did Mr. Potter say so?"

"No, but I can tell."

"How can you tell?"

"You'll be too big for my dresses next year."

"I could wear Mrs. Havighurst's dresses. She's as big as a house."

"No, when you're too big for my dresses, Randy, you'll be too big for dresses altogether. Do you understand?"

"Sure," I said.

"Do you really, Randy?"

I knew what she meant: she meant it was time to stop acting like a little kid, time to grow up. I knew it was time. She didn't have to tell me.

"Sure," I said again, and then suddenly jumped to my feet,

just as she did, at the sound of the ground-floor door opening below.

"Oh my god," she gasped. She ran through the kitchen and shouted down the stairway. "Pug! You're back so early. Is something wrong?"

"Tim Baxter—sprained ankle—" Even before I heard Pug's answering voice I had run into the bedroom, thrown her scarf on the bed, unbuttoned the sleeves of her dress, and was reaching behind me for the buttons in the back. I got the top two. The third one tore. The fourth one tore. It was hopeless: I could never do it in time. I scooped up my clothes and shoes, ran through the living room, unlocked the door to the hall, closed it behind me, turned immediately into my room, and closed the door. I heard the Foresters' door open again. With my clothes and shoes still in my arms I stepped into my closet, closed the door, and sat on the floor. The door to my room opened; my roller skates dropped on the floor. My door closed and the Foresters' door opened and closed. Then their voices through the wall:

"Who was that? Who just went out that door?"

"What are you talking about?"

"For Christ's sake, Gwen, somebody just went out that door. Who was it?"

"I don't know what you're talking about. Nobody went out the door."

"Teacups? Cookies? All by yourself?"

I heard their door open, then Pug running down the hall toward Mr. Potter's room, then her voice, now in the hall outside the door to their apartment:

"Don't be an idiot, Pug. He's in Ohio. He won't be back until tomorrow."

Doors opened and closed at the end of the hall; Pug's footsteps crossed the hall into the can, then headed back toward the apartment. Mrs. Forester's footsteps turned back into the apartment. Pug's footsteps followed her, their door closed, the lock turned.

"Would you listen to me for a minute?" Her voice, soft.

"Somebody was here, damn it."

"Betty Gilkey was here. She came for a chat after lunch. We had some tea. She left an hour ago, Pug, an hour ago." How simple, I thought. Mrs. Gilkey was one of Mrs. Forester's friends from town. All she had to do was call her later and tell her what to say in case Pug ever asked. We were saved.

"Well, why didn't you say so for Christ's sake?"

"How could I say anything with you acting like a madman? Thank god the boys are on vacation—you'd have made fools out of us forever."

"You've already done that, Gwen. Just thank your lucky stars Prissy Pants wasn't there. I'd have made something worse than a fool out of him."

Pug's footsteps receded toward the bedroom, followed by the faint sounds of Mrs. Forester taking away the tea things. Still sitting in the dark on the floor of my closet, I cautiously began to unbutton the back of her dress, wincing as my fingers reminded me of the two torn buttons. I undid the final two buttons without tearing anything, then stood up and pulled the dress over my head. Everything was quiet in the Foresters' apartment. I unsnapped the padded bra, opened my clothes hamper, and stuffed the dress and bra underneath the shirts and underwear and socks already in it. Then I opened the closet door, picked up my clothes and shoes, sat on my bed, and started to get dressed. Her scarf was tangled up in my shoes. I went back to the closet and stuffed the scarf underneath everything else in the hamper. I looked at my watch: it was four o'clock, two hours till dinner. I finished dressing, picked up my roller skates, opened my door, and walked quietly down the hall to the can. There, in the mirror, I saw a boy with roller skates slung over his shoulder and a pink ribbon in his hair. I snatched the ribbon off, stuffed it into my pocket, pushed my hair back off my forehead, took a leak, went down the stairs, put on my skates, and coasted down the walk toward Mayberry Hall.

Mr. Forester came to dinner alone that night. He sat at the same table I was at. Everybody was talking about Tim Baxter's accident. They asked me why I hadn't gone on the hike; I said it was because I was skating. After supper I played ping-pong in the seniors' rec room in Hamilton Hall. It was quiet in the Foresters' apartment when I got back to my room. I looked in my clothes hamper. Her dress and scarf and bra were gone. That was why she hadn't come to dinner. I thought of her coming into my room looking for her dress and finding it stuffed in the hamper under my dirty clothes, all wrinkled, two buttons in the back torn loose, her beautiful pink scarf streaked with dirt from my shoes. She must have wanted to weep. I wanted to run to her, weep with her, beg her forgiveness, tell her how much I loved her. I had ripped the buttons of her beautiful dress, just like she was afraid I would. I had put my dirty shoes all over her beautiful scarf. I lay down on the bed and buried my face in the pillow. It was after midnight when I finally undressed, got under the covers, and went to sleep.

She didn't come for lunch on Tuesday but she came for dinner Tuesday night, the last night before school started again. She and Pug came in with the Havighursts and sat with the Butterfields and Butlers. I could smell the sherry on their breaths all the way over at my table. I sat with the flunking seniors and the Baxter brothers and Mr. York. I could see her from where I sat, but I carefully didn't look at her until I accidentally raised my eyes while passing Jamie Baxter the white sauce for the brown betty; she was looking directly at me. She smiled, and I smiled back, but they weren't like the simple little smiles we used to give each other.

I'm sorry about your dress, my smile said.

It wasn't your fault, her smile said.

I love you, my smile said.

I love you too, her smile said, but we mustn't see each other again.

I know, my smile said, and we both looked away.

Gwen Forester and I never spent another moment alone together during my three remaining years at Tremont. I wasn't in another play until fifth form, when I played male roles in *Libel* and *R.U.R.* In sixth form Mr. Potter cast me in the leading role of Teddy Deakin in *The Ghost Train*, for which I won the award for the best performance of the year. But although we were never again alone together, there were countless times—in the dining hall, in chapel, in the stands at a game—when our eyes would meet and linger for a moment, until she smiled, and I smiled, and we turned to look at someone else. One of the first times that happened was on a Saturday evening in May, about a month after our tea party, when she came to dinner in the dining hall wearing her green silk dress, her pale pink scarf draped over her shoulders, and a pink ribbon in her hair. Three boys at her table scuffled to hold her chair, but Pug pushed them away and held it for her himself. I saw her eyes searching the room to see what table I was at the moment grace had been said, and when she found me she gave me a really big smile that anyone could have seen, and then looked away quickly before I could give her one back. The pink ribbon in her hair reminded me that I had never returned the one that was in my hair the day I ran from her apartment. I still have that ribbon today somewhere, in with the cups, plaques, yearbooks, and other stuff one saves from school.

Fortunate Traveller

LYNDA HULL

Dazed and voluptuous, Monroe sways through
the casino toward Gable. The last film.

Her soft face, like her voice, breathless
   above subtitles, the Spanish premiere

     of *The Misfits*, thirty years late. The line had wound
the block beneath a sky, stagy
   and ultramarine, swept with klieg lights,
     sherried autumn air. Like a trapdoor opening

   in time, ladders and tunnels, the metro's
        black underground winds beneath the theater,
blue signal flash. Each platform's arched and tiled, columned
   and inscribed, resplendent as memory palaces

   monks once constructed, lavish scriptoriums
of the mind for arcane texts, scrolls and histories.
   I'd wanted to hear American voices, the velvet
   curtained hush framing spectacular faces.

   Los Perdidos, the translation skews, the clement
     darkness violined as the stars navigate
tawdry celluloid orbits through the bungled script
of drifters whose luck dissolves at desert's edge.

   Tossed dollar bills crisp around her ankles,
Monroe shimmies, the barroom scene, hair musical, those
     naked humid eyes. Houselights, dim, benevolent.
   This morning, the Opera stop's electric

   no-time, then the metro's plunge into the tunnel.
     Swaying from the handgrip on the way from
the doctor, his ancient fluoroscope that verdigrised
   everything it touched, my reflection rippled,

   insubstantial in the coal-blacked pane, tangled in
layers of reflection, circus posters tumbling
   half-naked spangled acrobats pentimentoed
across the glass. Everyone I talk to these days

  is both here and not here, entranced by leaf-smoke,
    coal-smoke. Anthracite, the blue enduring flame.
Bituminous, yellow flame, burning quickly,
    volatile. Billowing tobacco clouds, the audience

    fans programs and onscreen the chemistry fails to
ignite but for this love scene, tender and confused,
    between Clift and Monroe. The alley outside the bar.
They'd kept forgetting their lines, passing between takes

    a silver flask of vodka, washing down
      barbiturates until finally the shooting stopped
and that's why the scene's so lost. *Los Perdidos.*
Crimson seconals, the tuinals and canary-yellow

    nembutals, the stoked hues of leaves dervished in the
      parks'
dry fountains, sherried autumn air. Like trapdoors in time,
    a yeasty breeze redolent as the breeze shaking
    winged maples in the park by the railroad station,

    the group of friends I had when I was young.
      Another city. Of all that group, I alone
am left to glimpse beneath these actors' faces
    other faces, behind Monroe's hand steadying

    herself on the torn car seat this hand fluoroscoped
green and fleshless, all arthritic whorls and ratchets,
    to see in those fanned bones the *transi*'s hand, caught
between life and afterlife, carved above

    the sandstone archway in the ruined monastery
      garden near our flat, already part of memory's
cluttered gallery. Here is the urn that holds
    the lover's ashes, the harp that plays

   the friend's delirium, the coal brazier measuring
time: anthracite burning blue, enduring, bituminous
  sulphur flames, the quick ones, black-bordered
    postscripts,
 those mistakes smudging police blotters. Of all that group

  I'd meet when I was young: a trapdoor opening in
    time—
   this one of the russet curls blown across a pale
    forehead,
this one I loved, rich laughter from a black throat like
 no other, the spark and groan of trains braking at

  the little station. Translation fails. The metro rumbles
beneath the theater as *Los Perdidos* reels suffused by
  harsh mineral desert glow. When the last
 shot of the actress's gone lovely face furls away,

  I alone will taste the foreign coffee, sweet
   and thick. I alone shall watch these hands vanish
in bewildering autumnal smokes, an evening
  at this century's end when wrought-iron streetlamps

  print wands and serifs over everything
they suffer to touch.
   Of all that group I'd meet when I was young . . .
 I can't recall what we spoke of—it meant so much.

The Spring House
KATHERINE SONIAT

sits astride this spongy hole in the planet.
Sycamores whiten at dusk, fruit bats

home in around the pond, and there's one
visitor that didn't make it in

for a drink: raccoon at rest by the spring
house, his scurry now settled into

carcass while the stove in the brambles
sprouts a welcome of newly warmed forsythia.

An unlaced work shoe, half-full of water,
leads me to look at my own bare feet,

damp with spring fever, the grass scattered
with feathers the mallard left, each quill

once a jade slash in white weather.
Tonight, new moon rising, this village

storefront holds sway as I pry open the door
on a dark wishing room of water.

Under these eaves, it will be afternoon
in a temperate zone all summer.

At School

MARIANNE BORUCH

They write and read to know everything worth knowing
each fall past snow to spring.
The yellow buses stop
and children wander off, this place a dream
their first dream
empties into. But the teachers
so real and quick, open their trunks
wide to the parking lot—woven bags they carry in,
books, bottles, all business this
early, the dim hall, dim
until they step there.

One teacher doubts herself, and the children
love that darkness.
She stands at the window
looking out so much she could be weather
or a kind of light they've seen in pictures,
scary, depending.
The room slips then, like ice
on ice. They fiddle at their desks,
walk around, know she knows at heart who
they are—fish or giant
ancient squids at seabottom, not kids at all.
Certain moments her darkness floods
the whole room at a thing
one says by accident
or because it sounded close. They watch her
whisper back
the awkward word or phrase, whatever it is,
whatever hung in the air those twenty seconds
like a kite wounded,
coming down.

At recess, she's in there, quiet.
She's in there, I know
she is, two of them say, two
who should be out on the playground, screaming.
Not one of them moves
though they want to—oh, they want to.
It's neither happiness
nor sadness
how they lean their heads
against her door that way.

Girl Writing a Letter
WILLIAM CARPENTER

A thief drives to the museum in his black van. The night
watchman says Sorry, closed, you have to come back tomorrow.
The thief sticks the point of his knife in the guard's ear.
I haven't got all evening, he says, I need some art.
Art is for pleasure, the guard says, not possession, you can't
something, and then the duct tape is going across his mouth.
Don't worry, the thief says, we're both on the same side.
He finds the Dutch Masters and goes right for a Vermeer:
Girl Writing a Letter. The thief knows what he's doing.
He has a Ph.D. He slices the canvas on one edge from
the shelf holding the salad bowls right down to the
square of sunlight on the black and white checked floor.
The girl doesn't hear this, she's too absorbed in writing
her letter, she doesn't notice him until too late. He's
in the picture. He's already seated at the harpsichord.
He's playing the G Minor Sonata by Domenico Scarlatti,
which once made her heart beat till it passed the harpsichord
and raced ahead and waited for the music to catch up.

She's worked on this letter for three hundred and twenty
    years.
Now a man's here, and though he's dressed in some weird
    clothes,
he's playing the harpsichord for her, for her alone, there's
    no one
else alive in the museum. The man she was writing to is
    dead—
time to stop thinking about him—the artist who painted
    her is dead.
She should be dead herself, only she has an ear for music
and a heart that's running up the staircase of the Gardner
    Museum
with a man she's only known for a few minutes, but it's
true, it feels like her whole life. So when the thief
hands her the knife and says *you* slice the paintings out
of their frames, you roll them up, she does it; when he says
you put another strip of duct tape over the guard's mouth
so he'll stop talking about aesthetics, she tapes him, and when
the thief puts her behind the wheel and says, drive, baby,
the night is ours, it is the Girl Writing a Letter who steers
the black van on to the westbound ramp for Storrow Drive
and then to the Mass Pike, it's the Girl Writing a Letter who
drives eighty miles an hour headed west into a country
that's not even discovered yet, with a known criminal, a van
full of old masters and nowhere to go but down, but for the
Girl Writing a Letter these things don't matter, she's got a
    beer
in her free hand, she's on the road, she's real, and she's in love.

Memorywork

SUSAN MALKA CHOI

In 1963 I was in Ann Arbor. I remember the usual things, like a blouse that I wore as often as I thought I could get away with it, and where I was the day they shot Kennedy. I think everyone must remember things like that. The blouse was thin and white, with no sleeves and a peter pan collar. Small buttons the milky color of imitation pearl. It was a flirtatious little blouse. Because I remember it so well I will always confuse myself in memory, thinking that it was a warm summer day when JFK died.

I was walking through the quad before I knew what had happened. The eeriest feeling of my life: something palpably malicious hung in the air, like a sharply drawn breath held trapped in the lungs for too long. There was something else strange, wrong, that gave me the thought of summer. It was biting cold yet the quad was peppered with small knots of people who stood absolutely still, shoulder to shoulder, their heads almost touching. Like tiny football huddles, engaged in silent prayer. At the heart of each group was a transistor radio, stuttering that terribly lonely, distant radio sound. I passed one group and heard a soft noise of choking, and later I knew it was weeping.

Kennedy had been to Ann Arbor the year before, to unveil the Peace Corps. I met Jay at the speech, and that is the source of another snag in my memory. I will always associate Jay with JFK, and this has me convinced that I cried the day that JFK was shot. I was in love, and my love threw an umbrella of tremulous, precarious emotion over everything. I felt dangerously alive, in pain, on the very brink of disaster all the time. I have never been happier than I was then. I am always happy to feel on the verge of death.

But the truth is that I didn't cry when JFK was shot. I reported for work, as a secretary's helper in the economics department. When they waved me away, I was glad to go. I went home, flipped on the news, and fell asleep. Years later I had to admit to Bettina that I slept through most of the sixties. I wore that peter pan collared blouse straight through for another decade, until the day it fell apart in the wash.

When I married Jay I agreed with him that we couldn't have any children until the dissertation was done. It would be impossible, he said. First things first: the dissertation, the degree, the job. Could I wait that long? It was funny, because we both knew that I was only acting disappointed for him. I didn't want children, ever. My pretending to yearn and to pine was a lie. He knew, but it wasn't until much later that he hated me for it. We would giggle together about Macready, fishing the first draft of his dissertation out of a sewer grating with a bent-out coat hanger. Macready was Irish, Catholic, married since his undergraduate years. His five children had fed the dissertation between the rusted teeth of the sewer grating, a page at a time. The only copy. Children! We giggled, made love, smoked fiercely.

I proofed Jay's dissertation for what seemed like ten years, but it must have only been four. I kept my job as a secretary's helper, and when the secretary was fired for being pregnant, I was promoted to full secretary. Jay wondered why I didn't take advantage of staff privileges, audit a class or two. It was another lie we shared. I pretended to be simple, and content with the helpful things I did. I corrected his spelling. I balanced our checkbook. "A Jew," he would confirm, with a tone of finality that strangely sickened me. Then, I always laughed.

There are some pictures of us, from that time when we were happy. Just a few stacks, taken three different days, maybe three years apart. All that time, and only this remains. It's strange to think that you buy a camera, and suddenly there's another form of selective memory, rivaling your own. The pictures are bent and fused together, cardboardy to the touch. They are edged with a border of white. When Bettina pulls them apart, the fronts cling to the backs and carry a papery fuzz away that cannot be removed. Strange, linty clouds float over our faces, obscuring our expressions.

Bettina is aggrieved. She is almost twelve, old enough to drag herself out of my enforced amnesia and insist upon having a past. She hauls old shoeboxes out of my closet, upending their contents onto the floor. Carbon copies of old letters, in no apparent order. Medical bills. Half the manuscript of a story that begins, *She stood by the window, day after day, watching the rain* . . .

"Bettina!" I bark. From my bed I snatch at the air.

"Where are they?" She is on her hands and knees, pushing stubbornly through the slum of yellowed paper.

"Where are what?"

"The pictures."

"You have the pictures right there in front of you."

"These are all the same day." She peers at them with irritation, pulling carefully. She winces when they part with the tearing sound that means they will be forever marred by fuzz. "There's no date on these," she complains. She is flabbergasted by my disregard for the past, for what she thinks is her past. She is angry that I haven't kept it in better shape for her.

I half-crane for a better view, half-cringe. I don't really want to see those pictures. "1963," I declare. There is the blouse. I am smiling as if I would break. That fantastic, sweet pain. It must have been early on.

"Where are the pictures of me? The pictures of me, when Dad was here?" Bettina is deliberately emotionless, businesslike. She is only cleaning, cleaning up this lousy mess I've made of our lives.

"I don't know," I tell her. "Now clean up that mess."

"*Are* there pictures of me?"

I waver between telling her No, telling her I don't remember, telling her Yes, somewhere. I don't want to say Yes. I don't want her to keep rooting around. I abruptly remember something I have been fighting hard to forget, a day I found Bettina shrieking in her room, a rare moment of hysteria. Even as a baby, she was usually sullen, glowering, silent. This day she wept until I appeared in the door, and then she hurled something at me. It might have been a lamp. Later I found the carbon, under her bed, of a letter I wrote to my sister that year, the year Bettina was eight. *When will I grow into this?* I had written. *When will it start? Everyone says I will learn to love her sometime . . . in answer to your question, No, she doesn't do a damn thing to help me. She's a kid. She doesn't do a damn thing.*

"I'll look for them," I tell her. For a moment, staring at the small, dark, truculent crown of her head, I am overwhelmed. She is a little foreigner, a little Martian. Sometimes, like this time, I love her. More often it is a struggle.

"Don't knock yourself out," she murmurs. She scoops the tattered salad of paper back into the boxes and leaves the room. A few minutes later I hear her music, the rock and roll that strikes a vaguely familiar chord in me whenever she plays it. If she is safely in her room, I will dance a little. I think it is the music from when I was young. I think I remember it.

Bettina is being taught a healthy respect for the past. It seems to be her classroom theme this year, the final year of elementary school. Next year she will be sent off to begin the harrowing career of a middle-schooler; maybe this is why the teacher is working feverishly, self-righteously, to instill the kids with a sense of history and worth. I went storming to the school in an indignant rage when Bettina told me the latest project. I had complied, even gone out of my way, for the other projects. I thought I was paying my taxes so that I could leave these things to trained professionals, but I did them. I taught her to bake bread for Know the Pioneers week. Another girl did hand-churned butter; Bettina's bread, unlike Bettina, was assimilated into the classroom scene with great success. Then I called my older sister for a crash course on the life of our mother, who had never bothered to know me, for Grandparentstory Week. I began to suspect that this unknown woman, this teacher, was using my child to teach me an unflattering lesson about myself, but I pretended great delight. I masqueraded as a normal, interested parent, until The Way They Were. When Bettina told me she needed a picture of her parents as young lovers, taken before she was born, I'd had enough. I would not have my child taught that every family was a Robert Redford love story. It seemed indecent, and insulting.

The classroom was in a temporary shack on blocks. When I opened the door I felt the need to duck, the door seemed so small, and I nearly fell into the room. I was fiercely blushing. I'd done myself up to be fearful but I knew I'd overshot and ended up pathetic. I was packed into a one-piece suit from my secretarial days, and it was too tight. The skirt crept up off the hips and bunched fretfully around my waist. I was teetering in heels. I stood uncertainly on the threshold, flushed and mortified. It had been so long since I'd made myself up, I was checking my rouge every other second in the rearview the whole way over. Now I was convinced all over again that it was much too bright.

The teacher was older than I had expected, perhaps even older than I was. Her hair was blonde but so abundant and fibrous that it could have been fake. Her face wore a matronly expression that defied any attempt to place her age. She had no wedding band, which surprised me.

"I'm Bettina's mother," I managed. I ventured unsteadily into the room and tried to look inquisitive. The large bulletin board was decorated with an elaborate racetrack, scattered across with cardboard cutouts of horses in flight. Each horse was slightly different, in color or in posture, and the lines were precise and delicate. I paused, admiring the care. They were emblazoned with names, the names proudly arcing across their flanks. I located Bettina near the lead. The board proclaimed: Attendance Winners!

It was true that she hardly missed a day. She never wanted to stay home.

"I'm Miss Shank," the teacher said, smiling broadly. The smile seemed to acknowledge the gracelessness of her name. "Bettina's right up there," she added. "It's a very close race this year."

"It's pretty." I nodded at the board.

"Oh." She waved a hand dismissively. "Horses are my great

passion," she said. She said it as though it were an admission. "I'm really thrilled to meet you at last," she continued quickly. "I was sorry you couldn't make Open House, but it looks like you're feeling better."

I registered this rapidly. Bettina never told me about an Open House, but this was the sort of omission she committed without forethought. I was surprised she'd said I was sick. Out of last minute embarrassment, or malice.

"I was very ill," I agreed, smiling.

Miss Shank dragged an adult-sized chair out of one corner and gestured to it. "They're big kids," she laughed, "but we're bigger, right?"

I nodded, numbly. I had imagined the visit as a flouncing through the door, a flinging of words, a quick exit. Now I was embarrassed and at a loss. She seemed so personable, so personal. I flirted briefly with suspicion, tried to suspect she was taking me in. I reminded myself of Grandparentstory Week and how much it had hurt me. My oldest sister played mother to me because our own mother was too old, too tired, too uninterested to care by the time I was born. So I was also an unwanted child, I know it's unfair. Then I thought of Know the Pioneers Week. I had to practice the bread secretly, two afternoons in a row, while Bettina was at school. I was always a lousy cook and it made me ashamed. It was another thing Jay had used to humiliate me, again and again, until he finally left.

"It's about The Way They Were," I began, and stopped abruptly. My hands worked anxiously around the edges of my purse. It was a tiny purse, a purse I never used. My real purse was huge, stained, hideous.

She nodded wisely. "Bettina was concerned. She explained that most of your old pictures were lost in the fire."

I absorbed this news without betraying shock. Of course: the fire.

She paused, eyeing me with a reserved empathy. "It's not really the pictures themselves that are important. The point is to teach the children a lesson they often learn too late, that their parents were once young, beautiful, excited about the future." She laughed. "Not to say that now all of you parents are old, ugly, and resigned."

I couldn't help it. I burst out laughing also, and she smiled appreciatively.

"It's just so hard for children to see beyond themselves, at this age. When they realize there was a time before they were born, a time when their parents actually existed without them, it teaches them something they may not show for a long time, but—" she held up a finger of warning—"it will come out one day. Children have to learn to esteem their parents as people, not just old windbags, disciplinarians, handservants. It's very hard." She sat back, a little breathless.

"Do you have children?" I ventured. I already knew what the answer was.

"No," she blurted out. After a slight pause she said again, "No, I don't."

I nodded carefully. I was cautious, afraid of appearing judgmental. Now I saw us as allies, as strategists. She seemed suddenly embarrassed.

"I know what you're thinking," she claimed.

"No, I think it's wonderful." My heart sank, unworthy of her project. "I really do."

She twisted one strange lock of hair, angrily. "You know, I lost my parents a few years ago, both of them. They weren't so old. It was an accident. I'd never imagined they would be gone one day, without warning." She nodded, without looking at me. "I'd always assumed there would be an interval, between knowing they would die, and death."

"Time at the deathbed," I offered. "A chance to say things."

"Yes." She caught my eye again, a little fiercely. She was not smiling anymore. "It's an old story, right? 'I never had a chance to say,' et cetera."

"I lost my mother when I was very young," I assured her. "I was angry, for years. Just sort of, I don't know, angry."

She nodded. We both looked away, at other parts of the room. In one corner I thought I could see an essay, tacked to the wall, in Bettina's hand. Her unexpectedly childish, cringing, disastrous cursive. I tried to look at my watch. I was always afraid when I left Bettina alone. Not afraid of what she was doing, but afraid of what she might find. I thought of the pictures, the letters, the furious disarray of my files. And Bettina picking through them with single-minded determination, and her unacknowledged fear of what she would find, what she would confirm about us both.

Miss Shank spoke up again, with formal caution. "Would I be too bold to assume . . . that there was never a fire?"

I smiled wanly. "Bettina thinks I'm sloppy. Maybe it seems like a fire to her." I wondered what made me find excuses for her. "There are some pictures of her parents, before we divorced. I haven't taken a whole lot of care with them." Briefly remembering my initial rage, I added, "It hasn't been a picture book life."

"I'm sorry," Miss Shank murmured. "It was an intrusion, a really thoughtless intrusion, and I'm sorry." She shrugged helplessly. My stomach became an anxious fist, unhappily aware that I was in the wrong. I didn't want her to surrender an apology to me, it made me stunned with shame. I wanted her to be severe with me, to be scolding, to exclaim that she had expected better. I realized I hadn't spoken.

"I feel so stupid," she added uneasily. "I guess I'm still stuck an angry child. I've never got to be an angry parent."

I stood up quickly, embarrassed. I wanted to say something that would dissipate our conversation like so much courteous hot air. "Bettina likes you very much," I offered. Bettina never spoke about her teachers at all, but when I said this I thought it was true.

Miss Shank took the cue, and stood also. "Bettina is very bright," she said mechanically. "Excellent in her reading, excellent in her memorywork. I'm enjoying having her."

I backed unevenly to the door. "Thank you," I said. It was a catastrophe, because I liked her. My incompetence infuriated me. I actually liked her.

"Thank *you*," she said stiffly.

Bettina's choice lies in a small envelope on the table. It couldn't be called a choice: it was the only one we found. A wedding picture. Suddenly, I remember a day at the height of summer—1965? 1964?—when Jay and I were renting a broken-down house in the country. I could put three things together and have the date exact, but I will not put three things together. Jay was teaching in the summer session at Eastern Michigan. Our porch had a trellis, choked with roses. I said, "They only grow if you don't care either way." We put bright green butterfly chairs in the yard, and took two pictures. One of Jay reclining in his chair, a pipe clamped between his teeth, a look of incredible audacity on his face. One of me stretched out in my chair, my eyes tensely closed, my body pale as a corpse.

I couldn't tell Bettina that it was always that way: he and I, alone. I couldn't tell her the truth: that our love never did endure company, and that we three would not have endured at all. She believes I cheated her out of a father, and her father believes the same. But what I want to ask is, If the child was so important, why am I the one who has her? If the child was the reason, how could he have gone without her? I want to ask this, but there is no decent way to do it. There is no decent woman who would say it.

So, there were always two of us. Never a third, to hold the camera and click. And the only picture of Jay and me together is on our wedding day.

Bettina was skeptical. I don't seem to do anything but give her fuel for her skepticism. "You didn't have any friends?" she demanded. "Any at all?"

"I guess we never had a friend and a camera at the same time."

Bettina shook her head, annoying me with her childish doubt. She peered closely at the wedding picture. It is a snapshot; there was no official photographer. Someone must have mailed it to us. It is a terrible picture, taken in the lounge of the University Chapel, a low room muffled by dun-colored drapes. The furniture is all orange and avocado, kitchen colors. Jutting into the frame at the left, the end of a folding table showing its metal legs beneath a white cloth. Stumbling out of the frame at the right, my sister. She appears to be my mother, both because she is old enough to have been my mother and because she is visibly disgusted. Jay and I stand in the middle, dressed only slightly better than the most casual guest. He is eating cake with his hand, staring off to one side. I face the camera flashing that explosive, murderous smile.

"I'm sorry," I told Bettina. I was, terribly, sorry.

"It's alright," she said. She regarded the picture with sudden, quiet understanding. As though the truth of it was what pleased her.

"Ain't no fairy tale, kid." I fought the urge to put my hand in her tangled hair and really mess it up. I kept still, looking over her shoulder.

"Mom," she said, leaning forward with an exaggerated air of secrecy. *"Truth is—"*

She made mocking eyebrows, letting the sentence dangle like an idiot question.

I waited for her to finish.

"Truth is, I've known it all along."

Today is the day that I have to get rid of it. I watch Bettina eat her breakfast, chewing every bite with a methodical fixity that amuses me. She is turning into a real person, this kid. She read somewhere that chewing every bite one hundred times could lead to weight loss, fooling the brain into filling the stomach with less. Now, in retrospect, she has proclaimed she has a weight problem.

I used to kill myself to love her. Now, without trying, I find myself liking her. More and more.

"Don't forget the picture," I tell her. The bus is blaring impatiently, but she is unflustered. She snatches up the envelope, throwing me a sly grin on her way out the door.

After she is gone I sit at the table a long time, willing myself to do it. I have to get rid of it because keeping it means hiding it, and hiding the ugly things about yourself gains nothing and loses so much time. It is only Bettina growing larger, angrier, increasingly articulate and demanding that forces my head out of the sand and commands me to do something. I remember passing a long window and being shocked by my own reflection: a squat little fireplug on legs. One moment of awareness in ten years. Later I told Bettina I wished I'd had a full-length mirror all my life. I always refused to own one, out of righteous indignation, or false pride. Now, I regretted it acutely. If I'd had one, maybe things would have been different. Maybe I would have paid better attention to what I looked like, and ended up a better person in the end.

"You can't be serious," she'd sneered. "You think your whole life would've turned out differently, if you had a bigger *mirror*?"

I go into my bedroom and pull the spare blankets out of a dresser drawer. Aside from what is discarded in the closet there are the things I'd truly hoped to lose. I empty the drawer and carefully slide my hand beneath the paper liner. There is only more paper, the sheets pressed carefully between the liner and the bed of the drawer like cherished leaves: a letter from Jay that made me vomit the first time I read it, and the carbon Bettina found, four years ago. Also, a very large photograph, an X-ray, in livid black and white. She does not know anything about it, but this is the picture Bettina is always looking for, a picture that offers some proof.

In it, the fetus is featureless and budlike, a lumpen blaze of light. At sixteen weeks everything is there, in grotesque proportion: the bulbous head, the delicate hinge of a leg, a hint of an arm. It is a poor X-ray, and the details are blurred. Still, you can see that something must accentuate the curl of that tiny body. The body is not simply shaped like a curl, it really *is* curling, clutching and clinging at something with inconceivable determination. Bent on being alive. The wisp of a thread betrays the prize in its fist, a prize it snatched like the brass ring off a merry-go-round. You may not be able to see it, but it's there. Impossibly, almost hilariously there. The baby is brandishing an IUD, and earning a place in Michigan medical history for us both.

I take the X-ray into the kitchen and set it on fire. It makes a rank smell from the developing chemicals and the gloss, but it burns. The corners cringe together, furling and swiftly blackening. When it is done I sweep the ashes together and throw them all over the yard. Then I make a tall glass of lemonade and play like it's summer.

Truth is, Bettina is right to be suspicious: I remember more than I admit. I remember that in 1967 we were in Ypsilanti, and preparing to leave. The prelude was complete: dissertation, degree, a job near the ocean. Jay and I shared the twin sense that the beginning had finally arrived, but our expectations were not the same. Jay had turned his unswerving attention to the accomplishment of children. For him children had always been the fourth term in the series, the next logical step. And it's true, I had always known this. But I was depending on a romantic change of scenery: we would walk near the sea and be battered by wind until our differences left us. Jay would realize it was just too soon for children, and then everything could start. I would pull myself together and do something of my own.

I'd started putting the Ypsilanti house into boxes months ahead of time. Those days were gigantic, emptied of everything but waiting. I was always alone. An eventless year is easiest to remember, in all its tiresome detail: the whirr of the electric clock, the morning light thick with dust. My flaking gold barrette and my plushy flowered housecoat. Always looking ahead, I lost track of the time. Summer seemed perpetual.

When I realized I hadn't been bleeding, I didn't know how many months I had skipped. There were no other symptoms. I knew the absence was a sure sign, but it was flatly impossible. After Jay banned birth control I had barely hesitated before visiting a doctor. I justified it as a necessary deceit, the only way to buy myself some time, and I was confident I could bring Jay around without his ever having to know. The thing would hang within me like a small pendant, a wire scrawl, undetectable. Jay and I would just happen to be unlucky, for six months or maybe a year, and soon it would cease to matter. It never occurred to me that the thing wouldn't work.

When the extraordinary circumstances of the pregnancy were explained to Jay, he was very quiet. The packing, abruptly suspended, had left the house with a vaguely exploded look. For days we picked carefully through the rooms, staring mostly at the floor. Our eyes met once over a teetering pile of books, once through the spidery stack of the butterfly chairs. I think he was grateful for the obstacles between us. When I finally sought him out, in his study, the X-ray lay on the desk between his hands. I stood at his back and felt the motionless rage there, hanging off him like a cape. I wanted to yank it away and be done with it. Things had changed and we had to let them change.

"Tricky thief." He could not see me nod at the picture.

"Like its mother," he said.

I was silent. It was already scripted, anything I could have said, and his response. If I'd wanted to wait: we'd waited. If I never wanted children: I'd lied. "Jay," I said. "Please turn around."

"I can't," he said.

Bettina will demonstrate her memorywork. I am very honored. She does not normally come to me with these things, but this time I asked. I wanted to know what it was. "I hear you're real good at it," I tell her. "Miss Shank said you were excellent." I pause over "excellent," and swell a little with pleasure. *"Excellent."*

Bettina frowns darkly. "Miss Shank told you? What'd you do, go and embarrass me?"

"Me? Embarrass you?" I wave her away with a grand gesture. "Go on. I was just trying to find out why you're doing so well. I thought you had some unholy arrangement with this woman."

Bettina turns very solemn. She puts on that you're-not-gonna-believe-this look again. "Mom," she says mournfully. "Truth is, I'm *real smart*."

She's a hell of a thief. I never wanted to admit how much of Jay she got away with, but lately I can see him standing in her place, and I can be captivated by it. I don't have to hate her for it.

"I know, kid. And I'm sorry."

Bettina grimaces and bolts out of her chair. She takes a place in the middle of the kitchen and tries to look resigned. "Well," she chants, "memorywork is both a means to an end and an end in itself. It fills the mind with well-known treasures and trains it to acquire even more. It is a skill!" Bettina flings with an arm and sighs with false passion. Her impersonation of Miss Shank is dead-on, and I have to laugh.

Bettina clears her throat severely. "I have a stunning repertoire. What would you like to hear?"

"What have you got?" I ask her. "Speeches? Poems?"

She gazes away, biting her tongue thoughtfully. "I have 'Four Score and Twenty Years Ago.' I have 'Two Roads Submerged.' I have a lot of weird political stuff, but only excerpts. 'King's Dream.' 'Kennedy's New Frontier.'"

I worry about making a good choice. I feel a little stupid. "A poem of your choice," I tell her. "Anything but that one about the roads."

"All right." Bettina looks anxious, but confident. "I have one that I kind of like."

"I'm ready," I tell her. I sit back and search for an attentive face, praying I won't be bored. I am almost always bored. But when Bettina starts to speak, straining her voice to be louder, I know she'll never bore me. Her poem is beautiful. Really, it is fantastic.

Party

NORMAN SAGE

Today I am seventy years old. I am amazed by that simple fact, but will not remark on it further than to express mild alarm and to remind myself that however hard one tries to forget, it is easier to contemplate the past than the future, and there is bound to be more back there than there is up ahead, and to remember that one's life slides by on the fluid crest of time, as they say. That is about as philosophical as I plan to get about it, although I can't help toting up this statistic: it has been one year, nine months, and thirteen days—at just about this hour.

Because I feel, in some obscure way, that the day should be noted, I am giving a party. It is to be catered by some young women who do that sort of thing and they are going to do it all, from drinks to snacks to a sit-down dinner. It will cost me a bundle.

I will go to the office this morning as usual—it is now nearly five-thirty—and I will discuss and probably argue about proofs and editing and jackets and other things more or less interesting, and then I'll come home in the heat of the day to bathe and dress and wait for my guests to arrive. I must remember to plump up the cushions on the sofa.

There will be fifteen for dinner and I have just realized that they all have cute names—Jan, Debbie, Kathi, Emmylou—and they will bring their current husbands or friends—Josh, Uriah, Bones, and Bobby Lee and so on. What ever happened to Tom, Dick, and Harry? I will greet them as they arrive with a peck on the cheek—we kiss thoughtlessly these days—for the young ladies and a firm handclasp for the men. I will be astonished—again—at their youth. These are the people I work with, and for the most part they are pleasant to have around. They pose a little, and some of them drink and smoke too much, but they are good people, and they like me, I think. In any event, they enjoy a good meal and a few drinks now and then and my parties, I know, are thought of kindly.

They will indulge me in my offerings of music—all on tape, for I will allow no one to touch my records. They will half-listen, or not at all, because they will all be busy laying bare their hearts to each other. But I will listen: It's the Talk of the Town, Ain't Misbehavin', Body and Soul, Lover Come Back to Me, Opus 3/4, Sugar—I've even worked in a bit of the last great movement of Dvořák's Fifth, just to see if anyone shifts gears noticeably.

I will watch them all and smile and lust after some of the young women, of course. I'll tell you something about seventy: it isn't necessarily *dead*. I will look particularly at Debbie, who is very beautiful if not terribly bright. She once thought the little junco at the bird feeder was on dope. But she is lovely to look at, and it seems to me that if one has the idea of a perfect late love it should be possible, and should involve such a person as Debbie—if the imagination is capable of establishing the proper circumstances, the active mind should have the power to bring them into actual being. Nothing, I have been told often enough, is impossible. If you think I don't know better, you are a dime short.

So I will look at them and marvel at their vigor and wonder when it was that I lost the moments which were there and those which I felt would someday come and didn't; and I will envy them their youth, but not their insouciance. I will imagine some of them unclothed, but I will not touch—I am very trustworthy in that respect. I will do my best to ignore the young men, in perfectly friendly ways, of course.

When the greetings have been made and the drinks passed around and the music is playing, and after we have observed the formalities of dinner, I will steal out and walk around the shore of our little lake, to hear the sweet evening sounds of spring and to remember seventy fleeting years. I will wonder how I came to this fearful state. I see the world now much as I have always seen it—bearing in mind the facts of four wars, a depression, unimaginable voyages to the moon, an assassinated president and a deposed one—and a world ill at ease with itself in the certainty of imminent destruction. I will hear the night cry of a catbird and the lonely call of a hound across the water. And I will remember the rise and fall of a woman's breast as she breathed her last harsh breaths.

My love was too proud to use a cane. Even when her leg hurt to beat hell she'd struggle along, leaning heavily on my arm. "Your little filly has gone lame," she said. "You limp, too, so folks will think we were both in an accident." Sometimes there was such pain in her eyes I could not bear looking into them, and I often had the feeling that I was somehow responsible, that I must have done something terribly wrong to curse her with that misery she felt every day of her life, every moment of it. When I suggested that possibility she said, "Of *course* it's your fault! Everything is your fault. You are personally responsible for all the evil in the world, and don't think I'm not going to get you *good* one of these days." She'd never say, simply, "You're wrong." She'd point out the absurdities in my logic, but she'd never accuse me of stupidity. "You just don't understand the joys of pain," she said.

When we first moved to Toddville we built a house (warm and friendly modern, the architect claimed) in the southeast corner of town only about a quarter-mile through an overgrown orchard to Millen Park, where there were stables for trotters and boarding facilities for the riding horses belonging to city folk. Jenny bought a two-year-old mare from Evert Reed, the kindest man, black *or* white, I've ever known, and she named her for him—Evvy. Jenny was in tune with everything sweet and natural. She looked at wildflowers with reverence and gratitude, and at the silliness of people with understanding and compassion. She regarded sex as perfectly natural, whether in humans or animals—a phenomenon quite like lightning—spontaneous and necessary, and sometimes a bit on the destructive side.

Once, when I was away from home for a few days, I returned to my hotel room just as the phone rang.

"Have you a woman in your room?" a voice asked.

"Certainly not!" I almost shouted.

"Would you *like* one?"

"Jen? Is that you, Jen?"

"You betcha," she said, "and I'm right in the next room and I don't got no clothes on."

Of course, that was before Evvy stepped in a gopher hole that steamy day in late August and fell on Jenny, crushing her left knee. Evert was there and got her to the hospital. By the time he found me, in tears himself, Ken Birch was there just looking at the X-rays.

"Looks like gravel in there," he said. He did the best he could and sent her to Granville where there is a good orthopedist, and he did the best he could, but it was a badly smashed joint. When she took her first steps with the walker following the final operation, I asked her how it felt.

"Stiff as a honeymoon prick!" she said, and wept.

She gave up horses altogether, not only because of her knee but also because Evvy had to be destroyed and that broke her heart, too. She took up art instead—something she could do seated with her gimpy leg stretched out to the left. It was not a good substitute. She punished herself by not using the crutches and in time got so she could walk without them, but at considerable cost to her in both pain and pride.

About a year after the accident some sort of systemic reaction took place and arthritis seized her entire body and every joint in it. Many operations did some good, but not much. Complete hip replacements did help some, but the bad knee was so messed up that a new joint there was out of the question. She was a bundle of constant and severe misery. She took what medication was available, knowing that the little relief it gave her would most likely shorten her life, but she was damned if she would become wedded to a wheelchair.

It would not be an exaggeration to say that I suffered along with her, but in different ways. I felt overwhelming guilt, as if taking responsibility for her condition would somehow influence chance in her favor. She was too miserable for love and she worried about that, I think, more than I did.

"If you find someone else, I'll understand," she said. "I'll hate her, but I'll understand." I looked, but I didn't buy. I think I had some idea that if she had to suffer so, the least I could do would be to suffer along with her, if only in that particular way. I may have thought that my own discomfort would in some mystical way gentle hers. I am not a wholly reasonable man.

And oh, yes, the party. I will think, My God! the promised time has come and gone, and I will try to tell myself that there is yet time for a good, warm, late love, but I will not believe it. I will say to myself, Let your breath come without willing it to do so, and do not write sorrow on the bosom of the earth—it has plenty without your small part. I will look at my guests and they will not know I have been gone, gone to that other place which flames in my heart. They notice only themselves. And seventy is quite beyond their comprehension.

The Book of the Dead Man (#6)
MARVIN BELL

ABOUT THE DEAD MAN'S SPEECH

Will the dead man speak? Speak, says the lion and the dead
   man makes the sound of a paw in the dirt.
When the dead man paws the dirt, lions feel the trembling of
   the pride.
Speak, says the tree, and the dead man makes the sound of
   tree bark enlarging its circumference, a slight inhalation.
Speak, says the wind, and the dead man exhales all at once.
Whoever told the dead man to be quiet was whistling in the
   dark.
To the dead man the dark is all words as white is all colors.
The dead man obliges, he cooperates, he speaks when spoken
   to, so when the dirt says Speak, he says what erosion says.

And when the air says Speak, the dead man says what a cavity says.

The dead man knows the syntax of rivers and rocks, the one a long ever-qualifying sentence for which no last words suffice, the other the briefest and most steadfast exercise in exclusion.

The dead man is a rock carried by a river, a pebble borne by air, a sound carved into frequencies infrequently registered.

MORE ABOUT THE DEAD MAN'S SPEECH

The dead man is part of the chorus that sings the music of the spheres.

Dead man's music uses the harmonics and parasitics of sound, in bands of low frequencies caught in ground waves that hug the terrain as they go, and in ultra-high megacycles that dent the ionosphere and refract over the horizon.

The dead man makes no distinction between the music he hears and the music he only knows about.

There are five elements in the dead man's music (time, tempo, key, harmony, and counterpoint) and two factors (silence and chance).

To the dead man, the wrinkled back of a hand is a score to be read.

The balding top and back of his head are a kind of braille awaiting a blind conductor.

The dead man's bone-sounds and teeth-clacks are a form of tuning-up.

Sad music brings artificial tears to the dead man's dilated eyes.

All things being equal, the dead man is not fussy about pitch and dissonance.

His inner ear is set to hear euphonic consonants.

The dead man sings in the shower, in good weather and bad, without knowing a song.

He hums the tunes of commercials without the words, sympathetic vibrations.

He has ideas for musical instruments made of roots and
 feathers, harps that use loose dirt something like an
 interrupted hourglass.
When the dead man, in a gravelly voice, sings gospel,
 hammers descend upon anvils.

The Departure

JAMES LAUGHLIN

They say I have to go away soon
On the long trip to nowhere.
Put things in order, they say.
But I've always been disorderly
So why start now?
Not much time, they say.
What to do with it?
Not much different, I think,
Than what I've been doing.
My best friends have always been
The ones in books.
Read a few pages here, a few there.
No complaints, few regrets,
Thanks to everybody.

At the End
JAMES LAUGHLIN

Let no mortician be her
last lover   I have sent

to Benares for two cords
of the finest sandalwood.

Untitled, 1968
JAMES GALVIN

for Mark Rothko

There's no such thing as an emergency.
                                        Betrayal is eventual.
The bridge is a river, when you think about it.
                                        River of blood,
when you think about it.
                         The Lord giveth.
                                   Highest echelons of
quietude.
         A veronica in each sunset.
                             In every blackening bandage
in the hospital's unspeakable bins, a veronica.
                                     Someone suffered
here.
        The elevator full of blood rose like any other.
                                             Why not.
Our nets were full of sunset when we hauled them in.
                                            The red sail

filled and pulled us darkward.
                              Blood in the drumroll blossomed.
The Lord giveth.
              Thou shalt.
                         Change the bandages when they blacken.
Don't think about it.
                  Set the red sail and disappear.
                                              Slow drip
in silence.
          Don't say a word.
                         Don't say the wineglass on the sill
is a sun-dried sangreal.
                      It's a landscape.
                                     You just can't bring
your body.
          The bridge is an inward horizon.
                                        The bridge has arrived
in time for us to cross.
                      I know because someone, or his assistant,
suffered here.

Translations from Colonial Swahili
SUE STANDING

A bad piece. A long arrow. Empty baskets.
Thick baobab trees. A hard bone. Heavy misfortunes.

She has beautiful buttons and a long chain.
The large islands have tall palm-oil trees.
The fierce drunkard has dry lips and a rotten head.

That arrow is broken. The basket has fallen down.
The baobab tree has fallen. The old person is dead.
The large bone is broken. The little child is dead.

The tall coconut tree has fallen. The cook is dead.
That drunkard has fallen down. He has built a house there.
This canoe is split. The child is lost.

Which baobab tree? Which chair? Which child?
What sort of bone is this? Which islands are those?
What sort of overseer is a blind person?

I have drawn a line. That old man dreamed.
The sweet potatoes have gone bad. You have tied yourself.
I have pained myself. Two thorns have entered the hand.

You will call the writer. The beautiful moon has gone down.
These months are good, those are bad. You were born.
I boasted yesterday, today I am sorry.

The mason built a secret room. Their spears are long.
The fisherman's heart is light. The man's voice is audible.
The children became blind. The broken water jars.
These bananas are redder and sweeter than yours.
He is weak today. It is true. A shadow which is not passing.

Emma Enters a Sentence
of Elizabeth Bishop's
WILLIAM H. GASS

Emma was afraid of Elizabeth Bishop. Emma imagined Elizabeth Bishop lying naked next to a naked Marianne Moore, the tips of their noses and their nipples touching; and Emma imagined that every feeling either poet had ever had in their spare and spirited lives was present there in the two nips, just where the nips kissed. Emma, herself, was ethereally thin, and had been admired for the translucency of her skin. You could see her bones like shadows of trees, shadows without leaves.

Perhaps Emma was afraid of Elizabeth Bishop because she also bore "Bishop" as her maiden name. Emma Bishop—one half of her a fiction, she felt, the other half a poet. She imagined Elizabeth Bishop's head being sick in Emma's kitchen sink. Poets ought not to puke. It was something which should have been forbidden any friend of Marianne Moore. Lying there, Emma dreamed of being in a drunken stupe, of wetting her eraser, promising herself she'd be sick later, after conceiving one more lean line, writing it with the eraser drawn through a small spill of whiskey like the trail . . .

In dawn dew, she thought, wiping the line out with an invented palm, for she knew nothing about the body of Elizabeth Bishop, except that she had been a small woman, not perhaps as thin as Emma—an Emma whose veins hid from the nurse's needle. So it was no specific palm which smeared the thought of the snail into indistinctness on the table top, and it was a vague damp, too, which wet Miss Bishop's skin.

Emma was afraid of Elizabeth Bishop because Emma had desperately desired to be a poet, but had been unable to make a list, did not know how to cut cloth to match a pattern, or lay out night things, clean her comb, where to put the yet-to-be dismantled elms, the geese. She looked out her window, saw a pigeon clinging to a tree limb, oddly, ill, unmoving, she. the cloud

Certain signs, certain facts, certain sorts of ordering, maybe, made her fearful, and such kinds were common in the poetry of Elizabeth Bishop, consequently most of Elizabeth Bishop's poems lay unseen, unsaid, in her volume of Bishop's collected verse. Emma's eye swerved in front of the first rhyme she reached, then hopped ahead, all nerves, fell from the page, fled. the bird

So she really couldn't claim to have understood Elizabeth Bishop, or to have read Elizabeth Bishop's poems, or fathomed her friend Marianne Moore either, who believed she was better than Bishop, Emma was sure, for that was the way the world went, friend overshading friend as though one woman's skin had been drawn across the other's winter trees. a cloud

Yes, it was because the lines did seem like her own bones, not lines of transit or lines of breathing, which was the way lines were in fine poems normally, lines which led the nurse to try to thump them, pink them to draw blood—no, the violet veins were only bone; so when death announces itself to birds they, as if, freeze on the branches where the wind whiffles their finer feathers, though they stay stiller there, stiffer than they will decay.

When, idly skimming (or so she would make her skimming seem), Emma's eye would light upon a phrase like "deep from raw throats," her skin would grow paler as if on a gray walk a light snow had sifted, whereupon the couplet would close on her stifled cry, stifled by a small fist she placed inside her incongruously wide, wide-open mouth. ". . . a senseless order floats . . ." Emma felt she was following each line's leafless example by clearing her skin of cloud so anyone might see the bird there on her bone like a bump, a swollen bruise. She was fearful for she felt the hawk's eye on her. She was fearful of the weasel 'tween her knees. fearful

Emma owned an Iowa house, empty and large and cool in the fall. Otherwise inhospitable. It had thin windows with wide views, a kitchen with counters of scrubbed wood, a woodshed built of now wan boards, a weakly sagging veranda, weedy yard. At the kitchen table, crossed with cracks and scarred by knives, Emma Bishop sat in the betraying light of a bare bulb and saw both poets, nearly breastless, touching the tips of their outstretched fingers together, whereas really the pigeon, like a feathered stone, died in her eye.

Emma was living off her body the way some folks were once said to live off the land, and there was little of her left. Elizabeth Bishop's rivers ran across Emma's country, lay like laminate, created her geography: cape, bay, lake, strait . . . snow in no hills

She would grow thin enough, she thought, to slip into a sentence of the poet's like a spring frock. She wondered whether, when large portions of your pleasure touch, you felt anything really regional, or was it all a rush of warmth to the head or somewhere else? When Marianne Moore's blue pencil canceled a word of Elizabeth Bishop's—a word of hers, hers only because of where it was—was that a motherly rebuke or a motherly gesture of love? Thou shalt not use spit in a poem, my dear, or puke in a sink.

There'd been a tin one once, long ago replaced by a basin of shallow enamel. It looked as if you could lift it out like a tray. It was blackly pitted but not by the bodies of flies. A tear ran down one side, grainy with tap drip, dried and redried.

How had she arrived here, on a drift? to sit still as pigeon on a kitchen stool and stare the window while no thoughts came or went but one of Moore or two of Bishop and the hard buds of their breasts and what it must have meant to have been tongued by a genius.

She would grow thin enough to say "I am no longer fastened to this world; I do not partake of it; its furniture ignores me; I eat per day a bit of plain song and spoon of common word; I do not, consequently, shit, or relieve my lungs much, and I weigh on others little more than shade on lawn, and on memory even less." She was, in fact, some several months past faint.

Consequently, on occasion, she would swoon as softly as a toppled roll of Christmas tissue, dressed in her green chemise, to wake later, after sunset, lighter than the dark, a tad chilly, unmarked, bones beyond brittle, not knowing where

or how she had arrived at her decision to lie down in a line of verse and be buried there; that is to say, be born again as a simple set of words, "the bubble in the spirit-level." So, said she to her remaining self, which words were they to be? grave behaving words, map signs

That became Miss Bishop's project: to find another body for her bones, bones she could at first scarcely see, but which now were ridgy, forming Ws, Ys, and Zs, their presence more than circumstantial, their presence more than letters lying overleaf.

She would be buried in a book. Mourners would peer past its open cover. A made-up lady wipes her dark tears on a tissue. Feel the pressure of her foot at the edge of the page? see her inhale her sorrow slowly as though smelling mint? she never looked better, someone will say. heaven sent

Denial was her duty, and she did it, her duty; she denied herself; she refused numbering, refused funds, refused greeting, refused hugs, rejected cards of printed feeling; fasted till the drapes diaphenated and furniture could no longer sit a spell; said, "I shall not draw my next breath." Glass held more heaviness than she had. Not the energy of steam, nor the wet of mist, but indeed like that cloud we float against our specs when we breathe to clean them. Yet she was all care, all

Because now, because she was free of phlegm, air, spit, tears, wax, sweat, snot, blood, chewed food, the least drool of excrement—the tip of the sugar spoon had been her last bite—her whole self saw, the skin saw, the thin gray yellow hair saw, even the deep teeth were tuned, her pores received, out came in, the light left bruises where it landed, the edge of the stool as she sat cut limb from thigh the way a wire passes the flesh of cheese, and pain passed through her too like a cry through a rented room. Because she had denied herself everything—life itself—life knew she was a friend, came near, brought all

Ask nothing. you shall receive

She was looking at the circular pull on the window's shade, her skin was drawn, her fingers felt for it, her nose knew, and it was that round hole the world used to trickle into her. With Emma down to her E, there was plenty of room, and then she, she would, she would slip into a sentence, her snoot full of substance, not just smell, not just of coffee she hadn't cupped in a coon's age, or fresh bread from back when, or a bit of peony from beside a broken walk, but how fingers felt when they pushed a needle through a hoop of cloth, or the roughness of unspread toast, between her toes a memory of being a kid, the summer's sunshine, hearty as a hug, flecks of red paper blown from a fire cracker to petal a bush, the voices of boys, water running from a hose, laughter, taunts, fear they would show her something she didn't want to know

red rows the clapboard shells her reading eye slid swallowing solemnly as if she'd just been told of someone's love, not for her, no, for the sea nearby in Bishop's poems, a slow wash of words on a beach hissing like fat in the flame, brief flare up before final smoke

Aunts trying hats, paper plates in their laps—no—dog next door barking in his sleep, how about that? the flute, the knife, the shrivelled shoes I spell against my will with two ells, how about that? her ear on the pull, the thread wrapped ring, swell of sea along sunsetted shore, Maine chance, I'm now the longing that will fill that line when I lie down inside it, me, my eye, my nips, finger tips, yes, ribs and lips aligned with Moore's, whose hats, maybe, were meant in the poem, the poem, the poem about the anandrous aunts, exemplary and slim, avernal eyed, shaded by brim, caring for their cares, protecting their skin. a cloud

Now I am the ex of ist I am the am I always should have been. now I am this hiss this thin this brisk I'm rich in vital signs, in lists I in my time could not make, the life I missed because I was afraid, the hawk's eye, owl's too, weasel's greed, the banter of boys, bang, bleeding paper blown into a bush, now I urinate like them against the world's spray-canned designs and feel relief know pride puff up for their circle jerk fellowship and spit on spiders step on ants pull apart peel back brag grope, since it is easy for me now, like sailing boats, making pies, my hair hearing through the ring the rumble of coastal water, rock torn, far from any Iowa window, now I am an ab, a dis, pre's fix, hop's line.

Out there by the bare yard the woodshed stood in a saucer of sun where she once went to practice screaming her cries and the light like two cyclists passing on a narrow road, the light coming in through cracks between the shed's warped boards, the ax she wouldn't handle, its blade buried in a white oak stump the shed had been built around so the stump would still be of service though its tree had had to come down, dad said, it would have a life like an anvil or a butcher's block because as long as you had a use you were alive, birds flew at the first blow, consequently not to cry that the tree'd been cut, groaning when it fell its long fall, limbs of leaves brushing limbs of leaves as though driven by a wind, with plenty of twig crackle, too, like a sparky fire, the heavy trunk crashing through its own bones to groan against the ground, scattering nests of birds and squirrels, but now she was screamed out, thinned of that, or the thought of the noble the slow the patiently wrought, how the oak converted dirt into aspiration, the beautiful brought down, branches lofty now low and broken, the nests of birds and squirrels thrown as you'd throw a small cap, its dispelled shade like soil still, at toppled tiptop a worm's web resembling a scrap of cloud, it should have been allowed to die in the sky its standing death, she'd read whatever there is of love let it be obeyed, well, a fist of twigs and leaves and birdspit rolled away, the leaves of the tree shaking a bit yet, and the web

whisperating

what was left

The house, like herself, was nowhere now. It was the reason why she fled facts when she came upon them, words like "Worcester, Massachusetts," dates like "February, 1918." Em had decided not to seek her fate but to await it. Still, suppose a line like that came to claim her. It was a risk.

I have lost this, lost that, am I not an expert at it? I lost more than love. I lost even its glimpse. Treefall. Branchcrash. That's all. Gave. Gave. Gave away. Watched while they took the world asunder. Now even my all is smal. So I am ready. Not I hope the prodigal or the brown enormous odor . . . rather a calm cloud, up the beach a slowing run of water

Circe

LAURA GERRITY

Men turn into animals; then they are mine.

My mother warned me: New York, for gods sakes, a seething little island like that? What can you expect? Still, it would have happened even at home, and where would I have been then? Argos, Pennsylvania. A town about as fun as an exhumed graveyard—dead, dead, dead. The tombstones of shops that were once fur boutiques and antique dealers, then turned into beauty salons and five-and-dimes. Now the only survivors are Sam's grocery, the drugstore, and the bowling alley, where the shoes have been worn so many times they feel like old leather slippers. If someone has hemorrhoids all of Argos knows because Rose, the cashier at the drugstore, can't keep her flapping mouth shut. Any prescription filled for VD, even the garden variety, means no nookie for the medicated. Rosie takes it upon herself to warn everyone to stop before the clothes hit the floor. That's what would have happened to me in Argos. I'm getting a reputation even here.

Still, it's a living.

I find a man somewhere, bring him home, give him wine, a meal, a warm bed. We roam the island together, sitting in the hot places. We talk about beauty, art, politics. It doesn't matter what he says; I'm watching his lips move, the soft skin brushing and cleaving. When a man opens his mouth, the lips part like skin peeling away from fruit, the teeth, tongue, and soft gums inside. After all this time that's what still gets me, that's when I believe in a man, when I watch his lips. I watch it all. The way his eyes shift, the way his spine curls and straightens his body across from mine. It would be easier to get to know him if he didn't talk. I'd learn him faster, just watching, without words clouding the subject. Of course I am interested in their bodies. But I don't get involved. It's business.

A man expects questions on these dates, conventions. So I ask if he likes his mother; the Oedipal thing can work to my advantage. One boy, Max, he's a real tiger now, put his head in my lap and I told him his world would disappear in a moment, that he'd be like a baby, my baby, my pet. I wasn't lying. But I do the usual preliminary screening with everyone. It's as if I'm asking them their favorite colors; their answers just different shades of the same hue. No one says plaid or houndstooth. Their responses tick along like seconds on a noisy watch; I'm not really listening while I look for the beast inside. I wait for the wildness.

The first man who turned on me was a rat. We met at one of those readings at the uptown Y, and he came to my place for coffee afterward. We were talking about Proust and the power that redredging the past unleashes. I'm this kid from Argos, been in New York all of one week, and I'm sitting there crosslegged in my Jordaches and Docksiders looking at this guy in a three piece tweed number with those little round glasses and Cole-Hahn loafers, thinking this has got to be God in a scratchy suit. After a while Proust gets peripheral and we lock gazes as if we are circling each other. Here I am, the magna cum A+ queen of Argos State without a clue in the world of what people can become. Pretty soon I'm touching his neck with the back of my hand and his head is between my breasts. He's breathing as if he is the lungs of the world and it's a small flimsy bed that breaks in the middle and we fall on the floor tangled in blankets and he seems a little irked to be flat on his ass in a dingy apartment and at that moment I feel like I will do anything to make him stay. So I look in his eyes and start to whisper and whisper and his jaw, which is all tensed up, goes slack and he stares at me with a little smile so I just keep whispering and moving my hair and my hands over his skin and I feel him relax under my fingers. I kept whispering long after he had fallen asleep.

In the morning I woke to a chirping noise, but then I realized it wasn't a chirp but a small shrill shriek. There was a light brown rat as long as my forearm in the blankets. He burrowed straight for me.

I grabbed him by the tail and threw him out the window. His head hit one of the bars and then he landed with a thick thud on the fire escape. I looked out after a minute, but he was gone.

I told myself the next guy I dated would be different. He was a Lithuanian actor who had gone to Harvard. I thought, oh, lovely to look at, intelligent, tells funny stories. They were long stories with beginnings, middles, ends, and moral lessons. I listened and listened.

Then one day he turned like milk. I was listening to his story about a car chase he was in in Venice, and midsentence it came to me that there are no cars in Venice and I looked at Markus and pictured him in this nonexistent Ferrari in this city of bullshit with boats as slow as slugs. I realized in that moment that he didn't stay underwater for ten minutes with a shark, that the other boy had not had a knife, that he had never set foot in Zimbabwe, that all of his stories were lies. Then I began to see the ass in him, that it had been there all along, and that it was only a waiting game, his flirtation with being a man.

He lasted a little while longer and then he turned into an ass. I came home from work and he was standing in the kitchen, braying, braying at me. I knew it was him because of the eyes, slightly crossed, the sad confused eyes that I see in all of them. He kept shaking his head and baring his huge blunt teeth—he didn't want to be an ass. But there he was. I led him down into the street, but he stayed in front of my building, whinnying at my window, until the police came to take him away.

I began to think it was my fault.

I told my friend Dusa about it. She doesn't have a normal love life either; guys just freeze up around her. We were having lunch, and she didn't seem surprised until I told her about the police. She looked up then, her head cocked, her hair wild about her head, her mouth in a small smile.

"The police?" she asked.

"Maybe it was the SPCA. I don't know. It was a big van. Looked official."

"But you just let them take him?"

"How could I take care of a donkey? I don't even have a backyard. . . ." Dusa reached over and covered my hand with her own.

"I wasn't suggesting you keep him." She paused. "I don't know how to say this, Cici, but I'm not an art dealer for nothing. I smell a million dollars here."

Dusa put me in touch with Herm Finkelstein at the Odyssey Circus. About acquisitions. I drove to Queens to talk to this guy, their head trainer who was also doing the late night thing with Dusa. I made an illegal left hand turn just to get down the little street to their warehouse. Everywhere the warehouses yawned like bored cats, gray and unimpressed. I parked halfway on the curb and walked to the entrance.

It was a huge bare place, its ceiling crisscrossed by iron beams, with walls that looked as if they had been laced together by the lines and ropes stretching from one side to the other. Lining the walls were animal cages: a few parrots, a lion, an elephant, and what looked like either a stray dog or a wolf. The floor was marked with chalk: one large ring and two smaller rings drawn on the gray cement. In the main ring, a small man in black was kneeling on the back of a camel. He had a wooden rod, and when he prodded the camel in the shoulder she knelt, when he poked her in the haunches she rose. The camel had just folded her knobby legs under her, lurching like a car out of gas, when he saw me.

"You Dusa's friend?"

"This is a circus?" He slid down one side of the camel and slapped her on the rump so she stumbled up again. He walked her over to me, holding the reins in one hand.

"First things first: I don't wanna know. You come up with what we can call paperwork—you got the zebra from your aunt, you got a cousin in Kenya—good enough. There's no truth as I see it, so I don't wanna know. You call me, I send the truck."

"What kind of circus is this? No spangles, no tent, no feather headdresses?" The camel curled her lip and shifted her back half from one hip to the other.

"You want the run of the mill variety, you sell to Dumb Dumb Brothers. They pay five figures, we pay four. But I'll tell you—they'll want papers. Legal papers." He pronounced each syllable. "Plus, I'll teach you to train."

"The animals?"

"Einstein. Whatever you get, I'll teach you to train."

"What's the number for the truck?" He pulled out a card. "Day or night?" I asked.

"Twenty-four hours. And Cindy."

"Circe."

"Whatever. Think Exotic."

About two weeks later, I was dating a sculptor from Louisiana. He turned at night. Imagine waking up in bed with a stallion. The bedroom was a shambles by the time the truck got there.

A wad of cash can make anything feel like a job. I began to think exotic. I learned to tell what kind of animal a man will be by the way he looks, the way he moves. Skin is a thin disguise. The lions with their barrel chests and thick glinting hair. The pumas with their sleek small heads and muscled taut bodies. When I knew what we needed at the circus I would look for the type—in clubs, in bars, I would hunt him down. When I guessed wrong there were always plenty of cages, but I didn't make many mistakes.

The first time I touch them I am sure.

Once, I was unbuttoning an investment banker's shirt. I undid the last button and pulled the tails out of his pants. Then I moved my hands, flat and splayed, along his chest. It was covered with dense brown hair, and I looked into his large eyes and reached down to his waist. He made a small rumbling noise in the back of his throat and I knew, *Bear*. I kept on top of the situation and hoped he wouldn't change in the middle. I didn't worry too much. Eventually I tamed them all, even the wildest ones eat from my hands. Herm (Hermes, he said, was his ring name) taught me to train, and he said I was a natural. The animals watched me, mesmerized, and once I had taught them a command they would perform as if hypnotized. Together, Herm and I taught them a complicated procession for that month's show. The rest of the performers were dancers that had gotten too chubby and beauties that had gotten too old. We had a couple of ex-Rockettes and a former Miss Teen Mississippi in the troupe. They liked me because I wore black sweatpants instead of a black unitard and so on opening night they could be sure that their husbands weren't checking out my legs.

I began to perform with the animals because I was the only one who could get the lions to do the quick mincing step on "Hurry up, please, it's time." When we performed I lost all sense of audience and attitude and coaxed, cajoled, and cooed my animals to their hops and hoops. I knew each one intimately, and they obeyed me like new lovers. Sometimes the girls would pause during the dance just to watch us. One of the dancers' brothers wrote reviews for the *Village Voice*, and she got him to slip us into the Style section. Pretty soon we were setting up double bleachers to pack the people in. Herm took to selling tickets and gave me the wilder animals to train. On my days off, I'd look for new ones.

One day I called Herm to come and pick up a land tortoise. When he came he brought a dolly with him and slid it under the mound of contracted tortoise.

"Reptiles reek," he shook his head. "I wouldn't have this sonofabitch in my apartment for five minutes." I held out my hand, and he reached into his pocket and peeled off a few hundreds from the steadily growing roll that never went to the bank. "You gotta meet the Greek. Alligator wrestler. Scar the size o' Jersey on his thigh—from the war, not the lizards. Little hard of hearing too. He shows up every once in a while, we put him up, though he doesn't deserve it. He'll get a kick out of you, but don't let him near that animal connection of yours." I wasn't paying much attention; I was already thinking about the next one, the insurance agent with llama potential. If I watched closely enough, it was like a science.

There was a rhino, a crocodile, a zebra, a gazelle, and a wildebeest in one month.

I noticed that it happened after long conversations, and I began to think it was because I knew something I shouldn't have. I had spent most of my life cramming myself full of useless knowledge. When I am with most men it is as if I am on a see-saw and everything in my head is like a weight that loads my side down. I sit on the ground, squinting up at him. He is flailing and powerless against the sun. This is what I see in their eyes when they turn.

I looked for the animals, but I always searched for the one who would keep the balance, who would have the gravity to play with me. I didn't believe it would happen. Herm and Dusa had broken off even their late night meetings, she claimed he couldn't look her in the eye. I looked at Herm and saw an Owl. I began thinking that being a man meant having the animal inside, that it only took a certain loss of control to release it. That didn't make them all the same. There are a million kinds of animals.

The more I whispered to them, the faster it happened. One, a chicken from the beginning, listened to me as if I were a priest. I could see him fade, halfway between sleep and love, into a trance. He sat, nestled on my couch, dazed and dull in the middle of cocktails. I talked to him until the change overtook him.

Soon, I began to get creative. It's not as if most men are purebreds. They would have the lips of a camel, the smile of a dolphin, the wings of a barn swallow, and the teeth of a hyena. In some, the different animals jostled within them, fighting for space. These were the difficult types; some would rather die than be tamed. Some tried to kill me.

With an iguana panther I waited until he was about to leave, heading for the door. I came up behind him, pressed my body against his back, my fingers trailing up his neck, into his hair, my whisper constant warmth in his ear. I turned him like this to my bedroom, my voice tumbling into him. He changed before dawn. I woke to see shining eyes in the corner of my room. He circled the bed slowly, his tongue flicking from his mouth. I was naked, and it occurred to me as I inched back against the headboard, *how stupid, not to have a gun.* The beast was twice my size and riled with anger. He looked at me and hissed, his triangular jaw opening like a trap—rows and rows of teeth.

I lived because the iguana panther did not know, could not comprehend how he had changed. I began to sing to him, as I would have sung to a child. My voice was shaking at first, but as he slowed and shook his head my song grew stronger. Soon he dropped, limp and heavy as a rolled rug, still watching me with his thin-lidded eyes. I went and sat beside him, stroking his smooth black coat. And for a moment, when I looked at him with his head in my lap, I wished he were a man.

Perhaps what I do is a gift, perhaps it is a curse, perhaps it has nothing to do with any god at all.

I had nightmares sometimes that I was being eaten by the animals I had created. I could die a thousand times—ripped limb from limb by a hyena, swallowed whole by the unhinged jaws of a boa constrictor. In each of these I lived to feel myself devoured.

In the Odyssey, they said I worked some kind of magic. I'll admit it was eerie the way the animals followed me around when they could, howled to get attention when I passed by their cages. And I could get a cheetah, or a boa constrictor, or a hippo with no trouble. Herm told me once in a matter of fact way that he assumed the animals had something to do with drugs. Illicit connections in other hemispheres. He didn't want to know, he added, searching my face for a confirmation. If I ever wanted out, though, I would still have work with him.

I didn't want to give it up. I was good at it. I'd decided against doing hybrids for now, so it was safe enough. And the animals came cheap: apartment damages, and a small finder's fee. As long as I came up with the creative paperwork no one at the circus asked any questions.

One day I came to the warehouse and Herm was on the floor, coloring flyers with a green magic marker. *Ulysses the Alligator Wrestler* captioned an outline of a man who was either wrestling with an alligator or had the animal tied around his waist.

"Think you could manage a couple alligators next week?" Herm asked. I shook my head. I was working on a couple of arctic wolves for the pooch parade. The men, Politês and Eurylokhos, were a tough pair. Politês was innocent and trusting enough, but Eurylokhos was wily and suspicious. Like most of the pure dog types, they were pack animals. I knew if I could get one away from the other he would be a dog by the next morning, but in bars and clubs they practically held each other's hands. Then it occurred to me to do them together.

They came to dinner and I spoke softly, making them lean forward to hear what I said, bringing us closer, warming them up. Then, before I even served dessert, one was lifting his leg on my sofa and the other was out on the balcony howling at the moon. I was standing in the doorway to the kitchen, holding the ice cream scooper for the Baked Alaska, and realized I had arctic wolves in my house. I stood there for a minute, watching, just watching the one on the balcony. His cry, aimed at the hazy stars, was long, low, and lonely. And suddenly I felt tired, just sad and lost and tired and I imagined my life going on forever like this, an endless procession of confused animals. I leaned against the doorway and closed my eyes, wishing that once it would be me and not them who would turn into the wild wondering thing.

Then one of the wolves turned and snarled at the other. I slid the kitchen door shut and called the truck.

The next morning I was sitting in the bleachers in the warehouse, inventing origins and donors while Politês and Eurylokhos paced in their cages, hungry and savvy now that they were limited by bars. They growled occasionally, but when I whistled to them they would whine and roll over, their long tails brushing the floor. Then I heard them both stop pacing. They were completely still, quiet. I looked up, and there he was in the main ring. I stared and kept staring at him because I couldn't see what he would become. For a moment I saw him as a lion, then a bear, a snake, a bird. He began striding up the bleachers toward me, talking about where he had come from and what he was looking for, but I didn't hear a word he said for all the animals I could see in him. There was a whole jungle in his face. I stood as he came closer to me to see if I could smell it—just a trace of what paced within him.

When I breathed in I only became dizzy.

This one would be a bit of a challenge. A rare animal. Not easily caught. Most of them give themselves away so quickly. In a minute, really. As I swayed from his scent, I reached over and put my hand on his arm thinking I would know from the first contact, the first touch skin to skin, I would feel it in him. But I could not. Instead of feeling the animal I could only feel this skin, this flesh warm against my own. And I stopped and looked in his face that was lined with human wrinkles, punctuated by human bones.

He admired the new additions, and his voice was not accusing but admitting me. He asked where I found them all, and I said I picked them up. Here and there. My hand was still on his arm.

When he moved my mind spun farther. We walked down the bleachers and onto the floor and I watched him. He moved like a wrestler, like a long line of elastic muscle that could stretch or contract itself at will. He could be a mongoose, a leopard, a lynx, an eel. Even his shrugs and crouches did not give him away. Perhaps, I thought, he is an animal I've never met. Or a mongrel of the worst kind. When we were walking next to the cages the animals moved with me, trotting alongside as far as their pens would allow, whinnying, clucking, hissing, and howling. When we left the arctic wolves behind with their pitiable whimpers he asked me what I did to them. I whisper to them, I thought, not so much, but enough to explode them out of their fragile skins, their unformed selves. I said, I bring them here.

He said I was a legend, that no one in the world could procure such animals. I knew that he was flattering me, wooing me, and I listened. I listened to the texture of his voice as he paced out his words, his tones low and intimate. I listened to the way he said *procure* and it seemed he was suggesting that these beasts had merely been solved of their humanity.

He said, your paperwork is shoddy. I laughed because it did not seem so much shoddy as fantastic. I agreed and shrugged and my shoulder brushed against his with a shock. I stepped back and stopped laughing. For a moment I had forgotten the animal inside him.

When I asked him for dinner I almost wanted him to say no, to prove that he was different. And we talked and I was watching, watching his face for changes, for that dull, thick expression that tells me that a man is no longer thinking, that his mind is beginning to stammer with his voice. I brought him home with me, with his fascinating fluid movements, with his weathered face and fresh body, with his voice that echoed through my skull. He would not stand still for a moment, he seemed to circle me when I cooked. A raven, I thought, a coyote. He seemed to be everything and for a moment I thought it would be too dangerous. If I turned him he would attack me, and I might have to kill him.

He did not slow down even when we sat. His gestures, large and various, kept his body in constant motion like some of the rodents I had known. But they were deliberate expressions that flowed into each other, one after the other. He was not parts but a mystifying whole. I whispered over the candle and our faces drew closer and closer until I could feel the heat of the candle flame rising under my chin. He watched my lips and did not succumb but responded. I could not eat. By the end of dinner, I was wild to know what he was.

Perhaps, I thought, the difference lies in knowing that he will leave, that he has only come to rest here for a while. He does not look at me as a destination, his eyes see through me to another horizon. Perhaps I will not be able to turn him.

I poured him some liquor that I saved for when I didn't want a fight. It could flatten the strongest of them, my liquor down their throats, my voice in their ears. Suddenly, I felt him behind me, his lips moving in my hair, his hands on my sides. My fingers loosened on the glass and it dropped to the carpet with a soft thud. I could hear a roar within me as my hands tingled and flexed. I turned my head and the four walls of my apartment seemed too close, moving in, containing me. And it struck me that there are female animals too. What was he trying to make of me? I heard his words soft next to my ear and I thought, who is this man and where has he come from and who but the gods could send this to me?

I turned my body to face him all at once and I put my forefinger to his whispering lips. He was silent, surprised, and then he smiled. His smile shocked me; he laughed at my desperate wildness. I began to murmur to myself to beat down what was within me. He watched me regain myself, waiting. I would beat him, I thought, shaking with frustration. I would turn him no matter what he was. But when I turned my voice to him he pressed his finger to my lips. And in that moment of stillness I realized how different this was to be. The fighting had ceased.

We stripped each other and were human and animal, everything.

He stays now. He sleeps in my bed, washes himself in my shower, smells of my soap and skin. After that night I knew I would not change him. We keep this balance, the urges trapped within us. And we train together and drink together and wake and cook and eat together. Once he asked me how many men there had been before him. I just looked at him and he shook his head as if he were waking up. It is only in moments that we forget that the rules have changed. At first I would see a monkey when he bent over, a seal when he raised his head from the pillow, a bull when he swayed in anger. Then the animals disappeared from my vision. He became, in his movement, man.

Even now he sleeps beside me, this man. And I know, because I have seen his eyes meet mine in a flash of anger, his hands stroke my sides with deliberate care, that it is only his strength that keeps him from turning. I have learned to tame myself, to keep the roaring reasoned within me. But it is so delicate, this truce which keeps us from what paces between the bars of our bones; sometimes I feel as if one word could explode us. Now he awakes, his eyes taking me in with the world. I put one hand on his arm, skin against skin. I do not use my voice; I am weary of spells. My hand grips him, my body asks, how will we keep this peace?

We Go to a Fire

JAMES TATE

Great blasts of hot air are pouring through broken windows
out into the night, a whistling contest for devils.
A powerful smoke ejector rolls up. Its huge, thick hose
looks like a giant caterpillar as it reaches into the warehouse
to suck out the smoke which is blinding the firemen.
Wearily, the firemen drive back to the station house and sleep.
"I suppose they dream of knot tying and gas masks
and tumbler locks, but what do I know?" I said, feeling
a chill come on. We walked on down the street to the café
and sat there contemplating. When, at the next table,
a young girl strikes a match, we dive for cover.
She's reading *The Sorrows of Young Werther* and ignores us.
Rolf claims he is in love and crawls around under the table
for a better look, and in this way we are preserved
from stultification. We are much impressed with the
    disharmony
of things, and, likewise, the occasional harmony,
such as when a fire chief gives orders to his men.
The serious problems of life, however, are never solved,
and, later, when Rolf asked for her hand in marriage,
she reported us to the authorities, and our flight-plan
was ultra-contemporary in no particular fashion.
"She's dark but her children will be blond," Rolf whispered.
And as I looked back at her, she began to darkle,
a rare, almost imperceptible, darkishness began
to tease her little fingers as we entered a murky cave
and bade farewell to the darling of this café society,
daughter of the dawn patrol, moccasin flower of radio-
luminescence, because nobody seems to worship her but
    ourselves.

Abundance and Satisfaction
PATTIANN ROGERS

1
One butterfly is not enough. We need
many thousands of them, if only
for the effusion of the wayward-
swaying words they occasion—blue
and copper hairstreaks, sulphur
and cabbage whites, brimstones,
peacock fritillaries, tortoiseshell
emperors, skippers, meadow browns.
We need a multitude of butterflies
right on the tongue simply to be able
to speak with a varied six-pinned
poise and particularity.

But thousands of butterflies
are surfeit. We need just one
flitter to apprehend correctly
the will of aspen leaves, the lassitude
of lupine petals, the sleep
of a sleeping eyelid. To examine
adequately one set of finely leaded,
stained wings of violet translucence,
one single sucking proboscis (sap-
and-sugar-licking thread), to study
thoroughly just one powder scale, one
gold speck from one dusted butterfly
forewing would require at least
a millennium of attention to all melody,
phrase, gravity, and horizon.

2
And just the same, one moon is more
than sufficient, ample complexity

and bewilderment—single waning crescent,
waxing crescent, lone gibbous, one perfect,
solitary sickle and pearl, one map
of mountains and lava plains, Mare
Nectaris, Crater Tycho. And how could
anyone really hold more than one full
moon in one heart?

Yet one moon is not enough. We need
millions of moons, glossy porcelain
globes glowing as if from the inside out,
weaving among each other in the sky
like lanterns bobbing on a black river
sea-bound. Then we could study
moons and the traversings of moons
and the multiple meanings of the phases
of moons, and the eclipsing of moons
by one another. We need a new language
of moons containing all the syllables
of interacting rocks of light
so that we might fully understand,
at last, the phrase "one heart
in many moons."

3
And of gods, we need just one, one
for the grief of twenty snow geese
frozen by their feet in ice and dead
above winter water. Yet we need twenty-
times-twenty gods for all the recurring
memories of twenty snow geese frozen
by their feet in sharp lake-water ice.

But a single god suffices
for the union of joys in one school
of invisible green-brown minnows
flocking over green-brown stones

in a clear spring, but three gods
are required to wind and unwind
the braided urging of spring—root,
blossom, and spore. And we need
the one brother of gods for a fragged
plain, blizzard-split, battered
by tumbleweeds and wire fences,
and the one sister to mind
the million sparks and explosions
of gods on fire in a pine forest.

I want one god to be both scatter
and pillar, one to explain simultaneously
mercy and derision, yet a legion of gods
for the spools of confusion and design,
but one god alone to hold me by the waist,
to rumble and quake in my ear, to dance me
round and round, one couple with forty
gods in the heavenly background
with forty violins with one
immortal baton keeping time.

Empties

ROCHELLE NAMEROFF

Not the sadness of the slag-heaps
or forests lost to garbage—
jobs lost to garbage
and the people inside them.
Now rains the tin cans

crushed perhaps through joy
to prove an all-over toughness,
and toilet tubes and sodden rubbers
tossed in fear a Father would see you—
though there were no more fathers

unless bar stools were a form of home.
Broken and bruised, the litter
of loneliness I used to think about
and feel sad and feel angry.
Not the sickness stuck inside me now.

I walk to the Turkey Hill Market,
head down to watch for dogshit and human shit
and broken glass left homeless for weeks.
It's the mindless carpet of my city
adrift in cigarettes, beer-spit, and sneers.

The sneer is mine as I push past
the nudie racks and lottery tricks and scan
beyond the hilltop of cigarette cartons
to locate food. I'm the only one here
buying milk, which sits somewhere near

the hasty lettered "beagels and cheez"
behind the stunted growth of produce
labeled "plumbs" and "tomato's,"
and for my special delectation
as if I believed anymore in irony

a proudly printed sign that lets me know
"All food prepared on the premise."
Of what? I want to ask the "huh's?"
who wait on me, but instead
stand breathing in my own stale secondhand

breath to avoid theirs. And snob! I want
a paper bag, and make them ask The Boss.
I should be ashamed of my disgust
but I'm lost in this stinkhouse of tragedy,
no longer charmed by jokes nor sweet

misery. I hurry home to my teevee
and watch the mirrors of decay
and think about nothing. "You can't
step on the same piece of water twice"
writes one of my students to quote

his philosophy class, to impress me.
But I've really stepped into it this time
and want to escape. I want to go home
to the world I believe in
which is outside this world.

So
which landscape is the smaller then—
the one great planet we all say we live on
or the tiny space of wilderness
that once housed my heart?

Permissions

Unless indicated otherwise, copyright is held by the author.

"Continuing" from *A Coast of Trees* by A. R. Ammons. Copyright © 1981 by A. R. Ammons. Reprinted by permission of the author and W. W. Norton & Company, Inc.

"Oleum Misericordiae" from *Self-Portrait in a Convex Mirror* by John Ashbery. Copyright © by John Ashbery. Reprinted by permission of Viking Penguin, a division of Penguin Books USA Inc.

"Saul and Patsy Are Pregnant" from *A Relative Stranger* by Charles Baxter. Copyright © 1990 by Charles Baxter. Reprinted by permission of the author and W. W. Norton & Company, Inc.

"Midwestern Villanelle" from *The Red Hour* by Robin Behn. Copyright © 1993 by Robin Behn. Reprinted by permission of HarperCollins Publishers, Inc.

"The Book of the Dead Man (#6)" from *The Book of the Dead Man* by Marvin Bell. Copyright © 1994 by Copper Canyon Press, PO Box 271, Port Townsend, WA 98368.

"Johnnieruth" from *Lover's Choice* by Becky Birtha. Copyright © 1987 by Becky Birtha. Reprinted by permission of Seal Press.

"Diamond Breakfast" from *View from the Gazebo* by Marianne Boruch. Copyright © 1989 by Wesleyan University Press. Reprinted by permission of the University Press of New England.

"At School" from *Moss Burning* by Marianne Boruch. Copyright © 1993. Reprinted by permission of Field Editions: Oberlin College Press.

"View Finder" from *What We Talk About When We Talk About Love* by Raymond Carver. Copyright © 1981 by Raymond Carver. Reprinted by permission of Alfred A. Knopf, Inc.

"Long, Disconsolate Lines" from *Green Notebook, Winter Road* by Jane Cooper. Copyright © 1994 by Jane Cooper. Reprinted by permission of the author and Tilbury House, Publishers.

"Confiteor" from *The Collected Poems of Coulette* by Henri Coulette. Reprinted by permission of The University of Arkansas Press.

"Each Bird Walking" from *Amplitude* by Tess Gallagher. Copyright © 1987 by Tess Gallagher. Reprinted by permission of Graywolf Press, Saint Paul, Minnesota.

"Gemini" from *The House on Marshland* by Louise Glück. Copyright © 1971, 1972, 1973, 1974, 1975 by Louise Glück. First published by The Ecco Press in 1975. Reprinted by permission.

"Another Elegy" from *The Museum of Clear Ideas* by Donald Hall. Copyright © 1993 by Donald Hall. Reprinted by permission of Houghton Mifflin Co. All rights reserved.

"Weed" from *Praise* by Robert Hass. Copyright © 1974, 1975, 1976, 1977, 1978, 1979 by Robert Hass. First published by The Ecco Press in 1979. Reprinted by permission.

"Reading Aquinas" from *The Man at Home* by Michael Heffernan. Copyright © 1988. Reprinted by permission of the University of Arkansas Press.

"From Commerce to the Capitol: Montgomery, Alabama" from *The Never-Ending* by Andrew Hudgins. Copyright © 1991 by Andrew Hudgins. Reprinted by permission of Houghton Mifflin Co. All rights reserved.

"At the Store" from *American Triptych* by Jane Kenyon. Copyright © 1978 by Jane Kenyon. Reprinted by permission of Alice James Books.

"Philosophy in Warm Weather" from *The Boat of Quiet Hours* by Jane Kenyon. Copyright © 1986 by Jane Kenyon. Reprinted by permission of Graywolf Press, Saint Paul, Minnesota.

"Under the Maud-Moon" from *The Book of Nightmares* by Galway Kinnell. Copyright © 1971 by Galway Kinnell. Reprinted by permission of Houghton Mifflin Co. All rights reserved.

"Zaydee" from *New and Selected Poems* by Philip Levine. Copyright © 1991 by Philip Levine. Reprinted by permission of Alfred A. Knopf.

"Power" from *The Black Unicorn: Poems by Audre Lorde*. Copyright © 1978 by Audre Lorde. Reprinted by permission of W. W. Norton & Company, Inc.

"Across These Landscapes of Early Darkness" from *History as a Second Language*, by Dionisio D. Martínez. Copyright © 1993 by Ohio State University Press. Reprinted by permission of the author and Ohio State University Press.

"Numberless" from *Hinge and Sign* by Heather McHugh. Copyright © 1994 by Wesleyan University Press. Reprinted by permission of the University Press of New England.

"Centerfold Reflected in a Jet Window" from *The Year of Our Birth* by Sandra McPherson. Copyright © 1973, 1974, 1975, 1976, 1977, 1978 by Sandra McPherson. First published by The Ecco Press in 1978. Reprinted by permission.

"The Houses" from *Opening the Hand* by W. S. Merwin. Copyright © 1993 by W. S. Merwin. Reprinted by permission of Georges Borchardt, Inc., for the author. All rights reserved.

"The Meal" by Sharon Olds. Copyright © 1981 by Sharon Olds. Reprinted by permission of the author and Alfred A. Knopf, Inc.

"For Ethel Rosenberg" from *A Wild Patience Has Taken Me This Far: Poems 1978–1981* by Adrienne Rich. Copyright © 1981 by Adrienne Rich. Reprinted by permission of the author and W. W. Norton & Company, Inc.

"The Power of Toads" and "Abundance and Satisfaction" from *Firekeeper: New and Selected Poems* by Pattiann Rogers. Copyright © 1994 by Pattiann Rogers. Reprinted by permission of Milkweed Editions.

"Remembering Brother Bob" by William Stafford. Reprinted by permission of the Estate of William Stafford.

"Translations from Colonial Swahili" from *Gravida* by Sue Standing. Copyright © 1995 by Sue Standing. Reprinted by permission of the author and Four Way Books.

"R for Rosemary" from *Bread Without Sugar* by Gerald Stern. Copyright © 1992 by Gerald Stern. Reprinted by permission of the author and W. W. Norton & Company, Inc.

"Farm Wife" from *Claiming Kin* by Ellen Bryant Voigt. Copyright © 1976 by Wesleyan University Press. Reprinted by permission of the University of New England.

The *Iowa Review*, 1970–1995

EDITORS

Merle E. Brown, 1970–1974
Thomas R. Whitaker, 1974–1977
Fredrick Woodard, 1978–1982
David Hamilton, 1978–1995

GUEST EDITORS FOR SINGLE ISSUES OR SECTIONS

Michael S. Harper, Darwin T. Turner, Al Young, 1975
Paul Engle, Hualing Engle, 1976
Henry Carlile, 1979
Marvin Bell, 1980
Jane Cooper, Gwen Head, Adalaide Morris, and Marcia Southwick, 1981
Donald Justice, 1981
James Alan McPherson, 1984
Marilyn Chin, Walter Knupfer, 1984
Stanley Plumly, 1985
Adalaide Morris, 1986
Lee Montgomery, 1994

CONTRIBUTING EDITOR

T. Coraghessan Boyle, 1977

ASSOCIATE EDITORS

Michael Ryan, 1972–1974
K. K. Merker, 1978–1979
Ed Folsom, 1979–1983

Adalaide Morris, 1979–1983
Mary Hussmann, 1992–1995

MANAGING EDITORS

Thomas Lux, 1971–1972
Jon Jackson, 1972–1973
Page Edwards, Jr., 1974
K. K. Merker, 1974–1977
Norman Sage, 1978–1982
John Van Gundy, 1982–1984
Sara London, 1984–1986
Lisa Schaefer Torrey, 1987–1988
Mary Hussmann, 1989–1991

BUSINESS MANAGERS

Norman Sage, 1970–1977
Mary Hussmann, 1982–1988

DESIGNERS

Irwin McFadden, 1970–1977
Kay Amert, 1977–1995

FICTION EDITORS

Wilfrido D. Nolledo, 1970–1971
David Hayman, 1971–1974
Robert Coover, 1975–1977
T. Coraghessan Boyle, 1978
Frederick Busch, 1979

POETRY EDITORS

Marvin Bell, 1970–1971
Norman Dubie, 1972–1973
Barry Goldensohn, 1972
Anselm Hollo, 1972

Donald Justice, 1972–1973
Helen Chasin, 1973
Michael Ryan, 1973–1974
Michael Burkart, 1974
Charles Wright, 1974
Sandra McPherson, 1975
Stanley Plumly, 1976, 1978
William Matthews, 1977

ASSISTANT EDITORS

James Perlman, 1978–1981
Beverly Butler, 1979–1980
Peggy Gifford, 1980–1982
Laura Julier, 1981–1982
Rochelle Nameroff, 1989–1992
Carolyn Jacobson, 1991–1992
Jules von Lieshout, 1992
Michael Fisch, 1993
Rebecca Childers, 1993–1995

ASSISTANT FICTION EDITORS

T. Coraghessan Boyle, 1974–1976
James Heckmann, 1977–1979
Irene Wanner, 1977–1978
Michael Cunningham, 1978–1979
Lee White, 1978–1979
Cathy Coats, 1979–1980
Douglas Glover, 1980–1981
Ethan Canin, 1982–1984
Jim Riley, 1983–1984
Toni Joseph, 1984
Dean Albarelli, 1985–1986
Mary Stefaniak, 1985–1987
Ann Reckling, 1987
David Madole, 1989

Nicole Cooley, 1990
Eileen Bartos, 1991–1992
Benjamin Anastas, 1992–1993
Lee Montgomery, 1994
Creston Lea, 1995

ASSISTANT POETRY EDITORS

David St. John, 1974
Ernesto Trejo, 1975
James Galvin, 1975–1976
Michael Sofranko, 1977–1978
Laurie Sheck, 1977–1978
Ilene Moskin, 1978–1979
Bruce Anderson, 1979–1980
Emily Chalmers, 1979–1980
David Groff, 1980–1982
Debra Hines, 1982–1983
Ginny Threefoot, 1983–1984
Robert Grunst, 1984–1986
Peter Junker, 1986–1987
Suzanne Webber, 1987–1988
James Boyd White, 1989–1990
Chris Foster, 1991–1992
Phil Kobylarz, 1992–1993
Eachan Holloway, 1993–1994
Laura Wilder, 1994–1995

EDITORIAL ASSISTANTS

1970s: Dwight Allen, Susan Aukema, Burt Blume, Edward Brunner, Michael Burkart, Jane Cogie, Susan Engberg, Catherine Gammon, Nicholas Gerogiannis, Gail Hanlon, Steve Holmes, Neil Ruddy, Mary Sterns-Sgarioto, Douglas Unger, David W. Young

1980s: Mary Adams, Mary Anders, Jon Anderson, Jocelyn Bartkevicius, Lizabeth Carpenter, Darrah Cloud, David Cole,

Christina Davis, Frank DePirro, Kim Edwards, Edwin Gentzler, Jessie Grearson, Chuck Hauck, Juan Felipe Herrera, Bruce Holpert, Carolyn Jacobson, Clair F. James, Anne Knupfer, Dennis Johnson, B. Colleen Junker, Fritz McDonald, Steve Parrott, Rosemary Regan-Gavin, L. Dale Rigby, Margarita Robles, Anne Schreiber, Brent Spencer, Paul Takemoto, Thomas Tyrer, Conlin Wagner, Sandy Wennenberg

1990s: Marilyn Abildskov, Paul Albanese, Scott Anderson, Aaron Anstett, Julene Bair, Kristen Bakis, Adam Barnard, Karen E. Bender, Nell Beram, Kristin S. Berg, James Bernard, Bennett Bridgers, Charlie Buck, Clay Carlson, Miriam Chancy, Lan Samantha Chang, Lisa Chen, Kimberley Chun, Adolfo Cisneros, Kristen Cleveland, Michael Connell, Peter Craig, Michael Daugherty, Jon Diller, Anelia Dimitrova, Karen Downing, LuAnn Dvorak, Hope Edelman, Evan Elliot, Jennifer S. Epstein, Jan Feeney, Brian Feltovich, Debbie Flapan, Phillip Fieseler, Kristen E. Gandrow, Karen Greenwood, Tom Grimes, Hernán Guaracao-Calderón, Chris Hallman, Laura Harger, Alyssa Haywoode, Corinne Heipcke, Kristen Hoyte, Meredith Jacobson, Heidi Johannesen, Rebecca L. Johnson, Michael Judge, Julie Kane, Stephanie Kelley, Janet Kenning, Mary Kraus, Steve Langan, Caroline Ledeboer, Darleen Lev, David Low, Fritz McDonald, Charles McIntyre, Tucker Malarkey, William Martin, Stephen Mayberry, Lisa Melsted, Lynn Mennenga, Amy Mueller, Kate Northrop, Robert Ohr, Andrew Osborn, Denise Osmundson, Lisa L. Owens, Diane Perry, Keith Peterson, Nancy Pickering, Tanya Pryputniewicz, Mark Rahe, Fred Redekop, Baron Reed, Kelly Ritter, Margarita Robles, Matthew Rohrer, Kate Roosevelt, Amy Scattergood, Annette Segreto, John Smick, Merrie Snell, Rebecca Soglin, Jacob Soll, Greg Spatz, Kirilka Stavreva, Craig Stein, Amy Stewart, Ned Stuckey-French, Mary Sylwester, Michael Taeckens, Michael Theune, Ruth Tobias, James Tweedie, David Van Fossen, Jennifer Veech, Kris Vervaecke, Anne E. Voss, David P. Wall, Julie Webber, Brenda Wiebler, N. S. Wilson, Rebecca Wolff, Brian Young

READERS FOR THIS ANTHOLOGY

Joshua Barkin, Andrew Berg, Teri Bostian, Kristin Brandser, Jill Britton, Alexander Chee, Laura Dubek, Angela Fasick, Karen Greenwood, Chris Harris, Eachan Holloway, Joshua Kotzin, Steve Lattimore, Elmar Lueth, Wendy McClure, Gina Pribaz, Mary Quade, Baron Reed, Matthew Rohrer, Trent Stewart, Ruth Tobias, Brady Udall, Laura Wilder

ADVISORY BOARD

David Baldus, Panayot Butchvarov, Frank Conroy, Maria A. Duarte, Charles Kremenak, Eugenia T. McGee, Allan Megill, Judy Polumbaum, Leslie Sims, Jeffrey Smith, Thomas Walz, Fredrick Woodard, Paul Zimmer